NATURE'S NEW DEAL

The Civilian
Conservation
Corps and the
Roots of the
American
Environmental
Movement

NEIL M. MAHER

OXFORD
UNIVERSITY PRESS

2008

OXFORD
UNIVERSITY PRESS

Oxford University Press, Inc., publishes works that further
Oxford University's objective of excellence
in research, scholarship, and education.

Oxford   New York
Auckland   Cape Town   Dar es Salaam   Hong Kong   Karachi
Kuala Lumpur   Madrid   Melbourne   Mexico City   Nairobi
New Delhi   Shanghai   Taipei   Toronto

With offices in
Argentina   Austria   Brazil   Chile   Czech Republic   France   Greece
Guatemala   Hungary   Italy   Japan   Poland   Portugal   Singapore
South Korea   Switzerland   Thailand   Turkey   Ukraine   Vietnam

Copyright © 2008 by Oxford University Press, Inc.

Published by Oxford University Press, Inc.
198 Madison Avenue, New York, New York 10016

www.oup.com

Oxford is a registered trademark of Oxford University Press

Library of Congress Cataloging-in-Publication Data
Maher, Neil M., 1964–
Nature's new deal : the Civilian Conservation Corps and the roots
of the American environmental movement / Neil M. Maher.
p.   cm.
ISBN 978-0-19-530601-9
1. Civilian Conservation Corps (U.S.)—History. 2. Conservation
of natural resources—United States—History. 3. New Deal,
1933–1939. 4. United States—Politics and government—1933–1945.
I. Title.
S930.M155 2007
333.720973—dc22   2007005032

9 8 7 6 5 4 3 2 1

Printed in the United States of America
on acid-free paper

In memory of my father
And for my mother and brother

env. history
+ U. S. history

ACKNOWLEDGMENTS

My father introduced me to the topic for this book when I was seven years old, when he took me, my younger brother, and our shaggy dog outside most weekends to explore New York's public parks. When we lived in the Riverdale section of the Bronx, this often entailed a journey to nearby Tibbetts Brook, a county park with an enormous public swimming pool built during the early years of the Great Depression. Years later, when my family left the city and moved up the Hudson River, my father continued these outings. He would take us by car to Bear Mountain State Park, up in the Hudson Highlands, whose miles of hiking trails, half a dozen artificial swimming lakes, and four-story lookout tower that offered views of the Empire State Building fifty miles to the south were also developed during the New Deal era. It was my curiosity about the building of these outdoor landscapes during the 1930s, and the impact they had on young people like my brother and me in the postwar era, that years later sparked this book.

This project began in earnest at New York University, in a graduate research seminar taught by Lizabeth Cohen, who became my primary adviser before leaving NYU for Harvard. While her own scholarship on New Deal politics has obviously influenced my work, her talents as a teacher guided the research and writing of this book from start to finish; no other person I've come in contact with during my career as a historian has pushed me harder to think analytically about the past. Liz always encouraged me to pursue environmental history, but to do so without losing sight of the larger historical questions affecting U.S. history writ large. "But how does your environmental history change the way we think about American history?" she asked me over

Worster +
KU

and over again while I worked on this project. It is because of this question that *Nature's New Deal* is as much about politics as it is about conservation.

This book would also not have been possible without Donald Worster. In the fall of 1996, in the middle of my graduate studies in New York, I asked Don if I could visit the University of Kansas for a semester to immerse myself in the field of environmental history. Not only did Don agree to let me come to Lawrence, he went out of his way to welcome me and to make me feel like a member of the KU environmental history community. Thankfully, he also generously agreed to serve as adviser on this project. While Don's scholarship, including that on the Dust Bowl, greatly influenced my own work on the New Deal, his moral passion and kindness continue to guide me as an environmental historian.

I would also like to thank the rest of my graduate advisers at New York University for their guidance and support. Thomas Bender continually encouraged me to keep the city in mind while I researched and wrote about remote forests, farms, and parks, and this book is much better because of that advice. Danny Walkowitz pushed me to make room for laborers in my work, and Walter Johnson, through his scholarship and teaching on slavery, forced me to think seriously about the bodily history of the New Deal era. I also want to thank the late Warren Dean, who first introduced me to the field of environmental history and allowed me to introduce him to hiking in the Hudson Highlands.

My classmates made the poverty-stricken years of graduate school one of the richest periods in my life. At NYU I want to thank the members of Liz Cohen's dissertation group, which included Katie Barry, Kirsten Fermaglich, Michael Lerner, Louise Maxwell, and Debra Michals, who read and commented on earlier versions of these chapters and always reeled me in when I blathered on too long about trees and dirt. As important were my four teammates on a pick-up basketball squad that gathered nearly every day, each week, for five years, to play against much younger and faster undergraduate opponents. Scott Messinger, Andrew Darien, Mark Elliott, Keric Brown, and I somehow figured out how to run successful fast breaks while simultaneously debating historiography and, quite often, providing one another with catchier book titles. My peers from Kansas also deserve thanks, including Jay Antle, Kevin Armitage, Karl Brooks, Kip Curtis, Sterling Evans, James Prichard, Adam Rome, Amy Schwartz, Frank Zelko, and fellow visitor Bruce Stadfeld. I also want to thank Brian Black, and especially Paul Sutter, both for sharing their own work on the interwar years and for their continuing friendship.

Between the streets of Manhattan and the plains of Kansas, dozens of archivists and librarians guided me through what felt like mountains of source material on the Great Depression and the New Deal era. I owe a debt to the staffs at NYU's Bobst Library, the Dartmouth College Library, and the Library of Congress. I also want to thank Michel Conan of the Dumbarton Oaks Garden and Landscape Studies Program, Cheryl Oaks of the Forest History Society, Tom Rosenbaum at the Rockefeller Archive Center, Annette Hartigan of the Great Smoky Mountains National Park Archives, and Bill Creech and Gene Morris at the National Archives and Record Administration. I am most grateful, though, to the amazing and talented people at the Franklin D. Roosevelt Library, including archivists Bob Parks, Alycia Vivona, and especially Nancy Snedeker for their help during the long hot summer I spent up in Hyde Park, and also to Karen Anson and Mark Renovitch for helping me locate many of the images that appear in this book. I would also like to thank the many institutions that provided financial support for my research on this project, including New York University's Graduate School of Arts and Sciences, the Organization of American Historians, the Dumbarton Oaks Garden and Landscape Studies Program, the Forest History Society, the National Park Service, Black Rock Forest, the Rockefeller Archive Center, and the Franklin D. Roosevelt Library.

Throughout these years of research and writing, numerous editors and colleagues provided invaluable feedback on portions of this manuscript. A much different version of chapter 4 appeared in the *Western Historical Quarterly* (Autumn 2000), and *Environmental History* (Summer 2000) published a portion of the third chapter as well. The editors of these journals, David Rich Lewis and Adam Rome, along with the anonymous reviewers of each article, provided me with suggestions that not only improved those chapters but also helped me focus and sharpen the entire manuscript. I would similarly like to thank the three anonymous reviewers for Oxford University Press for their extensive and insightful comments, which allowed me to take this manuscript to the next level. My friends and colleagues from the field of environmental history also improved this book, both through serious feedback at conferences and during lighthearted chats in conference hotel bars. I'd especially like to thank Thomas Andrews, Mark Fiege, Emily Greenwald, Sara Gregg, Mark Harvey, Lynn Heasley, Ari Kelman, Matt Klingle, Kim Little, Kathy Morse, Linda Nash, Cindy Ott, Sarah Phillips, Sara Prichard, Gingy Scharf, Ellen Stroud, Louis Warren, Marsha Weisiger, and Bob Wilson. I'd also like to thank Bill Cronon, both for his extensive comments on this manuscript and for helping to promote such a close-knit community within the field of environmental history.

I was fortunate enough to land an academic job just across the Hudson River from my New York City home, in Newark, New Jersey. I am thankful for such wonderfully supportive colleagues in the Federated History Department at the New Jersey Institute of Technology and Rutgers University, Newark, including Richard Sher, Doris Sher, John O'Conner, and Stephen Pemberton at NJIT, Susan Caruthers, Jon Cowans, Gary Farney, Jim Goodman, Jan Lewis, Clem Price, and Beryl Satter at Rutgers, Newark, and Julie Livingston, Phil Pauly, Susan Schrepfer, and Keith Wailoo down at Rutgers, New Brunswick. NJIT's College of Science and Liberal Arts and the Rutgers Center for Historical Analysis also provided me with generous funding that I used to revise this manuscript. I would like to thank my undergraduate and graduate students, too, especially Holly Estes, who painstakingly helped me locate images for this book.

It is difficult to explain how lucky I feel to have been invited to lunch, while attending a history conference in Providence, Rhode Island, by Susan Ferber of Oxford University Press. From the moment we sat down to eat and discuss my project, to the day I handed in the final text, she has been the ideal editor. Susan has read every line of this manuscript, made handwritten comments on every page, and always understood exactly what I was trying to do with my writing, even when I was having trouble doing it. Her amazing ability to remain calm and to keep nervous first-time authors calm even as daunting deadlines approach is an added, and rare, bonus. I cannot imagine a better publishing experience than that given to me by Susan and her team at Oxford University Press.

Finally, and most important, I want to thank my family. Quite simply, this book would not exist without their continual love and support. Thanks to the Elfers and the Healy clans, who for the past five years, at each family holiday, asked in a kindly, supportive way, if the book was done yet. My brother, Chris, my best friend since those walks years ago with our father in New York's public parks, has continually supported my dream to become a historian and, more recently, helped out by also sometimes picking up dinner tabs. I am also thankful for his wife, Stephanie, one of the most capable women I have ever known, and for their two daughters, Charlotte and Olivia, who have all breathed new life into our family. I cannot thank my mother enough, for her love for our family, for her faith in me, and for the strength she always seems to find in herself. Most of all, though, I want to thank my father, the late Neil Maher, Sr. It is he who started it all, back with wonderful adventures to Tibbetts Brook and Bear Mountain. Since that time he has read every word I have written. Though the words that follow won't make it to his reading list, I know how excited he would be to crack open this book. I am so happy to dedicate *Nature's New Deal* to him.

CONTENTS

NATURE'S NEW DEAL

INTRODUCTION
New Deal Conservation

In late April 1933, a young man named John Ripley climbed a solitary pine tree atop the Massanutten Mountains in George Washington National Forest, ten miles west of Luray, Virginia. After catching his breath on the uppermost branch, which bowed dangerously under his own weight, Ripley took a short-handled ax and with awkward strokes chopped the top off the slender pine. He next attached a rope and pulley to the tip of the tree, shimmied from his perch, and began working his way down the trunk of the thirty-five-foot evergreen, hacking off branch after branch until the young tree stood straight and bare. Near the bottom, Ripley wiped his brow before tying the other end of the rope to an American flag. At the base of the tree, where a crowd of locals from nearby communities had gathered along with newspaper reporters, magazine photographers, and film crews from across the country, a cheer quickly went up. Then, as if on cue, John Ripley's colleagues, who were all dressed in identical olive-green uniforms, pulled on the rope and hoisted Old Glory high above Camp Roosevelt, the first Civilian Conservation Corps (CCC) camp in the nation.[1]

While the conversion of a pine tree into a flagpole by young CCC enrollees may alarm contemporary environmentalists, it nevertheless hints at a number of important historical changes set in motion by Franklin Roosevelt's New Deal. Most obvious was the modification of the natural landscape, in this case a mountaintop pine grove, which Corps enrollees altered through their physical labor. The more than 3 million young men who joined the CCC between 1933 and 1942 undertook similarly transformative work, planting 2 billion trees, slowing soil erosion on 40 million acres of farmland, and developing

800 new state parks.[2] As the Corps' first director, Robert Fechner, explained in 1939, the CCC dramatically "altered the landscape of the United States."[3] Yet John Ripley's arboreal exploits indicate other changes as well. The hoisting of an American flag up a pine tree pole in April 1933 suggests that while the CCC was altering American nature, it was likewise transforming American politics.

Those interested in exploring the roots of this relationship between conservation and politics in the United States have tended to ignore places such as George Washington National Forest, focusing instead on a landscape on the other side of the continent. The Hetch Hetchy Valley in Yosemite National Park has long been the poster child for explaining conservationist ideology during the early twentieth century. According to the most basic version of events, the controversy over whether or not to dam the valley to provide water for San Francisco involved two competing conceptions of conservation. On the one hand there was Gifford Pinchot, first chief of the U.S. Forest Service, who supported the dam as the most efficient use of the region's natural resources. Criticizing Pinchot's view of conservation as "wise use" was John Muir. The nature writer and founder of the Sierra Club openly campaigned against the dam to preserve the valley as an aesthetic and spiritual resource for the American public. Congress's decision in 1913 to dam Hetch Hetchy, so the story goes, not only broke the spirit of John Muir, who died the following year, but more important, divided the conservation movement into conservationist and preservationist camps.[4]

Along with symbolizing the ideological schizophrenia of early conservationists, Hetch Hetchy is similarly trotted out to illustrate the shifting political terrain of turn-of-the century America. Gifford Pinchot's belief in scientific foresters, in concentrated authority such as that located in the U.S. Forest Service, and in the rational use of natural resources in places like Hetch Hetchy represent on a small scale the larger political structure of the Progressive Era. Progressives as a whole also believed in experts, centralized decision making, and the "gospel of efficiency" when dealing with a host of issues from urban political reform to rural road building.[5] Yet Progressive conservation did more than merely mirror Progressive politics; it played a vital role in transforming political power in Washington, D.C. The efficient use of trees, soil, and water located primarily in rural regions helped to extend the political reach of authority emanating from the nation's capital. It also incurred resistance on the local level aimed less at conservation in principle than at the undemocratic tendencies of Progressive conservationists.[6] Conservation like that at Hetch Hetchy thus linked natural resource policy to contestation over the expanding power of the federal state.[7]

The Hetch Hetchy landscape is paraded about to explain the connection between conservation and politics during the post–World War II period as well. According to this all-too-familiar tale, although Muir and the Sierra Club lost the battle over the valley in 1913, their preservationist ideas won the war against Pinchot's conservationists by successfully opposing similar dam projects after 1945. Here, Echo Park in Dinosaur National Monument is often held out as the final chapter in the Hetch Hetchy saga. In a near-repeat performance of the battle in Yosemite, during the 1940s the Bureau of Reclamation proposed a dam at Echo Park inside Dinosaur National Monument, which straddled the Utah-Colorado border. Although opponents initially criticized the proposed dam for destroying wilderness, as at Hetch Hetchy, they relied as well on two additional arguments: the project would reduce recreational opportunities and would upset ecological balance within Dinosaur National Monument.[8] The defeat of the Echo Park dam in 1955, this story concludes, not only added recreation and ecology to the debate between conservationists and preservationists, but it also unleashed the rising environmental tide of the post–World War II era.[9]

Just as the fight for Hetch Hetchy reflected Progressive Era politics, the Echo Park battle influenced and was influenced by its postwar political context. In the decades after Echo Park, those involved in the civil rights, New Left, antiwar, and women's movements embraced interest-group politics, relied on activism from the bottom up, and were less concerned with economic efficiency than with correcting social inequalities. Postwar environmentalists acted similarly to achieve these same liberal goals. Opponents of the Echo Park dam, for instance, fought the federal government with a sprawling coalition of more than 175 organizations spread across the country; through reliance not only on scientists but also on thousands of "amateur" conservationists who wrote letters, signed petitions, and lobbied local, state, and national politicians; and by emphasizing "quality of life" concerns over efficient natural resource use.[10] The result was a more grassroots movement that, unlike resistance during the Progressive Era, successfully countered the political power of conservation experts on the national level. The defeat of Echo Park thus not only foreshadowed environmentalism, but also mirrored the political upheaval of postwar America.[11]

For those studying this delicate dance between conservation and politics during the twentieth century, the question then becomes: how did the United States get from Hetch Hetchy to Echo Park? From a reliance on scientific experts to dependence as well on grassroots activists? From policies promoted by conservative Republicans to those embraced by liberal Democrats? From book's purpose

a narrow focus on natural resources located primarily in rural areas to a broader concern, often expressed by city dwellers and suburbanites, for the preservation of open space, outdoor recreation, and ecological balance, or what one historian has called "beauty, health, and permanence"?[12] Quite simply, how did Americans get from Progressive Era conservation to post–World War II environmentalism? As important, what was the impact of this transformation from conservation to environmentalism on the American political system?[13] *Nature's New Deal* answers these questions by exploring neither Hetch Hetchy nor Echo Park but instead landscapes across the country like that created by the CCC atop the Massanutten Mountains in George Washington National Forest.

In many respects, this focus on landscape and landscape change grew organically from the New Deal era, a period that perhaps more than any other in U.S. history witnessed the transformation of public space by the federal government.[14] Today, we drive on roads laid out by the Works Progress Administration, drop off our children and pick up books at schools and libraries built by the Public Works Administration, and even drink water flowing from reservoirs constructed by the Tennessee Valley Authority. These and other New Deal programs, including the Agricultural Adjustment Administration, the Soil Conservation Service, and the Resettlement Administration, not to mention the Civilian Conservation Corps, dramatically transformed the natural environment. They also altered American politics by introducing the New Deal to the American public in ways that raised popular support for Roosevelt's liberal welfare state. Analyzing in detail how one conservation program altered the landscape while helping the president to promote policy sheds light on the important link between American nature and national politics during the New Deal era.

Landscape is also a useful organizing principle for those today who are interested in examining the environmental history of the New Deal period. Defined here as "nonhuman nature altered by human labor," landscape represents the nexus of interactions between society and the natural environment, between culture and nature.[15] Landscape is thus neither solely the ecological nature of trees, soil, and water nor the socially constructed nature of ideas about the natural world, but rather a fusion of the two. Methodologically, then, landscape complements environmental history's emphasis on the interrelationship between the human and the nonhuman, while also helping practitioners to sidestep two problems that continue to plague the field. Landscape lets environmental historians off the hook, so to speak, when it comes to defining "nature," on the one hand, and in pinpointing the exact causes of ecological change, on the other.[16] Landscape, in other words, makes room for definitions involving both material and cultural nature, while at the same time focusing historic analysis less on the causes of ecological change and more on its consequences for human and nonhuman worlds alike. Rather than blaming society for degrading ecosystems, which has become a familiar refrain in the field, landscape helps environmental historians to explore instead how nature and culture change in tandem, and how such transformations affect history.

The concept of landscape proves equally useful for those interested in the New Deal's political history. Because landscapes are partly cultural, they can be "read" as one would read court records, census tracts, and government documents for clues to the society that created them. Similar to abrupt jumps or shifts in these more conventional source materials, which often suggest realignments of power within a given society, landscape changes similarly reflect not only ecological disturbances taking place within the natural environment but also associated political transformations occurring within cultures. As everyday landscapes change in appearance, so too do people's political outlook.[17] Instead of serving as a historic backdrop, a contextual filler for more important cultural events, landscape and landscape change are literally where nature and politics met during the New Deal era.

The landscape of George Washington National Forest is just one example of such a meeting. Long before the Corps arrived in the Massanutten Mountains and ran an American flag up a pine tree pole, conservationist thought and Progressive politics together had shaped the surrounding forest. This process began during the nineteenth century, when timber companies logged the forest to feed local iron furnaces situated throughout the Shenandoah Valley. Repeated cutting deforested the mountains while increasing soil erosion, stream flooding, and wildfires that burned repeatedly over the region during the late 1800s.[18] Alarmed at such waste in the valley and across the country, Progressive reformers lobbied Congress to take political steps to more efficiently manage the nation's natural resources, including its timber reserves. One result was the creation in 1905 of the Forest Service, which Gifford Pinchot ran until 1910. Another was the Weeks Act, which gave the federal government the power to buy degraded woodlands like those in the Shenandoah Valley and transform them into places such as George Washington National Forest, created in 1917 as one of the first national forests in the eastern United States. For the next twenty-five years, the Forest Service put Pinchot's wise use philosophy into practice on the nearly 200,000-acre landscape.[19]

At first, Camp Roosevelt enrollees undertook work projects in George Washington National Forest that continued the conservation efforts of the previous quarter century. Under the direction of Forest Service technicians, the 200 young men stationed at Camp Roosevelt left their barracks at 6 o'clock each morning and headed out into the Massanutten Mountains to undertake what the Corps called "timber stand improvement" projects. "The work," explained one reporter covering Camp Roosevelt during the summer of 1933, "consists of thinning overcrowded stands, clearing out dead standing trees and windfalls, and reforestation where new species are desired."[20] Camp Roosevelt enrollees also constructed dirt fire roads across the forest to help halt the devastating blazes that had burned over the valley since the late nineteenth century, and even traveled deep into the forest to physically fight fires when they broke out. Ironically, while many of these young, untrained men had never heard of Gifford Pinchot nor of scientific forestry before joining the Corps, at the outset of the New Deal they and millions of other enrollees stationed across the country applied his notion of conservation as wise use to thousands of landscapes like George Washington National Forest.

During the mid-1930s, however, Camp Roosevelt, like CCC camps throughout the nation, began expanding its efforts beyond the conservation of natural resources to include as well the construction of outdoor recreational amenities. In many respects, such efforts by the Corps in the Massanutten Mountains also had deeper historical roots, linked not to natural resources in rural areas but rather to residents in American cities. Here, the thinking of Frederick Law Olmsted rather than Gifford Pinchot influenced Corps work projects. For planners like Olmsted, an urban park represented an antidote to the hustle and bustle of the American metropolis, an oasis where nature could rejuvenate city dwellers physically, mentally, and emotionally. Olmsted was thus an older type of environmentalist; he believed that one's natural surroundings, or environment, influenced social behavior.[21] In the mid-1930s, this same philosophy guided CCC conservation work in rural areas as well. In George Washington National Forest, for example, the 200 enrollees stationed at Camp Roosevelt constructed campgrounds, picnic areas, hiking trails, and even motor roads that helped to transform this piece of the Shenandoah Valley into the Elizabeth Furnace, New Market Gap, and Little Fort recreation areas.[22] This recreational infrastructure provided city dwellers with a healthful respite from enervating urban environments while pushing conservationist thinking beyond the wise use of natural resources to include a concern for "human resources" as well. The CCC's campgrounds, hiking trails, and motor roads also indicated that the federal government had begun weaving political concern for both natural and human resources into a single conservation policy.

preservation + conservation + ecology

While foresters and park planners like Pinchot and Olmsted would no doubt have approved of the Corps' work in George Washington National Forest, others were less pleased. In particular, during the mid-1930s, the intellectual heirs of John Muir began criticizing the CCC's recreational development projects. The construction of campgrounds and picnic areas, hiking trails and motor roads by millions of Corps enrollees, argued wilderness advocates such as Bob Marshall, destroyed the primitive quality of national forests.[23] Comprehensive conservation, they countered, must include wilderness protection. While these preservationist concerns had lost out in Hetch Hetchy, in the mid-1930s this opposition to CCC recreation work slowed the pace of such projects and helped to redefine wild nature in ways that reinvigorated the fledgling wilderness movement. It also helped to set the stage after World War II for a new round of wilderness advocacy; when Congress passed the Wilderness Act in 1964, some of the first landscapes singled out for inclusion were those that had been saved from CCC development in places such as George Washington National Forest.[24] Thus, while CCC recreation work initially raised interest among conservationists for natural environments that improved public health, opposition to these same projects sparked a debate, not unlike that at Hetch Hetchy, over the proper place of preservation within the conservation movement.

Opponents of the CCC did not limit their criticism to Corps recreation projects aimed at conserving the nation's human resources. A minority disapproved as well of CCC work that conserved natural resources, such as trees and soil. Wildlife ecologists, including Aldo Leopold, spearheaded this opposition and at first trained their sights on the Corps' wildlife conservation projects in places like George Washington National Forest. In order to increase animal populations in the forest, Camp Roosevelt enrollees "stocked the mountains with deer" while "stocking the streams" running through the Massanutten Mountains with fish.[25] Although scientists like Leopold at first approved of these projects, and even labored on them alongside CCC enrollees, as the 1930s wore on they began criticizing such work for upsetting ecological balance. They similarly condemned the Corps' forestry efforts, arguing, for instance, that reforesting entire hillsides, often with nonindigenous species planted in perfectly straight rows, was not ecologically sound. True conservation, these critics argued, must take ecology into account. Such criticism of CCC efforts to conserve natural resources ignited yet another public dialogue during the New Deal, this time over the role of ecological science within conservation practices.

"middle landscape" took *"illustrates"*

As the work of the nation's first CCC camp illustrates, a good twenty years before the controversy at Echo Park, Americans were already debating the very meaning of conservation. Was conservation the wise use of natural resources, as Gifford Pinchot espoused? Or did it entail as well the conserving of human resources, in this case the American public, through increased access to healthy recreational facilities, as the followers of Frederick Law Olmsted argued during the mid-1930s? Or did true conservation need to take into account wilderness preservation and ecological balance, as Bob Marshall and Aldo Leopold advocated at the end of the decade? By integrating the conservation of natural and human resources into federal conservation policy, the Corps and its work projects generated similar debates in every corner of the country, suggesting that places like George Washington National Forest represent a new kind of "middle landscape," one that is not only a mixture of nature and culture, of machine and garden, but also a place between Hetch Hetchy and Dinosaur National Monument.[26] Most obviously, such New Deal landscapes sit chronologically betwixt the Yosemite of the 1910s and the Echo Park of the late 1940s and early 1950s. Yet the Corps, its work projects, and the landscapes they created are flanked on either side in other ways as well. For instance, they sit smack in the middle of conservation and environmentalism, on the one hand, and Progressive and postwar politics, on the other.

Nature's New Deal illustrates how CCC landscapes transformed conservation during the Great Depression in ways that helped environmentalism to blossom after World War II. The Corps did this on two different, yet related, levels. As happened in George Washington National Forest, Corps work projects across the country set off a national debate that expanded the meaning of conservation beyond the efficient use of natural resources to include as well concern for human health through outdoor recreation, for wilderness preservation, and for ecological balance, all of which became central to postwar environmentalists. This is not to say that such concerns were absent during the Progressive Era; Frederick Law Olmsted and John Muir obviously promoted outdoor recreation and wilderness preservation long before the arrival of the CCC. Yet by wedding the conservation of natural and human resources within a national conservation program, the Corps forced conservationists to rethink exactly what conservation was during the New Deal era, and to reimagine what it would become after World War II.

As suggested by the large crowd gathered at the Camp Roosevelt flag-raising ceremony in April 1933, the Corps also broadened the conservation movement's composition during the Great Depression era. Progressive conservation at the turn of the century had a small following among scientists and government bureaucrats, and to a lesser extent among rural landowners and hunters, all of whom shared a belief in efficient natural resource use. During the 1930s, however, the Corps democratized this movement by continually introducing the theory and practice of conservation to the CCC's working-class enrollees, to residents of local communities situated near Corps camps, and finally to the country as a whole through national media coverage of this extremely popular New Deal program. Americans across the country, for example, saw CCC enrollees working near their homes, read about Corps camps in local newspapers and national magazines, and even watched full-length feature films portraying CCC conservation projects in forests, on farms, and throughout parks. Due to this publicity, lay conservationists from the public at large who learned about conservation from the CCC joined ranks for the first time with professional conservationists from scientific and government circles who had been practicing conservation for decades. The result was a more broad-based movement that mirrored, and to a certain extent helped to produce, the grassroots character of post–World War II environmentalism.[27]

Nature's New Deal similarly shows how Corps landscapes straddled Progressive and postwar politics by helping Franklin Roosevelt to forge his liberal New Deal coalition. The CCC accomplished this first by raising support for the welfare state in every region of the country. The Corps and its work projects appealed to foresters in the West, to farmers in the Dust Bowl and in the soil-eroded South, and to easterners who could now recreate in hundreds of new state and national parks in their cities' backyards. It also attracted both urban youths flocking into the program and rural Americans who benefited economically from nearby CCC camps. Franklin Roosevelt was well aware of the political support he could raise, not to mention the political power he could wield, through the strategic placement of Corps camps and work projects nationwide.[28] Thus, while the public works of the CCC introduced conservation to the nation, altering the conservation movement in the process, the work relief of the Corps presented the welfare state to the American people, and in doing so helped to raise broad geographic support for the New Deal.[29]

While the CCC helped Roosevelt to introduce his policies to every corner of the country, the Corps appealed across ideological divides as well. The New Deal program was popular both with liberal working-class families, which received Corps paychecks every month because of sons enrolled in the program, and with conservative upper-class business owners, who each day sold

FDR's pol. insight "This book"

goods and services to CCC camps. It proved equally attractive to local politicians, from both political parties, who had Corps camps assigned to their districts, and to federal administrators in Washington, D.C., whom Roosevelt rewarded with key CCC appointments. Just as he was sensitive to the broad geographic appeal of the Corps, so too was Franklin Roosevelt aware that the CCC could bring together often competing special interests under the banner of New Deal liberalism. The president consciously used the CCC's popularity among both the working and upper classes, on the local and the national levels, and on the political Left and political Right, to knit together an ideologically diverse political constituency that supported the New Deal.[30]

This book begins the exploration of conservation and politics during the Great Depression by tracing the intellectual origins of the CCC idea. The most obvious ideological source for the Corps was the president's early experiences with the Progressive conservation movement in his native state of New York. Less well known, however, but equally important, is the impact of Roosevelt's lifelong involvement with the Boy Scouts on his decision to create the CCC. Like the Corps, the scouting movement promoted the notion that young men's behavior could be improved through exposure to nature, an idea that scoutmasters borrowed from old-style environmentalist reformers such as Olmsted. Franklin Roosevelt transferred this idea from the Boy Scouts to the CCC, which also took young men from unhealthy urban settings and placed them in salubrious outdoor environments. He also knew from experience that creating jobs in nature could raise political capital; as governor of New York, Roosevelt had established a popular program that also put unemployed urban men to work in rural areas. The Corps idea thus not only introduced the Boy Scout philosophy to conservationist thought. The immediate popularity of the CCC also helped the new president to jump-start the New Deal.

Nature's New Deal next traces how the two strands of thinking that informed the Corps' creation in turn altered the American landscape by influencing the types of conservation projects undertaken by CCC camps. Although Corps conservation work appeared haphazard throughout the 1930s, it evolved over time and involved two types of labor on a trio of rural landscapes. While the Corps began its work in the nation's forests, primarily in the far West, the Dust Bowl of 1934 forced CCC enrollees onto the country's farms as well, both on the Great Plains and in the soil-eroded South. This first type of conservation work, involving both reforestation and soil conservation, embodied the goals of Progressive conservationists, who advocated above all the efficient use of natural resources. Such work simultaneously popularized the New Deal throughout these rural regions. Yet during the later 1930s, the

book "illustrates" & "focuses"

Corps expanded its work projects once again, this time into state and national parks where CCC enrollees built hiking trails, campgrounds, and even motor roads to increase public access to outdoor recreation. This second type of Corps work echoed the Boy Scouts' call for healthful contact with nature, but extended this experience from young men working outdoors to the American public playing in parks. In doing so, Corps recreation work helped to broaden conservationist ideology to include a concern for public health.

As the Corps altered the American landscape, it transformed the more than 3 million young men who enrolled in the New Deal program during the 1930s and early 1940s. *Nature's New Deal* illustrates how Corps enrollees changed intellectually as they learned about conservation both on the job during the day and in classes offered by the CCC at night. Hard, manual labor out-of-doors altered these young men physically as well; by their own accounts, the great majority gained weight, developed muscles, and increased their overall bodily health. While such ideological changes helped to convert many of these working-class enrollees to the conservationist cause, thus expanding the movement's composition, the young men's bodily transformations added what the Corps called "human conservation" to the movement's agenda. Enrollees' bodies similarly influenced the New Deal body politic. Roosevelt used the restorative character of CCC labor in nature, not only to court the urban working class, but also to ease nativist concerns regarding his administration's ties to working-class immigrants, who were often blamed for the Great Depression. Thus while Corps work projects proved attractive to those living in rural regions throughout the country, labor in the CCC appealed to urbanites. By directly influencing the gender politics of the Roosevelt administration, Corps bodies thus became key components of the New Deal political landscape.

Corps enrollees were not the only ones affected by CCC conservation work. Residents of local communities situated near the more than 5,000 CCC camps scattered across the country also experienced changes during the New Deal era. Here *Nature's New Deal* focuses on two communities in particular and their relationship with nearby Corps camps. In Coon Valley, Wisconsin, located next to a CCC soil erosion project, local residents quickly embraced both conservation and the New Deal as agricultural production rose on local farms that cooperated with the CCC's conservation efforts. Residents from a second community, situated near Corps camps developing Great Smoky Mountains National Park for outdoor recreation, also welcomed conservation and the Roosevelt administration but for quite different reasons. In the

Smokies, locals supported the CCC because Corps recreation projects such as the building of campgrounds, visitor centers, and motor roads promised increased tourism to the national park. While Franklin Roosevelt consciously used work projects like these to promote both conservation and the New Deal locally, often in more conservative rural areas, during the mid-1930s a vocal minority in each of these two communities began criticizing the Corps in particular, and the Roosevelt administration by association, for being environmentally reckless. This early opposition to the CCC, led by Aldo Leopold in Coon Valley and Bob Marshall in the Great Smokies, would significantly shape both the conservation movement and New Deal politics during the later Great Depression period.

This volume next follows the local dispute over Corps conservation work to the national level, where it became a full-fledged public debate during the late 1930s. This process began as a steady stream of positive media coverage in newspapers, in magazines, in films, and on radio during the early and mid-1930s transformed the CCC into the New Deal's most popular program, and perhaps more important, made it synonymous with conservation. Simultaneously, however, a small but increasingly vocal group of Americans began publicly criticizing Corps conservation work, and the president promoting it, for threatening American nature. Marshall and Leopold, while supporting many of Roosevelt's conservation efforts, led this critique on two distinct fronts. While preservationists throughout the country agreed with Marshall that CCC recreation projects destroyed wilderness, biological scientists followed Aldo Leopold's lead by claiming that even the Corps' forestry efforts upset ecological balance. The result was a national dialogue about the very meaning of conservation that not only made the movement more grassroots but also helped Roosevelt to knit together a broader New Deal coalition.

Finally, *Nature's New Deal* examines how the popular national debate over the meaning of conservation influenced the politics of federal planning during the so-called "third New Deal." It does this by exploring Franklin Roosevelt's failed attempt, beginning in 1936, to rekindle support for his administration by reorganizing the federal government and in the process creating a cabinet-level Department of Conservation. Although this conservation department never materialized, the political controversy over reorganization greatly influenced both the conservation movement and federal politics from the later New Deal years into the immediate postwar era. On the one hand, the debate forced Roosevelt to embrace a new, more holistic, and increasingly ecological approach to federal planning best exemplified by the administrations' desire to

Book "concludes" + "ends"

make permanent, through reorganization, the National Resources Planning Board. The drive for reorganization similarly pushed Roosevelt to publicly promote a more inclusive, integrated, and cooperative federal conservation policy most fully developed in the CCC's work for the Tennessee Valley Authority during the later 1930s. While this more ecological form of national planning, along with its counterpart involving increased cooperation among a diverse array of government conservation agencies, never became institutionalized within the federal government under Roosevelt, *Nature's New Deal* concludes that the president's failure forced these two practices into the public sphere in the immediate postwar era. The result was a new form of special interest politics best expressed in grassroots movements such as environmentalism.

Although Congress refused funding for the CCC in 1942, effectively terminating the New Deal program, the Corps nonetheless cast a long shadow across the political and natural landscapes of the postwar era. *Nature's New Deal* ends by examining this legacy, first through the Corps' former enrollees, thousands of whom took jobs with conservation agencies and became actively involved in a host of environmental groups across the country. The Corps did likewise through the creation of a slew of postwar state conservation corps, and through copycat federal programs that continue to function even in the twenty-first century. Most important but less obvious, however, are the thousands of actual landscapes left behind by the CCC, which are scattered across the nation's forests, farms, and parks. Atop the Massanutten Mountains in George Washington National Forest, for instance, where in April 1933 the country's first CCC enrollees hoisted an American flag up a pine tree pole, visitors today will find a public campground with two sets of trails. Those interested in exploring the surrounding forest can head into the mountains on hiking trails built by CCC enrollees during the 1930s. Tourists more interested in the Roosevelt administration's New Deal policies can instead stroll the former footpaths of Camp Roosevelt, past the foundations of the kitchens, barracks, and recreation halls that fed, housed, and entertained CCC enrollees. What follows in *Nature's New Deal* explores on a national scale both types of trails, one into the forest and the other into politics, to better understand the important link between nation building and nature during the Great Depression era.

ONE / IDEAS
Franklin Roosevelt's Progressive Era Influences

Early in 1933, Joseph D. Wilson began a personal letter-writing campaign to the president. In numerous correspondences addressed to the White House during the following three years, the thirty-six-year-old unemployed electrician and father of two repeatedly claimed that he, not Franklin Roosevelt, had originated the idea for the Civilian Conservation Corps. In his letters, Wilson asked for a job with the CCC as payback for having furnished the Corps idea. Wilson even went so far as to contact several newspapers, telling reporters that the president stole his idea and refused to give him credit.[1] When the White House finally wrote back, stating that Roosevelt had conceived of the Corps while governor of New York, Wilson decided to take up the matter directly with the commander in chief. Telling his wife that he was going out to look for work, the Atlanta native left his home and traveled north to Washington, D.C., where on October 7, 1936, he demanded a meeting with the president to clarify the dispute concerning the origins of the CCC. When two guards denied him access to the executive office, Wilson became despondent, pulled a knife from his pocket, and cut his wrists in an unsuccessful attempt to take his own life.[2]

Although extreme, Joseph Wilson's desire to be anointed as the intellectual founder of the CCC was far from unique. Throughout the 1930s, dozens of individuals laid claim to having conceptualized what was often heralded as the New Deal's most popular program. British forester Richard St. Barbe Baker was perhaps the first of such claimants, arguing that he suggested the CCC idea to Franklin Roosevelt during a meeting in Albany just before the presidential election of 1932. A Brooklyn, New York, resident named

Major Julius Hochfelder also wrote several letters to CCC headquarters stating that he was the ideological creator of the Corps, and should therefore receive a job with the New Deal program. Such claims were nothing new to CCC director Robert Fechner. "We have letters from a large number of individuals...who feel they first conceived the idea of this organization," Fechner wrote to one of Hochfelder's supporters. "I merely point out these things so that you may know that Major Hochfelder is not alone in thinking that he was entitled to some reward for suggesting the CCC plan to the president."[3]

Similar to the debate between these individuals, contemporaneous accounts of the Corps' genesis also differed. Articles and books written during the 1930s generally highlighted four influences behind the CCC's birth. One of the most common explanations concerned the essay titled "The Moral Equivalent of War," written by Harvard philosopher William James in 1906. According to James, "instead of military conscription" the United States should adopt "a conscription of the whole youthful population to form for a certain number of years a part of the army enlisted against Nature."[4] Other accounts of the Corps written during the Great Depression emphasized the establishment after World War I of youth work programs in several European countries, including Bulgaria (1921), Switzerland (1924), and especially Germany (1925), whose German Labor Service was most often compared to Roosevelt's CCC.[5] Rising juvenile delinquency during the early years of the Great Depression was yet another cause often cited by newspaper reporters for the creation of the Corps. An article in the *New Republic*, for instance, stated that the president established the CCC "to prevent the nation's male youth from becoming semi-criminal hitch-hikers."[6] Finally, commentators during the 1930s often portrayed Franklin Roosevelt's practice of conserving natural resources prior to becoming president as a major factor in his decision to establish the CCC.[7]

During his presidency, Roosevelt did little to clarify this debate. Not only did he claim that he had never read William James's essay, but he also failed to acknowledge the influence of other nations' youth work programs on his own thinking. Instead, Roosevelt repeatedly responded to queries concerning the ideological roots of the Corps by referencing similar programs he had initiated while governor of New York, which likewise put unemployed men to work in state parks and forests, thus pushing the origin question back in time rather than answering it.[8] When forced to respond, as when *Time* magazine editor I. Van Meter personally wrote to the White House in 1939 for a cover story on the CCC, Roosevelt was equally evasive. The president "cannot find that the idea of the Civilian Conservation Corps was taken from any one source," replied Roosevelt's private secretary, Marguerite LeHand. "It was rather the obvious conflux of the desire for conservation and the need for finding useful work for unemployed young men."[9] Although the Roosevelt administration refused to elaborate further regarding this conflux, mapping the intellectual geography of the Corps is nevertheless central to understanding how the New Deal program altered not just the American landscape but the country's political terrain as well.

In scouting the ideological origins of the CCC, it is best to begin with the congressional action that created the New Deal program. Although Congress passed the bill establishing the CCC on March 31, 1933, the events creating it began several weeks earlier when, on March 9, Franklin Roosevelt sketched out rough plans for putting 500,000 unemployed men to work on conservation projects throughout the country. Over the next few days, he fine-tuned his thinking, deciding to limit enrollment in the program to young men between the ages of eighteen and twenty-five who were willing to send $25 of their $30 monthly pay back home to their families, all of which had to be listed on state relief registers. Roosevelt also decided to house these enrollees, as they were called, in 200-man camps located in national and state parks and forests, and to run the New Deal program cooperatively. While the Department of Labor would coordinate enrollee recruitment and the Department of War would be responsible for the daily functioning of the CCC camps, the Department of Agriculture would supervise the conservation projects in national and state forests and the Department of the Interior would oversee the work performed in national and state parks. After outlining these ideas to brain truster Raymond Moley on March 14, the president asked the secretaries of war, interior, agriculture, and labor to coordinate plans for putting the proposed program into operation and to report back to him. One week later, Roosevelt formally asked Congress to establish the CCC.[10]

Roosevelt's March 21 message to Congress represents his most developed thinking regarding the Corps prior to its creation. Entitled "Relief of Unemployment," the president's message began by drawing attention to the most obvious crisis then gripping the nation: the fact that 13 million, or one in four working-age citizens, remained jobless. "It is essential to our recovery program," wrote Roosevelt, "that measures be immediately enacted aimed at unemployment relief." After warning the members of Congress that the "enforced idleness" associated with joblessness threatened the "spiritual and moral stability" of the nation, and reminding them that the "overwhelming majority of unemployed Americans ... would infinitely prefer to work," the

unemp. + environment [handwritten annotation in top margin]

president proposed three types of work relief initiatives, one of which was the CCC. "I estimate," he wrote to Congress regarding the proposed Corps, "that 250,000 men can be given temporary employment by early summer if you give me authority to proceed within the next two weeks."[11]

Although the message suggested that the unemployment emergency was paramount in Roosevelt's thinking, it was not the only crisis on his mind early in 1933. The state of nature also alarmed the president, and he expressed this as well to Congress in his March 21 correspondence. After warning of the dangers posed by joblessness, Roosevelt directed the politicians' attention to "the news we are receiving today of vast damage caused by floods on the Ohio and other rivers," due in large part to deforestation along their banks. The president dismissed the notion that these disasters were natural and instead blamed human negligence, arguing that the floods had occurred because "national and state domains have been largely forgotten in the past few years of industrial development." To make up for such neglect, the federal government had to take action to "conserve our precious natural resources" located on these important public lands. The CCC was Roosevelt's first step in this process. "I propose to create a civilian conservation corps," he wrote to Congress, "to be used in simple work, not interfering with normal employment and confining itself to forestry, the prevention of soil erosion, flood control and similar projects."[12]

While the president's message identifies his dual concerns over unemployment and a degraded natural environment, it does little to answer the more significant question regarding how these ideological strands became interwoven in his early New Deal thinking. This is especially important considering that earlier in the century such concerns had been quite distinct. During the Progressive Era, the conservation movement had promoted the efficient use of natural resources such as timber, soil, and water but rarely, if ever, concerned itself with how such increased efficiency might affect workers' lives.[13] Conversely, Progressives interested in unemployment reform refrained from promoting conservation as a means of decreasing idleness in youth.[14] How, then, did Roosevelt decide to fuse the needs of nature with those of young jobless men in March 1933? Part of the answer lies in the evolution of Franklin Roosevelt's ideology regarding both conservation and youth relief prior to becoming president, a period when these two strands of thought were anything but in conflux.[15]

Franklin Roosevelt first experienced the deterioration of natural resources while growing up on his family's estate in Hyde Park, New York. Located approximately halfway between New York City and Albany, the 1,200-acre parcel of land sloped steeply upward from the eastern bank of the Hudson River to a level bluff, on top of which sat the family home. Although the Roosevelt family acquired the property, which they called "Springwood," in the early nineteenth century, Dutch settlers had worked much of the estate's land for more than 200 years. This became all too obvious to Roosevelt when in 1910, at the age of twenty-eight, he took over management of the property from his mother, Sara. After learning from estate records that his ancestors had grown prize-winning corn at Springwood in 1840, Roosevelt became understandably concerned that seventy years later the property produced only half of what it had in the mid-nineteenth century. He also became alarmed at the large gullies that had formed and continued to widen along the property's steepest slopes, slopes that had been cleared decades before for cultivation. With every rain, these gullies washed fertile topsoil off the property down into the Hudson River.[16] The rest of the estate suffered similarly; the yields of grain, pasturage, fruit, and vegetables were far below average because the rocky Hudson Valley soil had long since passed its peak. As Roosevelt put it, "I can lime it, cross-plough it, manure it and treat it with every art known to science, but it has just plain run out."[17]

Similar to his encounters with a deteriorating natural environment, Roosevelt's awareness of natural resource conservation also began early in life. In 1891, while vacationing with his family in Europe, Roosevelt bicycled through the countryside near Bad Nauheim, Germany, and encountered a small town with a large municipal forest on its outskirts. From discussions with local residents, the nine-year-old cyclist learned that the forested tract had been carefully managed for the last 200 years to yield an annual timber crop that offset the town's expenses. "The interesting thing to me, as a boy even, was that the people in the town didn't have to pay taxes," remembered Roosevelt many years later. "They were supported by their own forest."[18] It was this type of thinking that Roosevelt brought back with him to Hyde Park.

Roosevelt began conservation efforts at Springwood when he took over the day-to-day operation of the estate in 1910. He first bought several adjacent farms, which had also been depleted by generations of poor husbandry, and in 1911 asked foresters at the University of Syracuse's State College of Forestry to develop a reforestation program for the enlarged estate "in the hope that my grandchildren will be able to raise corn again—just one century from now."[19] On the foresters' recommendations, Roosevelt supervised the planting of a few thousand trees in 1912 and continued an annual planting regimen until his death in 1945, at which time he had overseen the planting of more than a half million trees covering 556 acres of the estate. In 1933 alone, the year the CCC was formed, he had 36,000 trees planted at Hyde Park. Thirty-two species were included in Roosevelt's plantings, the most common being Norway and Canadian spruce; Scotch, Norway, and white pine; and tulip poplar, which was his favorite tree. He introduced a number of exotics as well, such as European and Japanese larch, Sitka spruce, Douglas fir, and Western yellow pine.[20] In light of this extensive effort, it is not surprising that each year when voting in Hyde Park Roosevelt listed his occupation as "tree grower."[21]

Although he referred to reforested plots similar to those at Hyde Park as "the most potent factor in maintaining nature's delicate balance," Roosevelt planted trees on his property for economic, not ecological, reasons. According to Nelson Brown, the Syracuse University forester who oversaw the plantings at Springwood, reforestation for Roosevelt was "not just a passing fancy or plaything—it is a very realistic and practical business endeavor" that often turned a profit. Throughout the 1920s and early 1930s, Roosevelt did indeed make small returns by selling fuel wood and sawlogs locally, as well as cross-ties cut from his woodlots to the New York Central Railroad, which ran a train line along a narrow strip of land between the Hudson River and the Roosevelt property. Roosevelt's most publicized foray into commercial forestry, however, began in 1926 when he planted the first of many plots of Norway spruce, which at the time were used widely as Christmas trees. Only nine years later, he cut and sold 132 of these trees for a modest profit of $134.55, and in 1937 harvested 1,000 trees for a total profit of $480. All told, the Johnny Appleseed of Springwood sold several thousand Christmas trees worth almost as many dollars during the 1930s and 1940s.[22] In the early 1940s, he also harvested more than 2,000 mature hardwood trees that yielded 445,000 board feet of timber for a net gain of more than $60 per acre.[23] "He realizes," explained Nelson Brown of Franklin Roosevelt, "that aesthetic considerations are in order about his home, but out in the forest, they play a very small—in fact, a negligible part." According to Brown, Roosevelt continually inquired about the price of various forest products and weighed the relative merits of growing species for pulpwood, sawlogs, fuel wood, cross-ties, and Christmas trees. "He believes in taking advantage of favorable market conditions when available," added the Syracuse forester.[24] (See figure 1.1.)

Just as he transported what he learned in Bad Nauheim back to Hyde Park, Roosevelt brought the conservation knowledge he gained at Springwood with him to the New York State Senate when he began serving in that body in 1911. Because of his statewide reputation as a "tree grower," Roosevelt's first appointment was as chair of the senate's Forest, Fish, and Game Committee. In that capacity, he publicized a number of threats to the state's natural

Figure 1.1 One of Franklin Roosevelt's favorite pastimes when home at Springwood, his Hyde Park estate, was inspecting his forests in his Ford Phaeton. In this photograph, Roosevelt drives Syracuse University forester Nelson Brown, who was responsible for the estate's forestry program, to an area of the property being logged, most probably for board lumber. During the 1920s, when Roosevelt looked out his car window at similarly felled trees, he, like most conservationists who came of age during the Progressive Era, undoubtedly saw dollar signs. During his early political career, at least, aesthetic and ecological concerns took a back seat to economics and efficiency when it came to forestry like that practiced at Hyde Park. (Photograph title: "Drives his car in the Woods with Nelson Brown," February 26, 1944. NPx 54–70, Franklin Delano Roosevelt Library, Hyde Park, N.Y.)

resources and introduced eight bills aimed at conserving them, including legislative initiatives regulating fishing, hunting, and the development of water power.[25] By far, Roosevelt's most intense senatorial battle, however, involved a bill he proposed in January 1912 that would, among other things, allow the state to regulate timber harvests on private land. The Roosevelt-Jones Bill, as it was popularly called, arose in response to a disturbing trend then occurring in upstate New York's Adirondack Forest Preserve. When a state constitutional amendment created the preserve in 1895, the legislature in Albany had delineated its geographic boundaries by "drawing" a "blue line" on maps around twelve counties in the Adirondack Mountains region of upstate New York. The result was a 3.3 million-acre reserve composed of both state and privately owned land in nearly equal parts. Private individuals, associations such as the Adirondack Mountain Club, and numerous lumber companies all owned large parcels of land within the boundaries of the state park. More alarming to Roosevelt was that although the constitutional amendment declared state-owned property within the preserve to be "forever kept as wild forest land," the law did not apply to the park's privately owned parcels, which during the first decade of the twentieth century became increasingly deforested.[26] The Roosevelt-Jones Bill was aimed at regulating, not outlawing, this cutting on private lands in the Adirondacks and throughout New York.

Roosevelt defended his bill in the senate and across the state in the same manner he defended his conservation efforts at Hyde Park; he argued that it made good economic sense. "It is an extraordinary thing to me," he wrote to one constituent concerning the lumbermen opposing his initiative, "that people who are financially interested should not be able to see more than about six inches in front of their noses."[27] By regulating logging on private property, Roosevelt argued, the Roosevelt-Jones Bill would reduce water runoff and soil erosion on adjacent state-owned land and thus assure the long-term financial security of the state's forests. To help promote the bill, Roosevelt invited the well-known chief of the U.S. Forest Service, Gifford Pinchot, to lecture before the assembly in Albany. Pinchot illustrated his talk with two lantern slides of a valley in China: the first slide was of a painting from the year 1500 depicting a lush landscape covered with trees, crops, and numerous signs of human habitation, while the second, a photograph taken four centuries later, portrayed the same landscape void of both vegetation and humanity. The message was all too clear: poor land use was suicide. The presentation confirmed Roosevelt's belief in the economic necessity of conservation and made such an impression that he publicly referred to Pinchot's slides numerous times during his political career.[28]

As important, the Roosevelt-Jones Bill also gave the young state senator his first taste of what conservation could do for his political career. Although upstate lumber interests successfully convinced the Albany legislature to strike the section permitting the state to regulate logging on private land, passage of the 1912 bill raised Roosevelt's political stature across New York. This was especially true among the state's conservationists who, like their counterparts nationwide, had become increasingly concerned about industrialization's devastating impact on water, soil, and timber supplies and wanted to take concerted action to scientifically manage such resources for future use. This desire to produce natural resources rationally—what historian Samuel

Hays has called the "gospel of efficiency"—was in fact the central tenet of the Progressive conservation movement.[29] The Newlands Reclamation Act of 1902, the creation of the U.S. Forest Service in 1905, and the passage in 1911 of the Weeks Act, which provided for federal acquisition of private forest land, were only the most well-known attempts by conservationists to improve resource production nationally.[30] The Roosevelt-Jones Bill did something similar on the state level, and in doing so illustrated to Roosevelt early in his career the important connections between conservation policy and political power.

Unlike other reform efforts during the Progressive Era, an emerging middle class in search of order did not orchestrate the conservation movement. Instead, while a triumvirate of scientific professionals, government bureaucrats, and businesspeople involved in resource extraction directed the reform from above, local landowners, ranchers, and hunters in rural regions both supported and sometimes contested such efforts from below.[31] Perhaps no single individual better epitomized the professional side of the movement than Gifford Pinchot. Born in 1865 to a wealthy Connecticut family, Pinchot grew up in Paris and Pennsylvania, graduated from Yale in 1889, and then traveled to France and Germany to study forestry. Upon his return to the United States in 1892, he began promoting the scientific management of the country's timber supplies and practicing what he preached, first as timber manager at "Biltmore," the Vanderbilt family estate near Asheville, North Carolina, and later as a forester for the federal government. Throughout his career, Pinchot viewed nature primarily in utilitarian terms. For instance, in his autobiography he defined conservation as "the development and use of the earth and all its resources for the enduring good of men."[32] To determine how best to produce and use these resources, Pinchot also developed a simple formula for the Forest Service to follow. In a 1905 memo written soon after becoming chief forester, Pinchot explained that, when faced with conflicting interests regarding the production of a natural resource, such as the situation Roosevelt encountered in the Adirondacks, the question should "always be decided from the standpoint of the greatest good of the greatest number in the long run."[33] This principle became the guiding philosophy not only of the Forest Service but of the great majority of Progressive conservationists as well.[34]

While Pinchot served as the unofficial spokesperson for conservationists, the movement itself was suffering from growing pains during the Progressive Era. Rumblings had begun to surface during the late nineteenth century, when another point of view concerning the natural environment emerged and slowly gained adherents. The most well-known promoter of this alternative vision was John Muir, foremost lobbyist for the creation of Yosemite National Park in

1890, founder of the Sierra Club in 1892, and an indomitable outdoorsman whose nature writing propelled him to minor literary celebrity around the turn of the century. Muir's early life could not have been more different from Gifford Pinchot's. Born in Dunbar, Scotland, in 1838 to overbearing Calvinist parents, Muir moved with his family at the age of eleven to a homestead on the central Wisconsin frontier. Unlike Pinchot, who studied at the best schools in America and abroad, Muir was a self-taught naturalist who attended the University of Wisconsin for only two years. Before leaving Madison, however, he encountered the writings of Wordsworth, Emerson, Thoreau, and a lesser known minister named Walter Rollins Brooks. From that moment on, transcendentalism influenced his philosophy regarding the natural world. According to Muir, natural objects were "the terrestrial manifestations of God," and nature itself was "a window opening into heaven, a mirror reflecting the Creator." Leaves, rocks, and bodies of water were "sparks of the Divine Soul."[35] Wary of Gifford Pinchot's utilitarian view, Muir believed in preserving nature's beauty for its own sake as well as for the spiritual sake of humankind. While Muir rarely used the term "conservationist" when describing himself, during the Progressive Era his preservationist philosophy and Pinchot's utilitarian vision existed side by side in an uneasy alliance.[36]

Muir and Pinchot first met in 1893 and became friends three years later while working and camping together as part of a federally sponsored survey of western national forests, which at the time were called "reserves." Members of the expedition were responsible not only for examining the reserves but also for recommending a federal policy for their management. During the trip, the two men found much in common, and often left the camaraderie of the evening campfire to discuss their mutual love of the outdoors and the future of the nation's forests, which both agreed needed protection from private, unscientific development. Each morning, Pinchot recalled years later, "we sneaked back like guilty schoolboys" to rejoin the other members of the expedition.[37]

When the survey party began preparing its report, however, the limits of the two men's common interest became readily apparent. Whereas Muir recommended that the federal government preserve the forests without provision for commercial use, Pinchot favored opening up all of the reserves to scientifically managed economic development. This ideological divide widened in 1897, when Pinchot publicly endorsed sheep grazing in the forest reserves, and broadened into a chasm in 1905, when Pinchot, acting as the newly appointed Forest Service chief, supported plans to dam Yosemite National Park's Hetch Hetchy Valley to create a reservoir that would quench the thirst of San Francisco's growing population. While Pinchot argued that the valley's high elevation in the Sierra Nevada mountains made it perfect for supplying both drinking water and electric power, Muir, whose Sierra Club had successfully opposed the Hetch Hetchy dam since San Francisco officials first proposed it in the 1890s, launched an eight-year nationwide campaign to protect the valley from development. In one of his most well-known statements regarding the controversy, Muir countered Pinchot's economic argument by emphasizing Hetch Hetchy's noncommercial attributes. "Dam Hetch Hetchy!" he wrote in 1912. "As well dam for water-tanks the people's cathedrals and churches, for no holier temple has ever been consecrated by the heart of man."[38] President Woodrow Wilson's decision in December 1913 to approve the Hetch Hetchy dam devastated John Muir, who died less than a year later. Perhaps more important, it splintered what was already a fragile alliance within the conservation movement into conservationist and preservationist camps.[39]

Although Franklin Roosevelt was well aware of the differences between Muir's and Pinchot's philosophies, his actions at Hyde Park and during his career as a New York state senator indicated that his thinking corresponded more with that of Gifford Pinchot. Roosevelt's desire to produce timber efficiently both on his Hyde Park estate and in the Adirondacks, as well as his reliance on experts such as Nelson Brown and Gifford Pinchot, placed him squarely in the conservationist camp. Moreover, Roosevelt's frustration with lumbermen who could not "see more than about six inches in front of their noses" and his desire to regulate private land for the sake of the state's public forests, echoed to a great extent Pinchot's philosophy of the "greatest good of the greatest number in the long run." Finally, unlike Muir's desire to preserve nature for spiritual and aesthetic reasons, Roosevelt believed that "aesthetic considerations ... play a very small—in fact, a negligible part." This is not to say that Roosevelt had no preservationist tendencies; while scientifically managing his tree plantings at Hyde Park, he also ensured that a stand of old growth forest located along the western edge of his property was left untouched so that it could be "preserved just as nature always has treated it."[40] While such openness to Muir's philosophy would become increasingly important to the CCC story as the Great Depression wore on, during the Progressive Era Roosevelt was clearly a disciple of Pinchot's gospel of efficiency rather than of Muir's transcendental church.

Franklin Roosevelt's inclination for Pinchot-style conservation was still very much intact when he became governor of New York in 1929, long after Progressivism was said to be dead and buried.[41] In his 1931 "Message to the

Legislature," for example, Roosevelt noted the alarming rate of farm abandonment throughout the state and proposed a solution that reiterated his utilitarian notion of natural resources. "Every acre of rural land in the state," he explained, "should be used only for that purpose for which it is best fitted and out of which the greatest economic return can be derived."[42] To help formulate this policy, the new governor also looked to experts, much as Progressive Era conservationists had. He appointed Henry Morgenthau, editor of the *American Agriculturalist*, to the post of New York state conservation commissioner, and relied often on the advice of George Warren and Carl Ladd of Cornell's College of Agriculture, whose land use studies advocated the removal of marginal and submarginal farmland from production. Yet perhaps most indicative of Roosevelt's persistent belief in Progressive Era conservation was his support of the Hewitt Amendment. Introduced by conservative senator Charles Hewitt in 1931, the amendment to New York's constitution authorized the state to purchase abandoned farmland, reforest it, and scientifically manage it as production forests.

Roosevelt once again put his political neck on the line to support this controversial policy. He had encouraged Hewitt to introduce the amendment, and once more enlisted his old friend Gifford Pinchot to campaign for its passage, this time without his lantern slides. He also steadfastly supported the amendment even when Al Smith, who continued to harbor presidential aspirations for 1932, openly criticized the measure as a "tree stealing" program.[43] The amendment's passage in 1931 not only indicated that Progressive Era conservation was alive and well during the early years of the Great Depression, but it also helped to propel Franklin Roosevelt toward the White House. As the *New York Times* reported in a front-page article, the Hewitt Amendment represented a "victory for Governor Roosevelt and add[s] to his prestige as the titular leader of his party in the State and, for the moment the leading Democratic aspirant for the presidential nomination."[44] As with the Roosevelt-Jones Bill earlier in his career, the passage of the Hewitt Amendment demonstrated once more to Roosevelt that conservation could expand his political power, this time onto the national stage.

Thus when Franklin Roosevelt asked Congress to create the CCC, his experiences with Progressive Era conservation both on his family estate in Hyde Park and in the state capital in Albany greatly influenced his thinking. Yet the deterioration of natural resources was not the only crisis worrying Roosevelt in March 1933. Unemployment, particularly among young men, also concerned the president. Not surprisingly, Franklin Roosevelt had a long history with youth relief during and after the Progressive Era that equally, if not to a greater extent, influenced his thinking concerning the Corps.

Franklin Roosevelt's March 21 congressional message drew attention to the unemployment problem then facing the nation, and proposed work in the CCC as part of the solution. Roosevelt's language throughout his message, however, suggested that the new president held specific notions about those who were jobless and the type of jobs the Corps would provide. For instance, he incorrectly suggested that unemployment during the early years of the Great Depression was primarily an urban problem. "The overwhelming majority of unemployed Americans," he explained to Congress, "are now walking the streets." Two months earlier, he had made similar remarks, telling a crowd, "there are hundreds of thousands of boys who only know the pavements of cities and that means that they can take only those jobs that are directly connected with the pavements of cities."[45] As a first step toward addressing this problem, immediately after Congress established the CCC, the president invited representatives from seventeen of the nation's largest cities to the White House to listen to his plans for employing young men and to ask for their help in recruiting the Corps' first 250,000 enrollees.[46]

Although the president viewed joblessness as an urban problem, he envisioned its solution as taking place in the countryside, where he planned to locate CCC camps. By establishing the Corps as quickly as possible, he wrote in his congressional message, "we can take a vast army of these unemployed out into healthful surroundings."[47] Removing the unemployed from cities and placing them in rural areas across the country was central to getting these people back on their feet. Thus, while Roosevelt the conservationist saw the countryside's natural resources as in dire need of scientific management, Roosevelt the unemployment reformer believed that the countryside was also potentially rejuvenating, especially for young urban men.

This belief that the countryside was a curative for urban problems was not new to Roosevelt; it had informed much of his thinking during the early years of the Great Depression. In August 1931, for instance, Governor Roosevelt gave a speech before the American Country Life Conference in Ithaca, New York, in which he painted a gloomy portrait of urban America. "In times of economic depression we expect to find a concentration of unemployed persons, and as a result a concentration of distress, in the cities," he explained. Rural America, on the other hand, had surpluses of foodstuffs and other benefits as well. "The country has added advantages that the city cannot duplicate in opportunities for healthful and natural living," Roosevelt told his audience. "There is contact with earth and with nature and the restful privilege of getting away from pavements and from noise." As governor, it was Roosevelt's responsibility to correct this demographic imbalance by promoting the migration of unemployed workers from New York's urban areas to its rural regions where the materials for healthful living were cheap and abundant. "The task," he concluded in his speech, "is to determine to what extent and by what means the State and its subdivisions may properly stimulate the movement of city workers to rural homes." The enthusiastic response of the conference attendees illustrated to Roosevelt that juxtaposing city and countryside was politically popular with Depression era Americans.[48]

Roosevelt was not alone in contrasting rural and urban America during the early years of the Great Depression. A loose coalition of individuals and groups from across the political spectrum also called for the resettlement of unemployed urbanites in the countryside.[49] In the late 1920s, Ralph Borsodi, a former advertising executive turned social critic, was the leading advocate of this anti-urban, back-to-the-land movement. Borsodi left Manhattan in 1922 and moved to the countryside near Suffern, New York, where he and his family built a stone house on seven acres of land, raised domesticated animals, grew their own food, and made their own clothing and furniture. Borsodi described his experiment in self-sufficiency in two bestselling books, *This Ugly Civilization*, published in 1929, and *Flight from the City*, written four years later.[50] Other liberal writers followed Borsodi's lead, publishing what became a whole genre of do-it-yourself guidebooks devoted to explaining in detail how one could leave urban industrial society and survive on one's own in rural America. Edward Parkinson's *The Retreat from Wall Street* (1931), Louise Owen's *Escape from Babylon* (1932), Katrina Hinck's *A Home for $130* (1933), and Maurice Kains's *Five Acres and Independence* (1935), which advised former clerks and factory workers how to operate a farm, were only a few of the best-known works written during the early years of the Great Depression in response to widespread urban unemployment.[51]

This Depression era back-to-the-land sentiment also gained credibility on the political Right through a group of southern intellectuals who became known as the Nashville Agrarians. Centered at Vanderbilt University, members of this informal group included English professors, literary critics, poets, historians, and economists such as Allen Tate, John Crowe Ransom, Donald Davidson, Frank Owsley, Robert Penn Warren, and Andrew Lytle. The Agrarians' central theme, put forward most succinctly in their 1930 collection of essays titled *I'll Take My Stand*, centered around what they believed to be an unavoidable conflict between industrialism and agrarianism. According to the Vanderbilt intellectuals, industrialism represented everything antitraditional, immoral, and deadening, while agrarianism stood for all that was stable, moral, and spiritually uplifting. Together, they viewed urban society as repugnant and eulogized life in the countryside. "A city of any sort," wrote John Crowe Ransom, "removes men from direct contact with nature, and cannot quite constitute the staple or normal form of life for the citizen."[52] Joining the Agrarians on the Right during the early 1930s was the Catholic Rural Life movement. Centered in the Midwest rather than the South and led by Fathers Luigi Ligutti, John Rawe, and W. Howard Bishop, this coalition promoted economic independence and family unity by encouraging the widespread ownership of farms. It accomplished this by funneling financial support to rural parishes and by establishing "rural-life bureaus," directed by priests, to facilitate the "colonization" of rural regions. The return of Depression era families to the land, wrote Howard Bishop in *Landward*, the Catholic Rural Life movement's official bulletin, symbolized "the foundation for a real civilization upon which an enduring Christian structure can be found[ed]."[53]

Roosevelt was well aware that his anti-urban, pro-rural rhetoric appealed to both the political Left and the political Right, and that such ideas were not novel in the early 1930s. Such sentiments were instead merely the newest incarnation of a much older movement whose ideological roots went back at least to Thomas Jefferson. Much of this sentiment had crystallized during the Progressive Era when concern over the deleterious effects of industrialization and urbanization was at its peak.[54] While some Americans accepted these changes, others resisted by joining unions, embracing populism, and becoming active in a whole host of Progressive reform efforts aimed at insulating the working class from urban dangers.

Before the turn of the century, these reformers, most of whom hailed from the middle and upper classes, practiced what historian Paul Boyer has termed "coercive moral reform," meaning they attempted to stamp out urban vices, such as prostitution, alcohol consumption, and gambling, through moral persuasion and legal repression. During the first decade of the twentieth century, however, a new strategy of social control linked to advances in behavioral psychology emerged to compete with these coercive reform efforts. While this novel approach shared the underlying moral assumptions and aims of the coercive efforts, it differed fundamentally on how to achieve these goals. Instead of overtly repressing urban vices, this new group of reformers hoped to create an urban setting where objectionable behavior would not be practiced and would thus wither away. Summing up this new philosophy, John Dewey wrote in 1908 that the most effective social control was not based on the legal enforcement of strict behavioral standards, but rather on "the intelligent selection and determination of the environments in which we act."[55] Those involved in reform efforts such as the city beautiful movement, city planning, housing reform, settlement work, and even urban sanitation thus believed not in good and bad people, but rather in good and bad environments.[56] These Progressives were thus environmentalists of a different sort, members of an old school environmentalism quite different from the newer environmental movement that would arise during the postwar period.

Progressive Era environmentalists believed that their reform strategy was particularly effective in influencing young adults, who many viewed as malleable putty ready to be sculpted into model citizens. One of the foremost promoters of this ideology was landscape designer Frederick Law Olmsted, who depicted city parks as having a "harmonizing and refining" influence "favorable to courtesy, self-control, and temperance," especially for city youths.[57] Olmsted's views shaped an entire generation of urban park planners and promoters. While landscape architects such as George Kessler similarly posited that the "green turf" and "waving trees" of urban parks produced "innocent, joyous" youngsters instead of "dirty, white-faced, and vicious gamins" prone to "immorality and vice," park boosters including George Washington Eggleston argued that when city dwellers "have Nature at hand, evil seems weakened [and] . . . the souls of children become freshened with joy."[58] Such ideas even influenced the playground movement, led by the Playground Association of America's Henry Stoddard Curtis, whose 1917 classic *The Play Movement and Its Significance* depicted urban youth as prone to congregate on street corners "where drinking and the sex lure are the main enticements." For Curtis, as for Olmsted, the answer lay not in repressing such activities but in creating what the playground advocate called "a different environment" as an alternative to the vice-ridden streets.[59]

Along with creating different environments within the metropolis, Progressive environmentalists were also interested in the healing potential of the nonurban setting. This belief in the rejuvenative power of the countryside was part of a larger trend that gripped middle- and upper-class Americans during the early decades of the twentieth century. Called "antimodern" by Jackson Lears, "a search for the simple life" by historian David Shi, and a "wilderness cult" by Roderick Nash, this Progressive nature craze had three main elements: a country life movement similar to the back-to-the-land sentiment of the early Depression years, a wilderness fad that focused on preserving and experiencing life in the wild, and finally an outdoor fresh air movement best exemplified by country vacations and summer camps.[60] The most vociferous promoter of this outdoor rage was Theodore Roosevelt, who during the last decade of the nineteenth century became increasingly convinced that urban America was becoming an "overcivilized man, who has lost the great fighting, masterful virtues." To counter this descent into "flabbiness" and "slothful ease," in 1899 Roosevelt began urging Americans to adopt what he called "the doctrine of the strenuous life," which entailed a "life of toil and effort, of labor and strife."[61] Central to this sort of living was direct contact with nonurban nature.

Progressive environmentalist reformers enthusiastically embraced Theodore Roosevelt's call for a more strenuous life, and went to great lengths to transport young urbanites beyond the city limits to more bucolic surroundings. This was especially true during the summer months, when many urban youths were out of school but unable to find employment. Edward Bok, editor of the *Ladies' Home Journal*, was a leading proponent of so-called fresh air funds, and helped to establish several in eastern cities to subsidize country vacations for out-of-work city-bred adolescents. According to Bok and his associates, the urban environment's filth, its wearying working conditions, and its general enervating influence could be overcome by spending a few weeks in the "simplicity and sincerity of nature."[62] Similar beliefs underwrote the youth camping movement, which became a fad in its own right during this period. For those "who cannot afford yachting trips and the like, and whose ideas of summer recreation are not attuned to the string band of a 'summer hotel,' " explained one youth camping advocate, "there is nothing that returns so much for the expenditure of strength and money as plain American camping."[63]

One of the foremost promoters of the youth camping movement during the Progressive Era was the Boy Scouts of America. Although Lieutenant General Sir Robert Baden-Powell officially founded the Boy Scouts in England in 1907, he borrowed heavily from a number of similar organizations already established in the United States. One such group was the Woodcraft Indians, founded by popular nature writer Ernest Thompson Seton. In a series of articles in Edward Bok's *Ladies' Home Journal* in 1902, Seton described how his new group organized boys into tribes, taught them games based on Indian legend and ceremony, bestowed awards for good conduct, and most important took them out of the city to camp in the countryside. Alongside Seton's Indians, Daniel Beard founded the Sons of Daniel Boone in 1905 as a circulation booster for an outdoor recreation magazine. Whereas Seton relied on Native American history and symbols to encourage young boys to take to the woods, Beard employed the frontier's pioneer heritage and focused on teaching outdoor survival techniques, such as fire building, map reading, and shelter construction. When a coalition of New York City youth reformers officially established the Boy Scouts of America in 1910, focusing enrollment in the program on adolescents and young boys between the ages of nine and twenty, it not only integrated these organizational forerunners but also found jobs for both Seton and Beard, with the former acting as chief scout from 1910 to 1915 and the latter serving as national scout commissioner of the United States from 1910 until his death.[64]

With its close ties to environmentalist thinkers such as Olmsted, it is no wonder that nonurban nature was an integral component of the Boy Scouts' reform efforts.[65] This affinity was perhaps best expressed in the Boy Scouts' first *Handbook*, which Seton wrote in 1910. A century ago, the *Handbook* began, American boys lived close to nature, but since then the nation had experienced "unfortunate change" marked by industrialization and the "growth of immense cities." The result, Seton warned, was "degeneracy" and an urban population that was "strained and broken by the grind of the over-busy world." The Boy Scouts' solution was not to eliminate urban dangers but rather to introduce scouts to "outdoor life... nearest to the ground" so that these boys could "live the simple life of primitive times." The *Handbook* also provided instruction in woodsmanship and camping in an effort to urge city boys to spend at least one month each year in the countryside.[66] To foster this, soon after its creation in 1910, the Boy Scouts of America began establishing campgrounds on the outskirts of metropolitan areas throughout the country.

Similar to his cousin Theodore, who became the Boy Scouts' first chief scout citizen in 1912, Franklin Roosevelt was deeply involved in the scouting movement. The younger Roosevelt's experiences with the Boy Scouts began in 1921, when he accepted the chair of the organization's Greater New York City Council. The following year, he helped to centralize the scouting movement in and around the city by creating the Boy Scout Foundation of Greater New York to coordinate the work of the five borough councils, which had previously maintained independent relationships with the Boy Scouts of America's national leadership. In 1922, Roosevelt also became president of the Boy Scout Foundation of Greater New York and remained in that position until he resigned in 1937.[67] (See figure 1.2.)

Throughout his sixteen-year involvement with the Boy Scouts, Franklin Roosevelt aggressively promoted a Progressive environmentalist agenda. This became only too clear at a Boy Scout dinner in March 1929, during which he emphasized the role of the physical setting in shaping young urbanites. "The records show," Roosevelt told the audience gathered in New York's posh Metropolitan Club, "that the question of environment is important."[68] At a similar Boy Scout event a few years later, he expressed the belief, also shared by Progressive Era environmentalists, that urban surroundings were particularly dangerous for

Figure 1.2 This 1930 photograph, of Governor Roosevelt trying out an archery set presented to him by a Boy Scout troop in Hyde Park, New York, illustrates a second set of Progressive Era concerns that would greatly influence the creation of the CCC. The bow and arrow hark back to the Boy Scouts' roots in Ernest Thompson Seton's Woodcraft Indians, which also tried to rejuvenate youths from urban areas by taking them camping in the countryside. Franklin Roosevelt, who at the time of this photograph served as president of the Boy Scout Foundation of Greater New York, similarly embraced this notion that healthy environments out in nature could benefit urban youths. The leather cover for the bow and arrow set lying across Roosevelt's lap, imprinted with an American flag, also suggests the nationalistic sentiment, and political power, inherent in the Scouting movement. (Photo title "Tries archery set just given him by scouts of the Dutchess County Council," October 12, 1930, Hyde Park, N.Y. NPx 60-33(8), Franklin Delano Roosevelt Library, Hyde Park, N.Y.)

city youths, especially those from working-class families. For "the city boy living in crowded conditions," Roosevelt explained, "artificial interests have been substituted. Normal, natural growth is threatened."[69] He likewise promoted the other side of the environmentalist coin, namely, that the countryside was a potential curative for the problems afflicting urban youth. When transported to the countryside, the urban boy "discovers that the woods, the birds, the fields, the streams, the insects speak a language he understands," Roosevelt wrote in a 1928 article on the Boy Scouts for the *New York Times.* "His new environment takes on the aspect of a vast nature-lore museum which beckons to him to enter its great domain of study and to discover for himself."[70]

For the Boy Scouts, and for Franklin Roosevelt in particular, the means of introducing city boys to the benefits of the nonurban environment was through camping in the countryside. When Roosevelt became chair of the Boy Scout Foundation of Greater New York in 1922, the organization maintained eighteen scout campgrounds in the Bear Mountain section of the Palisades Interstate Park, located on the western bank of the Hudson River approximately halfway between New York City and Roosevelt's Hyde Park estate. Reputed to be the largest camping facility for scouts in the world, the Bear Mountain camps varied in size and together accommodated at any given time approximately 2,200 young men, most of whom spent three weeks in the park.[71] Although more than 6,000 boys camped at Bear Mountain during the summer of 1922, two-thirds of New York City's 20,000 scouts were unable to do so because of a lack of camping space. Franklin Roosevelt was especially concerned, stating years later that "we realized then that our camping facilities were inadequate."[72]

Roosevelt responded to this dearth of camping opportunities for urban unemployed youths by initiating a campaign to increase the number of scout campgrounds throughout the state. "It is probable that next year we will increase our capacity so that we can take care of as many as 3,000 boys daily," wrote Roosevelt to a Boy Scout backer in 1921, "and I would not be surprised if within the next three to five years we would have as many as 5,000 to 10,000 boys in camp at one time."[73] During the next several years, Roosevelt raised funds to acquire land in upstate New York for campground purposes, and in 1929 began developing a 10,600-acre tract located about 100 miles north of New York City in Sullivan County, where he estimated that 100,000 scouts could experience outdoor living each summer.[74] As the Boy Scouts of America's national leadership reported that year, experiences in these camps would include "many outdoor activities which bring Scouts closer to nature."[75]

Just what the Boy Scouts of America meant by "closer to nature" was evident in the daily operation of scout camps nationwide during the early years of the organization's history. With its roots in both Seton's Woodcraft Indians and Beard's Sons of Daniel Boone, the Boy Scouts understandably promoted outdoorsmanship and woodcraft in their campgrounds rather than nature study. Scoutmasters regularly taught the young boys to pitch tents, blaze trails, and build fires, but rarely how to appreciate or understand the countryside around them. In fact, the Boy Scouts' official camping program included only one test among many that involved the identification of trees and animals.[76] This desire to dominate or subdue nature was perhaps best epitomized by the Boy Scout hatchet, which the organization sold to the boys in such numbers that early on it became a standard addendum to the scout uniform. The teaching of trail blazing, the use of wood for rustic bridges and fences, and the continual search for firewood in and around Boy Scout campgrounds all encouraged a slash-and-burn style of outdoor living. Each year, for instance, scouts visiting the Bear Mountain camps stripped bark from birch trees as high as they could reach, often while posing for publicity photographs.[77] Such young men were obviously ignorant of the conservation efforts under way 50 miles upriver on Franklin Roosevelt's Hyde Park estate, or 100 miles north in the Adirondack Forest Preserve.

The Boy Scouts of America thus had much in common with Franklin Roosevelt's CCC. Both were concerned with unemployed male youths and associated this problem with the urban setting. Each also promoted the relocation of young city dwellers to camps in the countryside as a curative. In doing so, the Boy Scouts and the Corps each reflected the thinking of urban reformers such as Frederick Law Olmsted, who believed that one's surroundings or environment shaped social behavior. Yet as the Boy Scouts' camping program indicates, the conservation of natural resources was not an integral component of the scout philosophy. Rather than teaching their charges how to efficiently use timber, soil, and water, scoutmasters allowed, and often encouraged, the waste of such resources. How, then, did the idea of conserving natural resources become linked, in Franklin Roosevelt's mind, to the notion of rejuvenating urban male youths?

Franklin Roosevelt first suggested the idea of introducing the ideology and practice of conservation to scouting soon after he became president of the Boy Scout Foundation of Greater New York. In a letter to foundation member and New York state conservation commissioner George Pratt in 1922, Roosevelt expressed his desire to correct the Boy Scout camping program's wasteful natural resource practices. "I shall do everything possible," he promised, "to expand what might be called the better understanding of nature by these city-bred boys."[78] That same year, he asked members of the Boy Scout camping committee to investigate the possibility of enlarging the study of forestry at the existing scout camps. He also asked the Palisades Interstate Park Commission if it would be possible to secure a small tract of land near the Boy Scout camps in the Bear Mountain section of the park "to be scientifically forested by the boys this summer."[79] Such a reforested tract, the commissioners enthusiastically replied, would "imbue the coming generations with a knowledge of forest conservation" and "[teach] business, not sentimental theory."[80] It would seem that as soon as Franklin Roosevelt became involved with the Scouts, the days of the boys' overactive hatchet were numbered.[81]

Roosevelt expanded his effort to promote conservation within the Boy Scouts in 1923. Rather than merely adding forestry study to the camping program already in existence, Roosevelt helped to establish new scout camps, also in the Palisades Interstate Park, dedicated specifically to the teaching and practice of natural resource conservation. The Boy Scout Foundation of Greater New York established the first such camp in 1923, and another the following year. Known collectively as the Franklin D. Roosevelt Conservation Camps, each could accommodate approximately sixty campers and accepted only scouts fifteen years of age and older, many of whom had trouble finding employment during the summer months.[82] Instead of pitching tents, building fires, and stripping birch bark, boys attending these special conservation camps would perform work such as cutting firebreaks, fighting forest fires, and planting trees. As one forester involved in the new program put it, the conservation camps would give the older scout "expert training . . . and familiarize him with one of the biggest economic problems of the day—Forestry."[83] In 1929, Roosevelt decided to expand the scout conservation program yet again by including forestry work in the development plans for the Boy Scout Foundation's new 10,600-acre campground in Sullivan County, New York.

During these early Great Depression years, there were signs that the conservation program initiated by Roosevelt in the Palisades camps was influencing Boy Scouts throughout the nation. In 1930, the Boy Scouts of America launched a five-year reforestation program known as the Nut Seed and Tree Planting Project. After gathering nuts from trees in Mount Vernon's Arlington National Cemetery and at Theodore Roosevelt's grave in Oyster Bay, Long Island, the organization dispersed them to scouts throughout the country for planting as memorial trees. Boy Scouts in Emmet County, Iowa, conducted the project's first tree-planting demonstration, and other troops followed, with scouts planting nearly 50,000 seedlings in Oshkosh, Wisconsin; 20,000 in Leominster, Massachusetts; and 4,700 in Massillon, Ohio. Scout troops from Roosevelt's home county of Dutchess, New York, planted 4,500 seedlings and received in return "that satisfaction that comes from planting trees."[84] All told, the Boy Scouts of America hoped to plant more than 5 million trees during the five-year project. Perhaps more important, the conservation of natural resources had finally been wedded to youth reform in the mind of Franklin Roosevelt.

When the stock market crashed in October 1929, Governor Roosevelt applied what he had accomplished with the Boy Scouts to the economic and environmental problems of the Empire State. Just a few months after Black Tuesday, Roosevelt asked the state legislature for an appropriation to fund a tree-planting program, similar to that initiated by the Boy Scouts, to provide jobs for New York's growing unemployed population.[85] In September 1931, the governor greatly expanded this sort of relief work when he established the Temporary Emergency Relief Administration (TERA), which along with providing food, clothing, and shelter to those in need also created jobs, many in the field of forestry. The forestry jobs created by TERA provided the labor necessary to physically convert the abandoned farmlands purchased through the Hewitt Amendment into public forests. Roosevelt named Harry Hopkins, former head of New York's Tuberculosis and Health Association, as executive director of TERA and directed him to coordinate the program's forestry work with Conservation Department commissioner Henry Morgenthau, Jr.[86]

Under Roosevelt's close supervision, TERA began its forestry relief work early in 1932. "We have lately undertaken a new project using our State relief funds in forestry work," explained the New York governor to Ovid Butler, executive secretary of the American Forestry Association. "On this project we are now employing 100 men in Central New York on a somewhat experimental basis to find out to what extent we can profitably use men from the lists of the unemployed to improve our existing reforestation areas."[87] The "experiment," as Roosevelt called it, proved so successful that TERA immediately created more than 10,000 conservation-related jobs for out-of-work New Yorkers.[88] Not surprising given Roosevelt's contemporaneous involvement with scouting, TERA's forestry work initiative shared numerous traits with the Boy Scouts' new conservation program. TERA laborers performed work such as the cutting of fire lanes, the clearing of dead wood, and the planting of seedlings that was nearly identical to that done by scouts in the Franklin D. Roosevelt Conservation Camps. Moreover, TERA conducted much of this work in the Palisades Interstate Park, literally a stone's throw from the Boy Scouts' conservation campgrounds. All told, by the end of 1932, Roosevelt's forestry work relief program was aiding more than 25,000 unemployed New Yorkers.[89]

The forestry relief work undertaken by TERA not only reflected the practices of the Boy Scouts, but also foreshadowed the birth of the CCC. Both TERA and the CCC housed their workers in camps located on public lands, and each program provided its participants with food, shelter, and an allowance in exchange for labor. In TERA's case, this pay came to $12 a month, about half what the Corps provided. TERA also administered the selection process of young men from New York who joined the CCC between 1933 and 1937.[90] Most important, the TERA conservation program soon went national, much as the CCC did, when in November 1931 state officials from across the country began praising New York's program and implementing similar ones of their own. Michigan and Indiana of the Great Lakes region, Mississippi and Virginia in the South, and Oregon and Washington state in the Pacific Northwest, among others, all established forestry work relief programs based largely on TERA.[91] California's forestry work relief efforts, often cited as the most advanced program in the country, also began soon after Roosevelt asked the New York state legislature to establish TERA.[92] Even President Herbert Hoover showed his affinity for Governor Roosevelt's forestry relief initiative by allocating funds for similar work in the national forests in January 1931, a year after Roosevelt asked the New York state legislature for an appropriation for tree-planting relief work.[93] Rather than the ideological source of the Corps, TERA was thus the intermediary step on the state level between Roosevelt's metropolitan scouting conservation initiative and his federal CCC program.

As Franklin Roosevelt's experiences before becoming president indicate, Joseph Wilson had it wrong when in October 1936 he tried to commit suicide at the White House after unsuccessfully trying to convince the president that the CCC was his brainchild. Instead, the idea for the Corps was very much a conflux of desire and need on the part of the newly elected president. Roosevelt's desire to conserve the nation's natural resources in light of the disasters occurring along the Ohio and other rivers was the first tributary in the ideological stream that led to the creation of the CCC. This desire had been influenced by the future president's involvement with the Progressive Era conservation movement while both managing his family estate in Hyde Park and during his stint as a politician in Albany. Yet previous encounters with conservation account for only one branch of the CCC's intellectual roots. The president also needed to put young unemployed men back to work, and his experiences expanding rural opportunities for New York City Boy Scouts shaped this process as well. When Roosevelt asked Congress in March 1933 to "create a civilian conservation corps," he thus drew heavily on these two distinct sets of activities.

In relying on his past experiences with both conservation and environmentalist reform, Franklin Roosevelt was more a synthesizer of existing ideologies than a creator of new ones. The president was original, however, in his desire to combine the conservation of natural resources with the conservation of young men. He initiated this process by establishing the Franklin D. Roosevelt Conservation Camps in New York's Palisades Interstate Park, and furthered it

when as governor of New York he created forestry relief work under TERA. Because of such actions, in August 1933, the newly elected president could confidently announce to thousands of cheering Boy Scouts at their annual Jamboree that "this Spring, because of my scout training, I took a leaf out of the notebook of scouting" and "started the CCC in this country, modeling it to a large extent after scouting."[94] What he failed to note to the scouts was that this new leaf embodied in the Corps would greatly influence the future of conservation in the United States.

Roosevelt's experiences with both Progressive conservation and environmentalist reform taught him a thing or two about politics as well. Early in his political career, he learned that promoting conservation policies such as the Roosevelt-Jones Bill and the Hewitt Amendment increased his political power base in New York state and beyond. He similarly understood that sponsoring social programs that relied on rural nature to alleviate urban ills, whether through the Boy Scouts or TERA, also helped him to piece together a diverse coalition not only of city dwellers and rural Americans, but also of conservatives like Father Ligutti of the Catholic Rural Life movement and liberals such as social critic Ralph Borsodi. Roosevelt brought this lesson in constituency building through conservation with him from Albany to Chicago, where on July 2, 1932, at the Democratic National Convention, he accepted the nomination for president. Although three months later he would defeat Herbert Hoover with this same coalition composed of rural southerners from the political Right and urban northeasterners from the Left, on that summer day in Chicago he focused on bringing the groups together.[95] "Immediate means of relief, both for the unemployed and for agriculture," he roared over the applause of Democratic conventioneers, "will come from a wide plan of converting many millions of acres of marginal and unused land into timberland through reforestation."[96] On this first official day of his presidential campaign, Roosevelt began situating a new landscape at the center of his New Deal. It was the CCC that would build this landscape from the ground up.

change; in nation's landscape

what CCC did

TWO / **LANDSCAPE**
The Evolution of CCC Conservation

During the summer of 1942, the Corps' second director, James McEntee, sat down at his desk in Washington, D.C., to write the CCC's final report. In an effort to record for posterity the enormity of the work undertaken by the Corps during the previous nine years, McEntee tallied the number of trees planted by CCC enrollees, computed the total acreage saved from soil erosion by Corps camps, and added up the miles of hiking trails and motor roads built in national and state parks by the New Deal program he oversaw. He then sat back in his chair and began contemplating the bigger picture, thinking about the overall impact of Corps conservation projects and how the labor of millions of young CCC men scattered across the country had altered the United States. After admitting that "the neglect, waste and destruction of many generations could not be repaired or restored in a decade," McEntee argued that since its creation in March 1933, "the Civilian Conservation Corps wrote its name into the economic, social, and educational history of this country." He then incorporated nature into the CCC's overall accomplishments. "It did even more than that," he explained, Corps conservation work "started a change in the landscape of a Nation."[1]

McEntee had good reason for hyperbole. From April 1933, when CCC enrollees first began working on conservation projects, until the summer of 1942, when Congress terminated the New Deal program, the Corps was responsible for planting more than 2 billion trees, slowing soil erosion on 40 million acres of farmland, and developing 800 new state parks. It also constructed more than 10,000 small reservoirs, 46,000 vehicular bridges, 13,000 miles of hiking trails, and nearly 1 million miles of fence, while simultaneously stocking America's rivers with 1 million fish and eradicating almost 400,000 predatory animals from the nation's forests, farmlands, and prairies. Such efforts, moreover, were only the tip of the iceberg. All told, conservative estimates indicate that Corps work projects across the United States altered more than 118 million acres, an area approximately three times the size of Connecticut.[2]

Mapping these landscape changes over time and across space is central to understanding how the pair of Progressive ideologies that came together in the creation of the Corps continued to have influence during the New Deal era. This is partly because during the program's nine-year existence the CCC did not always undertake the same types of conservation projects. Some kinds of work were eliminated and others introduced, suggesting that the very notion of what constituted Corps conservation was fluid during the New Deal years. Tracing the temporal evolution of Corps conservation projects thus identifies in which directions conservation politics were being stretched, pulled, and pushed during the 1930s and early 1940s. It also helps to explain how the geography of CCC work began to influence New Deal politics by raising support, in this case in rural regions of the country, for Franklin Roosevelt's administration. Understanding how the CCC "wrote its name into the economic, social, and educational history of this country" is therefore dependent on the very landscape that Corps enrollees left behind.

Before the CCC could begin its work, the Roosevelt administration had to determine the geographic distribution of Corps camps and their nearby conservation projects. Due to his desire to conserve natural resources on a national scale, and because he was already conscious of the political clout such work had on the local level, Roosevelt made sure that the Corps spread its camps and conservation projects across the entire country. "I want to personally check the location and scope of the camps," he wrote in April 1933.[3] Although placing CCC camps throughout the western United States, where federal property was abundant, was relatively simple, the administration had more difficulty east of the Mississippi, where there was a dearth of public lands. To alleviate just this situation, Congress allowed for the federal acquisition of private land when it passed the act creating the Corps in March 1933. "The President," stated the act, "shall be authorized to acquire real property by purchase, donation, condemnation, or otherwise."[4]

Roosevelt used the law to begin a land-buying frenzy that continued throughout the New Deal years and culminated in the acquisition of more than 20 million acres of private land, enlarging federal holdings by 15 percent.[5] It was these land purchases, the great majority of which lay east of the Mississippi River, that allowed the Roosevelt administration to place CCC camps and their nearby conservation projects in every state in the union as

no. of projects varied + look at type of conserv.

well as in each territory (see figure 2.1).[6] Such purchases also enabled the president to spread New Deal funding, and thus to curry political favor, over a broader geographic area than would have been possible by relying solely on public lands. By buying lands in the East, Roosevelt in effect transformed the CCC into a national program. As the *New York Times* reported in July 1933, "the camps are scattered along the Pacific Coast, all through the Rockies, along the Appalachian chain in the East, down into the Great Smokies in Tennessee and up into the White and Green Mountains in New England . . . in the Middle West, the Ohio and Mississippi Valleys."[7]

While Corps camps and conservation work remained widely distributed during the Great Depression, the number of projects in each region, and across the country as a whole, varied greatly over time. This was due in part to the CCC's status as a temporary New Deal agency. Because Roosevelt originally authorized the Corps for a single six-month enrollment period, only to reauthorize it with varying amounts of congressional funding every six months for the next several years, the number of CCC camps and conservation projects fluctuated biannually (see figure 2.2).[8] Additionally, as enrollees completed conservation projects, the Corps shuffled camps between the Departments of the Interior and Agriculture, which were responsible for overseeing CCC conservation work (see table 2.1). The number of conservation projects assigned to the Department of Agriculture's Forest Service in 1933, therefore, was different than the number of conservation projects under Forest Service jurisdiction in 1936 or 1938 or 1942.[9]

As the number of CCC projects fluctuated, so too did the type of conservation work undertaken by Corps enrollees. This was partly because as the number of camps shifted between the Departments of Agriculture and the Interior, so did the type of work undertaken by camps under each department's jurisdiction; a camp overseen by agriculture's Forest Service might perform reforestation work for six months only to begin a recreation project after being transferred to interior's Park Service. During the 1930s, CCC conservation work also changed on its own, regardless of department and the number of Corps camps in operation. While CCC director Robert Fechner's first annual report listed 62 varieties of Corps conservation work, a year and a half later the list had grown to include no less than 100 different types of projects, and by 1937 the director was boasting that "more than 150 types of work [were] undertaken" by CCC enrollees.[10] This expansion in the scope of CCC conservation projects meant that camps under the jurisdiction of the National Park Service, for example, were not necessarily performing the same type of conservation work in 1933 and in 1941.

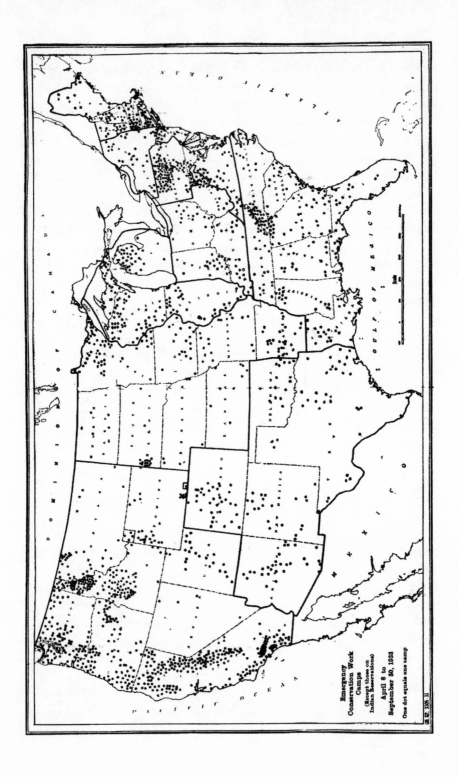

Emergency
Conservation Work
Camps
(Except those on
Indian Reservations)
April 8 to
September 30, 1933

One dot equals one camp

Figure 2.1 The small dots on this CCC map from 1933 depict the distribution of Corps camps nationwide during the program's first six-month enrollment period. To locate enrollees and conservation projects in the eastern United States, where federal land was scarce, Franklin Roosevelt, through the law creating the CCC, had the federal government purchase more than 20 million acres of private land, much of it east of the Mississippi River. Thus along with illustrating the early geography of the Corps, this map also represents the beginning of a dramatic landscape change, initiated by the New Deal, involving the transfer of enormous amounts of private land into a greatly expanded public domain. ("Emergency Conservation Work Camps," map located in CCC Director Robert Fechner, First Report of the Director of the ECW, Record Group 35: CCC, Entry 3: Annual, Final, and Special Reports, NARA, 27)

P 7DR0 trees

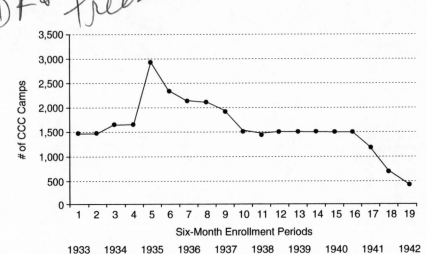

Figure 2.2 Total Number of CCC Camps by Enrollment Period. (Created by author)

While bureaucratically confusing, the variability of Corps work projects over time is central to understanding the historic importance of New Deal conservation. The ever-shifting focus of Corps conservation work, which as we shall see jumped from resource to resource during the Great Depression, was in fact far from random. Beneath the seeming disorder lay a rational pattern that marked the nation's public landscape, particularly its forests, farms, and parks. This pattern not only suggests a progression in Corps conservation work, but likewise illustrates an evolution in the way the Roosevelt administration envisioned conservation and its role within the New Deal political order.

Although Franklin Roosevelt did not clearly define the parameters of CCC conservation work when he asked Congress to establish the New Deal program, during its first year and a half of operation the Corps quickly became associated with one resource in particular: the nation's forests. This is perhaps understandable given Roosevelt's passion for tree planting at Hyde Park, as well as the early ties between the federal land acquisition program initiated through the law establishing the CCC and the expansion of the national forest system.[11] Both the president and Corps director Robert Fechner did little to dissuade this early association. Roosevelt's office frequently called enrollees' living quarters "reforestation camps," and Fechner, especially in his early communications, continually linked Corps work to forestry. In speeches and press releases, the CCC director repeatedly referred to the law creating the Corps as "the reforestation and relief bill," to the CCC itself as "the President's reforestation program," and to the enrollees as "young forest

Table 2.1 CCC Camps by Department Affiliation and Six-Month Enrollment Period. (Created by author)

Enrollment Period	Dates	Department of Agriculture	Department of the Interior	War Department	Total Number of Camps
1	April 1, 1933–Sept. 30, 1933	1264	173	31	1468
2	Oct. 1, 1933–Mar. 31, 1934	1128	305	35	1468
3	Apr. 1, 1934–Sept. 30, 1934	1135	471	34	1640◊
4	Oct. 1, 1934–Mar. 31, 1935	1124	491	25	1640
5	Apr. 1, 1935–Sept. 30, 1935	2105	699	108	2912
6	Oct. 1, 1935–Mar. 31, 1936	1650	571	101	2322
7	Apr. 1, 1936–Sept. 30, 1936	1530	503	76	2109
8	Oct. 1, 1936–Mar. 31, 1937	1511	501	78	2090
9	Apr. 1, 1937–Sept. 30, 1937	1387	488	51	1926
10	Oct. 1, 1937–Mar. 31, 1938	1086	372	41	1499
11	Apr. 1, 1938–Sept. 30, 1938	1053	360	22	1435
12	Oct. 1, 1938–Mar. 31, 1939	1061	438	0	1499
13	Apr. 1, 1939–Sept. 30, 1939	1065	449	0	1514
14	Oct. 1, 1939–Mar. 31, 1940	1014	484	0	1498
15	Apr. 1, 1940–Sept. 30, 1940	1012	483	2	1497
16	Oct. 1, 1940–Mar. 31, 1941	1007	482	11	1500
17	Apr. 1, 1941–Sept. 30, 1941	711	388	28	1127
18	Oct. 1, 1941–Mar. 31, 1942	380	205	41	626
19	Apr. 1, 1942–Sept. 30, 1942	224	126	49	399
Average % of camps		71%	26.5%	2.5%	100%

◊Additional CCC camps authorized in response to Dust Bowl drought during summer of 1934.

workers," a "vast forest army," and an "army of forest workers."[12] It is no wonder that early on the national media responded by nicknaming the Corps "Roosevelt's Tree Army."[13]

Widespread anxiety over the state of the nation's timber supplies was another factor linking the CCC to forestry work during the early New Deal years. Fear that the country's logging industry was cutting forests at a much faster rate than they could regrow was nothing new; individuals had expressed similar concerns since the early 1860s, and in 1872 the commissioner of agriculture had even warned that "a timber famine" was imminent. This apprehension reached its zenith between 1900 and the beginning of the Great Depression, when lumber production rose to heights never attained before or since, and professional foresters began publicly sounding the alarm. One of the shrillest voices was that of Gifford Pinchot, who

Pinchot

Table 2.2 CCC Camp by Supervising Agency and Six-Month Enrollment Period. (Created by author)

Enrollment Period	Department of Agriculture			Department of the Interior			War Dept.***	Total Number of Camps
	USFS	SCS	Other*	NPS	SES	Other**		
1	1255	—	9	172	0	1	31	1468
2	1097	—	31	300	0	5	35	1468
3	1104	—	31	423	34	14	34	1640◇
4	1095	—	29	421	51	19	25	1640
5	1434	544	127	590	—	109	108	2912
6	1157	398	95	489	—	82	101	2322
7	976	454	100	424	—	79	76	2109
8	964	456	91	422	—	79	78	2090
9	853	432	102	408	—	80	51	1926
10	639	364	83	291	—	81	41	1499
11	624	349	80	289	—	71	22	1435
12	630	355	76	306	—	132	0	1499
13	624	365	76	311	—	138	0	1514
14	614	393	7	308	—	176	0	1498
15	606	391	15	308	—	175	2	1497
16	682	318	7	308	—	174	11	1500
17	396	306	9	242	—	146	28	1127
18	183	190	7	118	—	87	41	626
19	108	112	4	89	—	37	49	399
Average % of camps	50%	18%	3%	20.5%	0%	6%	2.5%	100%

* Includes camps supervised by the Bureau of Biological Survey, Bureau of Animal Industry, Bureau of Plant Industry, and Bureau of Agricultural Engineering.

** Includes camps supervised by the Bureau of Reclamation, Fish and Wildlife Service, Grazing Service, and General Land Office, but excludes nonstandard camps under the jurisdiction of the Bureau of Indian Affairs.

*** Includes camps supervised by the U.S. Army, U.S. Navy, and U.S. Corps of Engineers.

◇Expansion of camps in response to the drought of the summer of 1934. Because the SCS did not exist at the time, these camps were placed under the jurisdiction of the USFS and NPS.

Pinchot

initiated a timber famine crusade in 1905 when he became the first chief of the U.S. Forest Service. Two decades later, he was still at it, warning in 1919 that the country would exhaust its timber supplies by the early 1970s, and cautioning again in the foreword to a popular 1928 book entitled *Deforested America* that logging companies were trying "to fool the American people into believing that . . . the industry is regulating itself and has given up the practice of forest devastation."[14] Pinchot refuted the timber industry's claim of self-regulation and had an extra 10,000 copies of the book printed and mailed to influential people and organizations across the country.[15]

Copeland Report

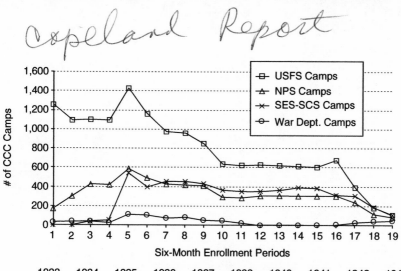

Figure 2.3 CCC Camps by Supervising Agency and Enrollment Period. (Created by author)

It was one thing to claim that the nation's forested landscape was on the verge of exhaustion and quite another to prove it scientifically. In an attempt to quantify Pinchot's "timber famine" rhetoric, in 1932 the federal government commissioned the *National Plan for American Forestry*, otherwise known as the Copeland Report, to reevaluate and update the Capper Report of 1920. According to this updated study, the amount of cutover forests poorly stocked stood at 83 million acres, almost identical to 1920 levels. While the gap between growth and consumption had narrowed, Americans were still consuming approximately twice as much total wood and five times as much saw timber as the country was producing annually. The result, stated the Copeland Report, was that "the forest resources of this country are being seriously depleted."[16] It seemed as if Gifford Pinchot's timber famine fears were not too far off the mark; studies by the federal government indicated that America's forested landscape was indeed in a degraded state.[17]

During its first year and a half of operation, the CCC responded to the timber famine threat by assigning the great majority of its conservation projects to the Department of Agriculture's U.S. Forest Service, which in turn located these projects in national, state, and, to a much lesser extent, in privately owned forests. This process began when the Corps allotted the first fifty camps in the nation to the Forest Service and continued throughout the CCC's history, with the Forest Service overseeing roughly 50 percent of all Corps camps ever in existence, while approximately half a dozen other federal agencies divided up the rest (see table 2.2 and figure 2.3).[18] Throughout the early New Deal years, Corps conservation projects focused on forestry to an even greater extent. During the

Table 2.3 U.S. Forest Service CCC Camps by Six-Month Enrollment Period. (Created by author)

Enrollment Period	United States Forest Service				
	National Forests	State Forests	Private Forests	Other*	Total
1	597	315	219	124	1255
2	439	324	223	111	1097
3	463	306	171	164	1104
4	467	305	177	146	1095
5	747	409	278	0	1434
6	567	345	213	32	1157
7	485	295	169	27	976
8	484	284	170	26	964
9	441	241	147	24	853
10	336	174	110	19	639
11	321	175	109	19	624
12	332	180	100	18	630
13	323	178	105	18	624
14	321	175	100	18	614
15	312	177	99	18	606
16	321	249	95	17	682
17	213	106	63	14	396
18	107	40	25	11	183
19	69	24	11	4	108
Average % of USFS camps	49%	29%	17%	5%	100%

* Prior to the fifth enrollment period, the majority of these camps performed erosion work in national, state and private forests. When the SCS was created at the outset of enrollment period 5 in April 1935, these Forest Service camps were transferred to this new agency. Thereafter, Forest Service camps in this category performed foresty work on TVA sites.

first six-month enrollment period, from April to September 1933, the Forest Service supervised the conservation work of 85 percent of all CCC camps.[19] As a Forest Service employee reported in 1934, "it seems perfectly clear, that the President and his advisers when the [CCC] was decided upon had in mind forest conservation as the major conservation activity that would be undertaken."[20]

Although the Corps undertook fewer projects in privately owned forests, such work worried Roosevelt during the early 1930s. Americans, he feared, might view such efforts as a boon to the timber industry or as political payback for certain well-connected landowners, in either case weakening support for the New Deal. To alleviate such concerns, the president went out of his way

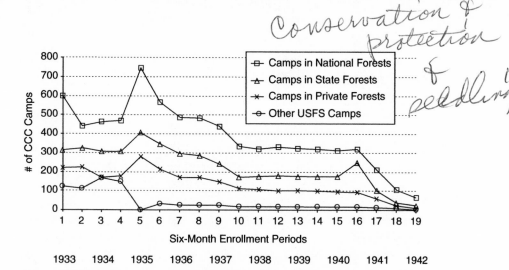

Conservation & protection & seedlings

Figure 2.4 U.S. Forest Service CCC Camps by Enrollment Period. (Created by author)

to limit the number and scope of such projects, and also to promote CCC conservation in private forests as being in the public interest, as he had in his defense of the Roosevelt-Jones Bill nearly two decades earlier (see table 2.3 and figure 2.4). "The cutting of firebreaks [on] privately owned forest lands," Roosevelt wrote to CCC director Robert Fechner, "will safeguard [nearby] publicly owned lands against fire."[21] Such work on private land would increase exponentially during the mid-1930s and, as we shall see, would initiate a new chapter in federal conservation efforts which prior to the Great Depression had been focused primarily on public lands.[22]

Once the Forest Service established its CCC camps in national, state, and private forests across the country, the Corps began working on a myriad of conservation projects. Although in 1934 the CCC listed no less than fifty-eight specific types of forestry work, all of these projects shared a common goal: to restore the nation's timber supplies. To accomplish this, the CCC took two approaches. "Our forests have been given greater protection," explained Fechner, "and our timber stands have been improved" through CCC conservation work.[23] At least during the early New Deal years, then, the Corps focused its conservation efforts on "improving" and "protecting" the nation's timber resources.

The forest improvement work most widely associated with the CCC both during and after the Great Depression was reforestation.[24] Before the Corps could begin planting trees, however, it had to collect seeds, nurture them into seedlings, and transport the seedlings to CCC camps across the country.

Corps conservation projects under the U.S. Forest Service were central to every step in this process. Young men in the CCC climbed trees to pick seeds, skimmed them off the surface of forest streams and lakes where floating seeds collected, and even " 'borrowed' excess seeds, nuts, and pine cones that [had] been hoarded by the squirrels for consumption through winter."[25] Such labor resulted in the collection of 875,000 bushels of cones and more than 13.5 million pounds of hardwood seeds, and vastly increased the capacity of federal and state nurseries already in existence.[26] By 1938, CCC conservation projects had also helped to establish 22 new government nurseries nationwide, raising the number of such institutions from 78 to 100. Due to such conservation efforts, Forest Service CCC camps increased national production to more than 370 million seedlings per year, a jump of more than 100 percent from 1933 to 1938. Such work, the Corps haughtily proclaimed, was "speedier and more efficient" than the reforestation techniques carried out by "Mother Nature."[27]

The Corps' Forest Service camps used this steady and varied supply of tree seedlings to reforest an enormous area during the New Deal years. In 1932, one year before Congress created the Corps, the Forest Service planted trees on only 25,000 acres of national forest land. With the aid of the CCC, the Forest Service raised this total to 70,000 acres in 1933, to 140,700 acres in 1935, and to more than 223,000 acres in 1936. Forest Service camps boosted tree planting in state forests as well, from a total of 154,302 reforested acres for the three years prior to 1933 to nearly 225,000 acres for the period from 1934 to 1937. All told, during its existence, the CCC planted 2.3 billion trees, or 12 for every Depression era American, on 2.5 million acres of previously barren, denuded, or unproductive land. This represents half of the trees ever planted in U.S. history.[28]

While the CCC's reforestation projects greatly expanded the nation's timbered landscape, a second type of forest improvement work promoted the development of trees that were already maturing. "When the CCC appeared on the scene," wrote Corps director Fechner in 1938, "large areas of forest, struggling for light and soil room, were badly in need of improvement." To correct this situation, Forest Service camps performed what the CCC called "timber stand improvement," which included "all classes of work that promote the growth and general welfare of publicly owned trees." These projects entailed clearing dead timber from the forest floor to enhance the growth of seedlings, thinning mature trees where forest growth was too thick, and removing low-value trees that interfered with the growth of more economically productive species so that, as the Corps put it, "the 'crop trees,' the straightest, tallest, and healthiest—those which were the most important commercially—could develop faster into better timber."[29] The forest area benefiting from such conservation work was extensive, increasing from more than 2 million acres early in 1936 to more than 3 million acres two years later and ultimately totaling more than 4 million acres of forest land during the CCC's nine-year existence.[30]

The second major category of conservation work undertaken by the CCC during the early New Deal years involved forest protection. Whereas forest improvement projects were intended to help trees grow more efficiently, forest protection work attempted to guard the nation's timber resources from destructive forces that could hinder this increased productivity. The Corps explained such work in an appropriately titled booklet, *Forests Protected by the CCC*, which described the threat to the country's timber reserves in biblical terms. " 'Three Horsemen' ride through American forests spreading destruction," warned the Corps. "Fire, Insects, and Disease. All three are deadly enemies." While fire, which the CCC nicknamed "the red horseman," was deemed the most spectacular, the most rapid, and the most destructive, equally threatening were diseases and insects that silently turned valuable timber into dying and decaying trees. "The loss to American forests from the 'Three Horsemen,' " the Corps cautioned in 1938, "is of staggering proportions."[31]

To prevent fires from igniting or from spreading if they did indeed catch, the Forest Service dedicated an enormous number of its CCC projects to physically altering the forest landscape in ways that decreased tree combustibility. During the New Deal, the Corps removed underbrush from well over 4 million acres of timberland, and strung almost 88,000 miles of telephone lines to speed communication among 3,116 newly constructed fire lookout towers. It also crisscrossed the national forests with more than 68,000 miles of cleared strips, called firebreaks, and a similar amount of fire truck trails. The longest of these firebreaks, called the Ponderosa Way, ran for an astounding 600 miles along the base of California's Sierra Nevadas in an effort to stop conflagrations starting in the brush-covered foothills from traveling up into more heavily forested elevations.[32] When these preventive methods failed and a fire did indeed break out, the Forest Service called on the CCC to physically suppress the blaze.[33] To slow the fire's spread, the Corps cut emergency firebreaks across the forest and used water tools, including hand-held and gasoline-powered water pumps, to extinguish the blaze and dampen the forest floor to prevent the flames' movement. Throughout its history, the Corps expended approximately 6.5 million man-days performing such work, compelling the *New York Times* to claim in 1934, "CCC men [have] buckled down to the task of fire-proofing the forests" of the nation.[34]

The Corps was equally militant in its battle against the two other "horsemen" threatening America's forests. To battle tree sicknesses such as Dutch elm disease and white pine blister rust, Forest Service camps destroyed the plants hosting the disease. Enrollees removed by hand 300 million ribes plants, mostly currants and gooseberries, in their effort to halt blister rust, and burned approximately 275,000 infected elm trees in New England, New York, and New Jersey to retard the spread of Dutch elm disease.[35] Forest Service camps fought insects in a similar fashion, combating the bark beetle in New England by burning trees hosting the insect, and the gypsy moth by destroying the insect's eggs across more than 3 million acres of northeastern woodlands in an unsuccessful attempt to maintain a "barrier zone" that would prevent the spread of the moth west of the Hudson River.[36] All told, CCC conservation projects protected more than 20 million acres of timberland from insects and tree diseases during the New Deal years.[37]

During the early 1930s, CCC forest improvement and protection work succeeded in restoring productivity to the nation's forested landscape. According to a 1943 study by the Society of American Foresters, of twenty-eight tree plots located in national forests stretching from Virginia to Georgia, CCC forest improvement work during the 1930s had not only increased the number of commercially valuable trees growing in these forests, but had also accelerated the growth rate of these trees. According to the study, trees treated by the Corps grew 38 percent taller and approximately 50 percent wider than untreated trees during the same period.[38] Nor were such findings geographically specific; surveys conducted by the Forest Service in South Dakota's Black Hills in 1939 and in the Ozarks of Arkansas in the 1950s reported similar results.[39] Even CCC fire prevention and suppression work, which drastically reduced the amount of timberland destroyed by fire from nearly 5 million acres in 1910 to approximately 500,000 acres in 1934, helped to increase overall forest productivity.[40]

This increased timber productivity would have made Progressive Era conservationists proud. Those like Gifford Pinchot, who saw the timber famine as the era's most pressing environmental problem, would have no doubt promoted political action such as that taken by the CCC to more efficiently manage the nation's natural resources. Indeed, Progressive conservationists still living during the Great Depression wholeheartedly endorsed the Corps' early forestry efforts. The Progressive belief in conserving trees thus did more than

alters
N D pol. order *gt. plains dust storms*

influence Roosevelt's thinking concerning the creation of the Corps. This idea also played out materially in America's forests. During the early New Deal years, in other words, Corps forestry projects were the political and physical manifestation of Progressive conservationist thought.

While the Corps' forestry work supported the conservationist status quo, it nevertheless began altering the New Deal political order. Although the Democrats won the 1932 election by an electoral landslide, Roosevelt's support was weakest in rural areas excluding the South, particularly in New England, the Mid-Atlantic states, the Great Lakes states, and, to a lesser extent, the far West.[41] Not surprisingly, soon after the election Roosevelt began placing Corps forestry projects in just these regions. The president located the great majority of CCC state forestry projects in the rural hinterlands of New England and the Mid-Atlantic region, which not only had a long history of state forest creation but which also expressed heavy opposition to the Democratic party and the New Deal during the 1932 election.[42] While Corps forestry work in national forests had a somewhat different geography, it too reflected Roosevelt's desire to raise political support from rural Americans. In the case of national forests, however, the president clustered the great majority of CCC conservation projects in nonurban areas farther west, particularly in the Great Lakes region, the Rocky Mountain states, and along the Pacific Coast, where national forests existed and where support for Roosevelt was less strong than in other areas of the country (see figure 2.5).[43] Franklin Roosevelt placed fewer Corps forestry projects in the South, Midwest, and Great Plains, where his support was strongest. During these early years of the Great Depression, CCC forestry work helped the new president to promote the New Deal to the most skeptical segments of rural America.[44]

The CCC first drifted out of the nation's forests on May 12, 1934, when air currents lifted soil from parched fields in western Kansas, Texas, Oklahoma, and eastern Colorado and carried it eastward across the continent where it darkened the sun over the nation's capital, sifted through the screens of New York City skyscrapers, and then wafted for hundreds of miles out over the Atlantic.[45] The dust from the drought-stricken Great Plains even made its way up the Hudson River, where it settled on the fields of President Roosevelt's Hyde Park estate. Commenting on the experience in a speech given soon after the event, Roosevelt told his audience that "the dust storms that a few months ago drifted from the western plains to the Atlantic Ocean were a warning to the whole nation of what will happen if we waste our heritage of soil fertility, the ultimate source of our wealth and of life itself."[46] A little more than one year after the CCC had begun its conservation work in the nation's forests, dirt

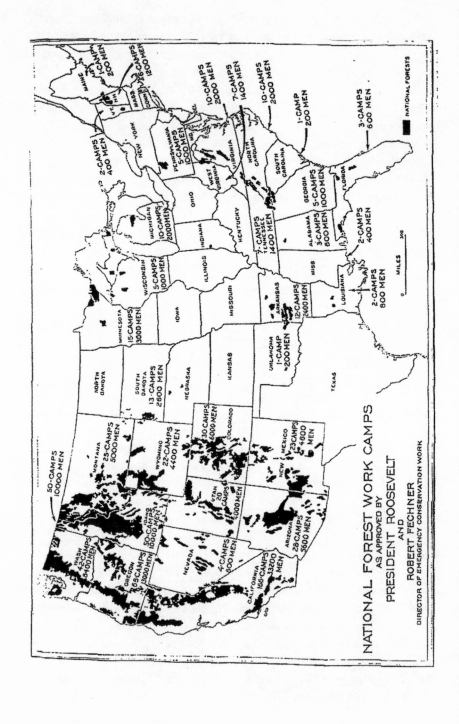

NATIONAL FOREST WORK CAMPS
AS APPROVED BY
PRESIDENT ROOSEVELT
AND
ROBERT FECHNER
DIRECTOR OF EMERGENCY CONSERVATION WORK

■ NATIONAL FORESTS

MILES
0   300

50-CAMPS
10000 MEN

2-CAMPS
400 MEN

1-CAMP
200 MEN

1-CAMP 1-CAMP
200 MEN 200 MEN

10-CAMPS
2000 MEN

7-CAMPS
1400 MEN

10-CAMPS
2000 MEN

1-CAMP
200 MEN

3-CAMPS
600 MEN

25-CAMPS
5000 MEN

22-CAMPS
4400 MEN

30-CAMPS
6000 MEN

23-CAMPS
4600 MEN

15-CAMPS
3000 MEN

13-CAMPS
2600 MEN

5-CAMPS
1000 MEN

10-CAMPS
2000 MEN

5-CAMPS
1000 MEN

7-CAMPS
1400 MEN

3-CAMPS
600 MEN

2-CAMPS
400 MEN

2-CAMPS
800 MEN

12-CAMPS
2400 MEN

1-CAMP
200 MEN

5-CAMPS
1000 MEN

20-CAMPS
4000 MEN

28-CAMPS
5600 MEN

166-CAMPS
33200 MEN

50-CAMPS
10000 MEN

42-CAMPS
8400 MEN

65-CAMPS
13000 MEN

4-CAMPS
800 MEN

Figure 2.5 This 1933 map not only depicts the geographic distribution and company strength of CCC camps located in national forests, but also hints at an early strategy employed by Roosevelt to shore up political support for his liberal New Deal agenda. Aware that enthusiasm for his presidential bid was weakest in the non-urban regions of New England, the Mid-Atlantic states, the Great Lake states, and the far West, once in office Roosevelt immediately began situating the majority of CCC forestry camps in these very locations. The president conversely placed fewer Corps forestry projects in the South, the Midwest, and the Great Plains, where rural support for his administration was already strong. When read in light of the 1932 election, then, this map illustrates that the new president quickly began using federal conservation policy to lure rural Americans into the New Deal fold. ("National Forest Work Camps," reprinted in *American Forests*, 39, no. 6 [June 1933]: 272)

from the Great Plains literally brought home the dangers of soil erosion to the president of the United States.

Franklin Roosevelt responded to the Dust Bowl much as the federal government had reacted to the threat of timber famine, by commissioning a national survey, in this case of the country's soil resources. As governor of New York, Roosevelt had successfully initiated a similar statewide soil study early in 1931, and he recommended a national soil inventory the following year while running for president.[47] Now, during the summer of 1934, he invoked the dust storms gathering over Washington, D.C., to raise political support for this task, and delegated responsibility for surveying the country's nearly 2 trillion acres to the newly created Soil Erosion Service and its director, Hugh Bennett.[48] Similar to the Copeland Report of 1932, which took stock of the nation's timber supplies, Bennett's Reconnaissance Erosion Survey of the United States inventoried the nation's soil resources and determined that approximately one-half of the land mass of the continental United States was experiencing moderate to severe erosion.[49] "The soil erosion reconnaissance survey showed erosion over the United States to be much more widespread and more severe than had been previously estimated," concluded the study, which was eventually published in 1935. "Soil erosion is one of the most serious problems facing American agriculture."[50]

Both the Dust Bowl and the findings of the national soil survey stirred fears throughout the country during the mid-1930s about the state of the nation's soil resources. In May 1935, just months after the Soil Erosion Service published its study, the *New Republic* printed an article explaining the survey's findings and warning of a future filled with "sand dunes rolling across as yet fertile districts" and "localities headed toward uninhabitable desert conditions."[51] Later that year, in a highly publicized congressional committee hearing, Chair Morris Cooke of the National Planning Board's Water Resources Committee concluded his testimony by mentioning Bennett's soil survey, explaining that "just as with bodily diseases such as cancer or tuberculosis which can be cured only in the early stages, so it is with soils built up through the ages."[52] Others picked up on Cooke's analogy and ran with it. Stuart Chase, one of the most widely read liberal economists of the Great Depression era, mentioned Cooke's testimony in his 1936 classic, *Rich Land, Poor Land,* and added the simple caveat, "erosion is an earth disease, and it spreads."[53] Whereas conservationists such as Gifford Pinchot had been concerned primarily with the timber famine during the years leading up to the Great Depression, by the mid-1930s the alarm had been sounded as well over an "earth disease" that threatened the nation's soil resources.

diseased landscape 19th century

This notion that the American landscape was in a diseased state was not new to the Great Depression era. The belief that a particular environment could itself be either healthy or sick had a long history in the United States.[54] While mid-nineteenth-century reformers, including Olmsted, saw garbage-strewn street corners as unhealthy for urbanites, western settlers during this same period viewed foul-smelling swamps and swollen, discolored streams far out in the countryside as diseased places in their own right. In cities, such sickly landscapes arose from human neglect and could be cured through street cleaning or the creation of spaces like Central Park. On the western frontier, this "geography of health" functioned somewhat differently; nature, not humans, made landscapes sick, while human labor such as agriculture transformed such places into more healthy spaces. In either case, environments during this period of American history were thought to have serious consequences for human health. As the statements of Cooke and Chase suggest, such thinking was alive and well during the mid-1930s. Yet whereas during the nineteenth century unhealthy environments had threatened the health of local inhabitants, in the midst of the Great Depression New Dealers began arguing that ailments, including earth disease, threatened the well-being of the entire nation.[55]

Prior to the Dust Bowl, CCC administrators had done little to cure the country's soil problems through conservation. Although the act creating the Corps allowed for "the prevention of soil erosion" by enrollees, such work remained severely circumscribed during the early New Deal years. This was because most conservationists at the time, Franklin Roosevelt included, perceived soil conservation narrowly as a beneficial side effect of forestry rather than applicable in its own right to the nation's farmlands. Planting trees slowed soil erosion in forests, conservationists agreed, yet most remained ignorant of soil erosion's threat to the nation's agricultural landscape.[56] Besides, farms were privately owned, and Roosevelt and Corps director Fechner were both wary of undertaking conservation work on nonpublic property. As a result, throughout the early 1930s, the CCC assigned what few soil conservation camps it had to the Forest Service, which in turn used enrollee labor to fight soil erosion primarily in public forests. Even after Congress established the Soil Erosion Service as a temporary agency in September 1933, and its director, Hugh Bennett, began lobbying to extend Corps conservation projects onto agricultural lands, the number of CCC camps fighting soil erosion on farms remained small. In April 1934, for instance, just one month before Great Plains dust blew into Washington, D.C., the Corps assigned only 22 out of 1,640 camps nationwide to Bennett's Soil Erosion Service.[57] As the CCC's

Table 2.4 Soil Erosion Service and Soil Conservation Service CCC Camps by Enrollment Period. (Created by author)

Enrollment Period	SES	SCS	Total
1	—	—	0
2	—	—	0
3	34	—	34◊
4	51	—	51
5	—	544	544
6	—	398	398
7	—	454	454
8	—	456	456
9	—	432	432
10	—	364	364
11	—	349	349
12	—	365	365
13	—	365	365
14	—	393	393
15	—	391	391
16	—	318	318
17	—	306	306
18	—	190	190
19	—	112	112
Average number of SES/SCS camps	42	362	324

* The Soil Erosion Service was renamed the Soil Conservation Service in April 1935 (enrollment period 5) and transferred from the Department of the Interior to the Department of Agriculture. During the Corps' first two enrollment periods, the SES acted as a research and educational agency for the CCC but was not assigned work camps of its own until April 1934. After the SCS was officially created in 1935, the majority of camps performing soil conservation work was placed under its jurisdiction.
◊ Additional CCC camps were authorized in response to the Dust Bowl drought during the summer of 1934.

director explained nearly a decade later, "erosion control...took up little space on the Corps' first work program."[58]

The Corps responded to the Dust Bowl of 1934 and the earth disease threat by greatly expanding its soil conservation work. After receiving an additional $35 million in emergency drought-relief funds from Congress at Franklin Roosevelt's behest, the CCC increased its enrollment by 50,000, and by July 1, 1934, had placed these young men in 172 additional camps.[59] The Soil Erosion Service received an ever-increasing share of these drought-relief enrollees, raising the number of camps performing soil conservation projects on farmland from 22 in April 1934, just before the Dust Bowl, to 34 in September of that year, and

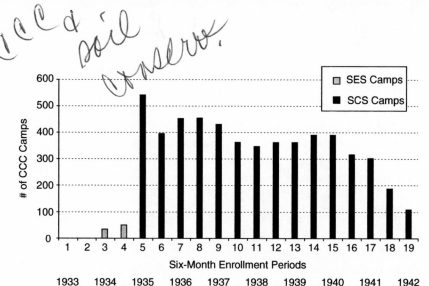

ccc & soil conserv. (handwritten annotation)

Figure 2.6 Soil Erosion Service and Soil Conservation Service CCC Camps by Six-Month Enrollment Period. (Created by author)

finally up to 51 camps in March 1935. During the next six-month enrollment period, the number of soil erosion camps skyrocketed to 544, 150 of which the Corps transferred from the Forest Service.[60] From that moment until Congress terminated the CCC in 1942, the Soil Erosion Service supervised approximately 30 percent of all Corps camps nationwide, with only the Forest Service responsible for more (see table 2.4 and figure 2.6). Yet another sign that soil had now joined timber as a resource worthy of federal conservation policy was evident on April 27, 1935, when Congress voted to make the Soil Erosion Service a permanent agency, to transfer it from the Department of the Interior to the Department of Agriculture and, most important, to rename it the Soil Conservation Service. "At first [CCC] camps were assigned largely to forest projects," explained Corps director Robert Fechner in 1936. "Since then the scope of the work has been broadened to include large-scale soil conservation work."[61]

The CCC undertook the great majority of its soil conservation projects on privately owned farms usually located within a fifteen-mile radius of an enrollee camp.[62] As with the few Forest Service projects on private timberland, the Roosevelt administration went to great lengths to portray the CCC's soil conservation work as being in the public interest. Corps work on private farmland, explained the president in 1936, was only undertaken "where there is a quasi-public character to the tracts on which the work is done."[63] Here the president continued to extend the reach of government conservation policy onto private property, a process he had begun back in New York with the Roosevelt-Jones Bill. To better ensure the public nature of such erosion projects, the Soil Conservation Service's Hugh Bennett made farmers sign a "cooperative agreement" that required them to contribute personally to the work being performed by enrollees and, perhaps more important, to maintain the improvements resulting from such work for at least five years. "The purpose" of such agreements, explained the CCC's Robert Fechner in 1938, "is that of demonstrating to all farmers how they may conserve soil and water most effectively and most economically."[64] Bennett echoed Fechner when he wrote one year later that the CCC's soil conservation work on private farms "serves as effective community erosion-control demonstrations," and thus has definite public value.[65]

With increasing numbers of farmers signing cooperative agreements, the CCC began a host of projects aimed at conserving the nation's soil. In arid, windy regions such as the Dust Bowl, this entailed keeping as much dirt and water as possible from blowing or running off farmers' fields. In more humid areas, such as the Piedmont in the South and the unglaciated portion of the upper Mississippi Valley, Corps soil conservation projects attempted to slow the rate of water runoff so as to decrease the amount of fertile topsoil carried from fields by rain.[66] In either case, the CCC relied on two basic types of soil conservation projects: the Corps used vegetative methods to better control the movement of soil and water on fields, and it physically altered fields in ways that regulated the resources flowing across them.[67]

New Deal agronomists such as Hugh Bennett were well aware of the role that vegetation could play in controlling the flow of soil and water on agricultural lands. Not only did vegetation hold topsoil that otherwise might blow away, but it also slowed the speed of water coursing across fields, thus decreasing the water's power to carry away soil while allowing more time for water to penetrate the earth.[68] Not surprisingly, one of the earliest uses of vegetation by the CCC involved halting erosion caused by running water in more humid regions of the country. In general, the Corps fought two types of water erosion, one that cut giant gullies across fields and a second form called "sheet erosion" that involved the even removal by water or wind of thick layers of soil from an entire segment of sloping farmland. Both types of erosion, argued Bennett, "sliced into the landscape of the nation."[69] To correct this situation, the Corps revegetated gullies and sheet-eroded fields with a variety of plants, including trees and shrubs such as willows and tamarisk, legumes and vines including kudzu and Virginia creeper and grasses, especially sod.[70] In total, such Corps conservation projects revegetated more than 1 trillion square yards of gullied terrain and 600,000 acres of sheet-eroded farmland between 1933 and 1942.[71]

strip cropping *Kudzu* *terraces*

Another vegetative technique undertaken by the CCC in its battle against soil erosion involved strip cropping. The practice of strip cropping entailed the alternate planting of ordinary farm crops with close-growing, erosion-resistant plants in relatively narrow strips running across rather than up and down a field's slope. By slowing water runoff, the close-growing plants reduced the water's capacity to pick up fertile topsoil from the adjacent rows of ordinary crops and transport it off the fields. The Corps helped farmers to strip crop more than 200,000 acres of land throughout the country. In the Corn Belt, the CCC alternated plantings with strips of small grains, while in cotton-producing areas it used hairy vetch, rye, and kudzu. On the Great Plains, Corps conservation projects also helped farmers with "wind strip cropping" by planting rows of ordinary crops at right angles to the prevailing winds, and alternating these rows with strips of wind-resistant vegetation such as Sudan grass and broom corn.[72]

Literally alongside these vegetative methods, the Corps undertook conservation projects that physically altered agricultural fields in ways that conserved both soil and water. Similar to the Corps' vegetative approach, CCC work involving the structural transformation of farmland also attempted to slow water runoff and thus decrease soil erosion while increasing the amount of rainfall absorbed by the ground. Here again, gullies were some of the first problems tackled by the Corps. When revegetative methods failed because a gully was too large or located in a region too dry to be controlled by planting, the CCC built small "check dams" to slow the rate of water coursing through the problem area. Corps enrollees constructed more than 6 million temporary check dams made of brush, wire, wood, or loose rock, which collected soil and water within each gully until protective plants could grow. When these temporary structures proved to be inadequate, CCC enrollees built permanent check dams of earth, stone, or concrete to slow water runoff and halt soil erosion. Between 1933 and 1942, the Corps constructed more than 300,000 temporary and permanent check dams on farms across the country.[73]

Corps enrollees working on soil conservation projects also restructured the country's agricultural lands by building field terraces. Similar in appearance to oversized steps, terraces act as shelves constructed at intervals across the slope of a field to help control water runoff. While in arid areas CCC camps helped farmers to construct terraces to catch and hold rain before it flowed downhill and off fields, in regions experiencing high rainfall Corps enrollees fitted terraces with special outlets that diverted the runoff from fields to nearby streams before the coursing water could carry fertile topsoil along with it. Whereas terraced fields in more humid areas aided farmers in halting soil erosion, the same structures helped to conserve water in places such as the Dust Bowl.[74] Overall, the CCC constructed more than 33,000 miles of terraces and more than 430,000 terrace outlets during the New Deal years.[75]

By far the most extensive structural change made to the nation's farmland by the Corps involved contour agriculture, which affected all other types of CCC soil conservation projects. Such farming entailed the plowing of fields parallel to the slope so that furrows throughout ran level, curving across hills rather than running straight up and down them. As with other soil conservation techniques, the CCC used contouring for different purposes in different geographic locations depending on climate and soil type. In regions with low rainfall, the primary purpose of contouring was similar to that of terracing: to conserve water and distribute it evenly throughout the field. In humid regions, enrollees helped farmers to contour plow their fields to slow the speed of runoff and thus reduce soil loss by erosion, much like planting cover crops or strip cropping.[76] Contouring was also important because it aided other types of CCC soil conservation work; revegetating gullies and planting cover crops was even more productive if done "on the contour."[77] Corps enrollees performed an enormous amount of this type of soil conservation work, helping farmers to build more than 150,000 miles of contour furrows throughout the United States, and maintaining more than 27,000 miles of preexisting contour crop rows.[78]

The Corps' soil conservation work, much like the program's earlier forestry projects, increased productivity, in this case on America's farmlands. According to Soil Conservation Service research published in 1941, terracing undertaken by the Corps in Texas increased cotton production by an average of 68 pounds per acre, and CCC contouring in the same state raised returns on grain sorghum by 128 pounds on a similar size parcel of land. When the Corps helped farmers to combine both terracing and contour furrowing, field output was even more impressive, increasing wheat yields on the southern Great Plains by 3.5 bushels per acre, bean production in New Mexico by 78 pounds per acre, and grain sorghum growth in Texas by an astounding 262 pounds per acre.[79]

Rising crop returns like those experienced by farmers cooperating with the CCC would have appealed to conservationists of the Progressive Era, who above all else valued the efficient production of natural resources. Yet most would have been surprised by the Corps' efforts on farms, since the movement at the turn of the century focused primarily on forests. By undertaking projects aimed at conserving soil in its own right, not merely as an addition to timber conservation, the CCC helped push another natural resource to the center of the movement's concerns, in a sense forcing conservationists like Pinchot to divide their attention between the timber growing above their heads and the dirt eroding under their feet. The curved and terraced landscape of farms cooperating with the CCC thus symbolized an expansion of conservationist thought. Soil, which Franklin Roosevelt called "the source of wealth and life itself," was now a key component of the conservationist agenda.[80]

Along with broadening conservationist concerns, CCC soil erosion work also began to influence New Deal politics during the mid-1930s by raising additional support across agricultural America for the Roosevelt administration's policies. To calm anxieties over the dust storms and the federal response to them, Roosevelt immediately increased the number of CCC soil conservation projects in the Dust Bowl, and announced that enrollees for these additional Corps camps would come primarily from the affected region, namely, the Great Plains (see figure 2.7).[81] Two years later, as the drought continued to scorch the plains, Roosevelt again used the CCC both to deflect dissatisfaction with the New Deal and to kick off his reelection campaign, this time by making a series of trips to Dust Bowl states to coordinate federal relief efforts, particularly those of the CCC. Not surprisingly, Roosevelt went out of his way to visit states filled with not only new Corps camps but also Republican farmers who were leaning toward his presidential opponent, Kansas governor Alf Landon.[82] While Landon spent most of the summer campaigning publicly against the New Deal, he continually endorsed the CCC, and even tried to take credit for an amendment to the original Corps bill.[83] To counter such claims, in Des Moines, Iowa, Roosevelt asked Landon directly and in person what he himself had done for farmers in the region. In the election that followed two months later, Landon lost the entire Great Plains region, including his home state of Kansas, to Roosevelt.[84]

One year after Dust Bowl winds blew the Corps from the country's forests onto its fields, CCC conservation work expanded once again, this time into the nation's parks. This process began on June 4, 1935, when the National Park Service announced that Americans from all walks of life were in the midst of an outdoor recreation renaissance. According to the Park Service, there were three reasons for this Great Depression nature craze: high levels of unemployment resulting in increased leisure time; the inexpensiveness of outdoor recreational pursuits such as camping, hiking, and hunting; and finally the widespread use of the automobile, which more and more Americans were using to get out of the city and into the countryside.[85] National Park Service director Arno B. Cammerer supported such claims by noting that visits to the country's national parks rose from just under 4 million in 1934 to well over 7.5 million by the summer of

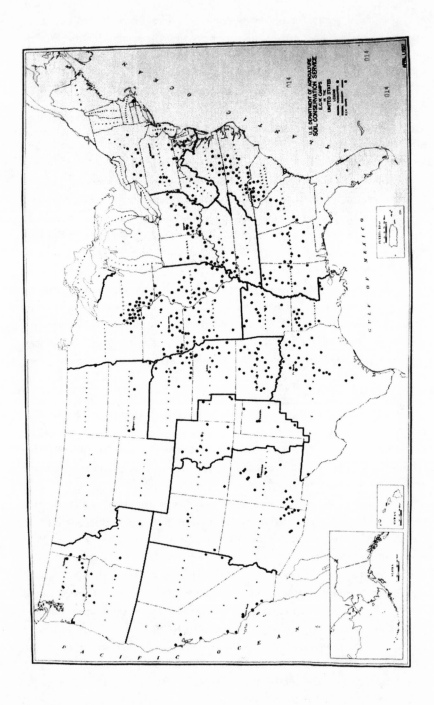

PLATE I

U. S. DEPARTMENT OF AGRICULTURE
SOIL CONSERVATION SERVICE
C.C.C. CAMPS
IN THE
UNITED STATES

Figure 2.7 Similar to other Corps maps that show camp locations, this one using dots to depict the distribution of soil conservation camps in 1937 also provides clues to New Deal politics. When the infamous Dust Bowl hit in 1934, Roosevelt responded by greatly increasing the number of Corps camps in the Great Plains and by stocking these camps with young men from the drought-stricken region. Two years later, Roosevelt returned to the area to kick off his first re-election campaign with a Dust Bowl tour that included widely publicized stops at Corps camps and soil conservation project sites. This strategy of using soil conservation as political leverage proved extremely successful. Not only did Republican farmers from the Great Plains vote overwhelming for the Democratic presidential nominee in 1936, but Roosevelt's opponent, Kansas governor Alf Landon, even lost his home state. ("U.S. Department of Agriculture, Soil Conservation Service, E.C.W Camps in the United States," 1 April 1937, RG 114: Records of the Soil Conservation Service, File 23, NARA)

1935. "It is believed," explained Cammerer, "that this figure will be greatly enlarged."[86]

Franklin Roosevelt responded to this outdoor recreation rage much as he had to anxiety over the state of the nation's timber and soil resources, by ordering another national study. He publicly endorsed a countrywide recreation inventory in mid-June 1935 and signed the survey into law one year later as the Park, Parkway, and Recreation Study Act. Not surprisingly, the survey, undertaken by the National Park Service, painted a gloomy portrait of what it called "the recreation problem" in the United States and recommended that "beneficial types of recreation appropriate to the areas should be developed and offered to visitors." The American people would greatly benefit if the federal government "provided a more suitable area for administrative purposes and for the accommodation of the public."[87] The survey concluded that CCC work in national parks could solve this recreation problem, much as other types of Corps projects helped to avert both timber famine and earth disease.[88]

Prior to the summer of 1935, CCC work projects involving recreational development had been extremely limited. While a few Corps camps assigned to the National Park Service undertook projects aimed at developing parks for outdoor tourism, the overwhelming majority performed forestry work within the boundaries of national and state parks. This hesitancy regarding recreational development was due in part to the National Park Service's ambivalent mission, which entailed both "conserving scenery . . . unimpaired" while simultaneously developing parks for "the enjoyment of future generations."[89] Building recreational amenities for tomorrow's visitors, many Park Service administrators felt, often impaired national park scenery today. Yet the decision during the early New Deal years to limit CCC recreation work in national and state parks also stemmed from the narrow concerns of the conservation movement, which during the Progressive Era focused on the efficient use of natural resources, primarily timber. Outdoor recreation such as that promoted by Olmsted was simply not a priority of the movement. It was thus perfectly understandable for Franklin Roosevelt, a Progressive conservationist, to restrict Corps work in parks during the early and mid-1930s.[90]

The rush of Americans into the great outdoors during the summer of 1935, much like the Dust Bowl the year before and the timber famine of 1933, forced Roosevelt and Corps administrators to rethink their policy of limiting CCC work in the nation's parks. This about-face was first evident in early June 1935, when the Corps announced that the National Park Service would oversee 120,000 enrollees for recreational development work during the upcoming

3 nee categories

year. This expansion meant an increase for the Park Service of approximately 30,000 CCC enrollees over the previous year, and raised the number of Corps camps under its jurisdiction from 421 in March 1935 to nearly 600 camps one month later, an overall gain in camps and enrollees of almost 30 percent (see table 2.5 and figure 2.8). According to the CCC, the reason for this enlargement was due to the national need for new and better recreational facilities, including hiking trails, campgrounds, motor roads, and other tourist amenities.[91] "Since the first camps were established on national forests and national parks, we have departed in some measure from that original program of objective," explained the CCC's director in an article for *American Forests* magazine in January 1939. "In addition to forestation and erosion work, the Corps has done a vast amount of recreational work."[92]

The Corps divided its recreational work into three main categories, all of which helped to foster outdoor tourism on the nation's parklands.[93] Corps enrollees first undertook structural improvement projects that welcomed visitors to the nation's parks and made their stay more comfortable. To better orient outdoor enthusiasts when they first entered these recreation areas, the CCC built dozens of visitor centers and more than 200 museums, interpretive sites, and park lodges. The Corps likewise created amenities to aid more intrepid park travelers, including the construction of more than 2,000 hiking shelters and nearly 2,500 rustic cabins in which hikers could rest during the day or sleep protected from the elements through the night.[94] Corps camps working on structural improvement projects also built sanitary facilities for visitors unwilling to rough it, and for hikers and campers coming in from long stints outdoors. Enrollees dug 13 million feet of ditches to supply the nation's parks with running water, built nearly 400 bathhouses, and installed nearly 2,000 drinking fountains between 1933 and 1942. They also constructed more than 12,000 latrines and toilets and installed just under 6,000 sewage and waste-disposal systems. Enrollees laboring on recreation projects built tens of thousands of additional structures, such as equipment houses, storage sheds, garages, and various administrative buildings, all of which helped national and state parks cater to tourism.[95]

To better control the movement of visitors once they left the lodge, museum, or latrine, CCC camps also undertook a variety of transportation improvement projects in parks across the country. One of the most common involved motor road work, which between 1933 and 1942 included the construction of 125,000 miles of new roads, the improvement of nearly 600,000 miles of old thoroughfares, the building of approximately 40,000 vehicular bridges, and the laying out of more than 8 million square yards of parking lots, an area equivalent in size to

Campgrounds

Table 2.5 National Park Service CCC Camps by Enrollment Period. (Created by author)

Enrollment Period	National Parks	State Parks	Other*	Total
1	70	102	—	172
2	61	239	—	300
3	108	315	—	423
4	86	335	—	421
5	115	475	—	590
6	50	398	41	489
7	59	329	36	424
8	45	341	36	422
9	60	314	34	408
10	41	224	26	291
11	61	208	20	289
12	47	233	26	306
13	68	219	24	311
14	97	165	46	308
15	118	151	39	308
16	106	158	44	308
17	113	103	26	242
18	79	32	7	118
19	75	14	0	89
Average % of NPS camps	24%	70%	6%	100%

* Includes camps in county parks, metropolitan parks, national monuments, national historic parks, military parks, and TVA park sites.

2,500 football fields.[96] The Corps undertook transportation projects that enhanced foot traffic as well. The CCC improved 100,000 miles of previously existing hiking trails and blazed more than 28,000 miles of new trails. Enrellees, for instance, improved and helped to complete the Appalachian and Pacific Crest trails, which each run for 2,000 miles along the spines of the Appalachian Mountains and Sierra Nevadas, respectively. Along these and other hiking trails, the CCC built more than 8,000 pedestrian bridges, almost always from local stone and wood, to help hikers ford streams, rivers, ravines, and other difficult terrain.[97]

While the CCC undertook structural and transportation projects to welcome tourists, enhance their movement, and make their stay in national and state parks more comfortable, the Corps also performed landscape and recreation work to improve and expand visitors' experiences in the great outdoors. For those desiring a more intimate visit with Mother Nature, the Corps improved nearly 40,000 acres of campgrounds already in existence, created more than 50,000 acres of new campgrounds, and cleared more than 15,000 acres of picnic

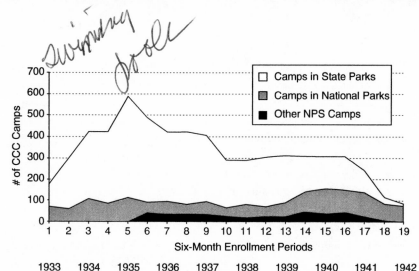

swimming pool

Figure 2.8 National Park Service CCC Camps by Enrollment Period. (Created by author)

areas.[98] Other landscape and recreation work focused on expanding the country's infrastructure for summer and winter activities. Enrollees not only built public swimming pools in national and state parks, such as the one at the very bottom of the Grand Canyon, but also constructed more than seventy-five artificial lakes, with beaches, mostly in state parks throughout the country.[99] The CCC helped to expand opportunities for winter sports as well by building ski trails in Yosemite, Sequoia, and Oregon's Mount Rainier national parks.

These projects in the nation's parks during the late 1930s, unlike earlier CCC conservation work in the country's forests and on its farms, were not aimed at increasing natural resource productivity. Instead, the CCC undertook recreational development work to accommodate and encourage visitors to the great outdoors. Here too the Corps succeeded, much as it did in increasing timber and agricultural output. Whereas less than 3.5 million people visited national parks in 1933, by 1938, just three years after the Corps expanded its work into the nation's parks, that number had skyrocketed to 16 million and rose again to 21 million by 1941, an overall increase during the 1930s of approximately 600 percent. During the same period, state parks across the country also set new attendance records.[100] As National Park Service director Arno Cammerer explained, the tourist boom on the nation's parklands was "due to the increasing facilities for recreation afforded tourists by the completion of trails, camp grounds, roads and other projects by the enrollees of the Civilian Conservation Corps."[101]

Although the construction of hiking trails, campgrounds, and picnic areas by the CCC attracted an increasing number of Americans during the late 1930s, such work would have appealed less to Progressive Era conservationists such as Pinchot. Instead, these recreation projects would have pleased reformers like Olmsted and others involved in the parks, playground, and city beautiful movements. They would also have interested the Boy Scouts, which took urban youths into the countryside for physical rejuvenation. Corps recreation work not only provided the same opportunity to the American public, who could now more easily restore themselves in state and national parks, but such projects also raised a novel concern for conservationists. "If conservation may be defined as the dedication of each particular resource to the use for which it is best suited," explained the Park Service in 1937 while in the midst of its CCC development boom, "the problem of recreational land use becomes a part of the general conservation problem."[102] As the Corps moved into the nation's parks, the Park Service suggested, outdoor recreation had begun nudging its way into the conservationist dialogue.

Along with influencing the conservation movement, Corps work projects in parks during the late 1930s, like CCC forestry and soil projects before them, also began to influence New Deal politics by raising rural support for Franklin Roosevelt, this time across the southern United States. Primarily because the South had a poor history of park development on both the state and national levels, and because Franklin Roosevelt wanted to maintain his broad-based support throughout the region, the CCC located an inordinate proportion of Corps recreation projects in the rural South. A large percentage of the 800 new state parks created by the CCC, and much of the expansion by the Corps of preexisting state parks from 300,000 to 600,000 acres during the 1930s, occurred in the southern United States.[103] Corps work in the region's national parks was equally intense. The dozens of CCC camps that Roosevelt assigned to Virginia's Shenandoah National Park and to Great Smoky Mountains National Park along the Tennessee and North Carolina border literally built both parks from the ground up by constructing a recreational infrastructure that included hiking trails, visitor centers, campgrounds, and motor roads.[104] Rural southerners kept supporting the New Deal in overwhelming numbers during the late 1930s partly because they understood only too well that such work by the Corps increased the potential for outdoor tourism, and with it a boost to the local economy in and around this new recreational landscape.[105]

When the Corps' second director, James McEntee, sat down at his Washington, D.C., desk during the summer of 1942 to write his final report, he thus had good reason to boast that his program had "started a change in the landscape of a Nation."[106] What began as work in state and national forests during the early 1930s had shifted onto the country's farms in the middle of the decade only to expand once again into the nation's parks by the later New Deal years. While reforestation and timber stand improvement had resulted in forests with taller trees planted in straighter rows, the Corps' soil conservation projects involving strip cropping and terracing on the contour had nearly the opposite effect, transforming rectilinear crop rows throughout the country into a more curvilinear farmscape. As one airplane passenger observed high above Oklahoma, "the crops are merged and wrapped around flow lines. The new field design . . . is marbled."[107] Corps work in the nation's parks during the late 1930s was different yet again. The unbroken expanses of many state and national parks had become crisscrossed with hiking trails and motor roads, and dotted with picnic areas, campgrounds, and visitor centers, all of which lured tourists to the wilderness being developed by the CCC.

Although Corps conservation efforts involved different types of projects in forests, on farms, and in parks, the result was a pair of landscapes with two very different histories. CCC forestry and soil conservation work traced its roots back to the Progressive conservation movement, with its emphasis on the efficient use of natural resources. Corps projects in state and national parks had resulted in a quite different landscape, rooted instead in the parks, playgrounds, and campgrounds of youth reform advocates. While this second recreational landscape reflected the Boy Scouts' belief in healthful contact with nature, it extended this experience from CCC enrollees laboring outdoors to the American public playing in parks. In both instances, the dual ideologies that influenced the creation of the CCC became physically realized during the New Deal era.

While the landscapes created through CCC conservation work had a deep past, they also immediately began influencing the present politics of both conservation and the New Deal. While Corps work on American farms introduced the novel notion that soil conservation was as important as guarding the nation's timber supplies, CCC projects throughout the country's parks raised the issue of outdoor recreation and its proper place within the conservation movement. Rather than separating recreation from the conservation of natural resources, as had been done during the Progressive Era, Corps work projects continued to weave Olmsted's philosophy with the ideas of Gifford Pinchot, just as Roosevelt had done when he created the CCC during the spring of 1933. The result was something new and represented the broadening of conservationist thought to include not just trees, but soil and parks as well.

These same landscapes created by the CCC also began to influence New Deal politics by physically representing the material benefits of the welfare state to millions of rural Americans from every region of the country. Franklin

Roosevelt understood this and used Corps landscapes as part of his constituency-building strategy. The location of Corps forestry projects, for example, helped Roosevelt to spread his New Deal gospel across the forested regions of New England, the Mid-Atlantic states, the Great Lakes area, and along the West Coast, where his support in the 1932 election was weakest. Similarly, situating CCC soil erosion camps throughout the Great Plains undoubtedly helped his reelection campaign in 1936 against regional favorite Alf Landon. Even Corps recreation projects in state and national parks in the southern United States helped Roosevelt to maintain solid support for his New Deal across the New South. Early on, the geography of Corps conservation became a key ingredient in the president's ability to create and maintain political support outside the nation's cities.

Although when James McEntee sat down to write his final report for the CCC in 1942 he may have been unaware of such political maneuvering on the part of the president, the Corps' director was nevertheless quite cognizant of the enormous amount of human labor that had been needed to alter the country's landscape. "The Nation awoke to find the landscape dotted with tented CCC camps and active young men," McEntee reflected in his report, "in the forests, on the western plains, in the mountains, on the banks of streams and lakes."[108] McEntee obviously understood that the sweat and muscle of millions of CCC enrollees were responsible for such changes. What he failed to acknowledge, however, was that this same outdoor work had also transformed these active young men in ways that dramatically altered both the conservation movement and the labor politics of the New Deal.

THREE / LABOR
Enrollee Work and the Body Politic

On the very first day that CCC enrollee Pablo Diaz Albertt arrived in Camp F-44 near Libby, Montana, he began contrasting his new surroundings to those left behind in his native New York City. "The majestic Rocky Mountains, covered with shining white blankets on top" and the "melody of the brooks and the beautiful western sunset," he mused, had replaced the "depressed days of New York" and "the streets I had walked so long seeking a decent job." During the next few weeks in camp, Albertt's thoughts also drifted to the labor he now performed each day on a CCC forestry project, as well as to its impact on the surrounding landscape. "The work was hard," he admitted. "I helped saw down large trees" to thin the forest for better growth, and "buil[t] roads" to aid foresters in their fight against fire. Only then, after getting settled in his new surroundings, did this Corps enrollee contemplate how such labor performed high in the Rockies had influenced his own physical well-being. "I grew stronger, I became more solid, I changed," he explained, from "working and living a healthy life in the 'Cs'."[1]

According to Albertt's fellow enrollees, the personal changes experienced while laboring long and hard outdoors on Corps conservation projects were not limited to the physical. In camp newspapers, essays reprinted in national magazines, and letters mailed home to family and friends, the more than 3 million young men who joined the CCC during the Great Depression went out of their way to describe the transformative character of their outdoor work.[2] "The Civilian Conservation Corps has benefited me in both body and mind," explained enrollee Frederick Katz of his labor at a CCC camp near Mount Union, Pennsylvania. "The actual work, digging, chopping, walking," added another enrollee, "are splendid means of bodily development and a sound body usually means a sound mind."[3] Corps administrators agreed. In a 1935 article in the *New York Times Magazine*, CCC educational advisor Frank Ernest Hill argued that enrollees' labor on conservation projects was "developing their minds as well as their muscles."[4] In this sense, Pablo Diaz Albertt's experiences were typical. As labor on Corps projects built up his body during the mid-1930s, Albert noted, "I learned things I never knew."[5]

Although working-class Americans like those enrolling in the CCC during the Great Depression are seen as central to Franklin Roosevelt's liberal New Deal coalition, labor has often been portrayed as problematic for nature.[6] Richard White, for example, argues that environmental historians too often equate work, particularly manual work, with the destruction of nature. According to White, this belief that nature is safest when shielded from human labor is dangerous because it masks the fact that human work has always intersected with the natural world and in doing so has historically imparted knowledge about nature to laborers. By digging, planting, harvesting, cutting, dragging, and even grazing livestock, farmers, loggers, and ranchers learn through their bodies about forests, fields, and plains. "We cannot come to terms with nature," White concludes, "without coming to terms with our own work, our own bodies, our own bodily knowledge."[7] Corps labor, however, can help us to come to terms with more than nature. Examining the impact of CCC work on enrollees' bodies and minds can also shed light on the shifting politics of both conservation and the New Deal during the Great Depression era.

From the moment Franklin Roosevelt conceived of the Corps, the concept of work was central to the mission and daily operation of the New Deal program. The president stated as much in his congressional message of March 21, 1933, in which he asked legislators to establish the CCC. "The overwhelming majority of unemployed Americans, who are now walking the streets and receiving private or public relief," Roosevelt wrote, "would infinitely prefer to work." Those enrolling in the program, he added, would "be used in simple work, not interfering with normal employment."[8] When Congress passed the bill creating the CCC just ten days later, labor was likewise of primary importance. According to the bill, the federal government established the Corps "for the purpose of relieving the acute condition of widespread distress and unemployment now existing in the United States" and "to provide for employing citizens of the United States who are unemployed."[9] Young men expecting their stint in the CCC to be a so-called walk in the park would be sorely disappointed. Labor, not leisure, was at the very heart of this work relief program.

Franklin Roosevelt's caveat that enrollees would "be used in simple work, not interfering with normal employment" was an attempt to alleviate the concerns of organized labor, which in the spring of 1933 reeled under a staggering 25 percent national unemployment rate. For the most part, the president's words fell on deaf ears. During joint hearings before House and Senate committees held in late March 1933, several union representatives interrupted an otherwise steady stream of supportive testimony to bitterly attack the CCC bill. American Federation of Labor (AFL) president William Green, who one week earlier had stated in the *New York Times* that the proposed reforestation program awakened "grave apprehension in the hearts and minds of labor," testified against the bill on three fronts, arguing that the army's control of CCC camps would militarize labor, that Corps enrollees would displace free laborers, and most important that the proposed compensation of $1 a day would depress wages for nonrelief workers. A. F. Whitney, president of the Brotherhood of Trainmen, opposed the Corps for similar reasons, stating that passage of the bill "would place Government's endorsement upon poverty at a bare subsistence level."[10]

Both Congress and the president went to great lengths to change the minds of organized labor. Partly in response to Green's congressional testimony against the establishment of the Corps, the Senate committee rewrote the bill to eliminate restrictive provisions concerning enrollment, discharges, and most important the highly controversial dollar-a-day wage rate, and instead simply authorized the president to organize and run the CCC "under such rules and regulations as he may prescribe."[11] Such changes allowed the AFL, which had been criticized by newspapers from across the political spectrum for its early opposition to the Corps, to quietly reverse itself and endorse, albeit reluctantly, the amended bill.[12] Yet even after the CCC became law, Roosevelt continued to woo union leaders. In August 1933, for instance, the president invited Green to accompany him on an inspection tour of five Corps camps in Virginia's Shenandoah National Park, where the two men lunched with an enthusiastic company of CCC enrollees on steak, mashed potatoes, green beans, and apple pie. In a letter to Roosevelt several weeks later, Green described the excursion as "one of the most pleasing experiences" of his life and admitted that, due to the president's commitment to the Corps, he "could not help but view the whole project in a most sympathetic way."[13]

Perhaps the most successful means of mollifying organized labor, however, was Roosevelt's decision to appoint Robert Fechner to the directorship of the newly created CCC. Born in Chattanooga, Tennessee, in 1876, Fechner grew up in the South and at age sixteen became a machinist's apprentice in the Augusta shops of the Georgia Central Railroad, where he immediately joined the union. In 1901, he helped to lead an unsuccessful strike for a nine-hour day and by 1914 had won election to both the general executive board of the International Association of Machinists and the vice presidency of the AFL. During World War I, Fechner worked as a labor policy advisor in Washington, D.C., where he first met Franklin Roosevelt, who was then assistant secretary of the navy. Nearly a decade later, while campaigning for the Democratic party during the 1932 presidential election, Fechner swung the machinist union vote to Roosevelt. His appointment to head the Corps, however, was less a reward for political loyalty than a presidential strategy for dealing with labor's opposition, which Roosevelt knew could be more easily ameliorated if one of their own was in charge of the program. Fechner's choice of another machinist, James McEntee, as his assistant director, soothed unionists yet again. Because of these maneuverings, organized labor, which during the 1930s occasionally butted heads with Corps administrators on issues such as wage rates for CCC contract work, never again openly criticized the New Deal program.[14] (See figure 3.1.)

Another indication that work was central to the newborn CCC was the fact that President Roosevelt assigned responsibility for recruiting enrollees to the Department of Labor. Due to time constraints as well as the desire to keep the Corps' bureaucracy to a minimum, the Department of Labor used agencies already in existence, specifically state unemployment relief bureaus, to identify, recruit, and enroll young men in the CCC. Quotas for each state were proportionate to population and enrollees were allowed to reenroll for up to four six-month periods for a total of two years in the Corps. Although decentralized, this system proved to be extremely efficient. Beginning the recruitment process on April 5, 1933, the Department of Labor had selected the CCC's first-year quota of 250,000 young men within two months. This system remained in operation throughout the Corps' nine-year life as the number of enrollees fluctuated, increasing to a peak of 520,000 in August 1935 then settling at 350,000 during the winter of 1937 before tapering off when Congress terminated the program in 1942 (see figure 3.2).[15] All told, the Department of Labor put more than 3 million young men to work for the CCC during the Great Depression, a mobilization effort dwarfing that undertaken by the U.S. military for World War I.[16]

The law creating the CCC stipulated that the Department of Labor adhere to a strict set of guidelines regarding the recruitment of enrollees. Most

Eleanor *Abbott's effort to get women CCC Camps*

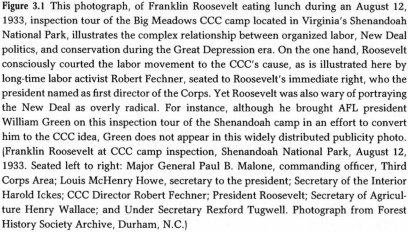

Figure 3.1 This photograph, of Franklin Roosevelt eating lunch during an August 12, 1933, inspection tour of the Big Meadows CCC camp located in Virginia's Shenandoah National Park, illustrates the complex relationship between organized labor, New Deal politics, and conservation during the Great Depression era. On the one hand, Roosevelt consciously courted the labor movement to the CCC's cause, as is illustrated here by long-time labor activist Robert Fechner, seated to Roosevelt's immediate right, who the president named as first director of the Corps. Yet Roosevelt was also wary of portraying the New Deal as overly radical. For instance, although he brought AFL president William Green on this inspection tour of the Shenandoah camp in an effort to convert him to the CCC idea, Green does not appear in this widely distributed publicity photo. (Franklin Roosevelt at CCC camp inspection, Shenandoah National Park, August 12, 1933. Seated left to right: Major General Paul B. Malone, commanding officer, Third Corps Area; Louis McHenry Howe, secretary to the president; Secretary of the Interior Harold Ickes; CCC Director Robert Fechner; President Roosevelt; Secretary of Agriculture Henry Wallace; and Under Secretary Rexford Tugwell. Photograph from Forest History Society Archive, Durham, N.C.)

obviously, enrollment was restricted to men, despite pleas from American women for admittance to the Corps and Eleanor Roosevelt's attempts to establish CCC camps for females. This decision to exclude women had less to do with the belief that they were physically unable to perform conservation work than with early twentieth-century thinking concerning public

Women's
CCC camp

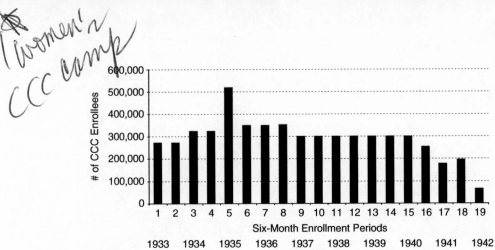

Figure 3.2 Total Number of CCC Enrollees by Enrollment Period. (Created by Author)

policy and the American female. New Dealers, like presidential administrations before and since, viewed men's labor as an inalienable right to be protected, if necessary, by federal action. Women's work was seen more as a family necessity or choice and therefore lay outside the purview of national social reform.[17] Thus, while Roosevelt considered male unemployment a civic problem to be corrected through federal programs like the Corps, he saw women laborers as less-than workers and therefore not entitled to the same economic rights. In part because of such thinking, there was only one CCC-like camp for women in the country, Camp Jane Addams, located in the Bear Mountain section of the Palisades Interstate Park. Not surprisingly, Camp Jane Addams trained its female enrollees not in conservation work but rather in domestic skills that could help their families weather the Great Depression.[18]

Franklin Roosevelt's gendered view of labor also determined which men could enroll in the CCC. In a conscious effort not to interfere with employment opportunities for male breadwinners, who were the primary focus of most New Deal legislation, those wishing to join the Corps had to be single and eighteen to twenty-five years old, the exception being a small number of World War I veterans, Native Americans, and what the CCC called "Local Experienced Men," all of whom could be married and over twenty-five.[19] As important, these youths had to be unemployed and willing to send between $22 and $25 of their $30 monthly paycheck back home to their families, which had to be already receiving public assistance.[20] By sidestepping competition with men's work and linking enrollee labor to the family, Roosevelt figuratively placed these youths alongside American women, including those at Camp Jane

Addams, who also served the familial economy. The president thus saw both unemployed women and CCC boys as of the working class but as not-quite workers.[21] While American women had little chance of altering their political status as laborers during the Great Depression, Roosevelt believed that the male youths joining the CCC could, through his New Deal, become full-fledged workers.

The selection criteria of the Department of Labor also ensured that while the young men joining the Corps would come from across the country, they would do so from similar economic backgrounds. Because of quotas based on state populations, CCC enrollees were a geographically diverse lot, hailing from every region of the country, the territories of Alaska and Hawaii, and Puerto Rico and the Virgin Islands. Enrollees were more homogeneous when it came to class categories, however. This is quite apparent in the Corps' own description of "the typical enrollee," a composite compiled from a census the CCC undertook in 1937. According to the data, the average young man joining the Corps had never held a full-time job, had been jobless for close to seven months prior to enrolling, and came from a family in which his father remained unemployed.[22] "The men who served as enrollees in the Corps came from economically insecure homes," explained the CCC's second and last director, James McEntee. "They were drawn almost entirely from that third of the population which President Roosevelt has described as 'ill fed, ill housed and ill clothed.' "[23]

Along with helping to determine the type of young men joining the CCC, the Department of Labor's selection criteria also influenced the sorts of work they performed. The Corps' own census indicated that less than one-third of the more than 350,000 enrollees in 1937 had experienced on-the-job training of any sort prior to joining the CCC, let alone training that provided them with technical know-how for conservation work.[24] As Robert Fechner wrote in 1938, "enrollees who come into the Corps are unskilled and untrained."[25] To accommodate such inexperience, the CCC planned and undertook conservation projects in forests, parks, and fields that could be completed with unskilled or semi-skilled labor. As a result, noted Corps educational advisor Frank Hill, the great majority of CCC enrollees "work with their hands."[26] Enrollee experiences support Hill's observations. "I have actually learned how to work with my hands," explained James Lowe in 1935 of the labor he undertook on a conservation project near Bedford, Pennsylvania.[27] It was precisely because of their lack of skill and training that enrollee labor was predominately physical.

peak strength

The manual labor that enrollees performed determined to a great extent the daily routine of CCC camps. A typical day in the Corps began at 6 o'clock in the morning with reveille, after which enrollees dressed, made their beds, cleaned their barracks, and ate breakfast before lining up for "work call" at 7:45. If the conservation project was located near camp, enrollees walked to the work site; if it was farther away, they climbed into trucks and drove deeper into the forest, park, or farmland until they reached the workplace. Enrollees then began laboring and continued, except for a short coffee break, until noon. If the conservation project was situated far from camp, lunch was brought to the work site rather than the men returning to camp for their midday meal. After eating, digesting, and resting for an hour, the young men recommenced work until 4 o'clock in the afternoon, when they headed back to camp. After dinner, which the camp kitchen usually served at 5:30, the evening belonged to the enrollees, many of whom spent the time playing sports, journeying to nearby towns for entertainment, reading in the camp library, or taking educational courses offered by the CCC. Camp lights flashed off at 10 o'clock and taps sounded fifteen minutes later. Corps enrollees then enjoyed eight hours of sleep before beginning another day of hard manual labor.[28]

According to this daily schedule, CCC enrollees performed an enormous amount of physical work. The Corps expected enrollees to labor eight hours a day, five days a week, for a total of forty hours per week. If inclement weather such as intense rain or severe temperatures prevented enrollees from working Monday through Friday, they made up the lost time on Saturday.[29] Each year, individual enrollees thus worked 2,080 hours, meaning that between August 1935 and mid-1936, when the New Deal program reached its peak strength of 520,000 enrollees, the CCC supervised more than 1 billion hours of enrollee labor. Throughout the Corps' nine-year history, the young men in the program performed approximately 4.5 billion hours of work, the overwhelming majority of it manual. Such figures do not include overtime labor undertaken during emergency activities, such as firefighting and flood control.[30] Robert Fechner was well aware of the central role played by such labor in determining the future of his program. "I believe that the general popularity of the Corps is due in large measure to the belief of the general public that it has not been conducted as a welfare organization but has engaged in useful worthwhile work," wrote the CCC director in 1939. "We have constantly tried to instill that spirit into the enrollees."[31]

Although Fechner understood the importance of labor to the success of his program, the young men joining the CCC were wholly unprepared for the new workplace that awaited them. While enrollees came in nearly equal numbers from cities and agricultural areas, the Corps situated its camps, even those undertaking soil conservation on farms, in remote locations on publicly owned lands, such as national and state forests and parks. "They put these camps mostly in the wildest places," explained enrollee Harold Fraine during the mid-1930s, "for it is usually in such spots that the forest can be most improved."[32] Such landscapes were unfamiliar to the young men joining the Corps. "After my company was transferred to northern Minnesota," wrote enrollee Dan Gately in December 1935, "I was put in an entirely different environment to which I had been accustomed." Kenneth Stephans described the view from his camp similarly, writing that "as far as the eye could see, stretched a vast forest of trees not familiar to me."[33] As with the surrounding flora, the young men joining the Corps were equally unacquainted with the fauna lurking around CCC worksites, leading one enrollee to pen a poem titled "Nature" that included the lines "until I started working here, just think—I'd never seen a deer!"[34] Because those joining the Corps often worked in foreign surroundings deep within woods and parks, explained enrollee Carl McNees in the late 1930s, the great majority "know little or nothing about good old 'Mother Nature' and her ways."[35]

The young men joining the Corps often feared what they did not know. Living and laboring in unfamiliar settings miles from what most considered civilization, many enrollees initially expressed repugnance for their new environs. "My first thought, when I descended from the bus and surveyed the camp-site, was one of aversion," wrote Robert Ross, an enrollee stationed in the Ozarks of Arkansas. "Mountains surrounded me and hemmed me in," he continued, "bushes with thorns on them, and the clinging vines that snarled and twisted around one's feet.... this was all so foreign to me, I hated it at once."[36] In some instances, enrollees acted on such antagonisms, lashing out at the natural environment about which they knew so little. When they first arrived in New York's Bear Mountain State Park, for example, enrollees went on a rampage, destroying dozens of garter, black, and meadow snakes along with other wildlife near their work project site, under the mistaken assumption that such animals were dangerous. The CCC boys "did some unnecessary killing of wild things they encountered," explained a park spokesperson in August 1934. "These boys, most of whom lived in the cities and few of [whom] had any ideas about an animal or a bird except that they were something to shoot at, were a threat to wild life."[37] Upon their arrival at camp, not only were many enrollees ignorant of the ways of Mother Nature, but they often acted out against her as well.

During their first few weeks in the Corps, enrollees were as mentally uninformed about their work as they were about the natural setting of their labor. Because less than 10 percent of those joining the CCC had graduated from high school and only 3 percent had attended some form of college, they were completely ignorant of the theory and practice of natural resource conservation. Of those who had gone to college, only a tiny fraction had taken courses in fields such as forestry, agronomy, and hydrology, or pursued a graduate degree in any of what the CCC called "the land sciences."[38] Most enrollees were upfront about their lack of knowledge. "Before I enrolled in camp," explained enrollee Wesley Kelley in 1935, "I knew nothing about the value of our forests and why so much care should be taken of them." When Joseph Swezey joined the Corps in mid-September 1934, he too "had absolutely no knowledge or interest in the natural resources of this country and nature in general," and neither did James Cordes, an enrollee stationed in a camp near Galeton, Pennsylvania, who stated simply that "before my enrollment, I knew very little about forest conservation."[39]

Corps administrators were well aware that the young men joining the CCC were intellectually unprepared for their new natural surroundings. "The mountains and forests of this country may seem a wilderness to those of the Civilian Conservation Corps who come from the cities and farms," explained a manual on woodsmanship published by the CCC for its enrollees. "They may feel that they are in strange surroundings and new ways of life."[40] The Corps also understood that its enrollees lacked the information required to perform much of the conservation work taking place in these wild regions. "They hadn't had any experience and were totally out of their element in the woods," stated a CCC camp supervisor from New Hampshire. "[T]he job was to teach them the various skills."[41] To achieve this, the New Deal program took two approaches, both aimed at instilling in enrollee minds the knowledge necessary to perform, and the reasons behind, CCC conservation work. The first strategy entailed informal on-the-job instruction given to enrollees while they labored on Corps conservation projects. The CCC supplemented this with a more formal camp education program for enrollees after work hours.[42] Both methods strove to replace enrollees' ignorance about their work and workplace with knowledge about the conservation of natural resources. The ultimate goal of this education, explained CCC director Robert Fechner, was to make enrollees' minds "conservation conscious."[43]

Informal learning through labor was a central tenet of Corps administrative philosophy.[44] According to the CCC, one unfortunate side effect of the formalization of the American educational system was a growing "separation

between the content of education and the workaday world, a separation between learning and doing." The academic, the Corps warned, had been set off
from the practical with the result that "work without thought and study" had
become "drudgery."[45] To correct this situation, the CCC placed several conservation professionals in each Corps camp to oversee work projects, to teach
enrollees the skills to undertake such projects, and to instruct enrollees in the
theoretical underpinnings of their conservation practices. In camps located in
national and state forests, such professionals were mostly trained foresters,
while work projects situated in national and state parks also involved an experienced engineer, several trained landscape men, and perhaps wildlife technicians.[46] The on-the-job instruction these professionals gave to enrollees, argued
the CCC's second director, James McEntee, represented "a new kind of education," one that he called "a scholarship in work experience!" (see figure 3.3).[47]

Figure 3.3 In an effort to teach CCC enrollees about conservation, the Corps conducted
on-the-job training in all of its camps. In this photograph, forester Frank S. Robinson from
a camp in California's Lassen National Forest teaches two enrollees about "How a Tree
Grows." Ironically, while these young men were learning about tree growth, the axes in
their hands suggest that when they labored on their camp's conservation project they
were in fact cutting trees down, most probably in an effort to thin the forest to ensure
more efficient growth. While the knowledge these and millions of other CCC enrollees
gained through similar on-the-job training converted many to the conservationist cause,
the actual work they performed, in this case thinning forests, would spark a backlash
against the Corps during the later 1930s that significantly altered both the conservation
movement and New Deal politics. ("Teaching Civilian Conservation Corps Workers
Basic Forestry Techniques, Lassen National Forest, California," U.S. Forest Service
photo courtesy of the Forest History Society, Durham, N.C. Forest History Society
image ID# FHS1186; U.S. Forest negative number 285389. Image taken 09/14/1933)

The result, concluded McEntee's predecessor, Robert Fechner, was that "enrollees have had an opportunity to learn first hand the necessity and the importance of conservation."[48]

The Corps supplemented on-the-job training with a more formal camp educational program. This began in April 1933 when the first enrollees in the nation trekked to their camp in Virginia's George Washington National Forest with an elementary manual on forestry packed away in their duffle bags. Drafted quickly and in plain, simple language by professionals in the U.S. Forest Service, the pamphlet explained the unfamiliar setting of the woods, recommended methods for using various tools, described poisonous plants and snakes, and defined in a rudimentary manner the meaning of conservation.[49] Robert Fechner greatly expanded such learning opportunities on May 29, 1933, when he authorized the establishment of libraries in Corps camps across the country and allocated funding for them to be stocked with 45 different periodicals and approximately 150 books, many of which were "educational volumes pertaining largely to forestry and nature study."[50] The CCC director hoped that enrollees interested in obtaining additional information about the conservation work they performed during the day would return to camp at night and make use of these libraries (see figure 3.4). Robert Ross, an enrollee stationed in a camp near Crystal Springs, Arkansas, did just this. "To learn more of the mountains and the trees, I turned to the library for information," wrote Ross in the mid-1930s. "It was mentally refreshing to read of things I had been totally ignorant of—soil erosion, restoration, protection of the forests, the uses of land, the damage of forest fires."[51]

The Corps' formal approach to conservation education, however, did not revolve around library circulation desks or brief pamphlets on forestry. Rather, it centered on a system of voluntary night classes held at all CCC camps. The Association of State Foresters first raised this possibility at its annual meeting in October 1933, when it passed a resolution urging the CCC to institute forestry instruction in enrollee camps throughout the country.[52] Franklin Roosevelt followed up on this in early November with a letter to Palisades Interstate Park superintendent Major William Welch regarding the possibility of an experimental after-work education program for enrollees stationed in the park's Bear Mountain section, the same section where Roosevelt in 1922 had established special campgrounds to teach Boy Scouts about forestry. "I am very anxious to try out in one or two places the idea of giving the men in the CCC camps some kind of informal instruction in forestry and the natural history of trees," wrote the president. "I wonder if you could get

Figure 3.4 After receiving on-the-job training in conservation during the day while laboring on CCC work projects, enrollees could return to camp each night and continue their conservation education by visiting their camp library. In this photograph, of the library at Camp Mormon Creek deep within Michigan's Hiawatha National Forest, Corps administrators lined the wall to either side of the fireplace with a wide variety of books, many of which pertained to forestry and nature study. Also seen here in the hands of several Mormon Creek enrollees are a few of the approximately forty-five journals and magazines to which all CCC camps subscribed; many of these periodicals also contained educational material on the conservation of natural resources. In early 1934, the Corps implemented a more formal camp education program consisting of voluntary evening classes that included courses on conservation-related fields such as forestry, soil conservation, and wildlife management. (The library at the Mormon Creek Camp, Hiawatha National Forest, Michigan, 1939, as reprinted in Stan Cohen, *The Tree Army: A Pictorial History of the Civilian Conservation Corps, 1933–1942* [Missoula, Mont.: Pictorial Histories Publishing Company, 1980])

somebody...to conduct voluntary classes at some of the Bear Mountain Camps this winter."[53] After this test run proved successful, on December 7, 1933, Roosevelt approved funds for a national enrollee education program under the auspices of the Office of Education, which early in 1934 began selecting "educational advisors" for CCC camps. Three years later, the Corps had hired more than 1,800 of these advisors, or approximately one for every camp in the nation.[54]

From the outset, the CCC organized these evening classes with the enrollees' daytime work in mind. During the program's early years, when the Corps lacked a comprehensive national curriculum, each educational advisor teamed up with the foresters, agronomists, or Park Service technicians in his camp and simply arranged a series of evening lectures, seminars, and workshops for enrollees. Although under this system each camp was responsible for its own course platform, the CCC administration in Washington, D.C., strongly recommended that these classes be "designed to supplement and lend background to the practical work the men do in the forests."[55] Even when, in the spring of 1935, the Corps developed an expanded national curriculum that included both literacy and vocational coursework in fields such as automotive repair, carpentry, and elementary masonry, CCC educational advisors still offered enrollees a core of conservation-oriented classes with titles including "Forestry," "Soil Conservation," and "Conservation of Natural Resources." Later that year, the CCC also formulated eight overall objectives for its evening instruction, the second of which entailed "instilling in the enrollees a deeper consciousness of the importance of conserving the nation's resources."[56] Thus, even as it matured, the CCC's formal education program never disassociated the coursework that enrollees performed at night from the fieldwork they undertook during the day.

Corps enrollees responded enthusiastically to the CCC's evening educational programs. Whereas only 35 percent of all enrollees took such classes in 1934, the first year they were offered, two years later nearly 300,000 young men, or 87 percent, participated in camp educational activities. As the Corps expanded the variety of course offerings during the mid-1930s, the percentage of enrollees taking classes after work increased, rising to nearly 92 percent by the end of the 1930s. "These figures," argued Fechner, "indicate strongly that at present the camps offer many effective educational opportunities."[57]

While the enormous number of enrollees attending CCC classes suggests that those joining the Corps studied at night what they were informally taught during the workday, the popularity of specific courses further confirms that the young men in the camps wanted to learn particularly about natural resource conservation. According to a CCC study undertaken in 1937, of the ninety-seven different classes offered in Corps camps during the six-month enrollment period covering October 1, 1934, to March 31, 1935, classes in forestry ranked second in popularity among enrollees, with only a required first aid course garnering more students. Other conservation-oriented instruction popular with enrollees included landscaping and nature study courses, both of which drew more students than two-thirds of the other classes offered.[58] Further evidence that CCC enrollees spent many of their evenings studying natural resource conservation comes from the American Tree Association, which late in 1933 donated 25,000 copies of its textbook, *The Forestry Primer*, to the CCC. According to the association, within weeks of this donation, requests for additional copies flooded in from Corps camps throughout the country. "Our Ohio boys are anxious to learn all they can and your publication is a valuable help," wrote an educational advisor from a Corps camp near Lake Arrowhead, California. The state forester of Massachusetts wrote a similar letter, explaining during the summer of 1933, "I certainly appreciate very much your kindness in sending the Forestry Primers which will be very helpful in the CCC camps of Massachusetts. We are organizing classes in forestry, geology, surveying and other subjects." In fact, so popular was *The Forestry Primer* with CCC enrollees that the American Tree Association printed an additional 100,000 copies of the textbook and distributed them to Corps camps nationwide.[59]

The CCC's instruction both on the job and in the classroom succeeded in educating the young men joining the New Deal program about the conservation of natural resources. "The classes in forestry have helped me differentiate the many types of trees which we see about camp," wrote enrollee Dan Gately in 1935 from his camp near Merrifield, Minnesota.[60] While forestry was a favorite topic of enrollees, through their labor they also learned about soil conservation. "The days work in the field is not all cream," admitted Frederick Carlsen, an enrollee stationed near Marion, Iowa. Yet because of instruction by CCC professionals, "I have learned a lot about soil erosion and how to prevent it."[61] Enrollee Harry Gough perhaps best summed up the overall impact of CCC education on the young men joining the Corps when he wrote from his camp near Flintstone, Maryland, "[T]hrough the Educational program I have learned a lot about . . . conservation. It has offered an opportunity for me to improve myself mentally."[62]

Thus, as CCC enrollees learned as they labored, and then learned again while studying in courses at night, they changed their minds about conservation. Whereas before entering the New Deal program they knew little, if anything, about conserving natural resources such as timber, soil, and water, a few months later after toiling on CCC projects they had gained an understanding of conservationist philosophy and the various techniques for implementing it across the American landscape. Corps work and the education that went along with it, however, did more than alter enrollees' thinking. While changing enrollee minds, labor on conservation projects in the nation's forests, throughout its parks, and on its fields also began to transform the bodies of the millions of young men in the CCC.

The majority of Corps enrollees were in poor physical condition prior to joining the New Deal program. By their own accounts, expressed over and over again throughout the 1930s, enrollees were aware of their physical deterioration during the Great Depression. "Due to insufficient food and worry, I was run down and not at all well," wrote enrollee Thomas Scott from his camp near Zanesville, Ohio. "Previous to my enlistment," added James Weister, "I was what most people would call a bag of bones." While frequently using terms such as "scrawny," "weak," and "poorly developed" to describe their physiques before joining the Corps, the young men enrolling in the CCC were not merely underweight; they felt unhealthy as well. Enrollee Paul Stone, for instance, complained from his camp in northern California's Redwood State Park that "when I joined I was gaunt and undernourished," and James Jensen likewise explained that "when I entered camp I was a rank tenderfoot, inclined to get colds and sicknesses easily." An enrollee stationed near Rushville, Illinois, could have been describing the experiences of many young men joining the CCC when he wrote in 1934 that "upon enrollment I was almost a physical wreck."[63]

New enrollees blamed joblessness in particular for sapping much of their corporeal strength. "Driven like a hunted dog through four years of unemployment," wrote enrollee James Kidwell of his search for work throughout the United States, Canada, and Mexico during the early 1930s, my "undernourished body [was] utterly without purpose in life."[64] Although the distances he traveled were unusually vast, Kidwell's situation was far from unique. According to data compiled by the Corps in 1937, the typical enrollee had been jobless for nearly seven months prior to joining the CCC.[65] In this respect, Charles Hiller was lucky. After graduating from high school and looking for employment to help his financially strapped family, Hiller became despondent. "In two months, I began to feel hopeless," he explained in March 1934. "Ill with worry, worn out in body, I was rapidly going to pieces." A few weeks later, Hiller enrolled his unemployed, weary body in the CCC, which assigned him to a camp in a state park near Clifton Forge, Virginia.[66]

Many of the young men enrolling in the Corps also faulted the unhealthy environments in which they were forced to live while unemployed for draining them of bodily vigor. Enrollees from cities were especially apt to emphasize the deleterious effects of the urban setting on their physical health. Between unsuccessful job searches in a central Pennsylvania industrial town, Charles Billmyer spent most of his free hours "with the pool room gang," which resulted in "a condition of habitual deviation from moral rectitude" accompanied by acute physical degradation. "I soon found myself,"

 *unhealthy enrollees*

Billmyer added, "in an environment not very desirable."[67] James Danner was more forthright in deriding the urban setting, describing his fellow enrollees in 1936 as "thin, hollow-chested, sharp-faced products of our big cities' slums with the threat of tuberculosis hovering over them."[68]

Enrollees' underdeveloped bodies led many of these young men to question openly their masculinity prior to joining the CCC. Enrollees expressed such insecurities in camp newspapers such as the *Thousand Islander*, published by a Corps company located in Fishers Landing, New York. On the illustrated cover of the paper's September 1937 issue stood a childlike enrollee holding Uncle Sam's hand while looking longingly at a sunset labeled "EMPLOY-MENT" (see figure 3.5). Another cartoon in the same issue similarly questioned enrollees' manhood by depicting a stork delivering a blanket-full of baby-faced rookie recruits to the New York camp (see figure 3.6).[69] Those joining the CCC often stated outright what the *Thousand Islander* suggested. "I enrolled as a boy, unsteady, groping, unsure," wrote Robert Miller from his camp near Pine Grove, California. "I had doubted my right to call myself a man."[70] Physically frail and unable to put in an honest day's work, many young men felt both emasculated and infantilized before enrolling in the CCC.[71]

The Corps was acutely aware of the poor physical state of the young men joining the New Deal program. According to the physical examinations of 100,000 enrollees conducted during the late 1930s by the army's Office of the Surgeon General, approximately 75 percent of the young men entering the Corps fell below what the army considered an acceptable weight and were therefore more prone to, or were already suffering from, physical ills such as tuberculosis, hookworms, and nervous exhaustion. "Thousands of these 'light-weights,' " as the army called them, "possess[ed] well developed or incipient ailments which—within a few months to a few years—would have produced total permanent disability or death."[72] As CCC director Robert Fechner explained, "thousands of under-weight, over-weight and unhealthy youths signed up last spring or early summer for the CCC camps."[73]

The CCC also echoed its enrollees in attributing the sickly bodies of those joining the Corps to conditions created by the Great Depression, namely, a lack of work combined with unhealthful surroundings. According to CCC directors, the young men enrolling in the program were sickly not only because "economic pressure" left them "undernourished," but also because unhealthy physical "quirks" had been "engendered by bad environments."[74] "The great bulk of CCC enrollees came from homes and from environments

Thousand Islander

EMPLOYMENT

SEPT. 1937
CO 1249

FAREWELL
ISSUE

FISHERS LANDING
NEW YORK

which, as a result of the depression, furnished an effective bar to development, social stability, or economic opportunity," explained one CCC administrator in 1942. Not surprisingly, the CCC reserved its harshest criticism for the American city. The nation's young men, explained a promotional article on the Corps written for *Forestry News Digest*, had to be rescued "from city streets, poor food, insufficient clothing and unventilated and unsanitary living quarters."[75]

Finally, the CCC shared enrollees' concerns that frail physiques, not to mention the lack of employment and unhealthful environments that caused them, threatened the masculinity of those joining the New Deal program. Director James McEntee admitted to such insecurities in his 1940 book on the Corps, which he rather wistfully titled *Now They Are Men*. After explaining that "many of the boys who make application for CCC enrollment have not had enough of the right kinds of food, and clearly not the right kinds of

Figures 3.5 (facing page) and 3.6 Corps enrollees often joined the New Deal program with undernourished and underdeveloped bodies that made them question their masculinity. While enrollees often kept such insecurities private, sometimes they were put on public display in the numerous camp newspapers that CCC enrollees wrote, published, and read on a weekly or monthly basis. These two cartoons from the *Thousand Islander*, a newspaper put out by a camp located in Fisher's Landing, New York, illustrates such insecurities by portraying Corps enrollees as young boys. Whether being guided by a paternal Uncle Sam or flown to their new camp by a stork representing motherhood, both illustrations suggest that when they joined the CCC enrollees saw themselves as young, physically frail, and in need of parental guidance. Uncle Sam suggests that many of these youths saw the federal government as one possible guide. (Uncle Sam cartoon, cover, and Stork cartoon, p. 11, *Thousand Islander*, September 1937, Official File 268: CCC, Folder: CCC Periodicals, August–December 1937, Franklin Delano Roosevelt Library, Hyde Park, N.Y)

exercise, to build up their bodies," McEntee further questioned enrollees' masculinity on the grounds that many had not worked prior to entering the Corps. "They would never become capable men," he wrote, "if they were unemployed, at home, supported by their fathers' meager earnings or relief allowances."[76] By reconditioning the young bodies joining the Corps, the New Deal program hoped to alleviate these threats to enrollee manhood. "Our purpose is not only to rebuild forests and lands," explained Fechner, "but to build men."[77]

The insecurity of Corps administrators and enrollees regarding the bodies of the young men joining the New Deal program reflected a broader cultural crisis involving gender roles during the Great Depression. The roots of this anxiety went back to the turn of the century, when many middle-class Americans began worrying that American men had become overcivilized, overly cultured, and physically soft—in a word, effeminate. Theodore Roosevelt's call at the turn of the century for "the strenuous life" was just one response to this widespread cultural concern. With the onset of the Great Depression, as American men lost their jobs in increasing numbers, this masculinity crisis resurfaced with renewed vigor and forced many Americans to question again American manhood. A host of sociological studies conducted during the 1930s and early 1940s with titles such as "The Unemployed Man and His Family: The Effects of Unemployment upon the Status of Men" attest to this widespread concern that male joblessness threatened male social standing. As these contemporary studies indicate, and as scholars of the New Deal era have argued since, manhood during the Great Depression was inextricably bound to both the flagging economy and the sagging physiques of American men.[78]

The Corps took a number of steps to rejuvenate the lackluster bodies that poured into the CCC during the 1930s and early 1940s. The program first eliminated those it felt were beyond redemption by requiring that all enrollees pass a physical entrance examination; during the Corps' nine-year history, it consistently rejected on average 10 percent of those applying. The CCC then began preparing the bodies of those passing the examination by placing new enrollees in conditioning camps for between one and three weeks, depending on the physical shape of each individual. Conducted on military bases and organized by the U.S. Army, the conditioning program consisted of immunization against diseases, light work details, good food, plenty of rest, and what Director Fechner called "a physical hardening process" that was necessary for "building up [enrollee] bodies generally for the arduous outdoor life to follow."[79] Early on, the Corps also instituted a fifteen-minute morning calisthenics regimen in camps across the country, complete with a *Physical Training Manual* containing photographs illustrating proper technique (see figure 3.7). "By means of systematic and wisely chosen exercises," explained the manual, "enrollees can bring into play many muscles which would not otherwise get a workout."[80]

The CCC's most important curative for the sickly bodies flooding into the Corps, however, was work in nature. Only hard, manual labor outdoors could reverse the physical deterioration caused by the unemployment and unhealthy environments of the Great Depression, and the Corps promoted it at every opportunity. Franklin Roosevelt first emphasized the physically rejuvenative character of outdoor work in March 1933, when he asked Congress to create the CCC in order to "take a vast army of these unemployed out into healthful surroundings."[81] Corps administrators followed the president's lead throughout the 1930s. In 1937, for instance, CCC educational advisor Samuel Harby described enrollee labor as "vigorous outdoor work" that "makes

Figure 3.7 In an effort to begin rebuilding enrollees' frail bodies, in 1933 the CCC instituted a fifteen-minute calisthenics exercise program that the young men undertook each morning before heading out to work on their conservation projects. In this photograph, of a morning workout at Camp Billis near San Antonio, Texas, enrollees do deep knee bends in clean white T-shirts to strengthen their physiques. As important to Corps administrators, however, was the setting of these exercises. While Camp Billis enrollees could have undertaken their morning calisthenics in the center of camp, surrounded by barracks, mess halls, and camp libraries, they instead exercised out in nature, in this case in the center of an open field. The Corps would eventually envision enrollee labor similarly. Not just work, but work in nature, the CCC would argue in much of its publicity literature, was central to rejuvenating the degraded male bodies joining the New Deal program. ("Setting up exercises at Camp Bullis, near San Antonio, in 1933," NARA, Stan Cohen, *The Tree Army: A Pictorial History of the Civilian Conservation Corps, 1933–1942* [Missoula, Mont.: Pictorial Histories Publishing Company, 1980], 13)

muscles strong and hard," while James McEntee argued that enrollee bodies would be restored through "healthful work in the outdoors, out in the forests, parks, and soils of this country."[82] By replacing joblessness with labor and sickly urban environments with a healthier setting in nature, the Corps hoped to rebuild enrollee physiques and in turn transform CCC boys into men.

The Corps succeeded, at least in the minds and bodies of the young men who joined the New Deal program.[83] The physical change first noticed by enrollees usually involved their muscles, which being underdeveloped prior to joining the Corps quickly became sore after a few days of laboring. "The first weeks on work detail remain to me still a black void of aching muscles and the sheer misery of exhaustion," remembered enrollee James Danner in 1941 of his work building a stone wall in a state park near Euclid, Ohio. "I could barely drag myself the one-hundred yards from work truck to bed" at the end of each day. After a few weeks in camp, however, Danner's body showed signs of adjusting to both manual labor and the natural setting in which it took place. "Slowly the wall grew, and slowly strength and health imperceptibly flowed back into my body," Danner wrote. "Suddenly, the first bitterness of toil had lessened, and I began to notice the beauty of the forest."[84] Enrollees from camps across the country similarly described how "sore" and "stiff" muscles became "stronger" and more "developed" from working outside on conservation projects in forests, parks, and fields.[85] Enrollees even noticed these changes in one another. The campmates who nicknamed Danner the "Ninety-Seven Pound Weakling" when he joined the Corps, rechristened him "The Bruiser" several months later after Danner lifted an enormous rock onto the stone wall they were constructing together.[86]

By developing their muscles, enrollees working outdoors for the Corps also increased their body weight. The gains experienced by the young men joining the CCC, however, had less to do with converting body fat into muscle tissue than with the enormous amount of free food the Corps fed its enrollees; the young men ate 375 pounds of meat, 228 pounds of potatoes, and 46 pounds of butter per year versus 115 pounds of meat, 163 pounds of potatoes, and 17 pounds of butter for the typical U.S. citizen. Because of this copious menu, the young men joining the Corps gained on average between eleven and fifteen pounds after spending three to four months in camp, a bodily change upon which they commented more than any other. Enrollee Joseph Weigel, for instance, proudly stated that he had gained sixty pounds during his stay in a camp near Toft, Minnesota, while James Bennett bragged of putting on twenty-five pounds by eating plentiful meals at his camp located thirty-five miles from Las Vegas, Nevada. Enrollees also grew taller while in the Corps than they would have under non-CCC conditions.[87] "Three times a day food quickly disappears from the tables in the mess hall," explained James McEntee, "as the healthy, hearty appetites of the boys are satisfied by generous helpings of body-building food."[88]

As they tightened their muscles and loosened their belts, enrollees laboring outdoors in forests, parks, and fields also experienced bodily changes involving their skin. When the young men first arrived in camp, they often described themselves as "pasty-faced," "pale," and "without good color at all."[89] During the next few weeks, however, the skin tone of CCC enrollees often turned from white to red. "Most of them are working without shirts," explained one visitor to a CCC camp located in a national forest near Riverton, Virginia, "and their skins are reddened" by the sun. Hands that had been soft and smooth before joining the Corps also changed as blisters arose on skin unused to manual labor.[90] Yet, as enrollees continued to work outside, their chameleon-like skin changed colors yet again, and blistered hands likewise became calloused. "I'd strip right down to a pair of pants and shoes and I'd get all tan after a while," explained Robert Buchanan, an enrollee stationed in a New Hampshire camp. Others proudly described themselves as "burned a deep brown," "brown as a berry," and "as brown as Indians."[91]

Outdoor work even altered the posture of many Corps enrollees. Prior to joining the CCC, the skeletal carriage of the young men suffered from both physical and mental deterioration. "It seemed to me I had never seen such an array of ragged, slouchy poor white trash," wrote Harold Buckles of his fellow enrollees, who like himself had just arrived at a Corps camp in Wyoming's Medicine Bow National Forest. "They didn't walk across the area; they shambled . . . stoop-shouldered." Two months after working outdoors eight hours a day, forty hours a week, Buckles noticed a significant change in the gait of these same young men. "When they move across the area today they don't walk; they stride," he explained. "Their shoulders are erect; they swing easily in their walk the way woodsmen do."[92] Harry Maynor, a camp advisor from Illinois, described a similar transformation when he wrote to his CCC superior in 1934 that "every boy is sturdier and stronger and walks straighter than he did before entering camp."[93] Even residents of enrollees' hometowns remarked on the improved manner in which the young men returning from a stint in the Corps carried their bodies. "In this community," wrote a resident of Romeo, Colorado, during the mid-1930s, "it is easy to identify the boys who have been in camps in the past, by their erect carriage."[94]

Finally, in causing many of these physical transformations, manual labor in nature bettered the overall bodily health of the young men joining the CCC. This was the conclusion of the army's 1937 study of 100,000 enrollees. While 75 percent of those joining the Corps had been so underweight and malnourished as to be either highly prone to disease or already afflicted, upon discharge the picture was quite different. After working outdoors and eating three square meals a day in the Corps for several months, the percentage of "light-weights" tumbled from 75 to 40 percent, and incidents of tuberculosis among CCC enrollees dropped to about one-fifth that of similarly aged young men in the general population. The army's survey also found that as a result of the physical, outdoor labor performed on Corps conservation projects,

bodies transformed + nature

enrollees were more physically fit than the citizenry at large.[95] Enrollee statements supported such findings. Lawrence Lescisco, stationed in a camp near Landisburg, Pennsylvania, described the experiences of many enrollees when he wrote during the mid-1930s that by working in nature he "gained weight, good firm flesh, and a more healthy, vigorous feeling."[96]

The bodily transformations experienced by CCC enrollees—from changes in muscle and skin tone to weight gain and improved overall health—altered these young men's relationship to the nature in which they labored.[97] This process began when Corps enrollees associated their renewed bodily health with the elimination of their unemployment. "The work is healthful," claimed enrollee John Goodspeed in 1934 from his camp near Kanosh, Utah. "The little aches and pains you experienced," added Herbert Junep, an enrollee stationed in California's Sequoia National Park, "were but in part payment for that magnificent physique and health which your work with this same gang has brought you."[98] To fully rebuild their bodies, however, many understood that such labor also had to take place in healthful environments. "Not an artificial mechanical world like that of the modern city, but a world alive with beauty more lovely than I had ever known," wrote enrollee Paul Stone in the mid-1930s of the natural setting in which he worked. "It was in this country that my health was renewed." Enrollee Virgil McClanahan agreed, stating simply that enrollees felt healthier because "the average CCC boy is in an environment that keeps him in contact with nature."[99]

By rehabilitating their bodies through outdoor labor, many Corps enrollees also believed that they had regained their masculinity. Over and over again, those in the Corps declared that their renewed physical strength had remade them into men. "I noticed my splendid physical growth and increases in weight," explained enrollee John McAdams after working for six months in the forests of central Pennsylvania. "I was a different boy, in fact I was really becoming a man."[100] Enrollees from a camp located near New Ulm, Minnesota, depicted this transition from boyhood to manhood quite literally in their camp newspaper, the *Cottonwood*, which in its July 7, 1939, edition included a before-and-after cartoon titled "But Wilbur Joined the CCC—and After a Year" (see figure 3.8). In the before frame, a thin, shoeless boy named Wilbur timidly asks his mother for permission to enroll in the Corps, while his father declares that the boy should not join the CCC because "He's pretty young and he's not so strong." The second frame shows a very different Wilbur returning home after spending a year in the CCC. Much to his parents' surprise, their son has gained weight, strides confidently into the room, and wears the trappings of an adult, including a suit, tie, and shoes.[101] Enrollees reading

Figure 3.8 Just as enrollees used cartoons in camp newspapers to portray their physical insecurities when first enrolling in the Corps, so too did they depict their newfound manhood after laboring long and hard outdoors on CCC conservation projects. In this illustration, which appeared in *The Cottonwood*, a newspaper published by a camp located in New Ulm, Minnesota, an enrollee cartoonist shows the transformation of a young boy named Wilbur into an adult after a year laboring in the Corps. While other enrollee newspapers also portrayed the CCC's outdoor conservation work as helping to convert boys into men, equally important in this cartoon is the indecisiveness and disbelief of Wilbur's parents. Here again, enrollees are implying that young Americans should rely less on their biological parents to help them through the Great Depression and more on federal programs like the CCC. (Anonymous, "But Wilbur Joined the CCC—and After a Year," *Cottonwood* [New Ulm, Minn.], July 7, 1939, Official File 268: CCC, Folder: CCC Periodicals, 1938–1939, Franklin Delano Roosevelt Library, Hyde Park, N.Y.)

the camp newspaper undoubtedly understood the juxtaposition; CCC work in nature transformed thin, shy boys into healthier, more self-assured men.

As they labored on CCC conservation projects, Corps enrollees thus experienced changes in their bodies to go along with those taking place in their minds. Yet these mental and physical transformations did more than teach broken-down boys about conservation while building them up into well-muscled men. The beefed-up brains and bodies of CCC enrollees also influenced national politics. In particular, by restoring their bodies and minds through outdoor work and classroom study, the young men in the Corps continued to transform both the composition and concerns of the conservation movement. On a more general level, these same intellectual and physical changes also altered New Deal political constituencies in ways that aided Franklin Roosevelt, especially during his more turbulent second term in office. Examining such changes is thus central to understanding conservation's evolving role in the rise of the modern welfare state.

Learning about conservation on the job and in camp classes converted many enrollees to the conservationist cause. Whereas before joining the Corps these young men had little or no knowledge of natural resource conservation, they soon began lauding such practices after spending several months in the CCC. "Our work is very interesting," explained enrollee James Brandon in 1935. "Being out in the open most of the time, we learn more about nature and the natural resources we are striving to conserve."[102] Enrollees across the country agreed.[103] "The work we do in the Great North woods gives us a greater understanding of what the word 'Conservation' really means," wrote enrollee Fred Harrison in the mid-1930s. Sounding more like Gifford Pinchot than a young man spending his first few weeks in the woods, Harrison added, "I am now a firm believer that conservation is necessary for the preservation of our forests."[104] By learning about topics such as forestry and soil erosion, millions of Corps enrollees like Harrison had indeed become conservation conscious.

This new consciousness represented an expansion not just of enrollees' minds but also of the conservation movement's political base. During the Progressive Era, conservationists were primarily urban, educated elites working in government or scientific circles and, to a lesser extent, rural landowners, ranchers, and hunters who also embraced conservation but often contested its implementation on the local level by wealthy nonlocals. The movement at the turn of the century, in other words, was divided between urban professionals and rural lay practitioners, between a more scientific form of conservation and a more popular counterpart.[105] The Corps added something new to this mix. No longer would elite city dwellers and rural amateurs serve as the sole guides of the movement. By converting into conservationists many of the city youths flocking to the program, the Corps broadened the movement's composition during the New Deal era to include for the first time in American history the urban working class.[106]

While the intellectual transformation of Corps enrollees helped to broaden conservation's political base, the bodily changes experienced by these same young men began altering the philosophy behind the movement as well. Similar to their Progressive Era counterparts, Corps administrators were openly alarmed at the wasteful use of natural resources, and even went so far as to blame such waste for causing the Great Depression. Yet, unlike Progressive conservationists, the CCC extended its concern about degraded resources such as timber, soil, and water to the bodies of the young men in the New Deal program. In other words, Corps administrators often expressed their anxiety that unemployment and unhealthy environments had weakened male bodies, and thus emasculated male youths, by directly comparing the physical deterioration of the young men joining the CCC to the material degradation of the country's natural resources.

The first step in this process was equating enrollees with natural resources. "The young men come to the Corps," explained Robert Fechner in 1939, "as a raw material from the cities."[107] Yet rather than simply comparing enrollee bodies to timber or soil, the Corps pushed this analogy even further by likening the sickly, undeveloped physiques of these youths specifically to degraded natural resources. The CCC's portrayal of enrollee Stanley Watson is a case in point. According to the Corps, after tramping for months across the Great Plains states, Watson's body became "sick and weak" from lack of food and shelter. The young man's trials and tribulations, the CCC concluded, were an all too common form of what it called "human erosion."[108] The New Deal program thus saw the atrophied bodies of those joining the Corps much as it viewed cutover forests and eroded soils: as a degraded natural resource in dire need of conservation.

Corps enrollees further redefined Progressive conservationist ideology by equating their own physical rehabilitation with the restoration of once-degraded natural resources. Whereas upon joining the CCC, enrollees had compared their sickly bodies to cutover forests and eroded fields, as Corps administrators had done, the young men working in CCC camps for several months soon began associating their manly physiques with restored trees and soils. "I am sure that the word 'conservation' means more than the conserving of forests," explained Robert Ross after laboring for several months on a CCC work project near Crystal Springs, Arkansas. "It means the saving of the young

"conserving people" - a new idea [handwritten margin note]

manhood of America!"[109] Enrollee Carl Stark likewise noted this alternative form of conservation in his essay titled "Conservation of Men in the CCC from My Own Experiences." "First of all, we are engaged in useful conservation work which will accrue to the benefit of both the present and future generations," Stark explained in 1941 of his camp's forestry project. "But secondly and far more important is the conservation of the individual." The CCC, he concluded, "was truly an organization that works for the conservation of the man as well as our natural resources."[110] Corps administrators agreed and continually portrayed healthy enrollee bodies and restored natural resources as two sides of the same conservationist coin. The physical rebuilding of these young men, the Corps concluded, was a prime example of what it began calling "human conservation"[111] (see figures 3.9 and 3.10).

Conserving people was a radically new idea for conservationists during the 1930s and early 1940s.[112] Although urban reformers such as Frederick Law

FDR
w/ Boy Scouts
in Mind

Figures 3.9 (facing page) and 3.10 These two publicity photos, published in a 1941 book titled *The CCC at Work: A Story of 2,500,000 Young Men,* show how Corps administrators intentionally publicized the program's projects as a means of conserving more than natural resources. In the first image, of a shirtless enrollee working on what appears to be a drainage canal, the Corps portrays the young man's body, tanned and muscled from laboring outside, directly alongside the natural resource he is helping to conserve. The second image is even more blatant; here the male body takes center stage, with the outdoor environment as mere backdrop. In both cases, however, the Corps' message to the American public was similar: through hard work in nature, the CCC was conserving not only natural resources but human resources as well. This notion of "human conservation" would later influence both conservation and New Deal politics. (Both images reprinted from Civilian Conservation Corps, *The CCC at Work: A Story of 2,500,000 Young Men* [Washington, D.C.: U.S. Government Printing Office, 1941], 33 and 43)

Olmsted embraced a similar philosophy, which promoted parks and playgrounds as a means of restoring enervated city dwellers, during the Progressive Era concern for human resources was separate from the conservation movement's interest in trees, soil, and water. The two movements, in other words, had remained distinct. The Corps began integrating these concerns when Franklin Roosevelt created the CCC with the Boy Scouts in mind, and continued this process when the Corps expanded its work projects into the nation's parks in an effort to rejuvenate the American public through outdoor recreation. Flexing enrollee muscles through labor in nature fused such concerns once again. Thus while the intellectual changes experienced by enrollees broadened the movement's composition by bringing urban workers into the conservationist fold, the bodily alterations encountered by these same young men helped to expand the movement's agenda from a narrow concern for natural resources to an interest in conserving human resources as well. The result not only marked a new chapter for the American conservation movement, but would also signify new politics for the New Deal.

The bodies and minds that joined the Corps during the 1930s and early 1940s were incredibly diverse. While Department of Labor restrictions ensured that all Corps enrollees hailed from the working class, an amendment to the bill creating the CCC forbade the program from discriminating "on account of race, color, or creed."[113] Thus even though the Corps placed African Americans in segregated camps, and established separate camps for Native Americans on Indian reservations, those joining the New Deal program came from a variety of ethnic and religious backgrounds. Corps personnel commented frequently on this heterogeneity, as did the enrollees themselves. For instance, on June 7, 1933, an army officer in charge of establishing a CCC camp in Beaverhead National Forest near Butte, Montana, met his company of new recruits as they disembarked at a nearby railroad station. "What a mob got off the train," he explained in a letter to his military superior, "they were large and small, Italians, Jews, and every other nationality."[114] Kenneth Stephans, an enrollee stationed in Two Harbors, Minnesota, described his fellow campmates in similar terms, writing in 1941 that he "worked and played side by side with young men from all walks of life, boys different in creeds and descent."[115] Corps enrollees thus joined the New Deal program not only with weakened bodies, but also with physical characteristics that suggested their various ethnic and religious identities.

Working-class immigrants such as those joining the CCC were not foreign to the New Deal; in fact they were central to the president's politics from the very start. Partly because the immigrant restrictions of the 1920s had successfully quieted nativist alarms, the Roosevelt administration welcomed immigrants to the nation and encouraged them in word and deed to become full-fledged Americans. "We gave them freedom," Roosevelt claimed of the country's foreign-born in a 1936 speech commemorating the fiftieth anniversary of the Statue of Liberty. "I am proud—America is proud—of what they have given us." They bettered the American nation while becoming fully American, he declared, and they have come to "appreciate our free institutions and our free opportunity."[116] Understandably, Roosevelt also hoped to welcome these same immigrants, who had recently become a powerful voting bloc across the industrialized North, into the Democratic party through participation in many of his New Deal programs.

Recent immigrants and their subsequent Americanization became even more politically controversial during the late 1930s, when congressional conservatives began attacking the New Deal for its radicalism. One of the most vociferous opponents of both the foreign-born and the Roosevelt administration during this period was the House Special Committee on Un-American Activities. Established by Congress in 1938, the committee was chaired by Texas representative Martin Dies, whose suspicion of all things "un-American" had begun in 1931, when he introduced a bill calling for a five-year suspension of immigration into the United States, and continued unabated into the mid-1930s, when he publicly blamed immigrants for the Great Depression. "If we had refused admission to the 16,500,000 foreign born who are living in this country today," Dies argued, "we would have no unemployment problem."[117] The House Special Committee on Un-American Activities was thus the perfect vehicle for Dies to extend his suspicions concerning immigrants to Franklin Roosevelt's New Deal. The chair wasted little time, immediately criticizing as un-American several New Deal agencies, including the Federal Theatre Project, the Works Progress Administration, and the National Labor Relations Board, and raising similar questions about a host of high-profile New Dealers, such as Department of Labor secretary Frances Perkins, Department of the Interior secretary Harold Ickes, and even First Lady Eleanor Roosevelt. Because the committee depended on the national media to publicize its proceedings, suspicions regarding the so-called subversive activities of both immigrants and the New Deal programs created to help them were front-page news for much of the late 1930s.[118]

The CCC was not immune to such partisan politics. In fact, criticism of the Corps as un-American began during congressional debates over the creation of the New Deal program, and continued throughout the 1930s and early 1940s. Such attacks emanated from both ends of the political spectrum. Concerned about the military's role in overseeing the daily operation of CCC camps, as well as the increasing popularity in Germany of Adolf Hitler, the American Left accused the Corps of fomenting fascism. "[Corps] work camps fit into the psychology of a fascist . . . state," warned Socialist party spokesperson Norman Thomas.[119] Father Charles Coughlin, the famed "radio priest," agreed, adding that the continuance of federal programs like the CCC was "a certain step towards fascism."[120] The right wing, on the other hand, branded the Corps a Bolshevik threat to the American political system. In June 1937, for instance, a special commission reported to the Massachusetts State Legislature that "communists were creating dissatisfaction, unrest and class consciousness among the young men in the [CCC] camps," a contention reiterated by Jersey City mayor Frank L. Hague.[121] Several conservative newspapers throughout the country were also quick to label CCC camps "hotbeds of radicalism," and to report on the few instances in which Corps enrollees expressed communist beliefs. As one such critic complained, the CCC "was hardly conducive to the development of qualities and attitudes needed for life in a democratic society."[122]

Partly in response to such criticism, the Roosevelt administration promoted many of its New Deal programs as having an Americanizing influence on the general public, particularly on recent immigrants. Since the CCC was one of the president's most popular projects, the program quickly rose to the forefront of this publicity campaign. Not surprisingly, the Corps put forth enrollee labor, enrollee bodies, and American nature as central to assimilating ethnic enrollees. "The [CCC] camps are civic melting pots in which youths from widely varying backgrounds . . . are taught the old-fashioned virtues of hard work," argued Robert Fechner in his annual report of 1939.[123] As important as enrollee labor were the corporeal transformations experienced by the youths in the New Deal program. Because of their newfound bodily knowledge, explained James McEntee, "those men knew within themselves that this is a great nation, a good nation, worth working for."[124]

Yet labor and the physical changes it caused did not on their own Americanize Corps enrollees. According to the CCC, it was specifically the natural environment in which such work took place that served as the catalyst in this assimilation process. As McEntee concluded in 1942, it was precisely because enrollees "helped to build America, reforest its barren spots, [and] keep its soil from washing away" by laboring outdoors that "Americanism, democracy, and a real love of country are not simply phrases or catch words to men who have served in the CCC."[125] The Corps, therefore, did more than make unhealthy boys into virile men. More particularly, and in direct opposition to the protestations of the Dies committee, the CCC promoted manual labor in nature, and the bodily changes such work engendered, as a means of transforming Italian, Polish, and Jewish boys into American men (see figures 3.11 and 3.12).

Corps enrollees often stated outright what CCC administrators suggested: the rejuvenation of their own bodies through work in nature strengthened their

Irish fully not white

Blacks have less opportunity

sense of citizenship. Central to this process was the belief that manual labor in American nature made enrollees more American. "Above all, I know what the word 'Americanism' means," wrote enrollee Kenneth Stephans in June 1941 of his experiences in the Corps. "This spirit is instilled in a person by work and toil such as we do in our protection and reproduction of our National Forests."[126] Other enrollees were more forthright in linking their own physical transformation while in the Corps to their assimilation. After explaining that he and his fellow campmates had gained weight and become recognizably stronger while working outdoors in the CCC, enrollee James Danner argued, "[I]t is not only physically that the CCC has been benefiting the youth of the nation." According to Danner, in strengthening their bodies through labor in nature, "second generation Poles, Slovaks, Italians, Hungarians, all are... finding a new pride in saying, 'We are Americans!' "[127] Enrollee Joseph Jurasek perhaps put this newfound patriotism most succinctly when he wrote from his camp in Coram, Montana: "I just love to work in the sun, getting a fine tan, building up one's body and yet doing a service to our country."[128] Enrollees thus not only felt healthier as they labored outside in parks, in forests, and on farms across the country, they felt more American as well.

As shirtless enrollees worked outside on their tans, there is ample evidence that through labor in nature they were in fact becoming more "white," at least if the past experience of American immigrants is any indication.[129] Long before working-class immigrants began joining the CCC in the 1930s, their forebears faced not only ethnic discrimination but racial prejudice as well. When Irish emigrants settled in the United States during the first half of the nineteenth century, for instance, it was by no means clear that native-born Americans viewed these newcomers as fully white. One means of becoming whiter was for these Irish workers to differentiate themselves from African Americans through labor, particularly free labor.[130] The same held true for a host of ethnic and religious immigrant groups during the postbellum years; through physical labor, they became more white while simultaneously becoming more American.[131] These links among manhood, whiteness, and nationalism remained a powerful historic force well into the twentieth century.[132] Ironically, then, as less-than-white Irish, Polish, Italian, and Jewish boys made their skin as "brown as Indians" through outdoor labor in the CCC, they were making themselves more native American as well.[133]

African Americans who joined the CCC during the Great Depression had a very different experience than did ethnic enrollees. Despite the amendment in its original charter stipulating that the Corps could not discriminate on account of race, African Americans found their opportunities in this and other New

Deal programs severely circumscribed. Due to racism both within the CCC and without, black enrollees had a more difficult time than whites getting into the Corps, found their segregated camps situated even farther away from nearby communities because of local protests in every region of the country, including the North, and were rarely allowed to take on administrative responsibilities in their own African-American camps.[134] Such difficulties for blacks indicate that while the Roosevelt administration used the Corps to lessen ethnic and religious tensions during the Great Depression, it was less concerned with using manly outdoor labor to heal the nation's racial problems.[135] Unable to become whiter by working in nature, African-American enrollees, like white and black women, remained outside the New Deal body politic.[136]

As the Corps promoted its role in Americanizing white enrollees, and as the young men joining the New Deal program in turn embraced this patriotic identity, the national media began publicizing the idea that CCC work in

Figures 3.11 (facing page) and 3.12 During the Great Depression, the CCC continually linked the outdoor labor performed on its conservation projects to an increased sense of national pride. This desire to build nationalism through nature is prominently displayed in these two CCC promotional images. In the first, a shirtless Corps enrollee labors literally in the nation's soil, beneath a horizon draped in the American flag. The second image is more subtle. Published during the early 1940s, this drawing of three Corps enrollees marching intently in unison across a field labeled "Spirit of the CCC" uses the country's imminent entry into World War II to link conservation to nationalism. The various tools used to conserve the pine bough in the upper right corner of the image, especially the fire-fighting water pump held by the enrollee farthest to the left, also suggest the weapons that will be employed by American soldiers in the impending war. (Civilian Conservation Corps, *The CCC at Work: A Story of 2,500,000 Young Men* [Washington, D.C.: U.S. Government Printing Office, 1941], cover; and Spirit of CCC, Civilian Conservation Corps, *Spirit of CCC*, Vertical File, Franklin Delano Roosevelt Library, Hyde Park, N.Y., n.d.)

nature created not only better bodies but better Americans. Much like the publicity garnered by Martin Dies's Special Committee on Un-American Activities, the coverage of the Corps' role in assimilating immigrant enrollees was extensive. For instance, in a *New York Times* article titled "The Forestry Army That Lives by Work," reporter Dorothy Bromley described both the physical labor performed by CCC enrollees in the nation's forests as well as its effect on their bodies. "The work that they are doing . . . whether it is chopping trees, digging out rocks, or building trails, looks hard, almost backbreaking," she explained. The bodily changes shared by these young men while working together outdoors, Bromley then went on to suggest, helped them to overcome many of their ethnic and religious differences. "They are one-hundred percent American," she concluded.[137]

This popular belief that the Corps helped to assimilate immigrant enrollees raised widespread political support for Franklin Roosevelt and his New Deal state. On the political Left, such backing was especially pronounced among working-class city dwellers, who saw in the CCC an invitation by the president to join the nation's civic family. One working-class mother from Baltimore, for instance, whose son joined the Corps in 1933, thanked God for the president and the CCC and pledged that "from now there will be nobody to tell me how to vote. I'll know."[138] The majority of working-class immigrants agreed with such sentiments. During the 1936 election, of the 6 million Americans who went to the polls for the first time, 5 million voted for Roosevelt. During the same election, the incumbent also received 80 percent of the vote of the poorest Americans and did especially well among ethnic minorities, most of whom lived in cities.[139]

The Corps' Americanizing influence on immigrants played equally well with the political Right. Newspapers historically opposed to Franklin Roosevelt during the Great Depression responded favorably to the Corps' assimilation campaign, helping in effect to muffle criticism like that from the House Special Committee on Un-American Activities. "Of all the New Deal agencies, the CCC has probably attracted the most attention," admitted the Houston *Post*, a conservative newspaper from Martin Dies's home state. "Democrats and Republicans, Socialists and Share-the-Wealthers," the paper went on to explain, "have joined in praising its objectives and accomplishments."[140] It seems that by transforming young, urban immigrants into full-blooded American men, the CCC raised popular support for Roosevelt's welfare state from across the political spectrum.

Enrollee Pablo Diaz Albertt was thus only partially correct when he described his transformation at a CCC camp in Libby, Montana. The "hard work" he performed "sawing down large trees" high up in the "majestic Rocky Mountains" did make him "stronger," as he put it, and most probably heavier, healthier, and more tanned, if the experiences of many Corps enrollees is any indication. The classes offered by Camp F-44 each night after work must also have taught Albertt a thing or two about the conservation of trees in the surrounding forest. The great majority of the more than 3 million young men who joined the CCC experienced similar changes while enrolled in the New Deal program. Long labor outdoors and serious study in camp classes had indeed benefited these enrollees "in both body and mind."[141]

Yet Albertt was less aware of the larger political implications of his physical and intellectual transformation. The youth from New York City failed to understand that while his newfound "conservation consciousness" helped to expand the composition of the conservation movement to include for the first time urban workers, the changes taking place in his body had similarly broadened conservation's agenda by incorporating concern for human resources into the movement. He was equally ignorant of the impact such changes had on New Deal politics. Outdoor labor in American nature made Albertt not only less of a boy and more of a man, but also less Hispanic and more American. Working outdoors in the forests near Libby, he explained, "rounded" him "into manhood" while at the same time making him "a better citizen."[142] The Americanization of millions of immigrant enrollees like Albertt helped Roosevelt to maintain a broad-based constituency that included those on the Left, such as socialist Norman Thomas, along with right-wingers such as the readers of the Houston *Post*. It similarly diffused criticism of the New Deal from conservatives like Martin Dies, who feared all things un-American. Thus although Albertt may not have realized it, by altering his body and mind, the Corps had transformed the politics of both conservation and the New Deal.

Pablo Diaz Albertt was also unaware of the impact that his conservation work had on his neighbors in Libby, Montana. Like residents of thousands of towns and villages across the country, those living in Libby quickly realized that having a Corps camp move in next door meant changes not just to the surrounding countryside but to their own community as well. Examining such community change is central to understanding how the transformations experienced by enrollees spread beyond the participants in this particular New Deal program and began to influence the wider American public.

FOUR / **COMMUNITY**
Locals and Next-Door Natures

In October 1934, the residents of Elkins, West Virginia, invited Corps enrollees stationed nearby in Camp North Fork to participate in their Mountain State Forest Festival. Held annually since 1929, the three-day festival involved pageants, contests, parades, and dances that drew tens of thousands of tourists from West Virginia and surrounding states. After accepting the invitation, the young men from Camp North Fork left their barracks in the Allegheny Mountains of Monongahela National Forest and journeyed to Elkins, where they participated in baseball games and boxing matches against locals citizens, built their own float for the festival's parade, and staffed information booths and a model CCC camp that explained the conservation work taking place in the surrounding mountains. The North Fork enrollees were also front and center in the many speeches given by visiting dignitaries. U.S. Secretary of War Henry Dern told the crowd at Elkins that Corps conservation projects such as those undertaken in Monongahela National Forest were central to national defense, while President Roosevelt, during his own personal visit to the Forest Festival, publicly praised the conservation efforts of Camp North Fork and other CCC camps across the country.[1]

As the Mountain State Forest Festival suggests, the landscape changes caused by CCC conservation projects did more than transform Corps enrollees. When the young men of Camp North Fork described the impact of their labor on the surrounding countryside during the three-day festival, local residents learned about the conservation of natural resources, many for the first time. As important, the CCC's conservation work in nearby Monongahela National Forest brought New Dealers, including Secretary Dern and the president himself, not to mention dozens of CCC and Forest Service administrators, to the remote town of Elkins, in effect making New Deal rhetoric a reality for people living far removed from the federal government. Similar situations occurred throughout the country during the Great Depression years as Corps landscape changes introduced both conservation and the welfare state to local community residents. The impact of CCC work projects thus went beyond the 3 million young men in the New Deal program, reaching deep into the towns and villages neighboring the more than 5,000 CCC camps nationwide.[2] As one local explained, the influence of Corps conservation work "was just like dropping a rock in the pond. The ripples spread out and out."[3]

Considering the warm relations between Elkins and Camp North Fork at the annual Forest Festival, it is surprising that during the early 1930s many local communities across the country initially opposed the location of CCC camps in their immediate vicinity. According to complaint letters filed with Corps administrators, such hostility took three forms. Most vociferous were those communities, even outside the South, that opposed African-American camps in their locale.[4] In addition, locals criticized new CCC camps for bringing urbanites and foreign-born immigrants into their overwhelmingly rural and homogeneous communities.[5] Finally, towns and villages opposed the announcement of new Corps camps in their area on the grounds that CCC enrollees were outsiders taking work from local laborers.[6] During the early New Deal years, long before enrollees even arrived to set up camp, the majority of local residents viewed these young men as "street-slum foreigners," "corner holders," and "bums."[7]

By the mid-1930s, this derision had subsided and been replaced by a newfound appreciation of what it meant to have CCC enrollees as neighbors. This about-face is evident in the increasingly steady stream of requests from local communities for new Corps camps in their vicinities. For example, in a random sampling of more than 200 letters written to the CCC in the mid-1930s by residents of towns and villages, a remarkable 85 percent requested additional camps or the maintenance of nearby camps already in existence.[8] When the Corps announced plans to close or transfer Corps camps, locals similarly rallied to keep CCC enrollees as neighbors. This support for the Corps on the local level reached its zenith in 1936, when the Roosevelt administration tried to reduce the number of CCC camps nationwide. Besieged with letters, petitions, telegrams, and phone calls from constituents in their home districts, congressional representatives rejected the proposed reduction and voted instead to increase funding for the popular New Deal program.[9] As CCC director

Communities
"Change of heart" *"I FDR"* *"greedy" lumbermen*

Robert Fechner explained in the mid-1930s, "for two and one-half years there has never been a time when we could begin to supply the demand on the part of communities for CCC camps."[10]

Accounting for this change of heart on the local level is central to understanding the history of the New Deal, especially since Franklin Roosevelt viewed the support and participation of communities like Elkins, West Virginia, as essential to his own political success. Roosevelt first expressed this faith in local politics in 1912 while delivering a speech on conservation before the Troy, New York, People's Forum. Environmental devastation, he warned his audience, "will happen in this very state if the individuals are allowed to do as they please with the natural resources to line their own pockets." To avoid such a fate, Roosevelt proposed what he called a new social theory that posited community cooperation as more economically efficient than individualism. "To put it in the simplest and fewest words," he explained to his audience, "I have called this new theory the struggle for liberty of the community rather than liberty of the individual."[11] Local communities, aided by government, must have the freedom to protect their interests from shortsighted individuals like greedy lumbermen. Two decades later, Roosevelt transferred such views from the state to the federal level, arguing that the CCC in particular, and the New Deal in general, were political means of protecting local liberties.[12] "It is not wise to direct everything from Washington," the president told Congress during his second term in office. "National planning should start at the bottom."[13]

Local communities like Elkins, however, tell only one side of the Corps story. Similar to the hundreds of CCC camps assigned to the U.S. Forest Service, Camp North Fork undertook work projects aimed at conserving natural resources, in this case timber. The hundreds of Corps camps assigned to the Soil Conservation Service during the 1930s and early 1940s did similarly by focusing on the natural resources of the American farm. Yet during the later 1930s, as the CCC expanded its work projects from forests and farms into the nation's parks, it began undertaking a second type of conservation aimed not at natural resources but rather at restoring the country's human resources through the development of healthful recreational amenities, including hiking trails, campgrounds, and picnic areas. This second set of landscape changes had a somewhat different effect on nearby towns. To fully understand the influence of the CCC on the local level, as well as Franklin Roosevelt's desire to direct his New Deal from the bottom up, it is therefore necessary to examine not only communities situated near Corps camps undertaking projects aimed at conserving natural resources in forests or on farms, but also communities located next to CCC enrollees working to restore human resources in the nation's parks.

The Coon Creek watershed in Wisconsin and the Great Smoky Mountains along the border of Tennessee and North Carolina contain within their geographic boundaries examples of such communities. Whereas the towns within Coon Valley sat near a CCC camp working with the Soil Conservation Service to restore agricultural production on surrounding farms, those in the Great Smoky Mountains were located near thousands of Corps enrollees developing Great Smoky Mountains National Park for outdoor recreation. These two types of conservation projects affected locals in Wisconsin and the Smokies in slightly different ways, yet the interactions between camp and community functioned similarly in each instance. In both regions, the changes in the natural landscape caused by Corps work altered local economies, which in turn resulted in ideological transformations among community members.[14] This unique interrelationship among ecologies, economies, and ideologies had implications not only for those residing within communities situated near CCC camps, but also for the American conservation movement and the expansion of the modern welfare state.[15]

Long before the Corps came to Wisconsin, nature set the stage for the communities that would eventually arise along Coon Creek. Flowing westward through La Crosse, Monroe, and Vernon counties in southwestern Wisconsin, the waters of Coon Creek carved a valley twenty-two miles long and seven miles wide through the heart of the so-called Driftless Area (see figure 4.1). While ice sheets spreading over large portions of North America during the Pleistocene era ground down and rounded off hilltops in their path, the Driftless Area remained unglaciated. Coon Valley thus escaped both the grinding power of ice, as well as the heavy deposits of organic material left behind after these glaciers retreated. Because of this, the valley maintained its sharp, steep slopes, which varied in elevation by as much as 400 feet in less than two miles.[16] Wooded forests grew along the sides of these slopes, while prairie grasses spread across the ridges and valley floor. Although the region's favorable climate ensured highly fertile soil throughout Coon Valley, the lack of glacier deposits meant that this soil proved extremely thin.[17]

The first white settlers in the region in the 1840s brought with them an economy that placed price tags on Coon Valley nature. At first Norwegian, German, and other Northern European immigrants cut much of the timber from the valley's slopes for local sawmills and to feed riverboat engines on the nearby Mississippi. Then, as grain prices rose during the 1860s and 1870s, locals began plowing up the prairie grass along the creek's ridges and valleys and replanting it with wheat. It was during this period, in the 1860s, that settlers founded the valley's three communities of Stoddard, Chaseburg, and the town of Coon Valley, each located along Coon Creek. Wheat remained the staple crop of the region until the early 1900s when drought, cheaper land to the west, and declining soil fertility forced residents to shift land use patterns once again. At first, locals tried raising beef cattle before finally settling on dairy farming. To feed their cows, residents began planting fodder crops such as hay, oats, barley, and corn.[18] By 1904, local farmers could ship their dairy products by rail to distant markets along a branch line running through Coon Valley to a main line on the Mississippi River.[19]

This combination of Coon Valley nature and white settlers' economics fostered the idea that nearby natural resources were commodities ripe for exploitation. This notion was perhaps best exemplified by the so-called square agriculture of Coon Valley's dairy farms.[20] Not only were "straight furrows" seen as the most efficient means of growing crops, they were "a pride to the operator" and symbolized a farmer's competence to the wider community.[21] The nearly total lack of conservation practices throughout the valley during this period was yet another indication that locals viewed the nature all around them as inexhaustible. While a few farmers close cropped a small portion of their land each year in an effort to slow soil and water erosion, the great majority avoided altogether conservation techniques such as strip cropping, terracing, and contour plowing. Nor did they limit grazing on the steeper sections of their land.[22] Coon Valley's Stromstad farm serves as a typical example. Field maps of the property reconstructed from aerial photographs taken in 1934 before the CCC arrived illustrate not only the dominance of straight row cropping in long rectangular fields, but also that the Stromstads ran their crop rows directly up and down the hillside in the very center of their 140-acre property.[23] As one commentator noted, "few effective erosion control practices were being followed" in Coon Valley prior to the 1930s because of the widespread belief that its "soils could not be exhausted."[24]

The desire to exploit Coon Valley's soil resources also fostered the idea among locals that federal authority was best when kept at bay. In many respects, such thinking went back to Thomas Jefferson, who used the Land Ordinances of 1785 to divide up western landscapes like Coon Valley into local communities that were independent of the nation's capital.[25] Throughout the nineteenth century, westerners settling in such communities often realized Jefferson's vision by circumventing federal laws through local, communal agreements.[26] The Northern Europeans who migrated to Coon Valley embraced this antipathy toward Washington, D.C., and kept it alive and well

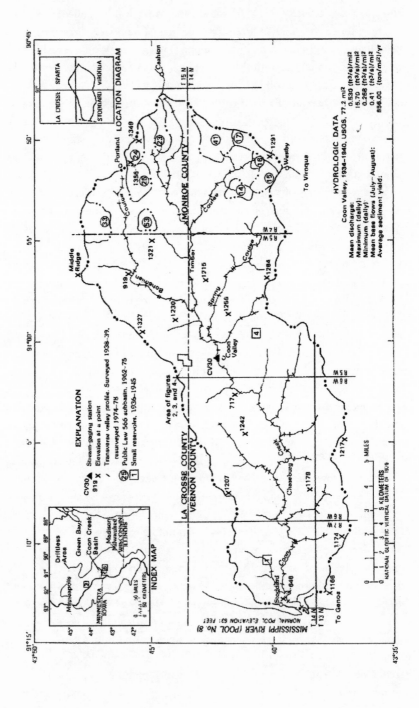

Figure 4.1 This hydrological map of Coon Valley, Wisconsin, provides clues to the ecology, economy, and ideology of the region prior to the arrival of the CCC in 1934. The twenty-two-mile-long valley, which runs along either side of Coon Creek from east to west, is blanketed with a thin, yet fertile, layer of topsoil that produced forests along the valley's slopes and prairie grasses across the ridges and valley floor. Such natural features in turn shaped the Coon Valley economy, which evolved from logging and wheat cultivation to cattle grazing and finally diary farming. Because such land use practices succeeded for several generations, local residents of the valley's three towns—Stoddard to the west near the Mississippi River, Chaseburg situated ten miles up Coon Creek, and the village of Coon Valley in the very center of the map—believed that the area's natural resources were inexhaustible. As a result, on the eve of the Great Depression, these self-proclaimed "rugged individuals" not only refrained from undertaking soil conservation on their farmland, but they were also extremely wary of federal officials and New Deal programs that promoted such practices. (Reprinted from Stanley W. Trimble and Steven W. Lund, Soil Conservation and the Reduction of Erosion and Sedimentation in the Coon Creek Basin, Wisconsin, Geological Survey Professional Paper 1234 [Washington, D.C.: U.S. Government Printing Office, 1982], 4)

individualism

into the 1920s. "The Coon Valley watershed," explained a reporter for *Collier's* magazine, "is owned by four hundred rugged individuals" who during this period adhered to the motto that federal bureaucrats "can't come in here and tell us how to farm."[27] Local voting patterns bear out such generalizations. During the three presidential elections of 1920, 1924, and 1928, residents of the three counties encompassing Coon Valley voted 86, 85, and 63 percent on average, respectively, for the Republican party.[28] On the eve of the Great Depression, Coon Valley farmers had spent a decade defending their fickle farming by supporting presidential candidates who campaigned for a small federal government little involved in local politics.

The practice over generations of square farming on round land, not to mention benign neglect from federal bureaucrats, had resulted in severe ecological problems for Coon Valley. One of the first to note such troubles was Aldo Leopold, who began visiting the region during the early 1930s after taking a faculty position in wildlife management at the University of Wisconsin in nearby Madison. Running crop rows and cattle up and down hillsides, Leopold warned, had caused sheet erosion and gullies, some three feet deep, to form throughout the valley. Both types of erosion stripped nutrients from agricultural soil, decreased the ability of farmers' fields to hold moisture, and even changed Coon Creek itself; what had been a narrow and deep water course at the turn of the century had become by the early 1930s a shallow, muddy stream increasingly prone to floods.[29] On the Stromstad farm, such gullies appeared in aerial photographs as white slashes running directly across valuable farmland.[30] "Great gashing gullies are torn out of the hillside," Leopold wrote of the Coon Valley landscape, "and gone is the humus of the old prairie which until recently enabled the upland ridges to take on the rains as they came."[31]

The ecological changes affecting Coon Valley's fields during the 1920s had a direct impact on local economies. As gullies and sheet erosion spread across farms in the region, crop yields declined; between 1930 and 1933 corn, grain, hay, and pasturage production decreased steadily.[32] Slumping farm productivity not only lowered Coon Valley incomes but also depressed land values from just over $44 an acre in 1929 to approximately $34 for the same piece of property just four years later. Since local banks during this period were increasingly reluctant to consider loans for Coon Valley farmers, tax delinquencies skyrocketed from less than 1 percent in 1929 to 5.2 percent in 1930 to 18.6 percent the following year. There is even evidence that the so-called standard of living of the 5,400 residents of Stoddard, Chaseburg, and the town of Coon Valley declined as well; the use of conveniences such as

aldo leopold

automobiles, electric lights, and telephones slumped in area homes between 1931 and 1934.[33] Such links between the ecological crisis cutting across Coon Valley's fields and the economic emergency moving down its main streets were not lost on Leopold. "Coon Valley," he argued in *American Forests* magazine, "is one of the thousand farm communities which, through the abuse of its originally rich soil, has not only filled the national dinner pail, but has created the Mississippi flood problem, the navigation problem, and the problem of its own future continuity."[34]

Aldo Leopold tried to solve Coon Valley's ecological problems and their debilitating impact on local economies by bringing the CCC to the rescue. This process began during the summer of 1933, when the Roosevelt administration asked Leopold to oversee Corps conservation projects in the Southwest, where he had been a forester for the U.S. Forest Service.[35] That fall, when Leopold moved to Madison to teach wildlife management, he brought along his interest in the CCC, and after several visits to Coon Valley he decided that the Corps could help local communities in this region as well. Specifically, he became convinced that Coon Valley was the perfect site for a new federal program then being implemented by the Roosevelt administration to demonstrate proper soil conservation techniques to local farmers.[36] After intense lobbying by Leopold and several of his colleagues at the university's College of Agriculture, in January 1934 Franklin Roosevelt and Soil Conservation Service chief Hugh Bennett selected Coon Valley as the first "soil demonstration area" in the nation. Four months later, 200 CCC enrollees arrived in Coon Valley, constructed Camp Coon Creek, and immediately began soil conservation work on the Coon Creek Demonstration Area.[37]

The new program in Coon Valley became a model for others across the country; the Soil Conservation Service established 175 soil demonstration areas during the 1930s and early 1940s. The concept behind these projects was to convince farmers within a single "representative" watershed to work with the Soil Conservation Service in implementing soil and water conservation techniques. The service would provide the technical expertise to help local farmers implement such practices, and these farms would then be showcased so that farmers from outlying regions could visit and learn how to undertake such agricultural practices on their own land. Unlike the Agricultural Adjustment Administration, the Soil Conservation Service did not pay farmers to participate. Instead, locals signed "cooperative agreements" in which they promised to maintain such conservation techniques for at least five years.[38] "People close to the land . . . want to be shown how to conserve," explained Bennett. "The answer to this demand is the demonstration."[39]

Demonstrations of all sorts were central to New Deal conservation policy and had deep roots in Franklin Roosevelt's experiences in New York. Following a precedent set by his friend and U.S. Forest Service chief Gifford Pinchot, in 1930 then Governor Roosevelt enlisted the aid of the State College of Forestry in Syracuse to develop demonstration tree plantings at his family estate in Hyde Park, where landowners from the surrounding region could observe proper forestry management.[40] Two years later, when Roosevelt became president, he brought his belief in demonstrations with him to Washington. During the New Deal years, the Roosevelt administration established hundreds of demonstration projects throughout the country to promote forestry, such as at Hyde Park, and for soil conservation, like that initiated in Coon Valley. During the mid-1930s, Roosevelt even expanded such practices by creating recreation demonstration areas to educate the American public on outdoor leisure.[41] "Effective demonstrations" in all of these areas, Roosevelt wrote during the summer of 1939, are "part of any education program" and "a vital tool" for promoting conservation.[42]

The Corps was essential to the success of New Deal soil demonstration programs. Although the Soil Conservation Service supplied the technical know-how by assigning agronomists to demonstration areas, the CCC supplied the muscle needed to physically alter farmers' fields in ways that halted soil and water erosion. By undertaking this work on hundreds of farms within a single watershed, Corps enrollees transformed landscapes such as Coon Valley into the Coon Creek Demonstration Area. The amount of such labor performed nationwide by the CCC was enormous. By January 1938, Corps projects on the nation's 175 soil demonstration areas affected approximately 11.5 million acres of farmland in forty-eight states. Corps enrollees helped farmers contour till nearly 2 million acres, strip crop more than 770,000 acres, plant cover crops on more than 250,000 acres, and terrace 1,136,553 acres of farmland throughout the United States.[43] "Through these demonstration projects and the work of the CCC camps," explained Hugh Bennett, "farming people throughout the country have had an opportunity to observe the effects of conservation farming and to learn how it is done."[44]

Corps work on soil demonstration areas would not only teach farmers how to halt soil erosion. It would also help the Roosevelt administration overcome one of its most vexing political problems: public concern that some Corps work occurred on privately owned land. This issue first arose in the early New Deal years, when the CCC undertook a minority of projects in privately owned forests, and resurfaced during the mid-1930s as Corps enrollees descended onto America's farms. "While it is legal to undertake projects on land belonging

soil demo area

in private ownership," wrote President Roosevelt to CCC director Robert Fechner in 1937, "I think it is a great mistake to do any more of this than we can possibly help" for fear that such work be seen as contrary to the public interest.[45] Soil demonstration areas could help the president to assuage such fears. By educating local community members about conservation, soil demonstration areas transformed CCC labor on private property into a form of public work. Corps labor, in turn, allowed the land within demonstration areas and the crops produced from it to remain private, but shifted the new agricultural landscape itself into the public domain.[46] Because of this, Fechner could confidently claim that Corps labor on private property within soil demonstration areas "was in the public interest generally."[47]

There was an enormous amount of private property in the Coon Creek Demonstration Area, which at 140 square miles, covering the entire 92,000-acre Coon Creek watershed, represented the largest soil demonstration project in the country. The Corps stationed its enrollees at Camp Coon Creek in the very center of the demonstration area near the small town of Coon Valley, approximately 10 and 5 miles upstream from the communities of Stoddard and Chaseburg, respectively.[48] As soon as they arrived in May 1934, the young men of Camp Coon Creek undertook conservation projects requiring that "the whole farming pattern be changed within a period of twelve to twenty-four months."[49] Those familiar with the region's land use practices quickly realized that the arrival of the Corps signaled a new era for Coon Valley agriculture. "We now see foregathered at Coon Valley," explained Aldo Leopold, "a staff of technicians to figure out what should be done; a CCC camp to perform labor . . . [and] a series of contracts with farmers, which, collectively, comprise a 'regional plan' for the stabilization of the watershed and of the agricultural community which it supports."[50] Leopold understood, perhaps more than local residents, that with the arrival of the CCC the private property of Coon Valley was poised to become the public landscape of the New Deal.

The transformation of Coon Valley into the Coon Creek Demonstration Area took an enormous amount of work by both local farmers and the 200 CCC enrollees stationed in Camp Coon Creek. Between May 4, 1934, when the Corps arrived, and July 1937, when the CCC transferred the camp to another location, enrollees and farmers together performed more than 1 million man-hours of work aimed at solving the valley's two main soil problems: sheet erosion and gullies.[51] To correct the former, Corps enrollees helped farmers to cut more than 1,700 acres of terraces into their fields to hold water, and to strip crop 77 percent of the valley's fields with alternating rows of vegetation to better hold soil in place.[52] Most important, Camp Coon Creek helped farmers to lay contour lines across their farms as guides for crop rows that would now run perpendicular to sloping land in order to slow water and soil runoff. Whereas such contour farming had been rare before the arrival of the CCC, by 1938 it had become standard throughout the valley.[53] "The first visible evidence of a new order on a Coon Valley farm," explained Aldo Leopold, "is a CCC crew stringing a new fence along the contour."[54] Leopold should know. In his capacity as extension advisor at the University of Wisconsin, he served as the unofficial monitor of CCC work in Coon Valley, and also secured jobs for his two sons, Luna and Starker, on the Coon Creek Demonstration Area project.[55]

Local farmers and CCC enrollees also joined together to fight gullies, which had cut into slopes and across fields throughout Coon Valley. To prevent gullies from growing and new ones from forming, the young men of Camp Coon Creek replanted all woodland above a 40 percent grade, converted 10,000 acres of sloping pasture into woodland, and replaced crop land on steep fields with 60 acres of wildlife habitat, 117 acres of hay, and 1,236 acres of pasture and woodland.[56] "The boys came over," recalled one farmer of nearby CCC enrollees, "and we fenced off the ravines and planted them to trees."[57] To repair gullies that had already formed across farms, CCC enrollees and farmers relied on dams made from dirt, brush, wood, and rock mined from quarries operated by Camp Coon Creek. Corps enrollees and local farmers built more than 1,000 permanent and temporary dams and planted gully slopes with nearly 200,000 square yards of trees and sod.[58] "Creek banks and gullies, as well as steep slopes, are being fenced and planted," Leopold explained.[59] So extensive was this cooperative effort against gullies and sheet erosion that by July 1937, when Camp Coon Creek left the region, CCC enrollees and local farmers had reworked more than 43,000 acres, or approximately one-half of the Coon Creek watershed.[60]

The combined labor of CCC enrollees and local farmers dramatically altered the Coon Valley landscape, especially on dairy farms like that owned by the Stromstads. Before the arrival of the CCC in May 1934, the Stromstads had planted alfalfa, grain, corn, and hay in straight rows within rectangular plots across right-angled fields. Such square agriculture was the norm throughout Coon Valley during this period and symbolized local farmers' belief that soil resources were unlimited. Yet crop maps of the same property in 1940, approximately five years after the Stromstads began working with the CCC, showed a decidedly different farmscape (see figure 4.2). Gone were the straight furrowed fields, replaced instead by contoured crop rows that hugged

new type of pig

the sloping hill in the center of the property.[61] This same transformation from rectilinear to curvilinear fields occurred throughout the Coon Valley landscape during the mid-1930s. "The Coon Creek project area presents a changed picture embedding a new pattern of agriculture," explained the Soil Conservation Service in 1939, less than two years after the CCC left the region. "The most noticeable change to the casual observer is the strips planted to alternating crops on slopes instead of the square or rectangular fields common in the area before erosion control work was started."[62] Gone too were the giant gullies cutting across the Stromstads' farm.[63]

The new agricultural landscape created by the CCC caused a host of ecological transformations throughout Coon Valley. As Corps enrollees and farmers contour plowed fields and built check dams across gullies, soil erosion throughout the valley declined. "As fields were reshaped and channel systems were removed or were healed the off-field and downstream transportation of erosional debris was decreased," explained a Soil Conservation Service study of the Coon Valley watershed.[64] Such declines were dramatic. Beginning in 1934 with the arrival of the Corps and continuing for the next forty years as locals maintained the soil conservation techniques initiated during the New Deal, annual upland erosion rates in the valley decreased by 75 percent while sedimentation plummeted by approximately 98 percent. "These reductions in erosion and sedimentation," concluded the Soil Conservation Service, "have been caused principally by improvements in land management" implemented during the CCC era.[65]

The ecological changes caused by Corps labor on Coon Valley farms soon began altering local economies in the nearby towns of Stoddard, Chaseburg, and Coon Valley. Such transformations began in "cooperator's" fields, where decreasing soil erosion and associated increases in soil fertility raised yields of hay, alfalfa, and other fodder crops from 23 million pounds of total digestible nutrients in 1934 to 28 million pounds in 1938, an overall increase of nearly 20 percent.[66] With more and better-quality feed, the dairy herds of farmers working with the CCC also began to produce more milk. Not only did the butterfat production of each of the cows expand from 166 pounds in 1934 to 207 pounds in 1936, but between 1940 and 1941 these farmers increased their sales of butterfat by 19 percent compared to a 12 percent rise in sales by those not cooperating with the federal program.[67] Such financial returns raised land values throughout the valley by as much as $10 an acre by 1940, and encouraged local banks to extend credit once again to cooperating farmers.[68] For most Coon Valley farmers, the proof was in their pockets. Between 1934, when the CCC arrived, and 1942, when Congress terminated the program, farm income

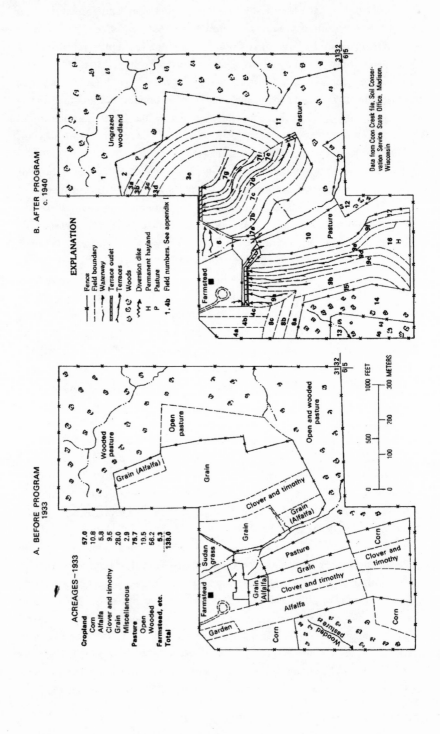

A. BEFORE PROGRAM
1933

ACREAGES—1933

Cropland	57.0
Corn	10.8
Alfalfa	5.8
Clover and timothy	9.5
Grain	28.0
Miscellaneous	2.9
Pasture	75.7
Open	19.5
Wooded	56.2
Farmstead, etc.	5.3
Total	138.0

Garden

Farmstead

Sudan grass

Grain

Grain (Alfalfa)

Grain Alfalfa

Alfalfa

Clover and timothy

Pasture

Grain

Grain (Alfalfa)

Clover and timothy

Corn

Corn

Corn

Clover and timothy

Wooded pasture

Open pasture

Wooded pasture

Open and wooded pasture

Open and wooded pasture

31|32
6|5

0   500   1000 FEET

0   100   200   300 METERS

B. AFTER PROGRAM
c. 1940

EXPLANATION

—x— Fence
—·—·— Field boundary
▬▬▬ Waterway
➤➤➤ Terrace outlet
⌒⌒⌒ Terraces
🌲🌲🌲 Woods
〜〜〜 Diversion dike
H Permanent hayland
P Pasture
1, 4b Field numbers. See appendix I

Ungrazed woodland

Farmstead

Pasture

Pasture

1
2
3a
3b
3c
3d
3e
4a
4b
4c
5
6
7a
7b
7c
7d
7e
7f
7g
7h
8a
8b
8c
9a
9b
9c
9d
9e
9f
10
11
12
13
14
16
H

31|32
6|5

Data from Coon Creek file, Soil Conservation Service State Office, Madison, Wisconsin

Figure 4.2 The stark visual differences between these two crop maps of the Stromstad farm in Coon Valley, Wisconsin, illustrate the dramatic landscape changes that occurred in thousands of local agricultural communities across the country when the CCC moved into the area. The first map, plotted from an aerial photograph taken in 1933 before the Corps arrived, indicates that the Stromstads practiced "square agriculture," involving straight crop rows running up and down hills in the middle of rectangular fields, and put little, if any, energy into conserving soil and water on their farm. By contrast the second map, created from another aerial photo taken in 1940, illustrates a dramatically altered farmscape. Contoured crop rows running around the hill in the center of the property and curving fields indicate that the Stromstads were still practicing the soil conservation techniques they had learned from the CCC, which left the region in 1937. Along with illustrating a newfound appreciation for soil conservation, the Stromstad new agricultural landscape also suggests a newfound reliance on the federal government. (Map showing crop patterns on the Stromstad farm, before and after CCC soil conservation efforts. Reprinted from Stanley W. Trimble and Steven W. Lund, *Soil Conservation and the Reduction of Erosion and Sedimentation in the Coon Creek Basin, Wisconsin*, Geological Survey Professional Paper 1234 [Washington, D.C.: U.S. Government Printing Office, 1982], 5)

of those participating in the Coon Creek Demonstration Area rose an astonishing 25 percent.[69]

As local ecologies began altering nearby economies throughout Coon Valley, farmers began thinking differently about their use of agricultural resources. "The progress of the program," explained Soil Conservation Service chief Hugh Bennett, "must be measured by the effect which these demonstrations have had upon agricultural thought."[70] According to such measures, Coon Creek was an ideological success. In interviews conducted in 1940 with 531 farmers who had cooperated with the CCC on demonstration areas in the upper Mississippi Valley, an area that included Coon Valley, 98 percent said they now believed that conservation was solving the erosion problem on their farms, and 99 percent stated their intention to continue practicing conservation indefinitely.[71] As important, this newfound belief in conservation had caught on with noncooperators as well; seventy Coon Valley farmers who had refrained from signing cooperative agreements nevertheless began practicing soil conservation on their own farms.[72] "A decided change has taken place in the attitude of most of those dwelling within the area," concluded the Soil Conservation Service of the Coon Creek Demonstration Area. "Cooperators and non-cooperators alike show that they believe in erosion control by adopting and continuing to use farming methods that check erosion."[73]

The spread of this new agricultural thought was not confined to the boundaries of the Coon Creek Demonstration Area.[74] Like the waters of Coon Creek, which eventually flowed into the Mississippi River, this new belief in conservation seeped beyond the watershed as farmers from the surrounding region visited the demonstration area, learned about soil conservation techniques, and implemented similar practices on their own land. By 1939, not only had more than 5,000 visitors toured the Coon Creek Demonstration Area, but the practice of contour strip plowing begun by 233 farmers in Coon Valley was expanding southward. A decade later, the practice had spread into neighboring Crawford, Grant, and Iowa counties, and by 1967 there were more than 6,400 farmers contour strip cropping their land in Wisconsin's Driftless Area.[75] A similar pattern occurred in the 174 other soil demonstration areas across the country during the New Deal era.[76] The dissemination of such soil conservation practices beyond Coon Valley, explained James Lindley, who oversaw CCC operations nationwide for the Soil Conservation Service, was the "sincerest form of flattery."[77]

As Coon Valley farmers began thinking differently about their fields, they embraced a new notion regarding the national government as well. Whereas during the 1920s these locals were extremely wary of federal involvement up and down their furrows, during the mid-1930s they encouraged just this by signing hundreds of cooperative agreements with the Soil Conservation Service for CCC work projects on their farms. Of the 812 farming families living within the watershed, 413, or slightly more than 50 percent, signed agreements with the federal soil agency (see figure 4.3).[78] Coon Valley residents likewise reversed their party affiliation; while throughout the 1920s those living in the three counties encompassing the valley had voted in overwhelming majorities for Republican presidents, just two years after enrollees moved into Camp Coon Creek these same locals voted for a Democratic party that in 1936 continued to promote a large federal government actively involved in local affairs.[79] Three years later, in 1939, Coon Valley residents also voted to create the Coon Creek Soil Conservation District, which would continue to provide technical information from federal soil experts in Washington, D.C., to local farmers long after the CCC departed from the region.[80] By the end of the Great Depression, then, residents of Stoddard, Chaseburg, and the town of Coon Valley had not only invited the New Deal into their communities, but had also taken steps to ensure that the benefits from federal programs such as the Corps remained in their crop rows long after Franklin Roosevelt left office.[81]

As the experiences of Coon Valley communities indicate, while the CCC transformed local nature it improved nearby economies in ways that promoted a newfound belief in natural resource conservation. Corps work on soil demonstration areas such as that along Coon Creek, asserted Aldo Leopold in 1935, fostered an "entity which many older conservationists have thought long since dead."[82] By bringing conservation to Coon Valley fields, the Corps simultaneously introduced the New Deal to nearby residents, who during the 1920s had actively opposed the intrusion of federal power on the local level. Yet Coon Valley illuminates only one aspect of the CCC's relationship with local communities. While Corps projects in private, state, and national forests altered local economies in ways that similarly publicized the idea of conserving natural resources, hundreds of CCC camps situated in state and national parks undertook a very different type of conservation work. Rather than focus their efforts on conserving water, soil, and trees, Corps enrollees in places like the Great Smoky Mountains labored to conserve something else.

The natural environment of the Great Smoky Mountains, like that of Coon Valley, greatly influenced the communities that settled in the region. Yet on a geological level, at least, the Smokies were in many ways the mirror image of Coon Valley. Whereas the waters of Coon Creek had cut a twenty-two-mile-long

COON VALLEY PROJECT
IN

WISCONSIN

LaCrosse

La Crosse
14 Miles

Coshton

Westby

½ 0   1   2   3   4   5
Scale in Miles

BLACK AREAS INDICATE FARMS ON WHICH
EROSION CONTROL PROGRAMS
HAVE BEEN ESTABLISHED

Figure 4.3 Although the federal government created this map of the Coon Creek Demonstration Area simply to identify the properties of Coon Valley farmers who signed cooperative agreements with the Soil Conservation Service, it also suggests a host of revolutionary changes taking place in Coon Valley communities during the New Deal era. As the Corps helped farmers transform the agricultural landscape of the valley through its soil conservation work projects, the local economy rebounded, which in turn forced locals to rethink their prior aversion to both conservation and the Democratic Party. Such changes, moreover, would seep beyond Coon Valley, as farmers from other regions visited the demonstration area, returned home, and undertook similar soil conservation measures in their own fields. The small black and white squares on this map are thus the first indication that the CCC would alter not just the Coon Valley landscape, but with it the ecology, economy, and political ideology of local residents. ("Coon Valley Project in Wisconsin," reprinted from R. H. Musser, "Coon Valley—4 Years After," *Soil Conservation* 4, no. 11 [May 1939]: 260)

nature - inexhaustible

depression east to west through the heart of the Driftless Area, plate tectonics 200 million years ago had uplifted the Appalachian range along North America's East Coast to form the thirty-six-mile ridge of the Great Smoky Mountains, which run north to south along the border of Tennessee and North Carolina. Thus while nature in Coon Valley includes lowlands surrounded on either side by steep ridges, in the Smokies the opposite is the case, with steep ridges running along the center of the region bordered on either side by lowland valleys. Agronomically, however, the Smokies resemble Coon Valley. Pleistocene glaciers had also bypassed the southern Appalachians, leaving the soil equally thin, the Smokies' 6,000-foot peaks similarly thick with forests, and the valleys below also covered with grasses, which grow as well on the cleared mountaintops known locally as "balds."[83]

The economic system brought to the Great Smoky Mountains by the first white settlers to the region was also the inverse, at least chronologically, to that transported to Coon Valley. Whereas in southwestern Wisconsin, the system began with logging and expanded into agriculture, in the Smokies economic development progressed in the reverse order. The first Euro-American settlers arrived in the region in the late 1810s and early 1820s and began practicing subsistence agriculture in the lowlands, hunting along the Smokies' forested slopes, and ranging domesticated livestock such as hogs, sheep, and cattle in upland areas, including the mountaintop balds.[84] To supplement their farm income, during the second half of the nineteenth century, locals also began small-scale, selective logging operations along the lower elevations of nearby mountainsides. By the turn of the century, however, lumber companies from the North increasingly looked to the Smoky Mountains as a new source of timber and began establishing larger-scale logging operations in the region.[85] The first of these, the Little River Lumber Company, began cutting timber in 1901, and by the early 1930s there were fifteen commercial lumber companies operating in nearly every Smoky Mountain watershed.[86] It was during this era that small towns sprouted on either side of the mountain range, with communities such as Townsend facing west toward nearby Knoxville, Tennessee, and towns including Bryson City and Smokemont anchored eastward toward the economy of Asheville, North Carolina.

As in Coon Valley, local nature and Euro-American economics fostered the idea among locals that the abundant natural resources of the Great Smoky Mountains were inexhaustible. This belief that nature was an exploitable commodity is perhaps best illustrated by the actions of one of the region's first lumber companies, and its relationship to local laborers. Between 1901, when W. B. Townsend established his logging operation, and 1938, when it felled its last tree, the Little River Lumber Company purchased more than 70,000 acres of timberland in the Smokies, cut between 750 million and 1 billion board feet in three different watersheds, and produced enough timber to build 100,000 modern three-bedroom homes. Perhaps most important, instead of selectively logging like early Smokies' residents, the Little River Lumber Company used industrial technology including logging railroads and steam-powered skidders to clear-cut much of its land, including old growth forests.[87] It also failed to reforest its property.[88] The other dozen or so lumber companies in the region did similarly, and by the early 1930s they had clear-cut approximately 60 percent of the Smoky Mountains' forest.[89] The employment provided by such operations had a direct impact on local ideas about nature. According to one visitor, who spent much of the 1920s in Bryson City, North Carolina, "the true mountaineer has no respect for a tree, feeling merely that the timber is there to be exploited and he is glad for the lumber operations that afford employment."[90]

Partly because they relied increasingly on timber work, Smoky Mountain locals also had little respect for federal intervention in local affairs. Although often wrongly portrayed as having "practically no contact with the outside world," the "mountain people" of eastern Tennessee and western North Carolina did remain quite isolated, physically and culturally, from national politics at the turn of the century. "The folks of Deep Creek, they mostly worried about what was going on in Deep Creek," explained Smoky Mountain local Winfred Cagle. "They didn't care too much for what was going on" in places like Washington, D.C.[91] Community residents even went out of their way to actively oppose federal meddling on the local level up through the 1920s. In 1925, for instance, when the U.S. Department of the Interior proposed limiting logging in the Smokies, local timber company owners took out full-page advertisements in Knoxville newspapers against the federal proposition and used their connections within the Republican party to oppose the proposal.[92] Working-class residents in the Great Smoky Mountains similarly embraced the idea of a small federal government with limited say in local issues; during the 1928 presidential election, more than 70 percent of those living in the five counties straddling the Great Smoky Mountains voted Republican. Four years later, when Franklin Roosevelt and his New Deal won a landslide victory across the nation, the mountain people of Blount, Cocke, and Sevier counties on the Tennessee side of the Smokies voted by majority for Herbert Hoover.[93]

The notion that Smoky Mountain trees represented limitless commercial timber, along with the desire to keep federal regulators out of the logging industry, resulted in a host of ecological problems during the 1920s. "The utter devastation the spruce logger leaves behind," explained local Paul Fink, left "the bare soil to erode and wash away under the heavy rainfall."[94] Discarded underbrush and branches also increased the likelihood of catastrophic forest fires, more than twenty of which occurred in the Smokies during the 1920s. Extensive clear-cutting even destroyed mountain habitat necessary for the survival of wildlife, such as white-tailed deer, turkeys, and black bears, and loosened mountain soil, which eroded down steep slopes into streams and rivers where it threatened fish and increased the potential for flooding in lowland hollows. "Fore we cut that timber in there them old big-horned owls, you couldn't sleep at night for them [calling]," explained Earl Franklin, a Smoky Mountain local who worked for the Little River Lumber Company. "Just as quick as the timber's cut them owls left."[95] Most important, deforestation stripped nutrients from mountain soil, making it difficult for forests to regrow naturally.[96] As one historian of the logging era in the Great Smoky Mountains put it, "the cutting of the later period brought with it the seeds of the virtual annihilation of the forest."[97]

The ecological degradation caused by logging throughout the Great Smoky Mountains during the first two decades of the twentieth century weakened local economies in communities such as Townsend, Bryson City, and Smokemont, and even hurt financial institutions farther afield in Knoxville and Asheville. As locals left their farms for work in logging camps and as deforestation destroyed hunting and fishing habitat, the subsistence lifestyle practiced by Smoky Mountain locals for generations became difficult if not impossible to maintain.[98] As important, deforestation forced logging companies to depart from the region in search of fresh stands in the West, leaving behind hundreds of unemployed locals.[99] The ecological crisis facing the Smokies' forests during the 1920s thus made the economic impact of the Great Depression even worse; by 1930, eight banks in and around Asheville had failed, while on the other side of the mountains near Knoxville six of eleven banks that had been in operation in 1920 had shut their doors by 1933.[100] Local relief organizations were similarly overwhelmed. The "burden" on the Associated Charities, explained the *Asheville Advocate* in April 1933, must be "materially lessened" in order for needy families in the region to be removed from "the charity list permanently."[101]

Like Aldo Leopold in Wisconsin, Bob Marshall was well aware of this link between the ecological degradation of forests such as those in the Great Smokies and the decline of local economies. Marshall began formulating this social critique of the American timber industry in 1925, after reporting to his first Forest Service assignment at the Northern Rocky Mountain Forest Experiment Station in Missoula, Montana. It was while studying the dynamics of postfire forest reproduction at the experiment station that Marshall visited logging communities in the Missoula region and began learning about their economies. Five years later, he wrote about these experiences, arguing in a 1930 *Journal of Forestry* article that proper forest management required protecting "all those who are part of the community in which the forest industry functions." Timber operators in the United States had failed in this regard, and as a result "abandoned towns and deserted farms have typified the unregulated pursuit of private profit in every forest region in the United States."[102] The Great Smoky Mountains were no different; here too local communities paid the price of poor timber management.

In response to the economic and ecological crises facing local communities in the Great Smoky Mountains, the Roosevelt administration sent the CCC to the region just two months after Congress created the New Deal program in March 1933. The Corps established its first camp in the mountains in May of that year, and followed up in July with nine more. The number of Corps camps functioning simultaneously peaked at seventeen in 1935, when approximately 3,500 enrollees labored on CCC work projects in the Smokies. All told, the Corps established nineteen new camps in the Great Smoky Mountains, more than any other two national parks combined, and built a total of twenty-two camps used by CCC enrollees at various times before Congress terminated the New Deal program in 1942.[103] The Corps divided these camps evenly between Tennessee and North Carolina, and situated them strategically throughout the mountains. The first CCC camp in the Smokies, for instance, sat along Laurel Creek, a tributary of the Little River on the Tennessee side of the Smokies. This and other Corps camps were located quite literally between ailing local communities like Townsend and the devastated landscapes abandoned by logging operations such as the Little River Lumber Company.

The arrival of CCC camps in the Great Smokies immediately helped nearby communities by funneling federal funds back into local economies. According to Corps studies, each CCC camp pumped approximately $5,000 per month back into the local economy through the purchase of materials and services.[104] As one owner of a small laundry reported, "my business grew with the coming of two CCC camps to our vicinity."[105] Approximately $2,000 in spending money from each camp also found its way every month from enrollees' pockets into local movie theaters, pool halls, bars, restaurants, and shops as the young men flocked to nearby towns for recreation on their days off.

A single Corps camp therefore injected approximately $7,000 per month into the nearby economy, or more than $80,000 a year.[106] Such estimates do not include the approximately $22,000 spent on the construction of each CCC camp, which during the early 1930s, before the Corps began using prefabricated barracks, involved the use of local materials and laborers.[107] "Hundreds of communities have discovered since the CCC was organized two years ago," reported *Business Week* in May 1935, "that the neighboring camp is the bright spot on their business map."[108]

The "bright spots" on the Smoky Mountains' business map jump-started local economies across the region. In 1935, for instance, the seventeen Corps camps in existence had cost the Corps approximately $374,000 to construct and more than $1 million to maintain, with much of this money finding its way into nearby bank accounts through the purchase of goods and services.[109] Each year, the CCC continued to spend money locally to keep up its Smoky Mountain camps; in 1936 the Corps spent approximately $540,000 to maintain the nine camps then in operation; $420,000 in 1938 for the seven camps then in existence; and $360,000 in 1941 for the remaining six camps.[110] All told, from 1933 until the Corps left the region in 1942, the New Deal program spent more than $5.5 million to build and maintain its camps.[111] This price tag does not include the more than $2 million of pocket money spent locally by CCC enrollees stationed in the Great Smoky Mountains during the Depression era.[112] As one Tennessee newspaper explained, local producers of "everything from septic tanks to ice cream" reported major increases in sales as soon as the CCC moved in.[113]

While having Corps camps as neighbors helped locals with their economic woes, the early conservation work undertaken by these camps focused on solving the region's ecological problems. "The mountains looked awful," explained CCC enrollee Frank Jackson of the surrounding forests.[114] To correct the situation, during their first year in the Smokies, enrollees like Jackson replanted portions of hillsides that had been clear-cut during the previous decade and labored on projects aimed at reducing fire hazards that had dramatically increased because of logging. In their effort to "fire proof" the Smokies, CCC enrollees removed slash debris from the forest floor, cut breaks to slow a fire's progress and fire roads to hasten the movement of firefighters, and constructed at least ten lookout towers connected by telephone wires on Smoky Mountain peaks.[115] The Corps even undertook conservation projects to increase wildlife in the park by "planting" fish from federal hatcheries in Smoky Mountain streams.[116] During these early New Deal years, the Corps thus spent most of its time cleaning up after loggers.

Although the arrival of CCC enrollees in the Smokies and their early conservation efforts focused on healing the economic and ecological scars of the late 1920s, neither would have lasting implications for local communities. As soon as CCC enrollees finished their conservation work, they would leave the region, relocated by Corps administrators to other needy areas, and take with them the New Deal dollars that had propped up nearby economies. Early CCC conservation work similarly failed to help locals financially since in 1934, a year after the Corps moved in, the Roosevelt administration officially established Great Smoky Mountains National Park, which outlawed logging within its boundaries. The forests that CCC enrollees were replanting and protecting from fire were now off-limits, at least economically, to those living around the park. During the mid-1930s, however, as the CCC expanded its conservation efforts nationwide into the recreational arena, Corps camps in the Smokies likewise shifted their work projects from restoring mountain forests to developing the new national park for outdoor recreation. This change signified not only an evolution in Corps conservation policy but, more important, a long-term economic solution for local communities.

The financial rewards of outdoor recreation were not foreign to those living in eastern Tennessee and western North Carolina. The same railroads that had helped loggers to remove timber from deep within the forests gave tourists easy access to Smoky Mountain nature. Yet while loggers sought the Smokies for their store of natural resources, tourists cherished the mountains for altogether different reasons. Some, desirous of escaping the industrial city for the more healthful climate of the Great Smokies, stayed in nearby Asheville, which became a mecca of sorts for such tourism during the 1880s and 1890s.[117] Others flocked to the mountains for more aesthetic reasons. Knoxville lawyer Harvey Broome, for instance, developed a passion for the Smokies during his first trip to the mountains, which he made on the Little River Lumber Company's logging railroad. "Such thrills!" he wrote. "We looked down on raw boulders in water, foaming and clear." For Broome, it was the intrinsic beauty of the forest that was "intensely desirable."[118] Yet whether they came for cures or the lure of mountain scenery, visiting tourists were welcomed with open arms by Smoky Mountain locals, who early on began establishing rustic hotels, mineral spring resorts, and guide outfits throughout the region.[119]

This faith in the economy of outdoor leisure also influenced locals who during the mid-1920s began advocating for a park in the Great Smoky Mountains. Although the seeds of such efforts were planted at the turn of the century, the park movement blossomed in 1923 when a wealthy Knoxville

nat'l park in Smokies

couple named Anne and Willis Davis vacationed in Yellowstone and noted the numerous businesses flourishing around that national park. When the couple returned to Tennessee, they promoted the idea of a park in the Smokies to local merchants, real estate companies, and the Knoxville Chamber of Commerce, to which Willis Davis, as general manager of the Knoxville Iron Company, belonged. The result was the formation in 1924 of the Great Smoky Mountains Conservation Association and the election of its president, David C. Chapman, who not surprisingly also served as director of the Knoxville Chamber of Commerce. Under Chapman, the conservation association immediately began courting businesspeople from Asheville, on the other side of the Smokies, as well as the general public by describing in detail the tremendous boon a national park would be to local economies. The creation of Great Smoky Mountains National Park, the conservation association argued in the *Knoxville Sentinel*, "will bring millions of extra dollars into the southland."[120]

It would also bring motor roads. "With the establishment of a national park in the Appalachian region," argued the same *Knoxville Sentinel* article, "roads would be built and maintained by the government."[121] This belief that improved motor roads would boost local economies was not unique to the members of the Great Smoky Mountains Conservation Association. During this period, the "good roads" movement in the southern United States was also promoting motorways as a means to economically develop the South.[122] The conservation association thus shared much with good roads enthusiasts. For instance, not only did Willis Davis launch his promotional campaign for the national park at a Knoxville Automobile Club board meeting in October 1923, but the conservation association and the automobile club also shared the same office space and board of directors.[123] In fact, so fuzzy was the distinction between the two organizations that Russel Hanlon, then secretary-manager of the automobile club, remembered that when either convened "it was often difficult to determine which group was meeting."[124]

Due to this belief in the economic synergy of roads and recreation, Smoky Mountain locals were understandably pleased when in the mid-1930s the CCC shifted its conservation efforts from forestry to development projects for the new national park. At first, Corps enrollees focused on expanding outdoor opportunities for visiting tourists by constructing nearly 700 miles of hiking trails, hundreds of picnic areas, and dozens of campgrounds throughout the Smokies. The CCC complemented such work by building a park infrastructure that included comfort stations, visitor centers, amphitheaters, observation towers, park headquarters, and two museums. All told, the more than 7 million man-hours of labor performed by CCC enrollees each year in the

Smokies dramatically increased the number and variety of recreational options throughout the region.[125] "Undoubtedly, the seventeen CCC camps stationed in this park have helped develop this park at a much more rapid rate than any other park ever built by the Federal Government," explained Great Smoky Mountains National Park superintendent Ross Eakin. "The park has advanced at least ten years."[126]

To make sure that tourists had access to these new recreational amenities, during the later New Deal years the Corps also improved and built motor roads throughout the national park. The CCC first began working on roadways in mountain valleys by converting many of the Smokies' old logging railroad lines into automobile thoroughfares. Corps enrollees removed ties, scrap metal, and rocks from the Little River Lumber Company railroad lines and installed culverts, drainage ditches, and a new roadway surface before reconstructing three bridges for car traffic across the Little River. "This type of construction is a new departure in this park," explained Superintendent Eakin of the stone automobile bridge near Elkmont (see figure 4.4).[127] In nearby Cades Cove, two CCC camps undertook similar work, rebuilding two bridges and a ford for cars on the lower part of Parsons Branch Road, and relocating a mile of the road along Forge Creek.[128] Between 1934 and 1938, CCC workers also stabilized the slope along Rich Mountain Road, which ran north out of the cove toward Townsend and Knoxville.[129]

Along with expanding motor road networks at the foot of the Smokies, the Corps also helped to reconstruct existing motor roads and to build new ones at much higher elevations. With enrollee sweat, the National Park Service reconstructed much of Newfound Gap Road, the only thoroughfare to run up and over the Smokies, in an effort to better link the Tennessee and North Carolina sections of the park. Corps enrollees extensively landscaped the motorway by grading its banks and cuts and by planting the slopes with native trees.[130] At the very top of this road, CCC enrollees also created the most famous view in the Smokies by constructing the Laura Spellman Rockefeller Memorial Overlook, as well as its adjacent parking terrace, which straddles the Tennessee–North Carolina border (see figure 4.5).[131] Finally, the CCC helped to construct the highest road in the Smokies, which ran 7.5 miles from Newfound Gap up to the 6,643-foot summit of Clingmans Dome. Corps enrollees bank sloped the shoulders of Clingmans Dome Road, expanded the parking area at the terminus of the dead-end motorway, and built a wooden rustic-style observation tower near the parking lot for motor tourists.[132] The Corps was so proud of this work that on September 2, 1940, when Franklin Roosevelt arrived to dedicate the Rockefeller Memorial on top of Newfound Gap, CCC enrollees stood at attention 1,000 feet apart as the president drove up the mountain road they had helped to reconstruct.[133]

Corps labor on Clingmans Dome Road actually marked the completion of just one section of a much grander road-building project planned for the Great Smoky Mountains. Called the "Skyway" by its promoters, this mountaintop road would run along the entire ridgeline of the Great Smoky Mountains and serve as the southernmost section of the Blue Ridge Parkway, then under construction, also with CCC labor, in Virginia's Shenandoah National Park. Members of the Asheville Chamber of Commerce promoted this thoroughfare in the early 1930s, much as their counterparts in Knoxville had publicized motorways during the previous decade, by arguing that the road would spur economic development.[134] In July 1932, Superintendent Eakin announced that the National Park Service would go ahead with the project, and two years later, in August 1934, the Department of the Interior's Harold Ickes sent Bob Marshall, then head of the Bureau of Indian Affairs' Forestry Division, to the Smokies to examine the proposal.[135] While Marshall hiked through the mountains scouting potential routes for the Skyway, Superintendent Eakin formalized plans to use thousands of CCC enrollees to build it.[136]

The conservation projects undertaken by Corps enrollees in the Great Smokies between 1933 and 1942 dramatically transformed the landscape of the new national park. During the early 1930s, as CCC enrollees conserved natural resources by replanting clear-cuts and limiting forest fires, Great Smoky Mountains National Park began to appear more natural, even though the tree stands planted by the Corps were as artificial as Coon Valley's new curvilinear crop rows.[137] Beginning in the mid-1930s, however, as the CCC began focusing instead on conserving human resources by developing the national park for outdoor recreation, portions of the Smokies took on a more artificial appearance as enrollees cleared stands of forest to make room for manmade structures such as campgrounds, picnic areas, parking lots, and motor roads. Ironically, whereas early CCC projects used the artifice of tree plantings and roadside vegetation to hide the Smokies' human history, Corps recreation work created more obviously artificial sites within the park in order to bring visitors closer to what they believed was untouched nature. Thus, while CCC conservation efforts in Coon Valley converted private land into a public landscape, Corps park development projects transformed the public land of the new national parks into public space for tourists.[138]

Although the two types of landscapes created by the Corps in the Great Smokies each blended the natural and the artificial, they caused quite different ecological changes in the national park. The forestry work first undertaken by

HISTORIC AMERICAN
ENGINEERING RECORD

SHEET

TN-35-9

1 OF 1

TENNESSEE

SEVIER COUNTY

ROADS & BRIDGES: ELKMONT VEHICLE BRIDGE

GREAT SMOKY MOUNTAINS NATIONAL PARK

GATLINBURG VICINITY

UNITED STATES DEPARTMENT OF THE INTERIOR
NATIONAL PARK SERVICE
RECREATIONAL DEMONSTRATION PROGRAM
ROADS & BRIDGES

DELINEATED BY: Edward J. Lagerstrom, 1994

ELKMONT VEHICLE BRIDGE
CONSTRUCTION PEEL-AWAY

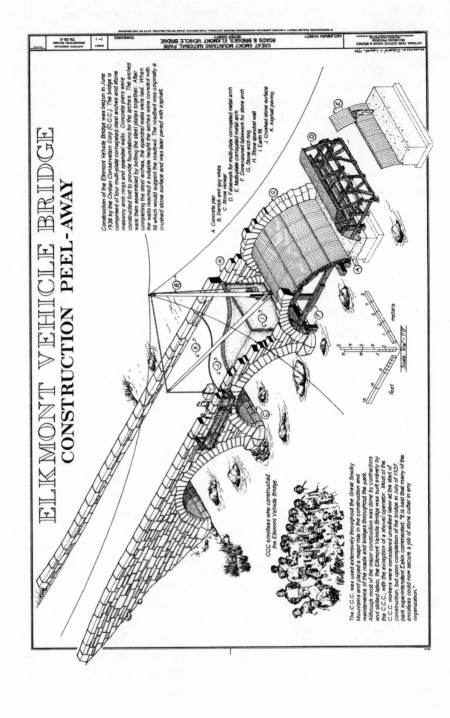

Construction of the Elkmont Vehicle Bridge was begun in June 1936 by the Civilian Conservation Corp (C.C.C.). The bridge is comprised of four multi-plate corrugated steel arches and stone masonry arch rings and spandrel walls. Concrete piers were constructed first to provide foundations for the arches. The arches were then assembled by bolting the steel plates together. After completing the steel arches, the spandrel walls were laid. When the walls reached a suitable height the arches were covered with fill which would support the roadbed. The roadbed was originally a crushed stone surface and was later paved with asphalt.

A Concrete pier
B Derrick and guy wires
C Stone veneer
D Falsework for multi-plate corrugated metal arch
E Multi-plate corrugated metal arch
F Dimensioned falsework for stone arch
G Stone arch ring
H Stone spandrel wall
I Earth fill
J Crushed stone surface
K Asphalt paving.

CCC enrollees who constructed
the Elkmont Vehicle Bridge.

The C.C.C. was used extensively throughout the Great Smoky Mountains and played a major role in the construction and maintenance of the roads and bridges throughout the park. Although most of the major construction was done by contractors and skilled labor, the Elkmont Vehicle Bridge was built entirely by the C.C.C., with the exception of a shovel operator. Most of the C.C.C. workers were considered unskilled labor at the start of construction, but upon completion of the bridge in July of 1937, park superintendent Eakin commented: "It is said that many of the enrollees could now secure a job of stone cutter in any organization."

meters

feet   Scale: 1/4" = 1'0"

Figure 4.4 Throughout the 1930s and early 1940s the CCC constructed hundreds of bridges like this one in the Elkmont section of Great Smoky Mountains National Park. Built between June 1936 and July 1937 by hundreds of Corps enrollees, the Elkmont Vehicle Bridge provided cars with easier access to the park, and in doing so drove increasing amounts of tourist dollars into nearby local communities that provided amenities to visitors. The new visitor centers, campgrounds, and hiking trails built by the Corps during the Great Depression did similarly for thousands of local communities situated near national and state parks across the country. Because of this newfound prosperity, many local residents began embracing park development work as conservation, albeit of a different sort than that practiced during the Progressive Era. These same locals also began switching their party affiliation and supporting Franklin Roosevelt's New Deal. ("Elkmont Vehicle Bridge: Construction Peel-Away," Historic American Building Survey/Historic American Engineering Record/Historic American Landscapes Survey, "Great Smoky Mountains National Park Roads and Bridges, Elkmont Vehicle Bridge, Spanning Little River at Elkmont Campground, Gatlinburg Vicinity, Sevier County, Tennessee." Call Number: HAER TENN, 78-GAT.V,6S-, Library of Congress)

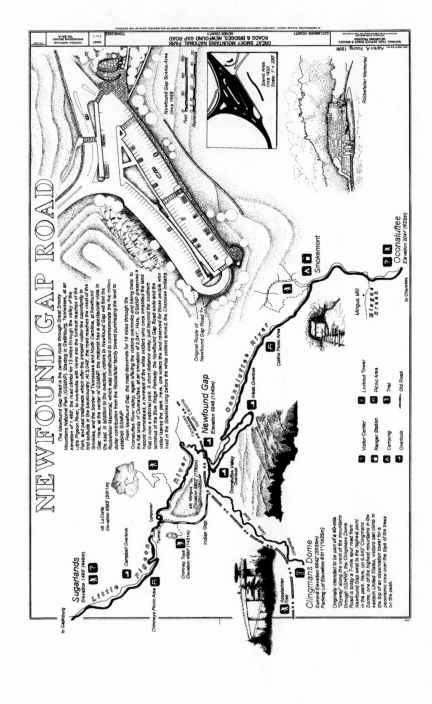

NEWFOUND GAP ROAD

The Newfound Gap Road is the central route through Great Smoky Mountains National Park (GSMNP). Starting in Gatlinburg, Tennessee, at an elevation of 1,465', the road climbs for 13 miles through the valley of the Little Pigeon River, to overlooks with views into the furthest reaches of the Park, and past trailheads which offer the intrepid visitor the opportunity to find solitude in the backcountry. At 5,048', the road reaches the crest of the Smokies, and the border of Tennessee and North Carolina, at Newfound Gap. Here, at the center of GSMNP, the motorist has a spectacular vista to the east. In addition to this overlook, visitors to Newfound Gap will find the Rockefeller Memorial, which was constructed to commemorate the five million dollar contribution from the Rockefeller family toward purchasing the land to establish GSMNP.

From Newfound Gap, the road descends for 16 miles through the Oconaluftee River valley, again offering the visitors overlooks and hiking trails to the flat lands of Oconaluftee, at an elevation of 2,041'. Here, GSMNP preserves a historic homestead, a remnant of the white settlers who once inhabited the land that is now a national park. A short distance away, just beyond the southern terminus of the Blue Ridge Parkway the Newfound Gap Road ends and the visitor leaves the park. Here, one enters the land reserved for those people who lived in the Smokies long before the white settlers arrived, the Cherokee Indians.

Sugarlands
Elevation 1465' (446m)

Clingmans Dome
Summit Elevation 6642' (2025m)
Parking Lot Elevation 6311' (1925m)

Originally intended to be part of a 40-mile "Skyway" along the crest of the mountains through GSMNP, the Clingmans Dome Road is today a 7-mile spur road from Newfound Gap west to the highest point in the park. Here, on 6,642' Clingmans Dome, one of the highest mountains in the eastern United States, visitors can climb to the top of an observation tower for a panoramic view over the tops of the trees on the peak.

Mt. LeConte
Elevation 6593' (2011m)

Mt. Mingus
Elevation 5802' (1780m)

Chimney Tops
Elevation 4880' (1421m)

Newfound Gap
Elevation 5048' (1540m)

Original Route of
Newfound Gap Road

Oconaluftee
Elevation 2041' (623m)

Smokemont

Mingus Mill

to Cherokee.

Webb Overlook

Collins Picnic Area

Oconaluftee Valley Overlook

Campbell Overlook

Chimneys Picnic Area

Tunnel

Loopover

Indian Gap

to Gatlinburg

Legend
- ① Visitor Center
- ① Ranger Station
- ⚠ Camping
- ① Overlook
- ① Lookout Tower
- ① Picnic Area
- ① Trail
- Old Road

GREAT SMOKY MOUNTAINS NATIONAL PARK
ROADS & BRIDGES, NEWFOUND GAP ROAD
SEVIER COUNTY
TENNESSEE

HISTORIC AMERICAN ENGINEERING RECORD
TN-35-A
SHEET
1-1

Scenic Area, circa 1933
Rockefeller Memorial

Newfound Gap Scenic Area, circa 1968

Scenic Area
Scale: 1" = 200'

DELINEATED BY: Karen A. Young, 1996

Figure 4.5 Along with building tourist amenities for outdoor recreation, the CCC also constructed thousands of miles of motor roads in national and state parks. In the Great Smoky Mountains, this road work included the conversion of old logging railroad lines into automobile thoroughfares at lower elevations, as well as the repair and reconstruction of an entire road network, pictured here, at the very top of the park. Corps enrollees extensively landscaped the shoulders of Newfound Gap Road, which ran up and over the Smokies, built the expansive Rockefeller Memorial Overlook and parking lot on the ridge of the gap, and helped to construct a brand new road, the highest in the park, which would wind from Newfound Gap up the peak of Clingmans Dome. While such CCC work opened up previously inaccessible areas of the park to visiting tourists, in the later 1930s projects like Clingmans Dome road would alarm many Americans who feared that its construction would destroy the wilderness character of national parks. This early concern for automobiles and wilderness, aroused in part by CCC work projects, would become a driving force of postwar environmentalism. ("Newfound Gap Road," Historic American Building Survey/Historic American Engineering Record/Historic American Landscapes Survey, "Great Smoky Mountains National Park Roads and Bridges, Newfound Gap Road, between Gatlinburg, Tennessee, and Cherokee, North Carolina, Gatlinburg Vicinity, Sevier County, Tennessee." Call Number: HAER TENN, 78-GAT.V,6A-, Library of Congress)

CCC enrollees in the Smokies actually reversed many of the environmental problems caused by logging. Reforesting cut-over areas not only increased wildlife habitat in the park but also decreased soil and water runoff on hillsides, which in turn lessened the potential of devastating floods in streams and rivers. As a result, populations of fauna, including white-tailed deer, black bears, and aquatic species such as trout, rebounded in the park during the late 1930s. Black bears, wrote park superintendent Eakin, now approached "numbers which they normally should have."[139] Yet the recreational development work undertaken by the Corps often had the reverse effect. Clearing forests for campgrounds, picnic areas, and visitor centers increased soil erosion and the potential for flooding while decreasing habitat for wildlife. Cutting hiking trails, firebreaks, and motor roads across the Great Smokies also threatened fauna by segmenting forest ecosystems.[140] In the end, the park's new motor roads brought cars and with them air pollution, which gave new meaning to the name Great Smoky Mountains.

Yet while Corps conservation projects caused divergent ecological transformations, together these two sets of environmental changes greatly improved local economies by expanding opportunities for outdoor recreation throughout the Great Smoky Mountains. The restored forest and returning wildlife resulting from early CCC conservation projects lured increasing numbers of outdoor recreationists to the national park, while the campsites, picnic areas, and motor roads built by the Corps during the later 1930s accommodated these tourists and brought them into closer contact with nature. "Through the efforts of hundreds of Civilian Conservation Corps workers," explained the *Asheville Advocate*, "a flood of tourists has been flowing through the new national playground."[141] What began as a trickle of approximately 40,000 visitors into Great Smoky Mountains National Park in June 1934, just before the Corps began its park development work, became a torrent of nearly 130,000 visitors during the same month in 1940.[142] To capitalize on this influx, continued the *Asheville Advocate*, "ample facilities for the entertainment of visitors are now found in cities and resort centers near the park boundaries."[143] Unlike the quick infusion of federal cash that would come and go with the arrival and departure of CCC camps, such recreational tourism had long-lasting economic impact; by 1955, visitors to the national park were spending $4.5 million annually in local communities.[144]

The ecological and economic changes set in motion by Corps conservation work in the Great Smoky Mountains transformed how locals in the region thought about the nature all around them. Before CCC enrollees arrived in 1933, locals viewed the Smokies' forest in utilitarian terms, as so many board feet of timber. As a result, ecological problems plagued Smoky Mountain communities, worsening an already dire economic situation. By the end of the decade, however, residents of communities around the national park were praising the CCC's conservation efforts. "There seems to be no phase of the work done...more universally popular than the Conservation Camps," explained a North Carolina Corps administrator in 1935. "The general public as represented by community opinion seems heartily in favor of the Civilian Conservation Corps."[145] Locals also now favored conservation. "Some of these folks said that five years ago they would have ridiculed the idea of planting more trees in the mountains," explained the *Asheville Advocate* in May 1934, "but now they are sorry that they did not plant at that time."[146]

While praising CCC work in general, locals during the New Deal period also began embracing a new notion of conservation, one quite different from that espoused by the Progressive conservation movement. Like old school conservationists, residents of communities in the Smoky Mountains region supported the conservation of natural resources such as timber. As the Knoxville *Appalachian Journal* proudly proclaimed, because of the Corps, "the dangers from severe forest fires and soil erosion are rapidly being eliminated." Yet for locals reading the *Journal*, CCC conservation was attractive precisely because it involved more than reforestation. Due to Corps recreation projects, explained the same Knoxville newspaper, "the genuine natural beauties of the Park are being made more accessible, conveniences for the growing number of visitors are being realized." Local support for CCC conservation, in other words, rested as much on the return of the tourist as on the return of the forest. "Here in the Great Smoky Mountains National Park," the *Appalachian Journal* concluded, "the work accomplished by these young men can indeed be regarded as a gigantic conservation project." Central to the size and scope of such work, the newspaper suggested, was the conservation of human resources, in this case park visitors, through the expansion of healthful outdoor recreational opportunities.[147] "The program is worth while," explained Mrs. Thomas O'Berry of the CCC's work in the Smokies, "and is actually conserving the social resources of the country."[148]

New notions of conservation also altered the way Smoky locals thought about national politics. Whereas during the 1920s, residents such as those in Deep Creek "mostly worried about what was going on in Deep Creek" and took action to keep federal bureaucrats from meddling in the local timber economy, throughout the Great Depression they did the opposite; they worried about the national economy and supported federal efforts to create local jobs that would ensure recreational tourism for years to come. Not only did hundreds of

Smoky Mountain youths become enrollees in nearby CCC camps, but the Corps also gave jobs to male community residents who were unable to join the New Deal program as enrollees because they were married or too old.[149] The Roosevelt administration's decision in 1933 to assign eight of what is called "local experienced men," or "LEMs," to every Corps camp in the country helped to appease local, unemployed laborers, who were hired as LEMs to show "green" enrollees how to work. The CCC employed more than 24,000 LEMs nationwide, approximately 200 of whom trained enrollees in the Smokies.[150] The LEM policy, like the Corps' cooperative agreements with local farmers such as those in Coon Valley, also allowed Roosevelt to actively involve community residents living near CCC camps in national politics, and in turn to raise popular support for his New Deal on the local level. Such political strategizing succeeded. On the more conservative Tennessee side of the Smokies in Blount County, for instance, the margin of victory for Republican presidential nominees plummeted 25 percent between 1932, before the arrival of the CCC, and 1940, after six years of Corps work in the new national park.[151] The results were even more decisive in North Carolina, where locals living in the Smokies' eastern foothills, who voted for Herbert Hoover in 1928, switched presidential parties in 1936 and 1940.[152]

When Corps enrollees left their barracks in the Allegheny Mountains to visit the Mountain State Forest Festival in Elkins, West Virginia, they did so to participate in parades and pageants, boxing matches and baseball games. The immediate goal of such activities, according to CCC director Robert Fechner, was for Corps camps to become "good neighbors." "The boys," he wrote of CCC enrollees, "have maintained such friendly and cordial relations with the communities with which they have come in contact."[153] Yet as the experiences of locals in Coon Valley and the Great Smoky Mountains indicate, the CCC's arrival in the neighborhood portended not just new social interactions, but novel, environmental, financial and intellectual relations as well. The same held true for thousands of local communities across the country situated near the more than 5,000 CCC camps. Corps conservation work near all of these communities transformed surrounding ecologies, nearby economies, and local ideologies.

Corps conservation work, however, functioned differently in different communities, depending on the type of labor undertaken. In places like Coon Valley, where Corps enrollees helped local farmers to halt water and soil erosion, the resulting increase in crop production spread a belief in conservation throughout the surrounding countryside. This newfound belief in conserving natural resources was actually quite old on the national level,

espoused since the turn of the century by Progressive conservationists such as Gifford Pinchot. This conservation ethic spread first to CCC enrollees as they labored on Corps work projects, and unfolded next in places like Coon Valley as locals began cooperating with the CCC. "A three inch rain sold me on soil conserving," remembered one farmer who had just contour plowed his field with Corps help. "There was practically no soil washing there."[154] Corps work projects were thus not only altering the nation's agricultural landscape but were once again broadening the composition of the conservation movement, democratizing it beyond Progressive Era elites and a small contingent of rural landowners and hunters to include a majority of locals from the nation's farm belt. The result was a more broad-based movement that better reflected the grassroots character of modern environmentalism.

At the same time, local communities situated near CCC projects in the nation's parks began redefining the idea of conservation itself. In the Great Smoky Mountains, for instance, community residents embraced early Corps work projects involving reforestation and fire protection not because it promised more efficient timber production, but instead because it restored forests that appealed to tourists. Locals thought similarly about CCC park development projects, which the Corps promoted during the later New Deal years as an alternative type of conservation, one aimed not at natural resources but rather at conserving human resources through the expansion of healthful outdoor recreation. While this novel brand of conservation had its roots in the urban parks movement of Frederick Law Olmsted, locals like those in the Great Smoky Mountains made it their own during the Great Depression, embracing it in part because healthy hikers brought fat wallets to the new national park and its surrounding communities. The expansion of conservationist ideas to include once again a concern for human resources, in this case outdoor recreationists, foreshadowed the broader considerations of environmentalists in the years after World War II.

By introducing conservation to nearby communities, Corps camps were also bringing the New Deal home to local residents. In some instances, as in Elkins, West Virginia, the CCC actually helped to introduce the president himself; Roosevelt traveled to the Forest Festival in part to promote the Corps and its work to locals. In other communities, the arrival of the New Deal was less obvious, but no less suggestive of a broader political shift. In agricultural regions such as Coon Valley, New Deal politics played out physically in farmers' fields; as curvilinear crop rows replaced the square agriculture of the 1920s, community aversion toward federal involvement in local affairs gradually gave way to an increasing acceptance of the welfare state. In

towns and villages near the country's parks, CCC conservation work functioned somewhat differently. As Corps enrollees planted both trees and the
roots of an outdoor tourist industry through the construction of hiking trails,
campgrounds, and motor roads in places like Great Smoky Mountains National Park, local residents similarly shed their fear of federal interference and
embraced Franklin Roosevelt's New Deal. Thus whether locals lived near
Corps camps conserving natural resources such as soil in Coon Valley or
human resources like the tourists hiking through the Smokies, the landscape
changes caused by CCC work projects altered community politics.

Although CCC work projects introduced both conservation and the New
Deal to local residents, not everyone was pleased with Franklin Roosevelt's
conservation from the bottom up. Even though enthusiasm for the Corps soon
spread from the local to the national level, making it the most popular New
Deal program, an increasingly vocal minority began criticizing the CCC during
the later Great Depression years. This opposition also began on the local level
before going national. Aldo Leopold, for instance, who had worked so closely
with the CCC on the Coon Creek Demonstration Area, began criticizing Corps
conservation projects for upsetting ecological balance in places like Coon
Valley. Bob Marshall similarly began to condemn the Corps during this period
but for quite different reasons. For Marshall, CCC park development projects
like the proposed Skyway across the Smokies, which he surveyed for the
Department of the Interior in 1934, posed a dangerous threat to wilderness.
Although the national debate between CCC proponents and this anti-Corps
crowd was quite complicated, unraveling it is essential to understanding not
only the transformation of conservation during the Great Depression era but
also the political difficulties that increasingly plagued Franklin Roosevelt
during the late 1930s.

CCC &
ads for
products

FIVE / **NATION**
The Great Conservation Debate

In late October 1934, the American Fork and Hoe Company sent Paul Criss, "the spectacular axe-man," to a CCC camp located near the Tennessee side of Great Smoky Mountains National Park. Surprisingly, Criss did not journey from the company's headquarters in Cleveland, Ohio, down to the Smokies to train Corps enrollees in the fine art of chopping wood nor to teach them how to properly fell a tree. Instead, the "axe-man" went to make an advertisement for a particular brand of ax manufactured by the company that would run in newspapers and magazines across the country (see figure 5.1). In the photograph for the ad, smiling young men from the Corps camp line up behind Criss, who stands holding a double-sided ax just above the exposed neck of a seated and understandably nervous CCC enrollee. Upon closer inspection, it becomes clear that the face and neck of the seated enrollee are slathered in shaving cream. "Axes are not going to replace razors," explains the copy just below the photograph, "but this again demonstrates the fine quality of Kelly Axes."[1]

Throughout the New Deal era, manufacturers similarly enlisted the Corps to hawk a host of consumer goods to the American public. D. B. Smith and Company of Utica, New York, used photographs of CCC enrollees fighting forest fires in ads for their Indian water pumps, while the Warren Tool Corporation, the Bartlett Manufacturing Company, and the Case Company all mentioned the Corps when selling forestry and gardening tools, including tree pruners, pole saws, and bush hooks.[2] Such ads were not limited to conservation-related products. The Mapleine Company of Seattle, Washington, used a picture of a CCC enrollee eating a plate of pancakes to sell maple syrup, and advertisers in agricultural regions employed images of the Corps'

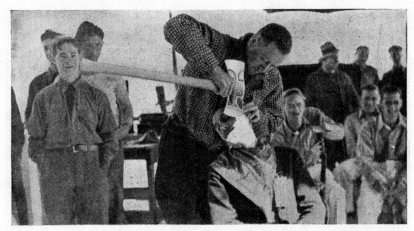

"... and it didn't hurt a bit!"

THIS photograph records an unusual incident during the 59th Annual Meeting of The American Forestry Association, held at the headquarters of the Tennessee Valley Authority (TVA), Knoxville, October 17-20, 1934.

The spectacular axe-man, Paul Criss, is demonstrating the possible keenness of a "Kelly Perfect" Axe. The photograph was taken at TVA, Camp 16.

That it was an interesting event is shown by the attention and evident amusement of the audience. The "Shavee" is the Secretary of the Great Smoky Mountain Hiking Association and the boys would not have been so complacent had they thought their pal was in danger. The result was a safe, easy, smooth shave; after which Paul showed the boys some expert chopping.

Of course, Axes are not going to replace razors, but this again demonstrates the fine quality of Kelly Axes.

Manufactured by

The AMERICAN FORK & HOE CO., Cleveland, O.
(Any Hardware Dealer Can Supply)

Figures 5.1 and 5.2 (facing page) Beginning in the mid-1930s, national companies began using the popularity of the CCC to hawk a host of products. In the first advertisement seen here, the American Fork and Hoe Company of Cleveland, Ohio, organized a publicity stunt in 1935 at a Tennessee Valley Authority CCC camp near Knoxville involving Paul Criss, the "spectacular axe-man." Here Criss's "razor," as well as the uniform of the enrollee standing in line for the next shave, would have been immediately identifiable to the American public as symbols of the Corps and its conservation work. The second advertisement indicates that as the 1930s wore on, and the Corps' popularity increased, manufacturers also tried to use the New Deal program to sell products that had little to do with the CCC or conservation. In this 1936 ad for Mapleine syrup, Americans again saw the familiar enrollee in Corps uniform staring back at them, but now he smiled over a steaming pile of pancakes. In case the public missed this visual cue, Mapleine placed this breakfast scene out in the forest and reminded readers in the text that the "C.C.C." serves Mapleine regularly in its camps. ("...and it didn't hurt a bit!" Advertisement for American Fork and Hoe Company, *American Forests* 41, no. 1 [January 1935]: 35. "Boy! That's Swell Syrup," Advertisement for Mapleine Syrup Company, *American Forests* 42, no. 7 [July 1936]: 332).

Boy! That's Swell Syrup

MAPLEINE
makes Syrup only
51¢ A GALLON

Cut your camp syrup costs in half with Mapleine!
It creates "lickin' good" syrup — only 51 cents a
gallon. America's leading restaurants, resorts,
camps and Uncle Sam's Army, Navy, C. C. C.
and Forest Service serve Mapleine Syrup regularly. To make it, just add Mapleine to hot water
and sugar. Easy, quick, and what swell syrup! Find
out more about Mapleine. Send for free sample
tomorrow — then put it on your purchase order.
Crescent Mfg. Co., 657 Dearborn St., Seattle.

FREE! WRITE FOR FREE SAMPLE —
MAKES TWO PINTS SYRUP!

MAPLEINE

soil conservation work when selling a variety of goods to farmers through mail
order catalogs and rural newspapers (see figure 5.2).[3] "I have been shown
some pages from farm papers illustrating how curved lines are taking the place
of straight lines in the background for advertisements," wrote New Dealer
Morris Cooke in the mid-1930s. The CCC's contour plowing practices, Cooke
concluded, "are obviously the inspiration for the advertisements."[4]

Such publicity suggests that, as the CCC altered the American landscape through its work projects, it was introducing conservation and the New Deal not just to the young men enrolled in the program and to the local community residents living near Corps camps but also to the wider American public. "The unemployed young men who moved by the tens of thousands from city streets and relief families into the forest and farm camps" were, in the words of the Corps' second director, James McEntee, "conservation evangelists."[5] Yet extensive media coverage of the CCC in print, on film, and across radio airwaves also exposed the New Deal and its most popular relief program to deeper scrutiny, especially by scientists and leaders of national conservation organizations, who began criticizing the CCC, and the President who created it, during the later 1930s. The result was a national debate over the Corps, its work projects, and at least four competing conservationist agendas that further transformed the politics of both the conservation movement and Franklin Roosevelt's liberal welfare state.

Throughout the 1930s, Roosevelt's CCC gained widespread notoriety as the best known of all New Deal programs. "No other relief agency has been so popular with the American people as the Civilian Conservation Corps," argued the *Pittsburgh Press* in August 1939. The *Mail Tribune* of Medford, Oregon, added, "Of all federal efforts to make the specter of insecurity take to its heels, the CCC has unquestionably been most popular and freest of public criticism!"[6] As New Dealer Rexford Tugwell wrote, "The CCC quickly became too popular for criticism."[7] While widespread, this popularity had not been immediate; opposition to the creation of the Corps had arisen from organized labor and from the Socialist and Communist parties. Illinois' Oscar de Priest, at the time the only African-American representative in the U.S. House, also opposed the bill establishing the Corps for its potential to discriminate against racial, ethnic, and religious minorities.[8]

During his first hundred days in office, Franklin Roosevelt took immediate steps to overcome such hostility to the CCC. Along with appointing labor organizers Robert Fechner and James McEntee to direct the Corps in an effort to appease unions, socialists, and communists, the president openly supported a nondiscriminatory amendment to the CCC bill proposed by Representative de Priest. Roosevelt even invited state governors from around the country to Washington, D.C., to teach them about the Corps and to ask for their support in getting the program off the ground.[9] Yet none of these efforts compare to the public relations campaign initiated by the Roosevelt administration to promote the Corps, and by association the New Deal, directly to the American people. To gauge public opinion about the CCC, Robert Fechner relied heavily on reports from the Press Intelligence Service, a federal agency created by Roosevelt to collect and analyze media coverage from across the country on various New Deal agencies. The CCC also attempted to mold popular opinion on the local, state, and especially the national level through a deliberate public relations campaign. Corps publicity director Guy McKinney oversaw this promotional effort from CCC headquarters in Washington, D.C., while Edgar Brown, the highest-ranking African American in the Corps' administrative hierarchy, supplied the black press with a similar stream of favorable copy.[10]

The CCC's promotional campaign used every available medium to publicize both the Corps and its conservation work. The Corps' publicity department sent out thousands of press releases to newspapers across the country, hundreds of feature articles to nationally syndicated magazines, and dozens of pamphlets on CCC work projects to forestry, farm, and conservation organizations as well as to community groups, such as chambers of commerce and town councils.[11] The CCC supplemented print media with word of mouth; the Corps' publicity staff wrote numerous speeches on the New Deal program for President Roosevelt, Director Fechner, and other government officials, while the CCC's "radio committee" often aired these speeches and even developed a series of radio programs aimed at educating the American public on the Corps and its conservation projects.[12] By 1935, the Corps had also created its own production company, which made more than thirty motion pictures depicting the CCC's work in the nation's forests, parks, and farms.[13] Fechner's publicity department even teamed up with the Works Progress Administration's Federal Theatre Project to bring a play written by two enrollees about life in the Corps to New York City's Broadway.[14]

The production by the CCC of press releases, radio programs, full-length feature films, and plays along the Great White Way, however, do little to explain how the program's work projects and the landscapes altered by them actually affected American citizens. In what ways did the Roosevelt administration promote the CCC and its conservation efforts to the country's voters? Did the national media simply accept this government propaganda, or did they translate it into something different for the public? Did the American people embrace a particular image of the Corps, and if so how did this image alter popular thinking about conservation and the welfare state? Answering these questions about the production, promotion, and consumption of the Corps' popularity illuminates how shifting conceptions of conservation during the 1930s and early 1940s in turn influenced New Deal politics.

The Corps' publicity campaign began soon after Congress created the CCC in March 1933 and at first focused on the program's earliest efforts to restore the nation's timber supplies. As enrollees during this period planted trees, thinned stands of trees, and fought forest fires, insects, and diseases, the Corps' publicity department in Washington, D.C., promoted such work to the national media. For instance, soon after enrollees from the CCC's first camp began protecting George Washington National Forest from fire by building lookout towers, constructing truck trails, and clearing combustible debris from the forest floor, the Corps sent out press releases to newspapers and magazines across the nation, stating that such work "greatly increased the value of the forest and added to its usefulness to the public."[15] Similar press releases followed throughout the 1930s and early 1940s, as did educational pamphlets and radio speeches that also described Corps forestry projects in detail.[16] "On a number of occasions during the last three years I have had the pleasure of talking to . . . the radio public generally about the Civilian Conservation Corps," stated Director Fechner on the National Broadcasting Company network in April 1936. "The work it is doing [will] gradually increase the usefulness and value of the nation's half billion acres of timbered lands."[17] The Corps even promoted such conservation work through film, producing several motion pictures on enrollees' forestry projects in New England and in California's coastal redwood region.[18]

In 1934, when the infamous Dust Bowl of the Great Plains forced the CCC to expand its work projects from the nation's forests onto its farms, Fechner's publicity department began publicly promoting the halting of soil erosion as an addition to the Corps' conservation repertoire. Soon after the CCC began helping Dust Bowl farmers to contour plow, terrace, and replant their fields with erosion-resistant crops, the Corps' Washington office sent out several press releases describing such work, and the following year the president himself undertook a nine-state speaking tour of the drought-stricken region to raise public awareness of both soil erosion and the CCC's efforts to halt it.[19] The Corps also ran feature articles on its soil conservation projects in magazines such as *Soil Conservation*, which in 1941 proclaimed that CCC enrollees were making "an invaluable contribution to the conservation of America's most vital natural resource—its soil."[20] Fechner's publicity department even helped the Soil Conservation Service produce a full-length feature film titled *The Heritage We Guard* on the dangers of soil erosion, and made several similar movies of its own to raise public awareness of Corps work projects aimed at conserving the country's soil resources.[21]

media picks up promo myths

In publicizing its work projects in the nation's forests and on its farms, the Corps was promoting a particular type of conservation. Robert Fechner defined what the CCC meant by conservation during these early New Deal years when he stated simply that Corps work was central in "the fight to conserve our natural resources."[22] Roosevelt used similar language in his fireside chat of May 7, 1933, when he told the American people that CCC projects on farms and in forests were "clearly enhancing the value of our natural resources," and Corps publicity director Guy McKinney repeated such sentiments when he explained that the CCC's "conservation films" depicted "the history of the destruction of our natural resources in this country and the steps being taken to remedy them."[23] This restoration of timber and soil resources by the Corps, President Roosevelt explained over and over again during the early 1930s to the American people, was a prime example of what he called "simple conservation."[24]

In promoting Corps work as "simple conservation," the Roosevelt administration was speaking the language of Progressives like Gifford Pinchot, who defined conservation narrowly as the efficient use of natural resources. Conservation, Pinchot often stated, entailed "the development and use of the earth and all its natural resources" for "the greatest good of the greatest number in the long run."[25] At the turn of the century, this utilitarian notion of conservation was known only within a small circle of scientists, government bureaucrats, and a narrow contingent of local landowners involved in natural resource extraction.[26] During the early 1930s, however, as the Corps began promoting its work in forests and on farms, the national media began picking up on the CCC's promotional efforts and publicizing to a new American audience the old idea that conservation meant restoring natural resources.

In response to the CCC's early promotional efforts, many newspapers, magazines, and radio programs incorporated well-worn myths and fables into their coverage of the CCC to spark interest and expand audiences. "Paul Bunyan was the daddy of all lumberjacks . . . he logged off the forests from Maine to Oregon," proclaimed *Popular Mechanics* magazine in an article titled "Rebuilding Paul Bunyan's Empire." The Corps, the article concluded, was now "putting back the forests he skinned off with his mighty ax."[27] Along with blaming Bunyan for the destruction of America's forests, the national media relied on military metaphors when describing Corps efforts to solve such problems. Magazines including the *New Republic*, the *Christian Science Monitor*, and *Popular Science Monthly* ran articles with titles such as "Roosevelt's Tree Army," "New Army Marches 'Over Here'," and "Army Recruited from Idle Men Wars against Fire and Flood" to gain and keep readers' attention.

As the *Christian Science Monitor* explained in April 1937, "When Franklin Delano Roosevelt . . . affixed his signature on March 31 to the bill facilitating his forest conservation-employment program, he in effect declared war on the waste and unproductive areas within the United States."[28]

The national media also publicized the Corps' soil conservation work, and here again newspapers, magazines, and radio programs relied on deep-rooted cultural symbols to arouse audiences. In this case, instead of spreading the CCC word through Paul Bunyan or "tree armies," editors and producers tapped into what historian Richard Hofstadter has called the "agrarian myth" in American culture, which idealizes independent farmers as the source of the country's democratic traditions.[29] "Pioneers indeed are the CCC enrollees who are fighting erosion in the Great Plains States," explained Ivy Howard in *Soil Conservation* magazine. "Trails blazed by them will be followed for generations . . . they pioneer in the field of erosion control."[30] Nelson Brown employed a similar migratory motif in an *American Forests* article on CCC enrollees titled "When East Goes West," in which he argued that "while the pioneer days have passed with the crossing of the last frontier, America is being rediscovered. Boys who would never have left the cities now appreciate the beauties and values to be found in the western part of the country."[31]

Whether they relied on military and agrarian metaphors or the fable of Bunyan and his blue ox, the national media often followed the Corps' lead and promoted CCC work in forests and on farms in terms that reflected conservation's Progressive Era roots. During the summer of 1935, for instance, the *Pittsburgh Press* sent a reporter to a "typical" CCC camp up in the mountains of southwestern Pennsylvania to write a series of articles that described Corps work projects as helping to "preserve our . . . natural resources."[32] The *Times* of Davenport, Iowa, similarly emphasized conservation as the efficient use of resources such as timber and soil. Corps conservation work in the nation's forests and fields, reported the *Times*, "can reverse a process by which the country was being denuded of much of its natural wealth."[33]

As the Corps promoted its conservation projects during the early New Deal years and as the national media publicized such work, ordinary Americans began to learn about natural resource conservation, many for the first time. The most obvious reflection of this newfound awareness was the flood of letters to newspaper editors that began soon after the Corps took to the woods. In a 1933 correspondence to the *New York Times* titled "Our New Kind of Army," for example, Cecillia Reber mixed her CCC metaphors when she compared Corps forestry work to "a war as vital as that of 1917–1918,"

news as source of Conservation enlightenment   *tree planting projects by women*   *schools alter curriculums*

and then noted that through such labor "our lost frontier is found again." Reber concluded with the simple statement that Corps conservation "destroyed the pests and hazards of the forests."[34] Similar letters written throughout the country suggest that unlike early conservationists such as Pinchot, who had to study forestry in Europe during the 1890s because there were then no forestry schools in the United States, ordinary people like Cecillia Reber could instead learn about conservation during the New Deal years simply by turning the pages of their local newspaper.

Americans in the 1930s, however, did more than simply read and write about the CCC and the conservation of natural resources; they replicated such work on their own as well. In particular, the general public was so enamored with the Corps' forestry projects that, soon after enrollees began such work, a tree-planting craze swept across the country. Women's groups were particularly active in this campaign, which began during the summer of 1933. As Milwaukee's Margaret March-Mount explained in August of that year, "since the popularity of the CCC... business and professional women have been credited with unusual interest in forestry." According to March-Mount, because of Corps efforts, the Democratic Women's Clubs of Wisconsin, the Minnesota Federation of Women's Clubs, and the Michigan Business and Professional Women's Clubs each planted memorial groves within their state's national forests.[35] By 1936, such efforts had spread nationally, with the General Federation of Women's Clubs launching a campaign in cooperation with the CCC to plant "Federation Forests" in every state of the union. That same year, the American Legion Auxiliary and the Daughters of the American Revolution initiated similar tree-planting drives with the help of the Corps and the U.S. Forest Service.[36]

Through the CCC's promotional efforts and the publicity generated by the national media, the Corps' soil conservation work also became quite popular with the American public. This newfound fame was most evident in the nation's schools, which during the mid-1930s began incorporating into their curriculum the study of soil erosion and the various methods of halting it. Drawing on the support and expertise of both the CCC and the Soil Conservation Service, teachers and administrators from elementary and secondary schools, colleges, and even entire school systems reformulated their curriculums, as one educator put it, to "bring soil conservation into the classrooms of the country."[37] The first step in this process involved educating teachers about soil conservation, which the CCC accomplished by inviting pedagogy classes from a number of institutions, such as the University of Seattle, Reed College, and the Tar Hollow Conservation Teaching Laboratory in Ohio, to nearby

public accepts program
CCC

CCC camps for training in the philosophy and techniques of soil conservation.[38] These teachers in turn took what they learned from the CCC and passed it on to their own students, often supplementing this hands-on training with written materials supplied by the Soil Conservation Service.[39] In the southeastern United States, for instance, the ten consolidated schools of Alamance County, North Carolina, developed their curriculum around the nearby CCC camp and its work on the Stony Creek Erosion Control Demonstration Area. Elementary and secondary school teachers from New Mexico to Missouri to Minnesota developed similar programs based on the premise that "the land is the text."[40]

As the Corps' forestry and soil work became popular with the American public during the mid-1930s, so too did the notion that conservation meant the efficient use of natural resources. Not only did private citizens create public organizations such as the Educational Conservation Society, which developed secondary school curriculums on "the conservation of the nation's natural resources," but interest in the conservation of timber and soil was on the rise outside the classroom as well.[41] As Indiana Department of Conservation commissioner Virgil Simmons explained, the "progress of Indiana's conservation program has been demonstrated in recent weeks with increased membership in conservation clubs, increased activity on the part of the clubs, and increased interest in the state's natural resources." According to Simmons, as the number of active conservation organizations in the state increased to an average of eleven groups per county, the number of conservation law violations decreased significantly because of the educational activities carried out by these conservation organizations in cooperation with government programs such as the CCC.[42] The situation was apparently similar on the national level. "I consider it a matter of great significance," explained Franklin Roosevelt to a supporter in 1939, "that now, according to the results of a recent poll of public opinion, the conservation of natural resources stands second in point of interest in the thoughts of Americans in all walks of life."[43]

Thus, in October 1938, when Corps director Robert Fechner wrote in *Forestry News Digest* that "the CCC has brought conservation into intimate contact with the daily lives of hundreds of thousands of American citizens," he had good reason to brag.[44] During the mid-1930s, as his office in Washington, D.C., began promoting the Corps' work in forests and on farms, and as the national media in turn publicized such projects in newspapers, in magazines, on radio, and in film, conservation became increasingly popular with the American people, influencing the charitable works of women's civic organizations, school curriculums, and even the way Americans sold products from saws to maple syrup. As important, during these early New Deal years at least, the American public was of one mind when it came to conservation, defining it in terms familiar to Progressives like Gifford Pinchot, who focused above all on the efficient use of natural resources such as timber and soil. Yet while popularizing this narrow notion of conservation, which Roosevelt labeled "simple conservation," the Corps' more expansive work in the nation's parks, involving the construction of hiking trails, campgrounds, and motor roads, began to publicize something quite different to the American public.

One year after the Dust Bowl blew the Corps from the nation's forests onto its farms, fear of a "recreation problem" in the United States sent the CCC scampering into the nation's parks, where Corps enrollees built a variety of recreational amenities. To validate and rally public support for such projects, the CCC's publicity office in Washington, D.C., began to promote this new type of work as conservation in its own right, albeit of a different sort. "In recent years an even broader concept of conservation has developed ... [which] has made clear the justification and necessity of preserving and conserving scenery for its social value," explained a CCC pamphlet entitled *The Civilian Conservation Corps and Public Recreation*.[45] Parks, the CCC began suggesting in the late 1930s, were social resources in urgent need of conservation.

In promoting recreational areas as social resources, the CCC argued that the development of parks by Corps enrollees helped to restore not forests or fields but the health and vigor of the American people. The initial step in this promotional campaign entailed educating the general public about the enervating effects of contemporary industrial society. "The complexity of modern life itself creates the need for recreation," wrote the Corps' publicity department in an educational pamphlet titled *The CCC and Its Contribution to a Nation-Wide State Park Recreational Program*. "The strain of urban living with its quick pace in business and social activities makes escape necessary to a person's well-being."[46] After describing the debilitating effects of city life, the Corps went on to promote its projects in parks as helping to reinvigorate the general public. By undertaking "park and forest developments for recreational ... purposes," explained a CCC pamphlet in 1941, "the Corps is making a vitally important contribution to conservation of the human wealth of the United States." This restoration of human resources, the same pamphlet concluded, "is helping to give expression to the highest meaning of conservation."[47]

The idea of conserving human resources was not completely foreign to CCC administrators. Healthful work in nature on CCC conservation projects, argued Director Fechner throughout the 1930s and early 1940s, would transform the sickly boys enrolling in the New Deal program into healthy American men. As the Corps expanded its work into the nation's parks, the CCC's publicity machine extended this logic from Corps enrollees to the general public. While enrollees' labor in nature would help to conserve the more than 3 million young men entering the New Deal program, increased access to outdoor leisure in parks developed by the CCC would conserve the health of American citizens. Corps recruitment administrator Frank Persons hinted at this expanded type of conservation in 1938 when he wrote, "Since 1933 the word 'conservation' has assumed new and significant meanings in our economic and social vocabulary."[48]

As soon as Corps administrators like Frank Persons began promoting the CCC's park development work as a form of social conservation, newspapers, magazines, radio stations, and film producers began to depict such projects as a means of conserving public health through increased access to outdoor recreation. At first, the national media touted the Corps' role in increasing access to previously remote areas for vigorous outdoor play. The building of roads and hiking trails by the CCC in Oregon's high country, argued *Oregon Motorist* magazine in June 1935, not only opened up "new worlds to conquer— new trout streams to fish, new mountain lakes to explore," but brought "the recreational benefits of these forest assets much nearer home to the average citizen."[49] The national media similarly praised the Corps for developing these newly accessible parks with a variety of outdoor recreational amenities such as swimming areas, campgrounds, and hiking shelters. "It is one thing to save timber and land, but quite another to build lakes and cabins and trails to the peaks," admitted a writer for *Recreation* in September 1935. "The park phase of the [Civilian Conservation Corps] took on great popularity ... because it combined conservation of resources for economic security and enjoyment of these resources in the furtherance of human happiness."[50] The national media thus enthusiastically embraced the CCC's promotional campaign; the Corps' park development work became the conservation of the American people in newspapers, in magazines, in films, and on radio shows across the country.

As the national media depicted Corps park work as helping to conserve public health, the notion that conservation involved human as well as natural resources became increasingly popular with the American people. This idea was especially important to outdoor enthusiasts, who during the late 1930s began to praise the CCC for helping Americans to become healthier. In Connecticut, for instance, anglers noted the social benefits of Corps efforts to restore trout populations in five of the state's streams through the construction

public approval — overwhelming

of small dams and current deflectors that helped fish to spawn. "Recreational outlets for the use of leisure time are essential to the economic welfare of the state no less than to its social welfare," explained Mary Pasco in an article on the Corps' Connecticut stream work.[51] Similar praise came from the New York Rod and Gun Editors Association, from numerous hiking clubs, and from the Izaak Walton League, one of the oldest and most active conservation organizations in the midwestern United States. "I am writing on behalf of the Housatonic Trail Club and speak for a group of nature lovers who have just had a hike through the Putatuck Forest, which is being developed by the CCC," wrote Ned Anderson to Franklin Roosevelt during the mid-1930s. "This State Forest adjoins our town, but not until your policy was put into effect has it meant anything to the public."[52] Corps labor, the hiker implied, had transformed this natural resource into a social one.

Thus, much like Corps work in the nation's forests and on its farms, CCC projects in the country's parks also helped to popularize conservation to the American public. "It has been on everyone's mind; it is on nearly everyone's tongue," wrote John Hatton in an article titled "New Things in Conservation." "It has had more inches of space in the columns of the press than any other single item of public interest." Yet whereas the CCC's efforts to restore the nation's timber and soil reserves helped to popularize conservation as the wise use of natural resources, the Corps' recreational development work in parks promoted something altogether different. "Conservation is more than forests; and the highest result in the conservation effort is best expressed in human welfare," continued Hatton, who concluded his article on new developments within the conservation movement by noting that the CCC and its work projects had popularized what he called "broader conservation."[53] "Conservation," agreed a journalist writing on the CCC for *Scientific American* in the mid-1930s, has become "a large word."[54]

Along with helping to redefine conservation in the public imagination, the Corps also transformed it into a more democratic movement, at least if the popularity of the Corps and its expanded conservation efforts are any indication. According to a Gallup poll conducted in 1936, 82 percent of those surveyed wanted the Corps to continue its conservation work both in forests and on farms as well as in parks. This support not only crossed party lines, with 92 percent of Democrats and 60 percent of Republicans in favor of maintaining the Corps, but spanned geographic regions as well; in no area of the country did approval for continuing the CCC fall below 80 percent.[55] A similar poll conducted three years later found that an astonishing 84 percent of Americans approved of the CCC and its conservation efforts.[56] In fact, so widespread was acceptance of the Corps that, by the end of the New Deal era, when the Gallup organization asked 1,500 Americans what they thought was the "greatest accomplishment of the Roosevelt administration," the third most-common response after the Works Progress Administration and banking reform was the Civilian Conservation Corps.[57] "It has been a good thing," admitted Republican congressman Charles Gifford, "Republicans and Democrats favor it."[58] "Broader conservation," it seems, had helped to broaden the composition of the conservation movement.

The Corps' widespread popularity also influenced the New Deal. Just as the CCC's work projects helped to democratize the movement and expand conservationist concerns during the 1930s and early 1940s, broader conservation similarly popularized Franklin Roosevelt's liberal agenda while simultaneously transforming it. On the most basic level, the CCC's fame undoubtedly rubbed off on the Roosevelt administration; by constantly referring to the Corps in public speeches, in radio interviews, and especially in his popular fireside chats, both the president and the New Deal basked in the CCC's glow. This popularity similarly helped Roosevelt to promote other New Deal programs associated with the CCC, such as the Soil Conservation Service and the Tennessee Valley Authority, both of which relied extensively on enrollee labor. "In creating this civilian conservation corps we are killing two birds with one stone," explained the president in one of his early fireside chats, "we are conserving not only our natural resources but our human resources." Roosevelt then continued his chat by linking this unique brand of conservation to New Deal plans for "the improvement of a vast area in the Tennessee Valley."[59] The Corps' broader conservation thus became a political advertisement for both the Roosevelt administration and a host of other New Deal programs.

In helping to popularize Roosevelt's liberal agenda, the CCC's expanded nation of conservation also altered New Deal politicking. This is perhaps most evident in the president's reelection efforts during the late 1930s and early 1940s. In 1936, for instance, Roosevelt made the Corps a staple of his stump speech, promising to make the temporary program permanent if given a second term, and he deliberately scheduled campaign stops around the country at Corps worksites, where the president continually emphasized the CCC's expanded conservation efforts.[60] "The men of the Civilian Conservation Corps, who have opened up Shenandoah National Park," explained the president in a speech at the park three months before the 1936 election, are "part of our great program of husbandry—the joint husbandry of human resources and natural resources."[61] Roosevelt did similarly during each of his reelection campaigns, in effect using

Corps work projects themselves as physical advertisements for the New Deal.[62] Although the impact of this campaign strategy is difficult to assess, in 1936, with the Corps' overall popularity standing at 82 percent, Roosevelt won reelection by the second largest popular vote in U.S. history. If CCC work projects had even a minimal impact on this landslide victory, broader conservation helped the president to embed political support for the welfare state quite literally across the American landscape.

Not everyone was happy with broader conservation, however. During the later 1930s, while the Corps was becoming ever more popular with the general public, an increasingly vocal minority began to criticize the CCC and its conservation projects. Much like support for the Corps on the local level, which depended to a great extent on the type of conservation work being performed nearby, opposition to the CCC also differed depending on whether critics were condemning Corps projects aimed at conserving natural or human resources. Aldo Leopold, for instance, who worked closely with the CCC in its efforts to halt soil erosion in Coon Valley, criticized the Corps for quite different reasons than those espoused by Bob Marshall, who experienced firsthand CCC work that developed Great Smoky Mountains National Park for outdoor recreation. Exploring these differences and tracing this pair of critiques onto the national stage are essential to understanding the conservation debate that took place during the late 1930s and early 1940s as well as its effect on New Deal politics.

During the early 1930s, Leopold was a CCC booster, overseeing Corps forestry projects in the Southwest and convincing the Roosevelt administration to bring the CCC to Coon Valley. Leopold even agreed to supervise a Corps conservation project at the University of Wisconsin's Arboretum and Wild Life Refuge during the mid-1930s. But as the Great Depression continued, Leopold's patience with the Corps and its conservation efforts faltered. Although he would later join those opposing CCC recreation work, at first Leopold restricted his criticism to Corps projects with which he was intimately familiar, namely, those aimed at restoring natural resources.[63] "The abstract categories we have set up as conservation objectives may serve as alibis for blunders," Leopold wrote in *American Forests* magazine in March 1936. "I cite in evidence the CCC crew which chopped down one of the few remaining eagle's nests in northern Wisconsin, in the name of 'timber stand improvement.' "[64] Two years later, Leopold's censure of the Corps had moved beyond the local. "The recent drainage of nearly the whole Atlantic tidal marsh from Maine to Alabama . . . was done with relief labor in the name of mosquito control," he wrote in 1938 of the CCC's work up and down the

Leopold's opposition

East Coast. "These marshes are the wintering ground of many species of migratory waterfowl and the breeding ground of others."[65] What had begun as opposition to Corps work in his own backyard, so to speak, became for Leopold in the late 1930s a more comprehensive critique of CCC conservation as a whole.

Leopold's opposition to the Corps on the grounds that it threatened wildlife was actually part of a more substantial condemnation of the CCC and its conservation work, one that he had begun articulating in March 1934 in a talk before the University of Wisconsin's Taylor-Hibbard Economics Club. Titled "Conservation Economics," Leopold's speech was his first public statement on New Deal conservation practices, and while he praised the Roosevelt administration for having made great strides in the area of conservation, he criticized programs such as the Corps for a lack of coordination that often led to "conflicts of interest" among New Deal agencies. "CCC camp crews were directed by brainy young technicians . . . each schooled only in his particular 'specialty'," Leopold complained. The result was a host of environmental problems. There were Corps "road crews cutting a grade along a clay bank so as permanently to roil the trout stream which another crew was improving with dams and shelters," argued Leopold, as well as "silvicultural crews felling 'wolf trees' and border shrubbery needed for game food." Even the Corps' reforestation work, which during the early 1930s had fostered a tree-planting fad, came up for criticism from Leopold because it caused the "setting [of] pines all over the only open clover patch available to the deer and partridges." The result of such uncoordinated conservation, Leopold concluded, was that "the ecological . . . limitations of 'scientific' technology were revealed in all their nakedness."[66]

The members of the Taylor-Hibbard Economics Club undoubtedly had difficulty understanding Leopold's reference in March 1934, since at this time the term "ecology" remained unfamiliar to most Americans. Although Ernest Haeckel, a German follower of Charles Darwin, had used the word in the late 1860s, in the United States during the 1930s the field of ecology was still developing as the interrelated study of plant and animal communities. Researchers interested in these ecological processes were particularly active in the American West and included Frederick Clements of the University of Nebraska, Victor Shelford from the University of Illinois, the entomologist Roger Smith from Kansas State Agricultural College, and Oklahoma ecologist Paul Sears. When Aldo Leopold gave his Taylor-Hibbard speech in 1934, few Americans beyond this tight-knit academic community were familiar with the term "ecology," let alone its biological applications. As historian

Worster   Leopold

Donald Worster has written of ecology in the 1930s, "up until this point, the conservation movement in America had been overwhelmingly dominated by a series of uncoordinated resource management programs" rather than by the "principles of scientific ecology."[67]

In opposing the Corps on ecological grounds, Aldo Leopold put forth his own definition of conservation, one quite different from that promoted by the CCC. "To apply conservation to the land," Leopold explained in a 1935 essay on his experiences in Coon Valley, New Deal programs such as the CCC must "reorganize and gear up the farming, forestry, game cropping, erosion control, [and] scenery ... so that they collectively comprise a harmonious balanced system of land use."[68] This interest in biological equilibrium and a more holistic approach to conservation appears repeatedly in Leopold's writings during the late 1930s. "Doesn't conservation imply a certain interspersion of land-uses, a certain pepper-and-salt pattern in the warp and woof of the land-use fabric?" he asked in a 1939 essay titled "The Farmer as Conservationist." Leopold's answer was that "the pattern of the rural landscape, like the config-uration of our own bodies, has in it (or should have in it) a certain whole-ness."[69] In opposing the Corps, Aldo Leopold thus put forth a definition of conservation that rested on neither natural nor human resources. Instead, he turned to the emerging field of ecology, and used its notion of biological balance to give new meaning to the Corps' conservation practices.

Opposition to the Corps on ecological grounds, and the promotion of an alternative conservation associated with biological equilibrium, quickly spread to a wider circle of scientists during the mid- to late 1930s. Not surprisingly, some of the first adherents of this ecological critique also taught and conducted research at the University of Wisconsin, where Leopold began working in September 1933. Conservation biologist Leonard Wing was the first of Leopold's colleagues to publicly oppose the Corps and its work. "In a few years, I fear, we shall look upon these early days of the CCC as a crowning blunder in conservation," Wing wrote in a 1936 *American Forests* article. "Lumber-farmers armed the CCC with saws, axes, shovels and matches and sent them on the trail of 'weed trees'." As a result, Wing explained, "the deciduous growth goes, the snags go, the fallen logs go; no browse for deer, no buds for grouse, no tender bark for rabbits, no holes for birds, no drum-ming logs for partridges." While criticizing the Corps for biological blunders Wing, like Leopold, put forth a more ecological view of conservation. "The conservation biologist is a new entry into the field of conservation," Wing wrote in the same article on the Corps. "He is the natural result of the need for better application of biological and ecological principles."[70]

[handwritten marginalia: "Fernald criticizes" written in top-left; "academia opposes CC media, too" written across the top]

The ecological critique of the CCC and its conservation work put forth by Leopold and Wing migrated from the Midwest eastward and took root in the academic halls of Cambridge, Massachusetts, and Philadelphia. In the latter city on May 20, 1938, before a scientific gathering at the Franklin Institute, Harvard botany professor Merritt L. Fernald delivered a scathing rebuke of the Corps, during which he called CCC enrollees "misguided and enthusiastic young men," and blamed the New Deal program for destroying rare and exotic plant species. "The building of artificial ponds, and bridges, the making of roads and the planting of introduced trees and shrubs is not conservation," Fernald explained to his audience of fellow scientists. "Indeed, it is just the opposite of true conservation, for it upsets the natural equilibrium which had become established long before man."[71] Ecological balance, not the wise use of natural and human resources, was central to Fernald's scientific definition of conservation.

Ecological opposition to the CCC, and the promotion by scientists of what Fernald called "true conservation," quickly made its way to the nation's capital and from there spread across the continent by way of the national parks. The journey began during the mid-1930s when George Wright, chief of the National Park Service's Wild Life Division, convinced his superiors to use CCC funds to hire wildlife biologists to monitor Corps conservation projects in national parks. As the number of wildlife biologists under Wright's command grew from three to twenty-seven by 1936, so too did their complaints against the CCC, especially regarding the Corps' forest fire protection work.[72] In the winter of 1934, for instance, Wright petitioned Park Service director Arno Cammerer to "reconsider" CCC fire prevention work involving the clearing of dead, combustible wood from forest floors because such projects changed park habitats in ways that threatened "wild life values."[73] Park Service wildlife biologists were equally alarmed at the Corps' war against forest insects and diseases. In a 1935 report on CCC work in Grand Canyon National Park, Victor Cahalane explained quite simply that his Wild Life Division "disapproves of insect control" by enrollees. The same year, after visiting Mount Rainier National Park, wildlife biologist Adolph Murie argued similarly that the Park Service should not "play nursemaid more than is essential." Instead, Murie advocated leaving forest insects and diseases alone, and "permitting natural events to take their course."[74] Letting nature be, these scientists believed, was sometimes the key ingredient to successful conservation practices.

As this scientific opposition to the Corps spread throughout academia and the Park Service, the national media also began to criticize the CCC for being ecologically irresponsible. Newspapers throughout the country and nationally syndicated magazines reprinted Leopold's essays about the Corps, and ran their own feature articles on his biological opposition to CCC work.[75] These same media outlets also covered scientists' critiques, especially that leveled by Harvard's Merritt Fernald, whose rebuke of the Corps at Philadelphia's Franklin Institute made the front page of the *New York Times* and was later picked up by a number of popular magazines.[76] Professor Fernald "was voicing an opinion which is becoming widespread among naturalists and plant lovers," explained *Horticulture* magazine editor Edward Farrington in June 1938. "Unless the work of the CCC is done under intelligent supervision, what has been described as a project in the interest of conservation, may become instead a serious menace." Farrington concluded his editorial by explaining to readers that "the balance of nature is a delicate thing [and] when this balance is upset, it interferes with the natural development of bird life, wild animal life and plant life."[77]

Along with criticizing the Corps on scientific grounds, newspapers and magazines throughout the country began to promote ecology as important to the conservation movement, much as Aldo Leopold had done. Of particular importance was the ecological belief in the interconnectedness of nature. "It goes without saying that conservationists admit the necessity of some control work that is being done," explained *American Game* magazine in 1935. Yet the conservation movement as a whole must "readily appreciate that conditions affecting one form of wildlife must, almost certainly, affect others."[78] Along with promoting a more holistic view of the natural world, reporters critical of the Corps also emphasized that in some instances conservation should entail no work at all. "Those persons having an interest in maintaining the natural environment," argued the same magazine, should be alarmed at "the prospect of having 250,000 [CCC] men working on forest land for a period of six months."[79] "True conservation," newspapers and magazines began to argue in the late 1930s, sometimes meant letting nature take its course.

As they read newspapers and magazines, listened to the radio, and watched films, the American public picked up on this ecological critique and began to express similar opposition to the Corps through a variety of means, not the least of which was writing directly to the president. "It is most unfortunate that the CCC, with its record of devastation ... has had to be turned loose on the Okefenokee," wrote Jean Harper to Franklin Roosevelt in May 1937. Harper was concerned specifically about the introduction of exotic Asian chestnut trees into the Georgia swamp, and used ecological language to scold the president, stating, "every real naturalist knows that the paramount policy in such an area should be non-interference with nature."[80] When bureaucratic channels in Washington proved ineffective, many Americans turned to their newspapers or wrote letters to the editors of their favorite magazines. "What I saw of the workings of the New Deal made me sick at heart and almost at stomach," wrote W. B. Sheppard in the *New York Times* of Corps forest protection work. Clearing dead and combustible debris from the forest floor "simply defeats Nature's processes and purpose, for it is rotting leaves and fallen logs that constitute the fertilizer and the soil itself."[81]

Citizens did not merely criticize the CCC, they too began arguing that ecological science was key to conservation. Perhaps the best indication of this was the increased involvement by the public during the mid-1930s in conservation groups working to promote ecological balance. The first of such campaigns involved the Emergency Conservation Committee, an organization composed of disgruntled Audubon Society members who wanted to make the bird group a more active participant in the conservation movement. Led by suffragist Rosalie Edge and funded by wealthy businessperson Willard Van Name, the committee in 1934 began railing against the CCC for its predator and rodent control work, which often involved poisons harmful to wildlife. "Most shameful of all is the teaching of our CCC boys to poison harmless and valuable wild creatures," wrote the committee in its 1934 annual report. The Corps' predator control projects, warned Edge five years later, "involves the whole profound study of ecology" and poses "a problem of the balance of all living things."[82] The Emergency Conservation Committee continued its eco- logical critique of the Corps into the early 1940s by mailing anti-CCC pamph- lets to thousands of conservationists and by writing a slew of letters critical of the Corps to newspapers and magazines across the country.[83]

Partly in response to criticism leveled by the Emergency Conservation Committee, which chastised other conservation organizations for not taking a tougher stand against the CCC, the Audubon Society initiated a nearly decade-long campaign of its own that also opposed the Corps on ecological grounds.[84] This initiative began in May 1935, when the National Association of Audubon Societies' executive director, John Baker, sent a string of letters to Corps director Robert Fechner complaining that the CCC's use of poison was contrary to "sound understandings of biological and ecological relation- ships."[85] Two years later, the society asked its members to write their own letters underscoring this point and mail them to both Fechner and President Roosevelt, and it also passed a resolution condemning CCC predator control work for disrupting the "natural balance" of mammal populations.[86] Through additional letter-writing campaigns and articles in Audubon publications such as *Bird-Lore* magazine, American citizens attacked other CCC projects as well—from the building of roads across wildlife habitat and the digging of artificial ponds for water conservation, to the draining of swamps in an effort to eliminate mosquito breeding grounds—all on ecological grounds. Such work projects, wrote Audubon Society member Warren Eaton in the July 1935 issue of *Bird-Lore*, are often mistakenly "heralded as conservation" when in fact they are "far-reaching in [their] effect on Nature...sometimes harmful in varying degrees."[87]

The efforts of citizens involved in the Emergency Conservation Committee and the National Association of Audubon Societies against the CCC were not isolated events. Similar campaigns opposing CCC work on ecological grounds occurred intermittently across the country during the later New Deal years. In Minnesota, for example, a coalition of conservationists led by the Izaak Walton League protested CCC road projects that threatened formerly inaccessible duck habitat in the northern reaches of that state, and ultimately succeeded in convincing the federal government to launch a full-scale investigation of such work.[88] Conservationists in New Jersey took similar action against CCC mosquito control projects by blocking fiscal appropriations for both swamp drainage and the allocation of CCC camps in various portions of that state.[89] Finally, in 1938, several conservationists frustrated with the administrative inconsistencies of New Deal conservation programs, including the Corps, joined together to create the National Wildlife Federation, which during the late 1930s and early 1940s publicly opposed the CCC's draining of swamps in the name of mosquito control.[90]

Thus, during the later 1930s, increasing numbers of Americans in every corner of the country followed Aldo Leopold's lead and began openly criticizing the Corps for being ecologically reckless. Scientists like Harvard's Merritt Fernald in the Northeast, concerned citizens such as Georgia's Jean Harper in the South, and members of midwestern conservation groups like the Izaak Walton League all opposed CCC projects for upsetting "nature's balance" and promoted instead what many were calling "true conservation" based on ecological science. While coming from a variety of backgrounds and regions, these opponents shared a common concern for those Corps projects aimed specifically at conserving natural resources such as timber, soil, and in many cases wildlife. Although the CCC's park development work aimed at conserving human resources did not worry these activists, it did alarm others who also began opposing the Corps during the later 1930s, but for very different reasons. Bob Marshall, for instance, became increasingly concerned with CCC recreation projects in Great Smoky Mountains National Park. While this second front against the CCC also began locally with individuals who experienced Corps park work firsthand, it too spread to the national stage and influenced the debate taking place nationwide about the very meaning of conservation, and New Deal politics, during the Great Depression.

Just as Aldo Leopold's early critique of the CCC grew from his local experiences in Coon Valley, Wisconsin, Bob Marshall's opposition to the Corps took root during a trip to the Great Smoky Mountains in August 1934. During that summer, the Roosevelt administration sent Marshall to the national park to scout a route for the Blue Ridge Parkway's southern terminus, which was supposed to run along the crest of the Smokies and join up with a thoroughfare called Clingmans Dome Road in the very center of the park. Marshall knew from experience that thousands of CCC enrollees stationed in the park had helped to construct Clingmans Dome Road, and that park superintendent Ross Eakin had already formulated plans to use these same enrollees to extend the road into a Skyway running along the entire ridgeline of the Smokies.[91] Marshall was also aware that this road work was not an isolated event. In part because of surplus Corps labor, during the early 1930s, the Roosevelt administration had floated similar proposals for the construction of "skyline" drives atop the crests of the Presidential and Green mountain ranges in New Hampshire and Vermont, and along more than 300 miles of the Blue Ridge Mountains running from Virginia's Shenandoah National Park to the Great Smoky Mountains.[92] Alarmed by such plans, Marshall had warned Emergency Conservation Committee funder Willard Van Name about "the prospect of needless roads building into the few wilderness areas which remain through the use of emergency funds" for CCC camps.[93]

Bob Marshall had planted the seeds of this opposition three years before CCC enrollees moved into the Great Smoky Mountains, in an article he wrote for *Scientific Monthly* magazine entitled "The Problem of the Wilderness." According to Marshall's essay, there were three societal benefits of untrammeled wilderness. Not only did it restore the body and mind of those weakened by modern living, but its beauty also bordered on the spiritual. "Wilderness furnishes perhaps the best opportunity for pure aesthetic enjoyment," wrote Marshall in "The Problem of the Wilderness." "The purely aesthetic observer has for the moment forgotten his own soul."[94] For Marshall, plans to build a Skyway across the Smokies with CCC labor would threaten wilderness as well as the mental, physical, and spiritual character of the American people.

While Marshall's critique of the Corps was quite novel, his desire to defend wilderness from development by the federal government harked back more than twenty years to the battle over Hetch Hetchy. Back in the early 1910s, however, it was John Muir who fought the federal government's plan to destroy wilderness, in that case through the construction of a dam in Yosemite National Park. Although Bob Marshall was a trained forester very much in the tradition of Gifford Pinchot, during the early 1930s he positioned himself squarely in John Muir's camp, and even mentioned the Sierra Club founder in his "The Problem of the Wilderness" article.[95] Wild nature, Marshall claimed, enabled a "number of America's most virile minds including . . . John Muir . . . to meditate, unprejudiced by the immuring civilization."[96] Whereas Muir fought dams in Yosemite, Marshall battled skyline roads being built with CCC labor along the crest of Great Smoky Mountains National Park.

While Aldo Leopold's ideas about conservation first filtered into academia, Marshall's concerns that the Corps threatened wilderness spread initially through government bureaus involved directly in CCC recreation work. During the early to mid-1930s, Marshall besieged fellow government officials, including Park Service director Arno Cammerer and U.S. Forest Service chief Ferdinand Silcox, with letters, telephone calls, and personal visits that called attention to the Corps' role in destroying wilderness. "The bulldozers are already rumbling up into the mountains," Marshall wrote to Silcox in 1935. "Unless you act very soon on the seven primitive area projects I presented to you a month ago, eager CCC boys will have demolished the greatest wildernesses which remain in the United States."[97] He similarly contacted Appalachian Trail creator Benton MacKaye, who had worked with the Corps as a Tennessee Valley Authority regional planner and as area supervisor for Corps work on the nation's Indian reservations, and Aldo Leopold, who was already criticizing CCC work in Coon Valley.

Such contacts proved to be especially important during Marshall's skyline drive scouting trip to the Smokies during the summer of 1934. It was on this trip that Marshall not only fortified his critique of CCC park development work but also took steps to institutionalize this opposition by discussing the Skyway and other ridgetop roads with MacKaye and Knoxville lawyer Harvey Broome. The three men met again in Knoxville the following year with Bernard Frank, a Tennessee Valley Authority administrator whose experiences with the Corps raised similar concerns, and together they decided to mail out an "Invitation to Help Organize a Group to Preserve the American Wilderness." The direct-mail piece, sent to individuals known to be deeply concerned about motor roads such as the Great Smoky Mountain Skyway, expressed the need "to integrate the growing sentiment which [they] believe exists in this country for holding wild areas sound-proof as well as sight-proof from our increasingly mechanized life."[98] The overwhelming response to the invitation encouraged these men in 1935 to establish the Wilderness Society in an effort to protect wild areas threatened by development.

Not surprisingly, those joining the Wilderness Society publicly denounced Corps road-building projects for destroying wild nature. Such attacks began in earnest in 1934 in an article written by society founder Benton MacKaye entitled "Flankline vs. Skyline." "The essence of wilderness is solitude," argued MacKaye, and the development of ridgetop motor roads like those constructed with CCC labor destroyed this quality.[99] Wilderness enthusiasts similarly criticized the Corps' forest fire protection work, which often included the construction of truck trails for the quick movement of firefighting men and equipment through national forests. "Considerable discussion and some objections have occurred among conservationists in respect to so-called 'truck trails,' proposed to be constructed by Civilian Conservation Corps camps," explained *Living Wilderness*, the Wilderness Society's official magazine.[100] In an effort to promote such concerns to a wider audience, Bob Marshall made a similar argument in the April 1937 edition of *Nature* magazine, explaining to readers in nontechnical, straightforward language that "the most prevalent destruction of wilderness comes from truck trails that are built for fire protection" by relief workers, including CCC enrollees.[101]

The Wilderness Society also blamed the Corps' other recreation projects in national parks and forests for destroying so-called "primitive" wilderness. "Today energetic CCC camps" constructing campgrounds, comfort stations, visitor centers, and the like "are busy turning nearly all these [wilderness areas] into public parks with all modern conveniences," complained Wilderness Society member Arthur Morgan in a 1936 edition of *Living Wilderness*.[102] Even the Corps' hiking trail work came under attack. "I saw with alarm the growing tendency to make magnificent mountain country, whose very aloofness from civilization is one of its greatest charms, extremely accessible to hordes of tourists," argued Wilderness Society member Georgia Engelhard, "not only by the construction of trans-mountain motor roads but also by the construction of well-groomed trails, whose equal might only be found in [Washington, D.C.'s] Rock Creek Park, and whose presence utterly destroys the virgin wilderness."[103]

Along with condemning Corps recreation work for threatening wilderness, the society claimed that such projects were equally dangerous for the conservation movement. "The Wilderness Society is born of an emergency in conservation," wrote Wilderness Society president Robert Sterling Yard in 1935 in the inaugural issue of *Living Wilderness*. The contemporary conservation crisis had arisen, Yard explained, because New Deal programs such as the

Corps want to "barber and manicure wild America as smartly as the modern girl."[104] To solve this predicament, the society put forth its own version of conservation that focused not only on natural resources such as timber and soil, and on human resources through the development of recreation areas, but also on undeveloped wild nature as a social resource in its own right. According to Yard, primitive areas, much like clean water, fertile soil, and ample timber reserves, are "a serious human need rather than a luxury and plaything."[105] By portraying wilderness as a social resource in need of protection from federal programs such as the CCC, the Wilderness Society was bringing concern for wilderness back into the conservationist fold.

The national media picked up on wilderness enthusiasts' critique and began to raise similar concerns about the Corps' park development work. *Collier's* and other national magazines, for example, began running their own articles criticizing CCC recreation projects. The *Saturday Evening Post* took the words nearly verbatim out of Robert Sterling Yard's mouth when it explained to readers that "there is a tendency at times" on the part of the Corps "to over-manicure the wilderness."[106] Even the *Journal of Forestry*, which throughout the 1930s and early 1940s overwhelmingly supported the Corps and its conservation efforts, had to admit to its readers in 1936 that CCC "road work is running somewhat ahead of present requirements."[107]

Along with blaming the Corps for destroying wilderness, the national media also began publicizing the preservation of wild areas as a new component of conservation. In October 1935, the *New York Times* placed the CCC's threat to wilderness squarely within a larger dialogue taking place among the state's conservation organizations, explaining in an editorial that " 'truck trails' ... built by CCC labor ... have become a lively topic of debate among local conservationists."[108] *Nature Magazine* also situated wilderness preservation within conservationist concerns by blaming the Corps for failing to live up to its name. "There is a new threat against the wilderness ideal far greater than all former menaces combined," warned *Nature* in 1935, and "curiously enough, this menace comes from an agency created in the name of conservation ... the Civilian Conservation Corps."[109] Two years later, the magazine was still situating wilderness within the conservation movement, calling opposition to CCC projects that threatened wilderness an important "hobby in conservation."[110]

As newspapers and magazines continued to publicize wilderness advocates' opposition to Corps park projects, the general public began to take notice. Following the Wilderness Society's lead, Americans in increasing numbers during the mid- to late 1930s began blaming the Corps and its conservation work, especially that involving recreational development in national parks and forests, for destroying the "primitive" quality of America's public lands. "The CCC cuts auto roads all through the forests... builds swimming pools, refreshment stands, playgrounds all over," lamented E. R. Lehnert in a *New York Times* letter to the editor entitled "Parking the Wilderness." "The CCC is making our forests as tame and artificial as city parks."[111] Another *New York Times* reader agreed. In a scathing letter to the editor titled "Conservation in Reverse," a self-proclaimed "habitué of the wilderness" described a summer visit to the redwood region of the Pacific Coast where he saw "with a feeling of despair, how the CCC men were performing the task of conservation by means of the axe."[112] While many Americans expressed similar views in the nation's newspapers and magazines, perhaps the best indication that the general public had begun to reincorporate wilderness preservation back into the conservationist agenda was the number of conservation organizations nationwide that joined the Wilderness Society's campaign against CCC park development projects.

The best known of these citizen efforts on behalf of wilderness during the mid- to late 1930s involved the Association for the Protection of the Adirondacks, which opposed Corps conservation work in New York state's Adirondack State Park. Founded as a public watchdog group in 1899 to ensure that the forest preserve would be kept "forever wild," as required by the New York state constitution, the association first expressed concern regarding CCC projects, including the building of truck trails and artificial ponds for fire control purposes, at the group's board meeting in May 1933. A year and a half later, members again took action against such work by dispatching an inspection team to examine Corps work sites throughout the forest preserve, and by organizing a statewide campaign involving twenty New York conservation organizations to oppose such projects. The Wilderness Society's Bob Marshall, who also served on the Adirondack association's board of trustees, even wrote a letter of protest to New York state conservation commissioner Lithgow Osborne. Because of such efforts, and to better assess CCC conservation work in the preserve, New York governor Herbert H. Lehman appointed an advisory committee, which after intense lobbying by the Association for the Protection of the Adirondacks, recommended that proposed Corps work on truck trails and artificial ponds in the forest preserve be abandoned.[113] "The truck trail program in the Adirondack Park in New York State, conducted since 1934 with the labor of the Civilian Conservation Corps... is now practically halted," boasted one Adirondack association member in November 1936. "This was largely due to objections by... conservationists."[114]

As news of the victory in the Adirondacks spread, citizen groups in other areas of the country similarly embraced both the Wilderness Society's critique of Corps work and the belief that wilderness preservation was central to conservation. In nearby Vermont, residents opposed a proposed motor road, to be constructed with New Deal labor along the crest of the Green Mountains, and campaigned against other Corps projects that threatened the wild character of that state. "Lacking other chores, a CCC gang was put in here to clear up the woods," explained Bread Loaf resident Walter Eaton. "Before they were stopped, the gang had 'improved' about twenty acres, converting a wild mountain forest to an imitation Central Park."[115] Similar complaints echoed from the Rocky Mountains. "No more will the traveler unsaddle his ponies to roll and graze on the bunch grass of the mountain tops . . . no more will the mountain man ride the high ridges," mourned Elers Koch soon after the Corps located several camps in the Selway-Salmon River valley of central Idaho. Instead, the "trucks roll by on the new Forest Service road" built by the CCC.[116]

Perhaps because of John Muir's legacy in the state, Californians were especially active in opposing Corps work on the grounds that it threatened wilderness. The Save the Redwoods League kept a vigilant eye on CCC camps in the northern coastal portion of the state, while other conservation organizations openly opposed Corps work projects in the Sierra Nevadas.[117] One such group was the Commonwealth Club of California, which in July 1935 voted to have its Committee on Forestry and Wildlife examine CCC road projects in the Sierras. Due to the committee's report, the club overwhelmingly passed a resolution condemning such work and warned that, if the Corps were allowed to continue, the "wilderness which has exerted such a fundamental influence in molding American character will be in the musty pages of pioneer books and the mumbled memories of tottering antiquarians."[118] Finally, a group of outdoor outfitters calling itself the High Sierra Packers' Association promoted what it called "wilderness conservation" through a campaign in April 1938 that included a petition drive against CCC road-building projects. According to one participant, only a "militant stand by conservationists will . . . save our back country from ultimate disappearance."[119] During the mid-1930s, a coalition of conservation organizations, including the Izaak Walton League, the American Nature Association, the American Wildlife Institute, the National Wildlife Federation, and the Sierra Club, also opposed road building by New Deal programs such as the CCC in the Sierra Nevadas, while promoting wilderness preservation in what eventually became Kings Canyon National Park.[120]

During the mid- to late 1930s, then, more and more Americans took Bob Marshall's philosophy to heart and began to criticize the CCC for destroying wilderness. Government administrators who had worked with the Corps including Benton MacKaye and Bernard Frank, concerned individuals such as New York City's E. R. Lehnert, and members of a host of citizen groups from the Association for the Protection of the Adirondacks in the East to the Sierra Club out West, all opposed Corps projects for threatening wild nature. Instead, this anti-CCC faction promoted what many were calling "wilderness conservation," which placed the preservation of wild areas centrally within conservationist concerns. Although these critics hailed from a variety of backgrounds and geographic regions, they shared a common concern specifically for those Corps work projects aimed at developing parks and forests for increased outdoor recreation. While other Americans during the New Deal era saw the construction of campgrounds, hiking trails, and even motor roads as means of conserving human resources through increased access to healthful outdoor play, those following Marshall's lead believed instead that these same projects threatened wilderness and thus citizens' ability to recreate in it.

In October 1934, when "the spectacular axe-man" Paul Criss shaved a CCC enrollee in a national advertisement for the American Fork and Hoe Company, he did more than promote the efficiency of Kelly axes. Criss was also publicizing the Corps to the American people. The national media did similarly by writing about, photographing, recording, and filming young CCC enrollees as they undertook work projects involving the conservation of timber and soil and the development of the nation's parks. Many of the citizens who encountered such publicity in turn embraced the conservation movement by planting trees in their communities, teaching soil conservation in their classrooms, and joining conservation organizations in increasing numbers across the country. Extensive media coverage of the CCC during the New Deal era thus helped to further democratize the conservation movement beyond the small group of Progressives already familiar with it, and the enrollees and local community residents who learned about it by laboring on, and living near, Corps work projects, to include as well ordinary Americans who read about reforestation in their newspapers, heard about soil erosion on their radios, and watched enrollees develop national parks for outdoor recreation in films at neighborhood movie halls. As *Scientific Monthly* explained to its readers in a 1943 article entitled "The CCC and American Conservation," by transforming the American landscape through its work projects the Corps "brought to the American people a better idea of conservation."[121]

In making the movement more grassroots, however, the Corps also altered the very definition of conservation during the New Deal era. "The CCC," argued the same *Scientific Monthly* article on conservation, "gave new meaning of the word to foresters, soil scientists, naturalists, and other conservationists."[122] It did the same for the American public and in the process sparked a national debate over what, exactly, conservation meant. Was Corps work an example of what Franklin Roosevelt called "simple conservation," a narrow definition that reflected Gifford Pinchot's Progressive Era concerns for natural resources such as timber and soil? Or was the CCC undertaking "broader conservation," as one reporter put it during the mid-1930s, aimed also at conserving "human resources" through the development of public parks like those built a generation earlier by Frederick Law Olmsted? During the later 1930s, those opposing Corps work promoted two additional definitions of conservation in newspapers and magazines, on radio, and in films. For Americans who read about Aldo Leopold's ecological critique of CCC projects in forests and on farms, "true conservation," as Merritt Fernald called it, entailed not just an interest in natural and human resources but a concern for "the balance of nature" as well. Finally, citizens familiar with the efforts of groups like Bob Marshall's Wilderness Society, which opposed CCC recreation work for destroying "primitive" areas, embraced instead what the High Sierra Packers' Association called "wilderness conservation," an idea first promoted by John Muir back in the days of Hetch Hetchy. During the later New Deal years, then, while the Corps conserved natural and human resources, and as CCC opponents raised concerns about ecological balance and wilderness preservation, the ideas of Pinchot, Olmsted, Leopold, and Muir came together under Franklin Roosevelt's New Deal and began changing the way the American public conceived of conservation.

The national debate over Corps work projects did more than transform the conservation movement. It also influenced New Deal politics. Most obvious was the way the CCC's overwhelming popularity across the country raised political support for both the Roosevelt administration and a host of other New Deal programs. The Corps' national reputation also altered the way Roosevelt promoted his liberal agenda to the American people, especially during his reelection campaigns of the late 1930s and early 1940s. By portraying himself in newspapers and magazines, in radio reports, and on film literally alongside CCC reforestation projects in national forests, at soil conservation sites on American farms, and near Corps recreation work in places like Shenandoah National Park, the president linked his New Deal to the new public landscape taking shape in every corner of the country during the Great Depression era.[123] In doing so, Roosevelt was building political constituencies for the modern welfare state literally from the ground up and rooting this support in a physical landscape that would endure long after he and his brain trust left the capital.

Yet while the popularity of the Corps and its novel form of conservation helped the president to spread the New Deal gospel to the American people, opposition to the CCC and its work projects would have the opposite effect. During the later 1930s, when many of Roosevelt's policies came under increasingly hostile fire from conservatives and liberals alike, criticism of the Corps for upsetting ecological balance and destroying wilderness by the likes of Leopold and Marshall fueled the flames of this anti–New Deal turn. While conservationists within the Roosevelt administration tried to address such criticisms through the creation of a new Department of Conservation, their failure to do so further weakened the New Deal. Examining these final years of Roosevelt's presidency is central to understanding how the Corps not only influenced the so-called "third New Deal" of the late 1930s, but also set the groundwork for the environmental politics of the postwar period.

SIX / **PLANNING**

From Top-Down Conservation to Bottom-Up Environment

On November 21, 1937, the naturalist and Pulitzer Prize–winning political satirist "Ding" Darling published a cartoon titled "The Kidnapping—or More and More Democracy" in the *Des Moines Register* (see figure 6.1). In the background of the cartoon, Darling depicted Secretary of the Interior Harold Ickes absconding with a child labeled "Forestry Service" into a waiting "Department of Interior" automobile, the drivers of which wear masks like thieves and welcome Ickes and his abductee into their getaway car with open arms. In the foreground of the cartoon stands Franklin Roosevelt, with his back to the scene and his arm raised in a Hitler-like salute, confronting five individuals, including Secretary of Agriculture Henry Wallace and chief of the U.S. Forest Service Ferdinand Silcox. "I don't want to hear a peep out of *any* of you! Understand?" demands the president. Such warnings, Darling's cartoon suggested, were quite unnecessary. Not only is Roosevelt depicted as pointing a gun, hidden under his trench coat, at Wallace, Silcox, and the others who watch helplessly as Ickes flees with the Forest Service, but all of the witnesses to this "kidnapping" are gagged and bound with their hands tied tightly behind their backs.[1]

Darling drew "The Kidnapping" in response to a proposal submitted to Congress by Franklin Roosevelt in January 1937 to extensively reorganize the federal government. If approved, the president's reorganization plan would have increased Roosevelt's power by creating six executive assistants, by replacing the ineffectual Civil Service Commission with a presidential administrator, and by giving more control over federal accounts to the president. It would also have made the National Resources Planning Board a permanent

Figure 6.1 This political cartoon by Ding Darling is just one of dozens he drew during the interwar years focusing on one of his favorite topics: conservation. Most of his other cartoons, however, focus on wildlife, the threats posed by over-hunting, and the possible solutions to this problem through Progressive-style scientific management. While his wildlife cartoons usually call for government action to protect, for instance, migratory birds, in *The Kidnapping* he argues for the exact opposite; Franklin Roosevelt is overstepping the bounds of democracy by allowing the "theft" of the Forest Service and the Biological Survey by Secretary Ickes and the Department of the Interior. *The Kidnapping* is thus novel, for Darling and for many Progressive Era conservationists, because it calls for less government intervention instead of more. This message would find an enthusiastic audience during the later New Deal years, when conservationists lost faith in the federal government's ability to conserve resources through programs like the CCC, and instead began looking to special interest groups. (Ding Darling, "The Kidnapping—or More and More Democracy," *Des Moines Register*, November 21, 1937.)

reorg. govt '37–'38 & consv. movement

central planning agency and given the president the ability to shuffle agencies from one bureau to another, all in the name of increased government efficiency.[2] It was this last part of the reorganization proposal that suggested to many in Congress and the public at large that Roosevelt planned to transfer the Forest Service from Henry Wallace's Department of Agriculture to Harold Ickes's Department of the Interior, which would be remade into a new Department of Conservation. Fear of this possibility is also what sent Ding Darling, whom Franklin Roosevelt appointed in 1934 as chief of the U.S. Bureau of Biological Survey, a predecessor of the U.S. Fish and Wildlife Service, back to his drawing board.

Roosevelt's attempt in 1937 and 1938 to reorganize the federal government has been called one of the most important events in New Deal history.[3] To many, it signified a watershed separating the early New Deal years, when Congress eagerly enacted proposals by the president for a host of emergency relief programs, from what has been called the "third New Deal" of the late 1930s, when the Roosevelt administration had difficulty not only passing reform legislation but also protecting programs already in operation from political attacks by institutions such as the Supreme Court and an increasingly conservative Congress.[4] The defeat of the reorganization bill in 1938 and the passage of a watered-down version the following year, several historians have argued, marked a turning point for Franklin Roosevelt's presidency and an early step in a half-century-long rollback of New Deal liberalism during the post–World War II era.[5]

Although less obvious at the time, Roosevelt's 1937 reorganization effort was also a defining moment for the American conservation movement. While presidents in the past had threatened to transfer the Forest Service from the Agriculture Department to the Department of the Interior, none of these threats had sparked such aggravated concern on the part of conservationists like Ding Darling. American Forestry Association secretary Ovid Butler expressed such anxiety in a 1937 *American Forests* article titled "Conservation at the Forks" when he wrote, "The President's plan appears to bring . . . conservation to the forks of the road for determination by Congress."[6] On one level, Butler's literary juncture served as a metaphor for the unknown future of the Forest Service, which under Roosevelt's proposal could end up in Harold Ickes's back pocket at a new Conservation Department. Yet on a deeper level, Butler was expressing growing apprehension over the way that New Deal politics in general, and CCC work projects in particular, had sparked a nationwide debate over the very meaning of conservation during the later 1930s.

*politics + conserv. interest group politics 2nd New Deal

Examining in greater detail the political battle over Franklin Roosevelt's reorganization plan illuminates the enduring connection between politics and conservation during the late 1930s. On the one hand, it demonstrates how the conflicting conceptions of conservation popularized by the national debate over CCC work projects during the mid-1930s continued to influence New Deal politics toward the end of the Great Depression. Conversely, the president's reorganization efforts similarly suggest how federal politics in turn kept reshaping these contested conservationist ideologies well into the later years of the Roosevelt presidency. At the very center of this interrelationship was planning. While New Deal plans such as federal reorganization would continue to alter the meaning and practice of conservation during the late 1930s, the competing interests debating CCC work projects also transformed national planning in ways that set the stage for a new politics of "the environment" in the early 1940s. It was this new form of interest group politics, forged around a fractured conservation movement that was increasingly resistant to federal coordination, which would blossom after World War II into grassroots environmentalism.

Franklin Roosevelt's desire to reorganize the federal government was a direct response to a variety of political problems facing the New Deal during his second term in office. While the president had successfully initiated a host of reform programs during the so-called first New Deal of 1933, including the CCC, and had continued those achievements into the second New Deal of 1935, Roosevelt's administration proved less able to pass and protect liberal policies on the national level after he won reelection in 1936. This was because during this third stage of the Roosevelt presidency, powerful constraints arose to check the strength and breadth of New Deal liberalism. Roosevelt thus had little time to celebrate his electoral landslide in November 1936; he and his administrators were well aware that powerful forces were creating a pair of political predicaments that were stalling his presidency.[7]

One of the most serious political problems facing Roosevelt during his second term in office involved threats to presidential power. As many historians have noted, this process began in earnest in the mid-1930s, when the Supreme Court declared the National Recovery Act (NRA) and the Agricultural Adjustment Administration (AAA) to be unconstitutional in 1935 and 1936, respectively. Such threats continued on the legislative level the following year, when during the midterm elections, an economic recession ushered into Congress a conservative coalition that actively opposed Roosevelt's reform agenda. In 1938, for instance, Congress defeated a number of New Deal proposals, including the Works Financing Bill, and dramatically cut funding *late 30's — erosion of pres. power Corps projects*

for others, such as the administration's work relief bill.[8] By the late 1930s, then, the Roosevelt administration was worried that inroads by the judicial and legislative branches on executive authority were weakening the president's ability to promote and protect his liberal New Deal policies.

The threat to executive power exacerbated a second political problem facing Franklin Roosevelt during the later 1930s. While early in his presidency Roosevelt had consciously created federal agencies and programs with related jurisdictions and responsibilities under the belief that competition between administrators spurred greater achievement, the speedy and haphazard expansion of New Deal programs during the mid-1930s had resulted in bureaucratic rivalries, programmatic repetition, and a host of governmental inefficiencies that threatened his administration's overall reform efforts.[9] "The Government has been compelled to undertake many new and diverse functions resulting in the multiplication of bureaus and agencies," complained Harold Ickes. "Some of them have been placed in the regular departments without regard for their relationship to the functions of the other bureaus with which they are associated" with the result that "over-lapping and needless duplication of services are general."[10] New Dealers like Ickes worried that as the Supreme Court and Congress eroded presidential power, making it tougher for Roosevelt to promote and protect New Deal programs, the diversity of such programs made the president less able to coordinate the administration's various relief efforts.[11]

While numerous scholars have examined how a lack of both centralized authority and programmatic coordination within the Roosevelt administration threatened the New Deal, few have understood how this same pair of political problems also plagued the conservation movement in the late 1930s. During the president's second term, conservationists, too, worried that their movement suffered from a lack of centralized decision making, and many blamed the CCC. Although the Corps became increasingly popular among enrollees, the inhabitants of local communities near CCC camps, and the public at large, as Corps projects expanded from reforestation in the early 1930s to soil conservation during the Dust Bowl years and finally to recreational development projects by the later part of the decade, professional conservationists as well as lay Americans began publicly debating the very meaning of conservation, with some worrying openly that the expansion of CCC work had weakened the centrality of natural resource conservation within the conservation movement. "The organization came into being as a CONSERVATION CORPS [and] I think all accepted that to mean the conservation of natural resources," complained forester Ovid Butler in a 1938 open letter to Corps director Robert

Leopold

Fechner published in *American Forests* magazine. "Unfortunately, the word 'conservation' of late has come to be used so loosely by many people that justification, I fear, has been found to spread the activities of the Corps over so diversified a field of work as to dim in the public mind its permanent and needful place in the field of conservation proper."[12] Ickes agreed, writing the same year that he was "strongly opposed ... to the divided and uncorrelated authority, which now characterizes the Federal Government's administration of the nation's natural resources."[13] Thus, while New Deal programs such as the CCC democratized and broadened conservation, conservationists worried that weakened federal authority regarding natural resources use had set their movement adrift.

Just as the various threats to executive power made it difficult for Roosevelt to manage efficiently the wide variety of New Deal reform efforts, the fracturing of authority over conservation because of the expansion of CCC work projects resulted in a lack of coordination among federal conservation agencies.[14] "One of our greatest handicaps in the pursuit of our conservation objectives is the number of separate divisions into which conservation may be segregated and each one claiming the title of conservationist," explained Ding Darling. "Foresters are conservationists for forestry; soil conservationists are conservationists of the soil. And there are conservationists of water resources, health, wildlife, and recreation, but all too few of them knowing the consequences of their single-track activities on the contingent agencies."[15] Aldo Leopold, who in the mid-1930s took the Corps to task for such disorganization, made a similar critique of New Deal conservation in general. "Almost all our present laws and appropriations are single-track measures dealing with a single aspect of land-use," he explained, concluding that "these measures frequently clash, or at best, fail to dovetail with each other."[16] Thus, along with worrying about decentralized decision making, conservationists also agonized that disconnected, uncoordinated, and what they called "single-track" land use practices increasingly afflicted their movement.

The so-called third New Deal therefore entailed more than political problems for Franklin Roosevelt. During the president's second term in office, he not only faced powerful political opposition to his reform efforts from the judicial and legislative branches, but his administration was also caught in a battle among conservationists that similarly threatened New Deal reform. As Ovid Butler explained in a 1937 article titled "Whither Conservation?" "the situation clearly presents a swiftly coming crisis in the public handling of our natural resources."[17] Yet the debate over Corps work projects likewise illustrates that these two threats to the Roosevelt presidency—one political, the other

N.D.
& planning   *Prog. & FDR*

conservationist—were part of the same predicament involving a lack of both centralized authority and administrative coordination within the New Deal administration. As important, these two dilemmas were mutually constitutive; as the U.S. Biological Survey's Walter P. Taylor explained of this shared history, "a conservation crisis, which means, doubtless ... a political crisis, continues upon us."[18] Roosevelt understood this connection as well, and began his second term in Washington by promoting a single solution—a new type of planning—to cope with the pair of crises plaguing his presidency.

Planning was always central to the New Deal, and the Roosevelt administration, perhaps more than any other presidential administration in U.S. history, used planning as a political tool in federal policy making.[19] New Dealer Rexford Tugwell was one of the most well-known and outspoken proponents within the brain trust of planning on the national level. "The cat is out of the bag. There is no invisible hand. There never was," argued Tugwell in reference to Adam Smith's economic theory soon after arriving in Washington, D.C., in June 1933. "We must now supply a real and visible guiding hand to the task which that mythical, nonexistent, invisible agency was supposed to perform, but never did."[20] Franklin Roosevelt agreed, admitting in an April 1932 presidential campaign speech that he favored "planning, not for this period alone but for our needs for a long time to come."[21] Years later, he was equally adamant. "Planning," he explained, quite simply, "is essential for the benefit of human beings."[22] It is no wonder, then, that the 1930s has been called the "New Deal Planning Decade."[23]

Not since the Progressive Era had planning assumed such importance within national politics. Although they worked on a wide variety of issues, Progressive planners fell generally into two distinct camps. There were conservationists, such as Theodore Roosevelt, who planned for the wise use of natural resources in rural areas by creating bureaus like the Reclamation Service in 1902 and the U.S. Forest Service in 1905.[24] During this same period, however, there arose another contingent of planners interested instead in reforming the American city. Progressives in this group prepared plans, often on the local level, to remake urban America by, for instance, improving public transportation, cleaning and beautifying city streets, building urban parks and playgrounds, and improving living conditions for poor immigrants in city slums.[25] Although these two groups often worked in isolation from one another, one conserving natural resources in the countryside while the other improved urban environments for city dwellers, Franklin Roosevelt had extensive experience early in life with each of these Progressive planning traditions.

As the examination of the CCC's intellectual origins has illustrated, as a young man Franklin Roosevelt embraced planning as a means of conserving natural resources, much as his cousin Theodore had done at the turn of the century. While growing up along the banks of the Hudson River, Roosevelt formulated tree-planting plans, with the help of Nelson Brown of the University of Syracuse's State College of Forestry, for his Hyde Park estate and planned as well with fellow New York state senators for more efficient timber production in the Adirondack Forest Preserve. Roosevelt later expanded such efforts to the entire state through a plan that studied and classified in 10-acre tracts the 30 million acres of land in New York to determine the best land use practices for each parcel. "Up to that time," Roosevelt argued, "little on a very large scale had been done for country areas."[26] Thus, long before he became president, Franklin Roosevelt embraced Progressive planning in order to conserve natural resources in rural areas.[27]

While Teddy Roosevelt's influence on his cousin's planning efforts are well documented, a second, lesser-known relative also exposed young Franklin Roosevelt to Progressive Era planning, albeit of a different sort. As Roosevelt explained in a 1932 article titled "Growing Up by Plan," written for the Progressive journal *Survey*, it was his uncle Frederic Delano who first introduced him to the urban planning movement. At the turn of the century Delano, who became a leading figure among Progressive urban planners, brought his railroad industry expertise to bear on a wide variety of plans aimed at solving problems in American cities. He worked closely with Chicago World's Fair architect Daniel Burnham on the 1908 City Plan of Chicago; with landscape architects Frederick Law Olmsted, Jr., and Charles Eliot II during the early 1920s on the National Capital Park and Planning Commission for Washington, D.C.; and with the Russell Sage Foundation's committee on a plan for the New York City area until 1932.[28] Young Franklin followed in his uncle's footsteps, formulating plans to clean up New York City's milk supply before 1910, and later he helped the Boy Scouts plan the expansion of their campground facilities for urban youths.[29] The latter effort, as we have seen, also shaped Roosevelt's thinking concerning the creation of the CCC. "My uncle, Frederic Delano, first talked to me about the City Plan of Chicago," explained Roosevelt in "Growing Up by Plan." "I think from that very moment I have been interested in not the mere planning of a single city but in the larger aspects of planning."[30]

The larger aspects of planning about which Roosevelt wrote in 1932 also appealed to a new breed of planners who during the 1920s began promoting planning as a means of addressing simultaneously the problems facing both

Marsh
& Powell planning

urban and rural America. To some extent, this new phase in planning had roots in the writings of George Perkins Marsh, whose *Man and Nature* of 1864 emphasized not only the importance of reforestry and floodplain protection in rural areas but also how the actions of humans, often living in far-off cities, created a need for such plans in the first place, and later through the work of John Wesley Powell, whose irrigation survey of the American West in the late 1880s implored Congress to limit migration to this intensely arid region.[31] Although the federal government ignored Powell's warnings, his ideas about planning for whole geographic areas resurfaced during the 1920s in the thinking of a diverse group of intellectuals, including architects Clarence Stein and Henry Wright, economist Stuart Chase, bureaucrats such as Louis Brownlow, and planners like Benton MacKaye. This contingent, along with their most well-known colleague, Lewis Mumford, institutionalized Powell's planning ideal in 1923 by creating the Regional Planning Association of America (RPAA).[32] Rather than focusing their efforts on urban or rural planning, as Progressive Era reformers had done, the RPAA envisioned the city and its hinterland as a single unit with an interrelated set of problems. For members of the RPAA, the solutions to such difficulties lay in a different type of planning, one that took into account not just the urban or the rural but entire regions encompassing both environments.[33]

The RPAA's planning vision was perhaps best exemplified by its first sponsored project, the Appalachian Trail. Formulated by RPAA member Benton MacKaye in 1921, the 1,500-mile hiking trail running along the crest of the Appalachian Mountains from Maine to Georgia would serve as a healthful retreat for those living along the urban corridor of the eastern seaboard and as a means of economically developing the Appalachian region; planned into the trail were rural logging and agricultural communities that would benefit not only from responsible natural resource use but also from visits by urban outdoor recreationists. Creating such communities, MacKaye argued, would require "a new deal in our agriculture system" as well as a "new deal" in forestry.[34] Quite ironically it would be a New Deal program, the CCC, that would complete MacKaye's Appalachian Trail, without the planned communities, in the late 1930s. Thus long before Roosevelt coined the phrase that would become synonymous with his administration, RPAA members were promoting a "new deal" in planning as a means of tying together the problems of city and country.

During the 1920s, regional planners such as those in the RPAA went out of their way to influence Franklin Roosevelt. In 1926, for instance, MacKaye contacted Roosevelt, then head of the Taconic State Park Commission, about plans to run a 120-mile section of the Appalachian Trail through several Taconic state parks lying between southwestern Massachusetts and Bear Mountain State Park in the Hudson highlands just south of Roosevelt's Hyde Park estate.[35] The RPAA similarly promoted its ideas in March 1931 when Clarence Stein lunched with Roosevelt to discuss regional planning in New York and to persuade the governor to attend a conference in Virginia on regionalism, and again the following year when the RPAA drafted a nine-page memorandum to Roosevelt urging him to develop a statewide master plan for the entire Empire State.[36]

While it is unclear whether or not Roosevelt read the nine-page letter sent to him by the RPAA, when he became governor of New York he nevertheless brought the organization's unique brand of planning with him to the state-house in Albany. "I am a great believer in the larger aspects of regional planning," he told the New York state legislature, "and in my judgment the time has come for this State to adopt a far-reaching policy of land utilization and population distribution."[37] To accomplish this, Roosevelt organized much of his gubernatorial legislative agenda around a comprehensive plan aimed at the state's urban and rural regions. To combat natural resource degradation in the countryside, the governor initiated a statewide soil survey and the refores-tation of marginal farmlands. He simultaneously formulated plans aimed at solving a host of urban problems plaguing several upper Hudson Valley cities, including Albany, Schenectady, and Troy. A key component of this statewide plan was the creation of the New York State Power Authority to oversee the construction of dams along the St. Lawrence River for the production of inexpensive hydroelectric power.[38] Although Roosevelt was unable to imple-ment most of this plan, due primarily to federal opposition to state develop-ment of the St. Lawrence waterway, he nevertheless remained an enthusiastic proponent of regional planning. "It is the way of the future," Roosevelt claimed in 1932. "Perhaps the day is not far distant when planning will become part of the national policy of this country."[39]

That day arrived on April 10, 1933, when a newly inaugurated President Roosevelt introduced the idea of regional planning in one of his first congres-sional addresses. "Many hard lessons have taught us the human waste that results from a lack of planning," he explained to the nation's legislators.[40] To avoid such waste, Roosevelt brought a team of regional planners with him to Washington, D.C., including RPAA founders Clarence Stein, Henry Wright, and Stuart Chase, all of whom consulted for the Greenbelt Town Program of Rexford Tugwell's Resettlement Administration. During his first hundred days in office, the new president also created several agencies that were clearly efforts at national planning. While the AAA brought planning to American farming by controlling the production of seven basic crops in an effort to raise farm prices throughout the country, the NRA attempted to plan production quotas, wages, and even prices for more than 500 U.S. industries.[41] It was a third New Deal program, however, that became the nation's poster child for federal regional planning. "It is time," Roosevelt told legislators in this same congressional address, "to extend planning to a wider field."[42] He then asked Congress to create the Tennessee Valley Authority (TVA).

Roosevelt's TVA extended regional planning to an extraordinarily wide field. Covering 40,000 square miles in portions of seven southeastern states, the Ohio-sized Tennessee Valley suffered from both economic and ecological degradation. Not surprisingly, such problems were interrelated and caused to a great extent by flooding, up and down the 900-mile-long Tennessee River, which hindered commercial navigation and eroded soil on adjacent farmland. Years of deforestation along the Tennessee River's banks had exacerbated such problems; without trees and their root systems, water and soil ran down banks, making annual floods even more severe. Because of this, on the eve of the Great Depression, 85 percent of the valley's 13 million acres of cultivated land suffered from erosion, with 2 million of those acres so deeply gullied that agronomists doubted that the land could be restored.[43] "In the Valley of the Tennessee River ... I had come to consider the fact of devastating floods that had existed for many generations," explained Roosevelt. "But worst of all, I had seen the splendid people living in parts of several states fighting against nature instead of fighting with nature."[44]

Through regional planning, the president hoped to tame the Tennessee River and in the process restore the Tennessee Valley both ecologically and economically. The first step in this process was the creation of a governmental agency with enough centralized power to formulate and implement plans for an entire watershed without outside interference. Taking his cue from his experiences in New York, where he had created a state power authority in an attempt to develop the St. Lawrence waterway, Roosevelt invested the TVA with an inordinate amount of power. As Franklin Roosevelt said of the TVA's special political status, "this Authority should be clothed with the necessary power to carry these plans into effect."[45] The TVA, for instance, was able to hire and fire its workers, remove residents from their homes and eliminate entire towns to make way for dams, build new towns in their stead and choose their residents, and even create hydroelectricity and sell it to those residents and to the public at large.[46] The TVA act, explained Senator George Norris, worried Washington politicians precisely "because it placed beyond their influence any possibility of interference which would disrupt or dismantle the organization set up under law."[47] Part independent federal bureau, part regional government, the TVA was unique in the amount of centralized power it wielded.

To help formulate plans for the Tennessee Valley, and to assist with New Deal planning overall, during his first hundred days in office, Roosevelt also created a federal planning agency. "It is not only necessary that a plan be formulated" for regions like the Tennessee Valley, explained Roosevelt, "it is necessary also that there be a continuous planning agency—one which is always functioning—with facilities to consider new inventions and new discoveries and new changes of continuous planning."[48] Created in 1933 as the National Planning Board, rechristened the following year as the National Resources Board, and renamed yet again in 1935 as the National Resources Committee, what finally became the National Resources Planning Board (NRPB) from 1939 until its dissolution in 1943 was the first national planning agency in U.S. history.[49] The president chose none other than his uncle Frederic Delano to head the new agency, and made it responsible for promoting local and state planning boards and developing various plans for federal agencies in a strictly advisory capacity.[50] The planning board, Roosevelt explained, would "collect into one place all the facts upon which planning can be based."[51]

Although the TVA wielded the necessary power and the National Planning Board helped to coordinate plans for the valley, a third New Deal program was instrumental in making these plans a reality. Much as it did for the U.S. Forest Service, the Soil Conservation Service, and the National Park Service, the CCC provided the manpower necessary to transform plans formulated on paper in Washington, D.C., into physical landscape changes up and down the Tennessee River valley. The Corps began this process during the fall of 1933 when it assigned twenty-five camps and 5,000 CCC enrollees to the TVA, and intensified such efforts in 1935, when the Corps reached its peak strength, by increasing the CCC's presence in the valley to thirty-eight camps with 7,600 enrollees (see figure 6.2). Such numbers do not include additional camps and enrollees that the Corps assigned to the Forest Service, the Soil Conservation Service, and the National Park Service that also performed conservation work in the Tennessee Valley. "These camps are vitally important in the Authority's long range program," argued TVA board member Harcourt Morgan in February 1938.[52] All told, throughout the Great Depression, 50,000 CCC enrollees passed through the nearly thirty Corps camps located up and down the Tennessee River valley.[53]

Corps enrollees made TVA plans a physical reality by performing an enormous amount of work in the Tennessee Valley. Throughout the Great

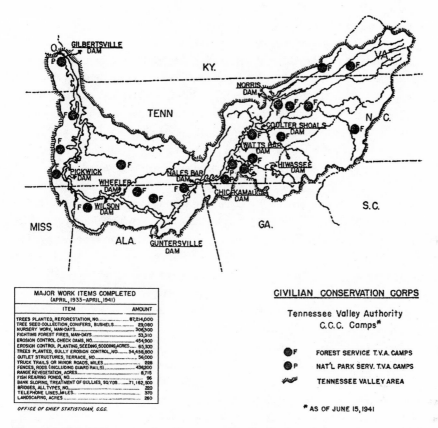

MAJOR WORK ITEMS COMPLETED
(APRIL, 1933–APRIL, 1941)

ITEM	AMOUNT
TREES PLANTED, REFORESTATION, NO.	87,214,000
TREE SEED COLLECTION, CONIFERS, BUSHELS	29,080
NURSERY WORK, MAN-DAYS	306,300
FIGHTING FOREST FIRES, MAN-DAYS	53,310
EROSION CONTROL CHECK DAMS, NO.	454,900
EROSION CONTROL PLANTING, SEEDING, SODDING, ACRES	65,300
TREES PLANTED, GULLY EROSION CONTROL, NO.	34,458,800
OUTLET STRUCTURES, TERRACE, NO.	56,000
TRUCK TRAILS OR MINOR ROADS, MILES	228
FENCES, RODS. (INCLUDING GUARD RAILS)	436,200
RANGE REVEGETATION, ACRES	8,715
FISH REARING PONDS, NO.	96
BANK SLOPING, TREATMENT OF GULLIES, SQ.YDS.	71,162,500
BRIDGES, ALL TYPES, NO.	220
TELEPHONE LINES, MILES	370
LANDSCAPING, ACRES	260

OFFICE OF CHIEF STATISTICIAN, C.C.C.

CIVILIAN CONSERVATION CORPS

Tennessee Valley Authority
C.C.C. Camps*

- F   FOREST SERVICE T.V.A. CAMPS
- P   NAT'L PARK SERV. T.V.A. CAMPS
-   TENNESSEE VALLEY AREA

* AS OF JUNE 15, 1941

Figure 6.2 This 1941 map noting the geographic distribution of the twenty-two CCC camps then under the jurisdiction of the Tennessee Valley Authority illustrates the central role played by the Corps in making TVA regional planning a reality. Although the map lists the names of dams alongside many CCC-TVA camps, enrollees stationed in the valley instead labored on projects involving reforestation, soil conservation, and park development. Also missing from this map is a visual depiction of the impact that the national debate over Corps conservation work had on federal planning both here in the Tennessee Valley and throughout the country. As more and more scientists and ordinary Americans began criticizing the CCC for upsetting the so-called balance of nature, Franklin Roosevelt began introducing ecological thinking into the federal government's regional planning efforts. The result would not only influence the Tennessee Valley but the conservation movement and New Deal politics as well. ("Civilian Conservation Corps: Tennessee Valley Authority C.C.C. Camps." RG 35: CCC, Entry 12: "Organization Charts, 1941–1942," National Archives and Records Administration, Washington, D.C.)

Depression, the approximately 5,000 young men stationed in TVA camps each year labored nearly 10.5 million hours annually for a total of more than 100 million man-hours between 1933 and 1942.[54] Their work was similar to that performed by CCC enrollees nationwide. At the outset of the Great Depression, the Corps focused its efforts on reforesting the valley, not to increase timber production but rather to decrease soil erosion and to control flooding along the Tennessee River. To aid this effort, the CCC established two nurseries in the valley that distributed to nearby Corps camps 153 million seedlings, enough to reforest one-quarter of the 40,000-square-mile watershed.[55] In the mid-1930s, as the Dust Bowl blew across the Great plains, the Corps also began conserving Tennessee Valley soil. Not only did enrollees help local farmers to halt soil erosion by contour plowing fields, building terraces, and erecting nearly 500,000 check dams, but at least three Corps camps were also assigned to the Muscle Shoals National Fertilizer Development Center, where they helped agronomists with chemical fertilizer experiments and the creation of demonstration farms, similar to those in Coon Creek, Wisconsin, which showcased soil conservation techniques to farmers from the Tennessee Valley and beyond.[56] "The CCC camps furnish virtually the only means of supplementing the landowner's efforts in dealing with those badly eroded lands," explained one TVA official.[57]

During the later New Deal years, Corps enrollees also began laboring on recreational projects for the TVA, building no less than seven public parks in the valley, most of which were situated adjacent to lakes created by TVA dams. One of these, Big Ridge Park, included two overnight campgrounds, scenic overlooks, hiking trails, and the creation of a swimming area in Norris Lake for visiting tourists.[58] Thus while Corps enrollees did not construct the enormous hydroelectric dams that became the international icons of the TVA, they were very much the muscle behind Muscle Shoals and the rest of Roosevelt's regional plan for the Tennessee Valley.[59]

During the early 1930s, the planning triumvirate of the TVA, the National Planning Board, and the CCC proved to be extremely successful in helping Roosevelt to build support for his liberal New Deal policies. "It was regional planning on a scale never before attempted in history," bragged Roosevelt.[60] The TVA and its army of Corps enrollees became so popular with politicians and the American public that in 1934 Congress by joint resolution asked the president for a comprehensive plan for several other major river systems. To undertake this study, Roosevelt turned to none other than the National Planning Board, which by 1935 had successfully created regional planning boards for New England and the Pacific Northwest, and had also helped to create forty-two state planning boards across the country.[61]

Other New Dealers were equally optimistic about the rising tide of regional planning within the federal government. "Long after the necessity for stimulating industry and creating new buying power by a comprehensive system of public works shall be a thing of the past," explained Harold Ickes during the early 1930s, "national planning will go on as a permanent government institution."[62] Throughout his first term in office, then, Franklin Roosevelt successfully transplanted the regional planning idea firmly within national politics.[63]

Five years later, however, the story was quite different. Whereas during the early New Deal years, the TVA's political clout had been unquestioned, in 1936 the Supreme Court approved, by only one vote, the authority's right to distribute hydroelectricity on the local level, a right the administration had all but assumed. Two years later, Congress made matters worse by blocking outright the creation of seven additional TVA-type river authorities.[64] The NRPB suffered similar setbacks; by the late 1930s it remained a temporary federal bureau with a part-time staff, no statutory authority, limited government funding, and little political support beyond the Oval Office.[65] As a result, while opponents weakened the authority of the TVA, critics also began attacking New Deal planning agencies such as the NRPB for their lack of overall coordination. Benton MacKaye, for instance, who worked for the TVA during the mid-1930s, lambasted the authority for fragmenting its planning among six different departments and two competing ideologies represented by what he called "beautifiers," who cared about aesthetics, and "engineers," who were interested instead in controlling water.[66] The CCC, which divided its work projects in the valley among the TVA, the Forest Service, the Park Service, and the Soil Conservation Service, was partly responsible for such criticism.

Such problems bring us right back to the twin crises of the third New Deal. The Supreme Court's slim endorsement of the TVA's right to distribute power was part and parcel of the political predicament facing the Roosevelt administration during the late 1930s, most often exemplified by the erosion of presidential power associated with the Supreme Court's decision to declare unconstitutional the NRA and the AAA. In a similar vein, a weakened NRPB unable to efficiently manage TVA planning was indicative of the conservation crisis also threatening Roosevelt in the late 1930s, which arose as the Corps expanded its single-track work projects in places like the Tennessee Valley through several uncoordinated New Deal conservation agencies. Federal planning during the later 1930s, in other words, suffered from the same pair of problems facing the New Deal in general: a lack of both centralized authority and coordinated management. In response, the president did not retreat from planning, as many scholars have insisted, but instead promoted a new type of planning aimed at increasing both his own political power as well as his ability to manage more efficiently his New Deal administration and its various conservation efforts.

The president reacted to the twin crises of the third New Deal, one political and the other conservationist, by promoting a plan to reorganize the federal government. "I am trying to leave behind an orderly and logical setup," Roosevelt explained, "which will take care of all the new work we have started ... and make it easier for my successor to carry on."[67] To help with this process, in March 1936, Roosevelt created a President's Committee on Administrative Management and appointed to it several prominent planners. Louis Brownlow, an early member of the RPAA, served as the committee's chair, while Charles Merriman and Luther Gulick, both of whom served on earlier incarnations of Roosevelt's NRPB, became committee members. In his instructions to the newly formed committee, the president told Brownlow that, instead of proposing specific agency transfers, they should take a big-picture view of government reorganization in the hopes of centralizing power and increasing coordination within his administration.[68]

After spending almost a year examining possible reorganization strategies, the President's Committee on Administrative Management published its findings in what became known as the Brownlow Report. Along with appointing presidential assistants, reinvigorating the civil service system, and reforming government accounting practices, the committee recommended the creation of a Department of Public Works and a Department of Welfare. Most important for the history of conservation and planning, Brownlow and his associates also proposed making the National Resources Planning Board a permanent federal agency and changing the name of the Department of the Interior to the Department of Conservation. Such proposed changes, Brownlow suggested to the president, would help to centralize authority and coordinate management both within the federal government and among the New Deal's numerous conservation agencies.[69] The proposed reorganization, in other words, would consolidate conservation planning firmly within the welfare state.

When Roosevelt first read the Brownlow Report in mid-November 1936, he was said to have exclaimed "one hundred percent!" while enthusiastically banging his fist on his desk.[70] Others in the nation's capital were less enthused. The following month, when the president sent the report to Congress, the *New York Times* claimed that legislators were "shocked," "flabbergasted," and "knocked breathless" by the audaciousness of the president's reorganization plan. So too were some conservationists, such as Ding Darling, who later that year sat down to draw the "Kidnapping" cartoon for the *Des Moines Register*.[71] Although Darling chose not to depict the CCC explicitly in his cartoon, both sides in this political skirmish nevertheless used the Corps to defend their positions. Supporters of the Brownlow Report, for instance, promoted reorganization as a new and improved form of federal planning, which, they argued, would unify the various strands of conservationist thought that had been unleashed by the national debate over Corps work. Opponents of the report criticized reorganization for similar reasons, fearing that a new Conservation Department would permanently institutionalize a conservation movement that had been splintered by the very same CCC projects. Examining the arguments on both sides of this controversy is central to understanding not only why opponents of the Brownlow Report ultimately won the battle over reorganization and sent the Department of Conservation down to defeat, but also how Roosevelt's distinct style of planning and conservation went on in the postwar era to influence environmental politics.

Besides Franklin Roosevelt, the foremost supporter of the Brownlow Report was Harold Ickes, who had first proposed the transfer of the Forest Service from the Department of Agriculture soon after Roosevelt appointed him secretary of the interior in 1933. Years later, in 1940, Ickes wrote to the president about his long-standing desire to control the forest agency. "I have had one consistent ambition since I have been Secretary of the Interior," explained Ickes, "and that has been to be the head of a Department of Conservation, of which, necessarily, Forestry would be the keystone."[72] Not surprisingly, Ickes turned to the National Park Service, one of the most powerful bureaus within the Department of the Interior, and to backers of the park movement for help in promoting Roosevelt's reorganization plan. No doubt at Ickes's behest, a group of park advocates met on November 17, 1937, at Chicago's Palmer House to create "an association of public-spirited citizens" to support the proposed Department of Conservation. Those present included former director of the National Park Service Horace Albright and president of the National Conference on State Parks Richard Lieber.[73] At the meeting, the group addressed a joint letter to the president, and several weeks later they met with Roosevelt before setting out to raise public support for his reorganization agenda.

Proponents of reorganization first defended it as a means of solving the political crisis facing the New Deal. Creating six new executive assistants, reinvigorating the civil service, and restoring control of accounts to the president, argued supporters of the plan, would reverse the erosion of executive authority that was occurring during the later 1930s. Roosevelt agreed wholeheartedly, dismissing the notion that reorganization was a presidential power grab and insisting instead that the plan would provide the "tools of management" that presidents so desperately need to make democracy function more effectively.[74] In making their case, supporters relied on patriotic rhetoric both to defend the plan and to criticize those opposing it. Augmenting presidential power "rests solidly upon the Constitution and upon the American way of doing things," explained Roosevelt in 1937.[75] Proponents of the Brownlow Report similarly tagged their opponents as being politically subversive. "Those who waiver at the sight of needed power are false friends of modern democracy," argued the President's Committee on Administrative Management. "Strong executive leadership is essential to democratic government today."[76] Providing the president with more political power through reorganization, proponents stated quite simply, was the American thing to do.

Reorganization advocates also promoted the Brownlow Report as a means of solving the second political problem plaguing the Roosevelt administration during the late 1930s, namely, a lack of programmatic coordination. Providing the president with the ability to rationally regroup agencies, as the Brownlow Report recommended, "will prevent overlapping and clashing and jealousies in the future," explained Harold Ickes.[77] Franklin Roosevelt concurred, stating that "there are a lot of Federal agencies, there are state agencies and there are local agencies, and our chief problem now is to work out a plan that all of these different agencies can carry out, working intelligently with each other and not crossing wires."[78] The ability to transfer certain bureaus, proponents claimed, would also help to ensure that New Deal programs remained a permanent part of the federal government, an idea particularly important in light of the actions by the Supreme Court regarding the NRA and AAA.

Yet Franklin Roosevelt and other proponents of the Brownlow Report did not merely advocate reorganization as a means of solving the political crisis of the so-called third New Deal. They also promoted it as an example of a new, more comprehensive style of national planning that would better coordinate New Deal programs and in turn help federal politics to function more smoothly. To do this, supporters of reorganization turned to the CCC and the public debate sparked by its conservation work in the later 1930s. As the examination of the Corps' popularity illustrated, some types of CCC conservation projects, including the planting of single species of trees in national forests, the eradication of "predators" from farmland, and the building of roads across the country's parks, had garnered criticism for being ecologically unsound. This critique began in Coon Creek, Wisconsin, where Aldo Leopold disparaged Corps conservation work for its "ecological limitations," before spreading to other professionals such as Harvard botanist Merritt Fernald and National

Park Service naturalist George Wright. When the national media similarly began criticizing some Corps projects for tipping the so-called balance of nature, the American public also took notice, as did conservation groups, including Rosalie Edge's Emergency Conservation Committee, the Audubon Society, the Izaak Walton League, and the National Wildlife Federation.[79]

Roosevelt was not immune to this ecological critique, and responded in the late 1930s by incorporating it directly into his administration's reorganization strategy. Initially, it was the philosophy of ecology, with its central tenets of interdependence, balance, and holism, which appealed most to New Dealers as a new model for federal planning.[80] "We no longer regard land as land alone; we regard it as one of the central and controlling elements in our whole national economy," explained Rexford Tugwell. "The recovery program brings us finally face to face with devising a plan which shall draw together our divergent efforts and look forward as far as possible toward permanent policy."[81] While Tugwell's drawing together of "divergent efforts" into a more integrated whole merely suggested ecological interrelationships, Franklin Roosevelt was more forthright in his incorporation of ecological ideas into federal planning policy. "Cooperating between all agencies," argued Roosevelt in 1936, entails "a plan of cooperation with Nature instead of going along with what we have been doing in the past—trying to buck Nature."[82]

The Roosevelt administration first began practicing this more holistic version of federal planning in the Tennessee Valley. Whereas during the early New Deal years, TVA planning had been divided among "six different departments" and "two competing ideologies," as Benton MacKaye had argued, by the end of the decade TVA administrators were consciously increasing coordination among the wide variety of plans in the valley and promoting such interdependence to the American public. In 1939, for instance, ecologist Paul Sears kicked off a TVA publicity campaign with a *Harper's* magazine article titled "Science and the New Landscape." Recent TVA planning efforts, he wrote, have "taught that man himself is not a watcher, but like other living things, is part of the landscape in which he abides." Due to increased coordination of work projects by programs like the Corps, Sears continued, the Tennessee Valley "landscape, including its living constituents, is an integrated whole."[83] The following year, in promotional literature on TVA planning, the authority extended this campaign beyond ecological philosophy to include as well the science of ecology. In a pamphlet titled *Forests and Human Welfare*, TVA administrators used before and after photographs of the Tennessee Valley to explain to the American public the scientific benefits of the Corps' reforestation efforts, and concluded that such balanced land use benefited both forests and local inhabitants alike.[84] The result was nothing less than a new ecological brand of national planning.[85]

Supporters of the Brownlow Report used this more ecological version of federal planning, exemplified by the TVA and its CCC work, to promote Roosevelt's reorganization efforts. In particular, they used the ecological metaphors of interdependence—between nature and culture, as well as among various New Deal relief programs—to promote the report's recommendation to make the NRPB a permanent central planning bureau. "A continuous planning agency," Roosevelt argued in a written statement that echoed the TVA's lesson in *Forests and Human Welfare*, would allow the president to better balance federal planning of both "natural and human resources."[86] Roosevelt added that a permanent federal planning agency like the NRPB would also ensure that "all the work that is being carried on" by New Deal relief programs will "have some relationship to the work that is being carried on at some other point."[87] It was this ideology of interdependence, so central to ecological thought and made popular in part through the national debate over CCC conservation efforts, which moved to the center of New Deal planning during the later 1930s.[88]

During the late 1930s, New Deal planners thus took a page from New Deal conservation in their effort to cure the political crisis of the third New Deal. As the CCC and its work projects came under attack for upsetting ecological balance, Franklin Roosevelt co-opted this criticism to take regional planning to a new level. The president accomplished this by first transferring the regional planning idea, promoted by a small group of intellectuals during the 1920s, onto the national stage through New Deal programs such as the TVA and the NRPB.[89] At the same time, Roosevelt transformed regional planning in ways that made New Deal planning distinct from earlier federal planning efforts. Similar to the regional planners of the 1920s, who envisioned the city and the country as a single, unified entity, Roosevelt used planning to solve problems affecting entire geographic areas such as the Tennessee Valley. Yet New Dealers went one step further by incorporating both ecological thinking and ecological science into their national planning efforts in order to integrate, balance, and make more "whole" a wide variety of plans involving both natural and human resources and dozens of independent federal agencies. "Our economic life today is a seamless web," Roosevelt explained of New Deal planning efforts. "We cannot have independence, unless we take full account of our interdependence."[90] The result was an ecological brand of national planning, unique in U.S. history, which would in turn transform New Deal conservation.[91]

Proponents of Roosevelt's federal reorganization plan similarly promoted the Brownlow Report as a means of solving the conservation crisis of the third New Deal, which also entailed a lack of centralized authority and coordination, but in this case among New Deal conservation programs. To tackle the former, the President's Committee on Administrative Management proposed remaking the Department of the Interior into a centralized Department of Conservation with the power to "administer the public lands, parks, territories, and reservations, and enforce the conservation laws with regard to public lands and mineral and water resources."[92] Harold Ickes immediately championed this recommendation as a means of increasing the federal government's authority over federal conservation efforts. "I think conservation ought to be under one department," he explained in an article for *Forestry News Digest*, so that "it can be administered more economically and more efficiently than if scattered among various departments of government."[93] No longer would responsibility for government programs like the CCC, overseen cooperatively by the Departments of War, Labor, Interior, and Agriculture, be dispersed among separate bureaus. Instead, a newly christened Department of Conservation, under Ickes's control, would administer all New Deal conservation efforts from one centralized office.

The proposed Conservation Department would also fix the second problem facing New Deal conservation, which involved a lack of coordination among federal conservation programs. Granting the president power to transfer various conservation bureaus into a centralized Conservation Department, argued supporters of the Brownlow Report, would increase coordination among federal conservation activities. The Forest Service was a case in point; its transfer from the Department of Agriculture to the proposed Department of Conservation, report advocates argued, would decrease bureaucratic redundancy and waste. Franklin Roosevelt agreed, explaining that the proposed Department of Conservation would avoid "ridiculous interlocking and overlapping jurisdiction" among New Deal conservation programs and thus enhance coordination of federal conservation efforts.[94] As important, the new Conservation Department could also serve as a clearinghouse of useful information for the numerous conservation organizations created by the public in response to the overwhelming popularity of the CCC and its work projects. The centralized Department of Conservation, in other words, could coordinate from above the numerous civic conservation efforts unleashed from below by the Corps.

Brownlow Report supporters, however, did not merely advocate reorganization as a means of increasing centralization and coordination among federal conservation programs. They went one step further, promoting it as a means of institutionalizing a novel, expanded, more inclusive type of conservation. To make their case, pro-reorganization advocates turned once again to the CCC and the national debate sparked by its conservation work during the late 1930s. As the examination of the Corps' popularity illustrated, when the CCC expanded its work projects from the nation's forests to its farms and finally into its parks, the very meaning of conservation began to shift, ultimately splintering into several competing ideologies. For some, "simple conservation" remained the wise use of natural resources, while others began advocating for a "broader conservation" that took into account human resources as well. Still others promoted what they called "true conservation," aimed at maintaining ecological balance, while yet another group promoted "wilderness conservation" as a means of preserving primitive, undeveloped areas. The result was a variety of single-track conservation efforts that, in Aldo Leopold's words, "failed to dovetail with one another."[95]

In an effort to bring these competing ideologies together under a single conservationist tent, the Roosevelt administration during the late 1930s began using the New Deal's unique brand of ecological planning to promote a novel type of conservation. Central to such efforts were the more integrated, balanced, and holistic plans for federal conservation such as those undertaken by the Corps in the Tennessee Valley in the late 1930s. "More and more careful planning has been done to insure a harmonious relation between the various conservation efforts and viewpoints," explained CCC director Robert Fechner of Corps work projects in his annual report of 1936. "In the practice of forestry," for instance, which entails the conservation of natural resources, "additional consideration has been given to wildlife values" that included a concern for ecological habitat. Similarly, the Corps' "recreational development" projects, which during the mid-1930s had been aimed solely at conserving human resources through healthful outdoor play, were by the later 1930s increasingly confined to "smaller areas" so as to preserve "the major portion of the areas for their other values," including wilderness. "This tendency will continue," Fechner concluded, "as greater familiarity with, and knowledge of, the various phases of conservation activities [are] more and more widely possessed by all engaged by the program."[96] In other words, as the "various phases" of CCC conservation work expanded from forests to farms and finally into parks, the Corps began embracing a more careful style of planning that harmoniously integrated the conservation of natural and human resources with the maintenance of ecological balance and the preservation of wilderness. During the later 1930s, then, the Roosevelt administration began to use the New Deal's ecological planning to better integrate the various types of conservation practiced by federal programs such as Corps.

While the CCC initiated this more holistic form of conservation based on the New Deal's unique brand of planning, its foremost cheerleader within the Roosevelt administration during the later New Deal years was Morris Llewellyn Cooke. An early supporter of Roosevelt's conservation efforts in New York state, Cooke became a powerful conservationist on the national level as an advisor to Gifford Pinchot, as an advocate of Soil Conservation Service chief Hugh Bennett, and as a member of several presidential natural resource committees, including the Great Plains Drought Area Committee and the Mississippi Valley Committee. It was while head of the latter, which like the TVA was responsible for outlining a scheme of natural resource development for an entire river basin, that Cooke, like Leopold before him, became alarmed at the federal government's various single-track conservation efforts. "In the conservation field," Cooke complained in 1940, "we have focused our attention on the detail of one or more of the 57 varieties, each one admittedly important in itself but by itself relatively unimportant in any comprehensive scheme."[97] By the end of the decade, Morris Cooke, too, had become concerned about the lack of centralized authority and coordination within federal conservation policy.

Similar to others in the Roosevelt administration, Cooke looked to planning to solve this conservation crisis. The creation of "an ultimate planning agency for the nation as a whole," he argued while in charge of the Mississippi Valley Committee, would centralize power over federal conservation efforts. Yet here again, run-of-the-mill planning would not suffice. Instead, like Fechner, Cooke promoted the New Deal's unique style of ecological planning based on integration and balance as a means of increasing coordination among various federal conservation efforts. "Such an agency" for the entire nation, Cooke argued, "could weld together for a common effort the conservation forces" that had been fractured by the CCC.[98] While Fechner had merely alluded to this new form of conservation when discussing Corps work projects in the late 1930s, Morris Cooke not only described it in detail but also named it. "This all-inclusive picture," he wrote, "I am calling 'total conservation'."

Just as ecology had influenced New Deal planning in the Tennessee Valley, so too did it shape "total conservation." "Planning is of special importance here," Cooke explained of this new outlook, because of the "numerous ways in which any one factor affects the others."[99] Cooke went on to use similar ecological metaphors, urging New Dealers to "plan the whole job," "seek an all-embracing theory," and "get the whole thing mapped out" in order to avoid criticism of single-track conservation efforts like those practiced by the CCC.[100] "The answer is for those who realize the gravity of the conservation situation to pool their knowledge and interests," he explained.[101] In particular, he implored "farmers" and "stockmen" concerned with natural resources to team up not only with "nature lovers" interested in both parks and wild spaces but also with "sportsmen," who focused on the ecological health of habitat for wildlife.[102] For Cooke, then, the New Deal's novel form of ecological planning could bring together under the unified banner of total conservation the contrasting conservationist ideologies highlighted by CCC work projects.

Ecological metaphors, however, were not the only influence on Cooke's more-inclusive brand of conservation. Ecological science also shaped total conservation. According to Cooke, this new approach to conservation was useful "not because we can define it exactly" but instead because it "may have the magic to make us all see our ultimate goals through a maze of ecological specialties having to do with soil, water, vegetation, wild life, and, of course, with man."[103] Not surprisingly, ecologists played a central role in Cooke's thinking. "The wise practice of 'total conservation' will involve the management of land in such a way as to create on it a community," he explained in language that played on, but was significantly different from, the "wise use" rhetoric of Progressive conservationists. "This means the planning of communities whose organizations roughly parallel the pattern set by nature."[104] Ecological scientists, he concluded, "must help in giving unity to the drive for 'total conservation'."[105] For perhaps the first time in American history, a federal bureaucrat was promoting nature as a guide for a new, more-inclusive type of conservation.

Although championed most forcefully by Cooke, during the late 1930s the idea of total conservation was increasingly popular among New Deal administrators, some of whom used it to promote Roosevelt's reorganization efforts. While Hugh Bennett endorsed what he also called "total conservation" in the magazine *Soil Conservation* and Benton MacKaye did similarly in letters to fellow planners such as Clarence Stein, TVA director David Lilienthal refrained from naming this new approach specifically but nevertheless gave speeches calling for the inclusion of the ecological sciences in Tennessee Valley conservation efforts.[106] Yet it was Harold Ickes who most directly employed this idea to support the Brownlow Report. "I am persuaded that we are not going to get very far in building up a real conservation policy for the government unless all the conservation activities are right in one department," he wrote in support of reorganization. A Department of Conservation, he continued, was a place where "all conservation problems can be handled with relation to each other, because there is an interrelationship."[107] The centralized Conservation

Department recommended in Roosevelt's reorganization plan, Ickes concluded, went hand in hand with a more integrated, scientific, and efficient form of conservation.

Thus, as New Deal planners were taking a page from New Deal conservation during the late 1930s and forging a new style of ecological planning on the federal level, New Deal conservationists were conversely borrowing from New Deal planners. The Corps' Robert Fechner, the Soil Conservation Service's Hugh Bennett, and the TVA's David Lilienthal, for instance, all embraced the more ecological style of planning promoted by Roosevelt during the later 1930s. The result was total conservation, a more-inclusive, scientific brand of conservation that integrated the competing conservationist ideologies unleashed by the public debate over the expanding character of CCC work projects. Under the umbrella of total conservation, there was room for the conservation of natural and human resources as well as ecological balance and wilderness preservation. Roosevelt's reorganization plan, proponents argued, sought to make this more-comprehensive form of conservation a permanent part of the federal government by placing it squarely within a newly christened Department of Conservation. Ecological planning, in turn, attempted to plant total conservation permanently within Roosevelt's liberal welfare state. Unfortunately for the president, opponents of reorganization thought otherwise.

Arguments in support of the Brownlow Report that relied on ecological planning and total conservation did not hold water for opponents of federal reorganization during the third New Deal. Not surprisingly, the most vocal critics of reorganization were those associated with the U.S. Forest Service, which under reorganization would most probably be transferred from the Department of Agriculture to the proposed Department of Conservation. Along with agriculture chief Henry Wallace, professional foresters were particularly active in the campaign against the reorganization plan through their group, the Society of American Foresters; as soon as the Brownlow Report became public in January 1937, the society began enlisting regional foresters, faculty members of forestry schools, and businesspeople from the timber industry in a nationwide letter-writing campaign against reorganization. Gifford Pinchot, who had founded the society in 1900 to promote the practice of forestry in the United States, spearheaded this effort by writing numerous letters to magazines and newspapers across the country and by attacking the reorganization plan in speeches before a variety of local groups, including garden clubs, granges, and conservation organizations.[108] The society also hired a professional lobbyist, Charles Dunwoody, to coordinate efforts to defeat the proposal.[109] Such actions helped to bring farmers and ranchers into this "Forest Service lobby," and prompted Department of the Interior secretary Harold Ickes to remark, "the Old Guard is marshalling its forces, but I know of no way to stop it."[110]

Similar to park advocates who supported reorganization, the Forest Service lobby first relied on arguments related to the political crisis facing the New Deal during the late 1930s. Yet whereas proponents of reorganization promoted increased centralized power as beneficial to what they called "modern democracy," those opposing the plan insisted the exact opposite, that reorganization would threaten the American way by giving too much power to the president.[111] Such fears were further inflamed by Roosevelt's attempt in February 1937 to pack the Supreme Court, a move repeatedly held up by those opposing reorganization as yet another example of Roosevelt's dictatorial tendencies. The Brownlow Report, argued Representative Hamilton Fish, "is just a step to concentrate power in the hands of the President and set up a species of fascism or nazi-ism or an American form of dictatorship."[112] Former Forest Service chief Gifford Pinchot, who had recently completed his second term as governor of Pennsylvania, used similar language to attack Ickes, who many viewed as the source of the reorganization idea. "Ickes and Hitler seem to have the same method," explained Pinchot after Ickes first tried to take the Forest Service from the Department of Agriculture. "I might add, [they have] certain very definite resemblances in character."[113]

Critics of the Brownlow Report also attacked the notion that reorganization would increase bureaucratic coordination and thus enhance programmatic efficiency within the federal government. Here, the labor movement joined forces with the Forest Service lobby, arguing that by providing the president with the political power to transfer bureaus as he saw fit, whenever he saw fit, reorganization would actually obstruct the day-to-day functioning of the administration. The American Federation of Labor specifically argued that the constant threat of immediate bureau transfers, and with it the possibility of federal layoffs, would paralyze government employees, many of whom were rank-and-file union members. Providing Roosevelt with this political power, argued AFL representatives in hearings before Congress in 1938, would "keep the Federal service in a state of constant anxiety and turmoil."[114] Thus, while reorganization supporters promoted the Brownlow Report as a means of solving the pair of political problems plaguing the Roosevelt administration during the later 1930s, opponents countered that it would instead create a presidential dictator ruling over an increasingly inefficient federal bureaucracy.

Those opposed to the Brownlow Report also believed that reorganization would do little to solve the conservation crisis of the third New Deal. For starters, they argued that centralizing authority in a new Department of Conservation under the direction of Harold Ickes would exacerbate, rather than resolve, this conservationist crisis. Reorganization opponents based such claims on the fact that the Department of the Interior, which according to the Brownlow Report would become the new Department of Conservation, had little experience conserving trees, soil, and water. The Interior Department "is organized not to manage natural resources," complained Pinchot to Roosevelt early in the reorganization fight.[115] Instead, interior was dominated by what the Society of American Foresters called an "urban ideal" based on a "recreational urge" that had been greatly enhanced by the CCC's development work in state and national parks across the country. This special interest among urbanites, argued reorganization opponents, violated Gifford Pinchot's conservationist mantra of "the greatest good of the greatest number for the longest time." According to such thinking, the proposed Department of Conservation, which would oversee parks created by the Corps and used primarily by city dwellers, failed to meet this democratic standard. "The good of the whole Nation," continued the Society of American Foresters, "means more to foresters than the unlimited and unregulated extension of the single urban objective of recreational monopoly."[116] Centralizing authority for conservation in a department run by former park administrators, these critics argued, enmeshed conservation in interest group politics.

The Forest Service lobby also dismissed the Brownlow Report's claim that reorganization would enhance coordination among federal conservation efforts. On the most basic level, opponents argued that too much coordinated management under a proposed Department of Conservation could actually hinder federal conservation activities and thus aggravate the conservation crisis of the third New Deal. In particular, opponents feared the creation of a permanent central planning agency, such as the NRPB, that would oversee the wide variety of conservation efforts undertaken by the proposed Conservation Department. "Each of these activities," Secretary of War George Dern argued of flood control, soil erosion, and wildlife preservation, "is a separate problem, to be handled by a special group of experts." According to Dern and others involved in opposing reorganization, "too much coordination" by an agency like the NRPB "might prove harmful," in part because it might place the concerns of a single interest group above the common good.[117] Thus, while Brownlow Report proponents such as Ickes promoted increased centralization and coordination as solutions to the conservation crisis, opponents countered that reorganization would actually make matters worse for the conservation movement.

In opposing Franklin Roosevelt's reorganization plan, the Forest Service lobby therefore rejected outright the idea, promoted by the Corps, Morris Cooke, and like-minded New Dealers in the later 1930s, that conservationists should broaden their purview beyond natural resources to include as well a concern for human resources, ecological balance, and the preservation of wild spaces. Instead, opponents of reorganization fell back on the old Progressive Era argument that conservation should entail the efficient use of natural resources. Trees were crops, the Forest Service lobby argued, and logically belonged in the Department of Agriculture, not in a new Conservation Department also overseeing parks. The Forest lobby, in other words, viewed reorganization less as a mechanism for coordinating forestry with other types of conservation efforts, in this case involving national parks, and instead as an attempt to supplant an old, familiar brand of conservation with something new. It was due in part to such opposition, and the call for a return to Progressive-style conservation, that in early April 1938 Congress defeated President Roosevelt's reorganization plan.

In the end, then, Ding Darling's "Kidnapping" helped to derail Roosevelt's efforts to reorganize the federal government. The cartoon's depiction of interior's secretary, Ickes, stealing the Forest Service while agriculture's secretary, Wallace, looked on, bound and gagged, captured perfectly the concerns of reorganization opponents regarding the dangers of increasing both authority and coordination within the federal government during the so-called third New Deal. The efforts of Gifford Pinchot, the Forest Service lobby, and the American Federation of Labor, not to mention political cartoonists, all weakened executive power, hindered administrative coordination, and made it even more difficult for Roosevelt to promote his liberal agenda during the late 1930s and early 1940s. "History will probably mark the crisis of President Roosevelt's political career," explained the New York *World-Telegram* on April 9, 1938, "by yesterday's defeat of the Reorganization Bill."[118] Darling's cartoon thus illustrates not only the continuing influence of conservation on federal politics during Roosevelt's second term in office, but also indicates the first wave in a half-century rollback of New Deal liberalism.

Yet less obvious in "The Kidnapping" is the inverse relationship regarding the impact of reorganization on the conservation movement. In winning this political battle, reorganization opponents like Ding Darling stalled a new era for conservation within the federal government. Due to opposition by the likes of the Forest Service lobby, the New Deal's more ecological brand of national planning based on integration, balance, and science faltered within the Roosevelt administration at the end of the New Deal. Similarly, total conservation, a broadened ideology practiced by the CCC and the TVA that integrated the conservation of natural and human resources with ecological balance and wilderness preservation, also receded within federal politics by the end of the decade. Instead, opponents of the Brownlow Report successfully reinstated a more restricted notion of conservation, based solely on natural resources, presided over by what Secretary Dern called "a special group of experts." The result was a retreat, at least within the federal government, back to the conservationist thinking of the Progressive Era, with its narrow set of concerns and small number of professional practitioners.

Yet it was precisely because the New Deal's novel type of conservation withered within federal politics during the late 1930s that it took root instead in the public sphere in the early 1940s. This process began on March 23, 1940, when approximately sixty individuals gathered at Washington, D.C.'s Wardman Park Hotel to create a new conservation organization called Friends of the Land. Presiding over this group were none other than Morris Cooke and Hugh Bennett, the very New Deal administrators who had failed to institutionalize total conservation during the federal reorganization debate. Not surprisingly, Friends of the Land immediately set out to promote a civic version of total conservation by linking the group's creation explicitly to the broadening of conservationist thought, caused in part by the expansion of CCC work projects. "With the conservation idea advancing to a wider outlook," involving a broad array of concerns for "soil, grass, trees, songbirds, game, flowers, livestock, landscape, or outdoor recreation," explained one Friends of the Land publicity brochure, "the time is right for such a society to form and act" in order to "unify all efforts for ... conservation."[119] This new group, in other words, accepted the diverse array of conservationist ideologies of the later New Deal period but hoped to unite them under a more inclusive, integrated conservation agenda. It also hoped to name this new way of thinking. This "wider outlook," wrote one Friends of the Land member in 1947, marked a new "recognition and acceptance of the responsibility that [humanity] adjust properly to [its] *total environment.*"[120]

As important, Friends of the Land deemed it necessary to guide this adjustment to the total environment not from Pennsylvania Avenue or the halls of the capital but rather from Main Street and the homes of ordinary Americans. Friends of the Land, explained an early membership flyer for the new organization, is "a nonprofit, nonpartisan society" aimed not just at professional foresters interested in conserving natural resources and scientific ecologists concerned with the balance of nature, but also at everyday "outdoor enthusiasts" who hiked, camped, and hunted in parks and wilderness areas. Cooke and his cohorts were particularly interested in attracting to their new organization America's youth. In an explicit reference to the Corps and its millions of young enrollees, Friends of the Land hoped to foster "the participation of the youth and youth organizations and especially unemployed youth, in a moral equivalent of war against wastage."[121] Thus, while the New Deal's novel brand of total conservation began within the federal government in programs like the CCC, by the early 1940s it had migrated outside the Beltway, so to speak, to become a concern of special interest groups like Friends of the Land.[122] Fortunately for all Americans, this migration—from a narrow conservation orchestrated from above by politicians in Washington, D.C., to a broader notion of the environment embraced from below by special interest groups appealing particularly to America's younger generation–blossomed in the postwar era into a new social movement.

EPILOGUE

New Deal Landscapes in the Environmental Era

During the spring of 1942, Corps enrollees stationed in Virginia's George Washington National Forest began dismantling Camp Roosevelt, the first CCC camp in the nation. They probably began by removing 200 iron cots and bedding from the six barracks located in the northern section of the camp. They carted out books, old magazines, desks, and chairs from the camp library, pool and ping-pong tables from the recreation hall, and cooking appliances, utensils, and dishware, used for nearly a decade to provide thousands of hungry young men with three square meals a day, from the mess hall and camp kitchen. They even removed the medical supplies from the infirmary, so that all of the camp buildings, except the pump house, could be sold off by the federal government and physically moved to other locations. On the last day of the camp breakdown, before the Corps left the Massanutten Mountains for good, these young men also probably gathered around the same pine tree flagpole created back in April 1933, just days after Franklin Roosevelt initiated the Corps, when a young enrollee named John Ripley climbed to the top of the tree and began stripping it of branches until the trunk stood straight and bare. The CCC enrollees who came together in 1942 next almost certainly watched as one of their colleagues pulled on a rope, attached to the tree by a pulley, and slowly lowered the American flag for the very last time from high above Camp Roosevelt.[1]

The closing of Camp Roosevelt during the spring of 1942 suggests that the New Deal continued to initiate important historical changes even at the end of the Great Depression. Most obviously, the lowering of the American flag in the center of the nation's oldest CCC camp symbolizes the slow descent of the

CCC opposition

New Deal political order, which began in the late 1930s with battles over federal reorganization and the Supreme Court and continued into the postwar era. Yet while the New Deal's political influence waned, the landscapes created during this period endured long after Roosevelt left office. Like all Corps camps across the country, when Camp Roosevelt packed up and left, it left behind a radically altered natural landscape, in this case comprised not only of stone foundations, dirt paths, and open fields where CCC enrollees once slept, walked, and did morning calisthenics, but also a transformed forest, extensive hiking trails, and numerous campgrounds and picnic areas that tens of thousands of Americans used after World War II.[2] The lowering of a flag down a pine tree pole during the summer of 1942 thus indicates that even as the Corps closed up shop, the landscapes it left behind continued to affect both American nature and American politics into the postwar decades.

The CCC's postwar influence began with the country's impending entry into World War II, which forced politicians in Washington, D.C., to begin debating the future, or lack thereof, of this New Deal program. "The Civilian Conservation Corps received what may be its death warning," explained *American Forests* during the summer of 1942, "when the bill providing appropriations for the Federal Security Agency was under consideration." During the three days of debate over the bill, representatives in Congress made numerous speeches opposing funding for the continuation of the Corps on the grounds that a dwindling number of young men were signing up for the New Deal program during the early 1940s, that a rising number of enrollees were leaving the CCC for work in the private sector, and most important that the Corps was using up manpower and federal funds that should be employed instead for the war effort. Not surprising in light of such arguments, the House of Representatives voted by a margin of 158–151 to liquidate the CCC, and then sent the bill terminating the New Deal program to the Senate where, as one writer for *American Forests* wistfully predicted, "Administration forces will make a determined effort to restore to the bill a continuing appropriation."[3]

Opposition to the CCC did not arise mysteriously in August 1942; it had begun during the late 1930s and early 1940s as concerns about American involvement in World War II raised questions about fiscal priorities within the federal government. In response to such criticisms, the Roosevelt administration made every effort to portray the Corps and its conservation work as central to the war effort. "You are dead right about the danger of forest fires on the Pacific Coast," wrote Franklin Roosevelt to Utah senator Elbert Thomas in March 1942. "It is obvious that many of them will be deliberately set on fire if

CCC
+ nat'l defense

the Japs attack there." Corps forest fire protection work in that region would defend against such foreign aggression. "I don't think people realize that the CCC [is] doing essential war work," concluded the president.[4]

While Roosevelt praised Corps conservation projects for aiding national defense, the CCC's second director, James McEntee, also emphasized the New Deal program's role in preparing the country's young men for military conflict. "The Corps has hastened and is hastening the day when this country will be adequately prepared for any aggressor or combination of aggressors," wrote McEntee in his annual report of 1940. "By continuing this man-building program, the Nation will continue to strengthen national defense by building up the health and skills of youths for selective service."[5] The CCC director proved prescient; approximately 90 percent of the more than 3 million young men in the Corps during the Great Depression era later served their country in the armed services.[6] Thus while President Roosevelt painted the Corps' work conserving natural resources as central to the country's defense efforts, McEntee promoted his program's role in conserving human resources, in this case the more than 3 million young men who enrolled in the New Deal program, as likewise helping the country to prepare for war.

Yet the Corps did more than merely portray the conservation work it had been performing throughout the New Deal era as an aid to military preparedness. During the early 1940s, the CCC explicitly began redirecting its entire conservation program toward national defense. This process began in June 1940, when Franklin Roosevelt's proclamation of a limited national emergency encouraged the Corps to begin training its enrollees for military service. Such defense training at first involved only classroom study, which excused enrollees from five hours of conservation work per week, but was extended in August 1940 to include also the drilling of CCC enrollees in simple military uniforms. By December of the following year, Corps director James McEntee had begun to assign CCC camps to military reservations where enrollees undertook a host of defense-related work projects, including the construction of target ranges, airplane landing fields, and military structures such as barracks.[7] In January 1942, the Corps again broadened such efforts by adopting a "Victory War Program," which according to McEntee "placed all CCC facilities squarely in back of the War effort."[8] By May of that year, McEntee had assigned approximately 175 camps and more than 12,000 enrollees to military reservations and forts, and by June the CCC was devoting all of its labor to war-related projects.[9] Such work projects, argued *American Forests*, represented "conservation in its broadest sense. It is America's saga to conserve freedom of thought, speech, worship, work, play, life itself."[10]

Thus, while the imminent entry of the United States into World War II threatened the future of the CCC, the Corps and its conservation projects in turn influenced the politics of military preparedness. The CCC not only portrayed its conservation as essential to the country's defense efforts but also altered the types of projects it undertook to help the military organize for war. The Corps even funneled the overwhelming majority of its enrollees directly into the military during the early years of the conflict. In the process, the Corps once again expanded the idea of conservation, this time to include a concern for protecting not natural or human resources, nor wilderness or ecological balance, but rather a variety of American freedoms that were threatened by World War II. In the end, though, the CCC could not deflect criticism that it was siphoning dollars from the war effort, and in late June 1942, the Senate followed the House's lead and also voted to abolish the New Deal program. As the *New York Times* proclaimed of the Senate vote, "Thus will disband the remnants of one of the most popular of the New Deal establishments."[11]

While the vote in Washington, D.C., meant flags like that flying over Camp Roosevelt would soon be lowered in CCC camps across the country, the Corps nevertheless continued to cast a long shadow over both conservation and politics in the postwar era. This impact was most immediately felt within the halls of government, where CCC conservation had taken its first steps. On the local level, cities and counties after World War II immediately began to establish a wide variety of programs that replicated the CCC and its conservation work. Atlanta, Georgia, and San Francisco, California, for instance, initiated their own Corps-like programs, as did counties throughout the country. The Montgomery County Conservation Corps of Maryland, along with the Marin Conservation Corps and the Tulare County Conservation Corps in California, were just a few of the local governmental programs that adopted the CCC idea, its nomenclature, and its practices after World War II.[12]

The Corps similarly influenced state governments during the immediate postwar period. While the great majority of CCC enrollees joined the military during World War II, many instead entered graduate programs at state universities in the "land sciences." As early as 1935, for example, the University of Idaho experienced an increase of 300 students, almost all former Corps enrollees, in its forestry program.[13] The states of Wisconsin, California, and New York also paid homage to the Corps by creating postwar conservation programs for prisoners that housed participating inmates in former CCC camps.[14] Perhaps the best indication that the CCC tradition lived on in state-houses across the country, however, were the numerous state conservation corps created during the postwar era that borrowed the name of the New Deal program and intentionally replicated its work. Among them were the California Conservation Corps, the New Hampshire Conservation Corps, the Arizona Conservation Corps, the Montana Conservation Corps, the Washington Conservation Corps, and the Michigan Civilian Conservation Corps.[15]

Finally, the postwar staying power of the CCC was evident nationally within the federal government. To begin with, many CCC enrollees simply took jobs with federal conservation bureaus.[16] "In camp I took some conservation courses," explained former enrollee Chuck Krall. "I credit the CCC experience as the main reason for my thirty-year career in the Soil Conservation Service."[17] Hundreds followed in Krall's footsteps, including ten enrollees from one camp near Highland, California, who left the Corps for Forest Service careers, fourteen enrollees who became regional forest directors in the northern Great Plains and Alaska, two enrollees who rose to the rank of superintendent at Mount Rushmore National Monument and Glen Canyon National Recreation Area, and at least one former Corps enrollee who served as assistant regional director of the National Park Service.[18] The federal government even proposed and enacted a slew of programs aimed at replicating the CCC in the postwar era. Although attempts to re-establish the Corps failed in 1950 and again during the late 1980s, when New York senator Daniel Patrick Moynihan proposed an American Conservation Corps, other efforts proved more successful.[19] In 1965 Lyndon Johnson created Job Corps, which was administered by a former CCC enrollee and housed its own young enrollees in abandoned CCC camps that were renamed Civilian Conservation Centers; in 1971 Richard Nixon signed an act establishing the Youth Conservation Corps; and in 1977 Congress initiated the Young Adult Conservation Corps.[20] President Bill Clinton followed suit in 1993 with AmeriCorps, which according to one newspaper reporter "considers itself the 'grandchild' of the original CCC [and] routinely does much of the same type work its 'grandparent' did."[21]

The Corps' lasting effect on local, state, and federal governments undoubtedly influenced both conservation and politics during the early postwar period. For instance, whereas the majority of government conservation agencies, including the U.S. Forest Service, the National Park Service, and the Soil Conservation Service, were administered primarily from the federal level prior to World War II, after the war, because of the CCC, an increasing number of towns, counties, states, and even regions initiated their own conservation programs and policies. As the New Deal came to an end, in other words, the federal conservation efforts initiated by Roosevelt began to trickle

postwar
CCC influence

down from the federal to the state and local levels.[22] Yet it was outside these formal government institutions, beyond town halls, county seats, statehouses, and the nation's capital building, that the CCC had its most enduring, and important, impact after the Second World War. This influence, moreover, had as much to do with the Corps and its conservation work as it did with the shifting political terrain of the postwar United States.

As the sun set on the New Deal, the country's political landscape began to evolve in two interrelated directions. On the one hand, postwar America experienced a dramatic rise in the number and power of nongovernmental groups that put pressure from the bottom up on elected government officials at the local, state, and national levels. While such grassroots politics had a long history in the United States, it flourished perhaps most fully in the postwar era.[23] The second transformation involved an associated shift in political priorities. Whereas New Deal liberals during the Great Depression had been concerned primarily with economic efficiency as a means of ensuring financial recovery for both the nation and its citizens, many of the new grassroots groups established during the affluent postwar era were more interested in correcting the social injustices of everyday life. The civil rights, New Left, antiwar, and women's movements were just a few examples of these special interest factions concerned with "quality of life" issues. Environmentalism was another, and in helping to foster it the Corps was furthering this novel form of postwar politics.[24]

On the most basic level, the CCC supported this postwar shift by sparking an increase in the number of nongovernmental citizens' conservation groups after World War II. This process began with Corps enrollees, who after leaving the New Deal program created their own organizations in various regions of the country that replicated much of the CCC's work. Former enrollees from upstate New York, for instance, formed an independent group called the Ex Civilian Conservation Corps Workers, while a second contingent from Kentucky got together to organize the American Conservation Enrollees.[25] In the Great Lakes area, Clarence Case, who had served in a CCC camp located near Lansing, Michigan, also founded Citizens for Conservation and Trustees of the Earth in 1953.[26] Former CCC enrollees even initiated a countrywide organization called the National Association of Civilian Conservation Corps Alumni. Created to preserve the memory of the original New Deal program, this CCC alumni association boasted 7,000 members by the end of the 1970s.[27]

Along with encouraging former enrollees to organize their own conservation programs after WWII, the Corps also spurred local communities to create independent citizens' groups. Beginning in 1942, a program called the

"Green Guards" trained more than 5,000 boys and girls from dozens of small towns across Oregon to undertake conservation work in nearby forests, much like the CCC had done during the 1930s.[28] Not to be outdone, in the mid-1950s college students initiated a similar program, the Student Conservation Association, which put university students to work on conservation projects near their college campuses. Urban communities were also involved in such efforts. In the 1990s the city of Durham, North Carolina, created the Durham Service Corps, which one reporter called "a back-to-the-future version of the Depression era's Civilian Conservation Corps."[29]

Such efforts were not confined to groups created by former CCC enrollees or local communities. The Corps' ability to foster nongovernmental copycat programs after the Second World War reached the national level as well. In the mid-1950s, the National Parks Association, created in 1919 as an independent watchdog agency to oversee administration of the country's national parks, began to lament publicly the limited resources provided by the federal government to the National Park Service. "For many years the national parks have suffered from lack of manpower," explained the National Parks Association in 1957. That same year the association responded by creating its Student Conservation Program. Similar to the original CCC, the program enrolled young Americans, in this case high school, college, and graduate school students, and put them to work helping "the National Park Service maintain the natural beauty of the parks while serving its visitors."[30] Unlike the original Corps, however, the National Parks Association was a citizens' group that administered its Student Conservation Program from the private sector.

Sparking a host of new, independent citizens' groups that replicated its conservation work beyond local, state, and federal governments, however, was only one avenue by which the Corps continued to influence conservation and politics in the postwar era. After the Second World War, the CCC also helped to shape the interests of these copycat programs. Not surprisingly, many of the independent conservation organizations that built on the CCC's legacy focused on the old Progressive Era concern regarding natural resources. Oregon's "Green Guards," for instance, put young boys and girls to work clearing combustible underbrush from forest floors, building firebreaks, and staffing lookout stations in forests near the youths' local communities, the very same jobs undertaken by CCC enrollees during the early 1930s, when the Corps focused primarily on the nation's timber resources.[31] While this interest was not new, local programs like the "Green Guards" in Oregon continued to push this concern for efficient natural resource use from its Progressive Era perch primarily within government agencies into the realm of the private citizen. The outdoor labor of a new generation of young Americans in programs like the "Green Guards" thus harked back to Roosevelt's Corps while simultaneously bringing forward into the postwar era the interest in "simple conservation" so central to progressives like Gifford Pinchot.

Along with propelling old governmental concerns into the public arena, the Corps also helped to create new special interests for citizens' groups after World War II. Unlike the progressives' concern for natural resources, however, these new interests were focused less on economic efficiency than on enhancing the quality of life for ordinary Americans. One new concern involved the conservation of human resources. Like the original CCC, the Durham Service Corps enrolled young Americans who were often unemployed, living in poverty, and physically unhealthy. "Durham's two-year old experiment," explained one reporter from the *Wall Street Journal*, "targets the town's toughest, most troubled youths" in the hopes that "CCC-like discipline" on work projects involving, for instance, the planting of "erosion-control seedlings," will rejuvenate both forests and youths alike.[32] While Durham followed the Corps' lead in conserving young people through outdoor labor, other CCC-like programs focused instead on rehabilitating the American public by developing parks for outdoor recreation. The National Parks Association's Student Conservation Program, for instance, put youths to work maintaining hiking trails, repairing visitor buildings, and restoring campgrounds in Grand Teton National Park.[33] The notion of a "broader conservation" involving both natural and human resources, which had roots in Frederick Law Olmstead's park movement and later flourished during the New Deal because of the CCC, was thus alive and well within a variety of independent citizens' programs that intentionally replicated the Corps after the Second World War.

A new interest in the philosophy and science of ecology also became important to many of the postwar independent programs inspired by the CCC. The group American Conservation Enrollees, created by former Corps boys from the Louisville, Kentucky, region, promoted, among other types of work, projects that protected vanishing wildlife by restoring the state's ecological habitat.[34] Citizens for Conservation and Trustees of the Earth, also established by former CCC enrollees, organized a similar ecological program for the entire Great Lakes region.[35] This new approach to conservation had influenced Corps projects and planning only during the later New Deal years, in places like the Tennessee Valley, after scientists such as Aldo Leopold began publicly criticizing certain Corps work for upsetting the so-called balance of nature. Although the CCC was late to embrace Leopold's "true conservation," the independent citizens' groups inspired by the Corps after World War II were quick to incorporate ecology into their various conservation efforts.

Finally, along with promoting interests in natural resources, human resources, and ecological balance, several programs that followed the Corps' lead also embraced a concern for wilderness preservation during the postwar period. Perhaps the best example of this was the Student Conservation Association. Founded by college students in the late 1950s explicitly as a means of continuing the Corps' efforts, the association exposed young Americans to wilderness and provided them with jobs aimed at protecting wild spaces. Students who enrolled in the program not only learned wilderness survival skills and patrolled backcountry areas but more important worked on projects aimed at reclaiming wilderness by, for instance, eradicating invasive species from wildlands and restoring aquatic areas that had been heavily affected by human use.[36] The "wilderness conservation" so dear to those like Bob Marshall, who during the 1930s began criticizing CCC road projects in parks for destroying wilderness, had moved to center stage in several Corps-like organizations functioning outside government bureaus after the Second World War.

Thus, along with influencing the country's entry into World War II and fostering a diversity of Corps-like programs within local, state, and federal governments, the CCC inspired a wide range of independent, copycat citizens' groups during the immediate postwar years. As the Corps' influence trickled down from the federal to the state and local levels, in other words, it also began to sprout up from the grassroots. At the same time, the CCC helped to shape these new groups' interests, which focused less on economic efficiency and more on quality of life issues such as access to healthy work and play, a belief in ecological stewardship, and a desire to protect some wild areas from development. This shift toward grassroots politics was due partly to the failure, during the late 1930s, of Roosevelt's reorganization plan, which pushed these special interests from the proposed Department of Conservation out into private organizations like Morris Cooke's Friends of the Land. Yet the shift was also dependent on postwar politics, which encouraged social movements to function similarly from the bottom up.

While many of the new interest groups inspired by the Corps continued to shape postwar America, the Corps' legacy perhaps endured even more through the landscapes it left behind in every corner of the country. During the Great Depression, the landscapes transformed by the Corps in forests, parks, and on farms had greatly influenced the enrollees constructing them, the residents of local communities living near them, and the public at large who read about them in newspapers and magazines, who watched and heard about them in films and on radio, and who visited them in enormous numbers during the 1930s and early 1940s. The impact of these public spaces continued after World War II and is perhaps best exemplified by Dinosaur National Monument and the national controversy it sparked during the immediate postwar era.

The story of Dinosaur National Monument is usually portrayed as a creation tale for the modern environmental movement. According to this narrative, although President Woodrow Wilson established the eighty-acre site in 1915 in northeastern Utah to protect prehistoric dinosaur skeletons, it wasn't until after World War II that the monument took on national significance. By then, Dinosaur National Monument had been expanded eastward across the Colorado border to cover 100 miles of deep canyons carved by the Green and Yampa rivers, both of which caught the eye of irrigationists, reclamationists, and hydroengineers within the federal government who saw the Green River in particular as the perfect site for a power-generating dam. The national debate that took place in the late 1940s and early 1950s over whether or not to build this dam in the Echo Park section of Dinosaur National Monument, as well as the project's ultimate defeat in 1955, many argue, unleashed modern environmentalism in the United States.[37]

At first glance, the controversy over the Echo Park dam in Dinosaur National Monument after the Second World War seems like a repeat performance of the fight over Hetch Hetchy Valley in Yosemite National Park during the first decade of the twentieth century. At stake, once again, was whether or not the federal government could develop a site within the national park system, in this case a national monument, for purely utilitarian purposes. Battling one another, also once again, were conservationists within the federal government, who believed the dam would ensure the wisest use of natural resources, against an alliance of preservationists from both within and outside the federal government who felt instead that the project would jeopardize the integrity of the entire national park system. In the end, however, the outcome at Echo Park was the exact opposite as that which took place at Hetch Hetchy. Rather than a tall, concrete dam holding back another artificial lake, the Green River today flows freely through the steep canyons of Echo Park.

Commentators at the time and since have put forth a variety of explanations for this reversal of fortune. The loss of Hetch Hetchy way back in 1913, many argue, taught preservationists an invaluable lesson that would help guide them to victory after World War II. Others contend that it was the grassroots political structure of the postwar era that helped dam opponents raise enough broad-based support to successfully counter the power of federal agencies planning to submerge Echo Park under millions of acre-feet of water. Yet few, if any, commentators have looked to the period in between, to the years in the middle of the Hetch Hetchy controversy of the Progressive Era and the Echo Park debate taking place after the Second World War, for answers. No one, in other words, has examined the New Deal decade for clues to the victory at Echo Park. As important, nobody has looked to the landscape itself, and in particular to the landscape changes caused by the New Deal and the CCC, for an explanation as to why the Green River's salvation flowed into a new environmental politics.

The omission is all the more surprising considering that if not for Franklin Roosevelt, the New Deal, and the CCC, there would have been no Dinosaur National Monument over which to fight in the postwar era. This is because in April 1938 Secretary of the Interior Harold Ickes encouraged the president to enlarge the original, tiny national monument in order to protect the surrounding canyons both for aesthetic reasons and to preserve their rugged "frontier" heritage.[38] Three months later, on July 14, Roosevelt responded by signing a proclamation that increased Dinosaur National Monument from 80 to more than 200,000 acres, in effect transforming in one pen stroke one of the smallest National Park Service sites into one of the largest; the monument now covered more than 360 square miles and crossed state lines into neighboring Colorado. Local residents immediately grasped the opportunities inherent in the president's actions. The "possibilities," explained two newspapers from the region that collaborated on a story about the enlarged national monument, "are almost unlimited, and whether it be fishing, bathing, scenery, history, or study, the tourist may find it there."[39]

The only problem was that tourists during the late 1930s were having difficulty actually finding the monument, let alone locating fishing spots or bathing beaches within it. This was due only partly to the monument's remote location in the desert southwest. Not only was it several hundred miles from both Salt Lake City and Denver, but the monument had no access roads running into its picturesque canyons. An added liability was the site's status as a national monument, which historically received far less federal funding for recreational development projects than national park sites. In 1938, for instance, Dinosaur National Monument still lacked a visitor center, and only a few hundred tourists each year visited the site.[40] Thus, although Franklin Roosevelt in effect put Dinosaur National Monument on the map by greatly enlarging it during the Great Depression, at the time the monument remained one of the most isolated and unknown Park Service sites in the country.

In an effort to make Dinosaur National Monument more accessible to the American public, during the late 1930s and early 1940s Franklin Roosevelt sent the CCC to the region. The Corps located four of its camps in the area and assigned approximately 800 enrollees to conservation projects that would help to develop that corner of the desert southwest for outdoor recreation.[41] The CCC accomplished this by assigning several camps and hundreds of enrollees to work projects that involved motor road construction to the south of Dinosaur National Monument, which opened up the entire canyon lands to automobile tourism.[42] Such Corps recreational development work eventually paid off; whereas one commentator noted during the early 1930s that "no one had ever heard of Dinosaur National Monument," by 1954 visitation rates had skyrocketed to more than 70,000 outdoor recreationists annually.[43]

The same New Deal policies that brought the CCC to Dinosaur National Monument, however, also encouraged other federal programs to formulate their own development plans for the area. The Bureau of Reclamation began setting its sights on the monument soon after Franklin Roosevelt's 1938 proclamation to enlarge it. Having already developed the lower Colorado River with the construction of Boulder Dam during the early 1930s and completed other dam projects in California's Central Valley and along the Columbia River in the Pacific Northwest, in 1939 the bureau sent surveyors, engineers, and geologists into the upper Colorado River basin in search of similar dam sites. It was while exploring the Green River, a tributary of the Colorado, that the bureau found tall canyon walls only a few hundred feet apart near Echo Park, which happened to lie within Dinosaur National Monument. This location just below the confluence of the Green and Yampa rivers was ideal for a large dam and reservoir, and by the end of the year the Bureau of Reclamation had begun drawing up detailed blueprints for a new dam in Echo Park.[44] It was these plans that ignited a national debate and a new national movement.

Supporters of the proposed dam at Echo Park defended the project in much the same way conservationists had defended the construction of the dam at Hetch Hetchy. Taking their cue from the Progressive Era, dam supporters argued that the Echo Park project represented the most efficient use of the region's scarce natural resources. As one scholar has noted, proponents of the Echo Park dam adhered to "a traditional conception of conservation—in this case, the wise use and management of the Colorado River."[45] They relied, in other words, on Gifford Pinchot's tried and true notion of "simple conservation." It was on such grounds that old school conservationists within the

Bureau of Reclamation, along with Secretary of the Interior Oscar Chapman, approved plans for the dam and in June 1950 sent the matter to Congress for public discussion.

Opponents of the Echo Park plan were also similar to those who rallied against the damming of Hetch Hetchy Valley back in the 1910s. The National Park Service, which had fought the dam in Yosemite because it would encourage comparable development in other national parks, opposed the Dinosaur National Monument project for similar reasons, while the Sierra Club objected, as it had during the Hetch Hetchy controversy, on the grounds that the new dam would mar the unique beauty of Park Service lands.[46] Yet at Echo Park these same Progressive Era preservationists were joined by new advocacy groups, born during the New Deal years when Bob Marshall began calling for "wilderness conservation," that greatly expanded both the constituency and political strength of the anti-dam bloc. Marshall's Wilderness Society, for instance, created in 1935 partly in response to growing concern over CCC road-building projects in places like Great Smoky Mountains National Park, publicly opposed the Echo Park dam for threatening wilderness in Dinosaur National Monument.[47] So did the American Nature Association, which had similarly criticized Corps road projects in the Sierra Nevada's Kings Canyon National Park.[48]

While conservationists and preservationists were again squaring off at Echo Park, much as they had at Hetch Hetchy, two new factions also came out against the proposed dam, but for very different reasons. The first of these arose in part because of the recreational development work undertaken by the CCC in places like the Utah-Colorado borderland. "[It is] essential for the good healthy lives of Americans that they should have out of door recreation areas," wrote one group opposing the Echo Park dam. Recreation projects like those undertaken by the Corps near Dinosaur National Monument, the group continued, "draw to them both children and adults and are the means of providing an incentive toward a more healthy rather than a less healthy form of recreation."[49] The proposed dam would destroy this opportunity for physical rejuvenation by placing much of Echo Park under water. Other outdoor recreation organizations also embraced this notion of a "broader conservation," involving both natural and human resources, first put forth by reformers such as Frederick Law Olmsted. The Izaak Walton League, for instance, which during the early 1930s had praised Corps recreation work in parks for regenerating the public's health, fought hard against the Echo Park dam after the war because its construction would lessen the recreational value of Dinosaur National Monument.[50]

Another new faction, interested in the emerging science of ecology, also became active in the fight against the Bureau of Reclamation's proposal for Echo Park. Freelance writer and historian Bernard DeVoto first voiced this ecological opposition in a 1950 *Saturday Evening Post* essay titled "Shall We Let Them Ruin Our National Parks." In language that echoed Aldo Leopold's call for "true conservation," DeVoto argued that Dinosaur National Monument was important "for the field of study of . . . the balances of Nature, the web of life, the interrelationships of species."[51] Agreeing with DeVoto were several postwar conservation organizations that got their start during the New Deal years in part by criticizing the CCC for being ecologically reckless. Rosalie Edge's Emergency Conservation Committee and the National Wildlife Federation, both of which had opposed the Corps' predator control work during the late 1930s, came out against the Echo Park dam because it would tip nature's balance in Dinosaur National Monument.[52] The Audubon Society, which had similarly condemned the CCC for building roads across wildlife habitat, digging artificial ponds for water conservation, and draining swamps to control insects, also worked actively against the dam on ecological grounds.[53]

As the debate over Echo Park illustrates, years after Congress halted funding for the CCC, the New Deal program continued to influence both conservation and politics in the United States. The Corps shaped the former by inspiring a host of copycat programs, both within the government and outside it, that kept popularizing conservation to postwar Americans. By simultaneously helping to shape the concerns of these groups, the CCC also kept publicizing novel notions of conservation that went far beyond the wise use of natural resources. Equally important were the thousands of landscapes that the Corps left behind throughout the country, such as those in and around Dinosaur National Monument. It was there, in the nation's parks, forests, and on its farms, that the conservation movement in the postwar era continued to evolve.

The lingering impact of the Corps on the conservation movement also shaped, and was shaped by, the shifting political terrain of postwar America. By inspiring a multitude of CCC-like programs after the Second World War, the Corps nurtured the growth of independent citizens' groups functioning outside government control. This new form of grassroots politics, in turn, helped to promote a new set of special interests focused less on economic efficiency, a central characteristic of natural resource conservation, and more on quality of life issues including outdoor recreation, ecological stewardship, and the protection of wild spaces. These new interest groups, which joined forces after World War II as a new environmental movement, were part and parcel of the postwar political order.

These postwar changes, however, were merely the latest illustration of transformations that had begun during the 1930s with the rise of Franklin Roosevelt's New Deal. From the very start, the Corps and its work projects began to expand the composition of the conservation movement, which during the Progressive Era included a small contingent of scientists and government bureaucrats, and to a lesser extent rural landowners and hunters. The Corps extended this base by introducing the theory and practice of conservation to the CCC's working-class enrollees, to residents of local communities situated near Corps camps, and to the public as a whole through national media coverage of this wildly popular program. The result was a more broad-based constituency that reflected, and helped to produce, the grassroots character of post–World War II environmentalism.

Yet as the CCC democratized conservation during the New Deal years, it also redefined it. This process began when Corps work projects sparked a national debate that expanded the meaning of conservation beyond the wise use of natural resources to include also concern for human health through outdoor work and play, the need for ecological balance, and interest in wilderness preservation, all of which became important to postwar environmentalists. What began the Great Depression as an ideology dominated by the likes of Gifford Pinchot, in other words, ended the New Deal era with additional intellectual baggage borrowed from thinkers such as Frederick Law Olmsted, Bob Marshall, and Aldo Leopold. The redefined and realigned movement that resulted reflected less the narrow constituency and limited concerns of Progressive Era conservation and increasingly the broadened base and expanded interests of postwar environmentalism.

As it altered conservation during the Great Depression, the Corps also transformed New Deal politics. The Corps did this first by raising support for the Roosevelt administration in every region of the country. The program and its work appealed to foresters out West, to farmers across the Dust Bowl and the soil-eroded South, and to easterners who could now recreate in hundreds of state and national parks only a few hours' drive from their homes. The Corps also attracted both urban youths flocking into the program as well as rural landowners who benefited financially from Corps work projects that increased agricultural and timber production as well as recreational tourism. Franklin Roosevelt immediately understood the political support he could raise, as well as the political power he could exercise, through the strategic placement of Corps camps and work projects through out the country. Thus, while the public works of the CCC introduced conservation to the nation, altering the conservation movement in the process, the Corps' work relief introduced the welfare state to the American people, and in doing so helped to raise widespread geographic support for the New Deal.

While helping Roosevelt to introduce his policies to all regions of the country, the Corps also shaped New Deal politics by appealing across the ideological spectrum. The CCC program was extremely popular both with liberal working-class families, whose sons enrolled in the program, and with conservative upper-class business owners, who profited financially from trade with nearby Corps camps. It proved equally attractive to local politicians, regardless of party affiliation, who had camps in their districts, and to federal administrators in Washington, D.C., who obtained CCC appointments. Just as he understood the broad geographic appeal of the Corps, Franklin Roosevelt was similarly aware that the CCC could help unify often competing political interests under the banner of New Deal liberalism. The president intentionally used the CCC's fame among both the working and upper classes, on the local and the national levels, and on the political Left and the political Right to weave together an ideologically diverse political following that supported the modern welfare state.

Widespread support for the CCC was also evident as recently as September 2001, when the National Association of Civilian Conservation Corps Alumni held its annual reunion for former CCC enrollees at the site of the original Camp Roosevelt. Approximately 300 of the more than 3 million young men who joined the Corps during the Great Depression made the trip that September up into the Massanutten Mountains of George Washington National Forest, to what had been the first CCC camp in the nation. They came from across the country to take walking tours of Camp Roosevelt's crumbling foundations, to break bread at long tables that reminded them of meals eaten as young men in CCC mess halls across the country, and to gather around a new flagpole, this one not made by stripping a pine tree of its branches, which today stands in the center of the old Camp Roosevelt grounds. But these men came, too, because they believed their hard work in the Corps all those years ago had a lasting impact, not only on their country's forests, parks, and farms, but also on its politics. They came because they believed, in their minds and in their muscles, the slogan they chose for the banner of their alumni newsletter, which read in big, bold letters "Before Earth Day There Was the CCC."[54]

NOTES

INTRODUCTION

1. There are several accounts of the establishment of the nation's first CCC camp. See especially Erle Kauffman, "Roosevelt: Forest Camp No. 1," *American Forests* 39, no. 6 (June 1933): 251; Captain Leo Donovan, "The Establishment of the First Civilian Conservation Corps Camp," *Infantry Journal* (July–August 1933): 245; and William Train, Jr., "Building Camp Roosevelt . . . the First Civilian Conservation Corps Camp in the U.S.," *National Association of CCC Alumni Journal* (November 1992): 6.

2. The literature on the CCC is scant. The best administrative history of the Corps is John Salmond, *The Civilian Conservation Corps, 1933–1942: A New Deal Case Study* (Durham, N.C.: Duke University Press, 1967). For a survey of CCC work under the U.S. Forest Service, see Alison Otis, *The Forest Service and the Civilian Conservation Corps, 1933–1942* (Washington, D.C.: U.S. Forest Service, U.S. Department of Agriculture, 1986). For CCC work under the Park Service, see John Paige, *The Civilian Conservation Corps and the National Park Service: An Administrative History* (Washington, D.C.: National Park Service, U.S. Department of the Interior, 1985); for an examination of African Americans in the CCC, see Olen Cole, *The African-American Experience in the Civilian Conservation Corps* (Gainesville: University Press of Florida, 1999). Nonscholarly histories of the CCC include Ray Hoyt, *We Can Take It: A Short Story of the CCC* (Cincinnati, Ohio: American Book Company, 1935); Charles Harper, *The Administration of the CCC* (Clarksburg, W.Va.: Clarksburg, 1939); and James McEntee, *Now They Are Men: The Story of the CCC* (Washington, D.C.: National Home Library Foundation, 1940).

3. Robert Fechner, *Annual Report of the Director of the Civilian Conservation Corps: Fiscal Year Ended June 30, 1939* (Washington, D.C.: U.S. Government Printing Office, 1939), 7, located at RG35: CCC, Entry 3: Annual, Special, and Final Reports, NARA. The reports of the CCC director are essential for understanding the history of the Corps. Locating them, however, can be difficult because reports from the early CCC years were not published for the public, while later reports were printed by the U.S. Government Printing Office. Thankfully, all of these reports are located at Record Group 35: Civilian

Conservation Corps, Entry 3: Annual, Special, and Final Reports, NARA. When citing any of these reports I have noted their location at the National Archives and, when applicable, also if they were published by the U.S. Government Printing Office.

4. Historians have recently begun unearthing a more complicated history of the Hetch Hetchy controversy. See especially Robert W. Righter, *The Battle over Hetch Hetchy: America's Most Controversial Dam and the Birth of Modern Environmentalism* (New York: Oxford University Press, 2005); and Char Miller, *Gifford Pinchot and the Making of Modern Environmentalism* (Washington, D.C.: Shearwater, 2001), 138–144. On Pinchot and Muir as more complicated individuals, see also Donald Worster, "John Muir and the Modern Passion for Nature," *Environmental History* 10, no. 1 (January 2005): 8–19; and Brian Balogh, "Scientific Forestry and the Roots of the Modern American State: Gifford Pinchot's Path to Progressive Reform," *Environmental History* 7 (2002): 198–225. The interpretation of Hetch Hetchy as a battle between conservationists and preservationists has become a staple of American environmental history. See especially Roderick Nash, *Wilderness and the American Mind* (New Haven, Conn.: Yale University Press, 1967); and Stephen Fox, *The American Conservation Movement: John Muir and His Legacy* (Madison: University of Wisconsin Press, 1981).

5. This reference comes from Samuel Hays, *Conservation and the Gospel of Efficiency: The Progressive Conservation Movement, 1890–1920* (Cambridge, Mass.: Harvard University Press, 1959). The literature on the Progressive movement is vast. See especially James Weinstein, *The Corporate Ideal in the Liberal State, 1900–1918* (Boston: Beacon, 1968); Gabriel Kolko, *The Triumph of Conservatism: A Reinterpretation of American History, 1900–1916* (New York: Free Press, 1963); Robert Wiebe, *The Search for Order, 1877–1920* (New York: Hill and Wang, 1967); and Richard Hofstadter, *The Age of Reform* (New York: Knopf, 1955).

6. Environmental historians have recently begun examining this local, grassroots form of Progressive conservation. See especially Louis Warren, *The Hunter's Game: Poachers and Conservationists in Twentieth-Century America* (New Haven, Conn.: Yale University Press, 1997); Karl Jacoby, *Crimes against Nature: Squatters, Poachers, Thieves, and the Hidden History of American Conservation* (Berkeley: University of California Press, 2003); and Richard Judd, *Common Lands, Common People: The Origins of Conservation in Northern New England* (Cambridge, Mass.: Harvard University Press, 2000).

7. For links between natural resource conservation and the growth of the federal state during the Progressive Era, see Elmo Richardson, *The Politics of Conservation: Crusades and Controversies, 1897–1913* (Berkeley: University of California Press, 1962); Clayton Koppes, "Efficiency, Equity, Esthetics: Shifting Themes in American Conservation," in *Ends of the Earth,* ed. Donald Worster (New York: Cambridge University Press, 1988); and Brian Balogh, "Scientific Forestry and the Roots of the Modern American State," *Environmental History* 7 (April 2002): 198–225. For material on the western United States, where the links between federal power and natural resource conservation were especially pronounced, see Donald Pisani, *Water and American Government: The Reclamation Bureau, National Water Policy, and the West, 1902–1935* (Berkeley: University of California Press, 2002); and Donald Worster, *Rivers of Empire: Water, Aridity, and the Growth of the American West* (New York: Pantheon, 1985).

8. According to Mark Harvey, the Izaak Walton League put forth this outdoor recreation argument during the Echo Park controversy. See Mark Harvey, *A Symbol of Wilderness: Echo Park and the American Conservation Movement* (Seattle: University of

Washington Press, 2000), 54. For the ecological argument against the Echo Park dam, see Bernard DeVoto, "Shall We Let Them Ruin Our National Parks?" *Saturday Evening Post* 223 (1950): 44, as quoted in Nash, *Wilderness and the American Mind*, 214; and Benton MacKaye, "Dam Site vs. Norm Site," *Scientific Monthly* 61 (October 1950): 214–242.

9. Many argue that the Echo Park controversy in Dinosaur National Monument helped to spark modern environmentalism. See especially Hal Rothman, *The Greening of a Nation? Environmentalism in the United States since 1945* (New York: Harcourt Brace, 1998), 34; Robert Gottlieb, *Forcing the Spring: The Transformation of the American Environmental Movement* (Washington, D.C.: Island, 1993), 41; and William Cronon, "Foreword: The Dam That Wasn't," in Harvey, *A Symbol of Wilderness*, xiii. On the postwar environmental movement in general, see also Philip Shabecoff, *A Fierce Green Fire: The American Environmental Movement* (New York: Hill and Wang, 1993); Kirkpatrick Sale, *The Green Revolution: The American Environmental Movement, 1962–1992* (New York: Hill and Wang, 1993); and Adam Rome, *Bulldozer in the Countryside: Suburban Sprawl and the Rise of American Environmentalism* (New York: Cambridge University Press, 2001).

10. For a history of the amateur wing of the conservation movement, see Fox, *The American Conservation Movement*. On environmentalists' emphasis on quality-of-life issues, see Samuel Hays, *Beauty, Health, and Permanence: Environmental Politics in the United States, 1955–1985* (New York: Cambridge University Press, 1987), especially 22; and Adam Rome, "Give Earth a Chance: The Environmental Movement and the Sixties," *Journal of American History* 90, no. 2 (September 2003): 530, 532.

11. For a more expansive examination of the links between environmentalism and other postwar social movements, see Rome, "Give Earth a Chance," 525–554; Gottlieb, *Forcing the Spring*, especially chap. 3, "The Sixties Rebellion: The Search for a New Politics"; and Terry Anderson, *The Movement and the Sixties* (New York: Oxford University Press, 1995). On ties between postwar environmentalism and civil rights, see Eileen McGurty, "From NIMBY to Civil Rights: The Origins of the Environmental Justice Movement," *Environmental History* 2, no. 3 (July 1997): 301–323; and Andrew Hurley, *Environmental Inequalities: Class, Race, and Industrial Pollution in Gary, Indiana, 1945–1980* (Chapel Hill: University of North Carolina Press, 1995).

12. Hays, *Beauty, Health, and Permanence*. Here I am consciously avoiding Hays's paradigm that associates Progressive conservation with production and postwar environmentalism with consumption. The two, in my opinion, have always been more intimately linked. For a discussion of environmental history's lack of scholarship on the New Deal era, see Paul Sutter, "Terra Incognita: The Neglected History of Interwar Environmental Thought and Politics," *Reviews in American History* 29 (June 2001): 289–297. Exceptions to this rule include Donald Worster, *Dust Bowl: The Southern Plains in the 1930s* (New York: Oxford University Press, 1979); and, more recently, Paul Sutter, *Driven Wild: How the Fight against Automobiles Launched the Modern Wilderness Movement* (Seattle: University of Washington Press, 2002); Sarah Phillips, *This Land, This Nation: Conservation, Rural America, and the New Deal* (New York: Cambridge University Press, 2007); Randall Beeman and James Pritchard, *A Green and Permanent Land: Ecology and Agriculture in the Twentieth Century* (Lawrence: University Press of Kansas, 2001); and Brian Black, "Organic Planning: Ecology and Design in the Landscape of the Tennessee Valley Authority, 1933–45," in *Environmentalism in Landscape Architecture*, ed. Michel Conan (Washington, D.C.: Dumbarton Oaks Research Library and Collection, 2001).

13. Although historians have refrained from examining this link between conservation and New Deal politics, many have analyzed the rise of the modern welfare state during the New Deal era. See especially Theda Skocpol, "Political Response to Capitalist Crisis: Neo-Marxist Theories of the State and the Case of the New Deal," *Politics and Society* 10, no. 2 (1980): 155–201; Skocpol, "Bringing the State Back In: Strategies of Analysis in Current Research," in *Bringing the State Back In*, ed. Peter Evans, Dietrich Reuschemeyer, and Theda Skocpol (New York: Cambridge University Press, 1985); Alan Brinkley, *The End of Reform: New Deal Liberalism in Recession and War* (New York: Knopf, 1996); Brinkley, "The New Deal and the Idea of the State," in *The Rise and Fall of the New Deal Order, 1930–1980*, ed. Steve Fraser and Gary Gerstle (Princeton, N.J.: Princeton University Press, 1989).

14. For a wonderful discussion of the New Deal landscape, see Phoebe Cutler, *The Public Landscape of the New Deal* (New Haven, Conn.: Yale University Press, 1985).

15. My conception of landscape comes most directly from readings in cultural and historical geography. See especially Carl Sauer, "The Morphology of Landscape," *University of California Publications in Geography* 2, no. 2 (12 October 1925): 19–54; J. B. Jackson, *Discovering the Vernacular Landscape* (New Haven, Conn.: Yale University Press, 1984); J. B. Jackson, "A New Kind of Space," *Landscape* 18, no. 1 (Winter 1969): 33–35; and D. W. Meinig, ed., *The Interpretation of Ordinary Landscapes: Geographical Essays* (New York: Oxford University Press, 1979). For an informative description of landscape as an organizing concept, see Mart Stewart, *"What Nature Suffers to Groe": Life, Labor, and Landscape on the Georgia Coast, 1680–1920* (Athens: University of Georgia Press, 2002), prologue, 11–12.

16. On the difficulty of defining "nature," see Raymond Williams, *Keywords: A Vocabulary of Culture and Society* (New York: Oxford University Press, 1976), 184–189. As Williams explains on 186, "any full history of the uses of nature would be the history of a large part of human thought." Environmental historians' difficulty in pinpointing causes for ecological change is due to developments within the field of ecology which show that, rather than reaching a state of equilibrium, ecosystems are in a constant state of flux. For an analysis of what this insight means for environmental history, see Donald Worster, "The Ecology of Order and Chaos," in his *The Wealth of Nature* (New York: Oxford University Press, 1993), 156–170; and William Cronon, *Changes in the Land: Indians, Colonists, and the Ecology of New England* (New York: Hill and Wang, 1983), 10–11. For a synopsis of this debate within the field of ecology, see Alan Berryman, "Equilibrium or Nonequilibrium: Is That the Question?" *Bulletin of the Ecological Society of America* 68 (September 1987): 500–502; Robert McIntosh, "Pluralism in Ecology," *Annual Review of Ecological Systems* 18 (1987): 321–341; S. J. McNaughton, "Diversity and Stability," *Nature* 333 (May 1988): 204–205; and Paul Koetsier, Paul Dey, Greg Miadenka, and Jim Check, "Rejecting Equilibrium Theory: A Cautionary Note," *Bulletin of the Ecological Society of America* 71 (December 1990): 229–230.

17. On the political meaning of everyday landscape change, see especially Pierce F. Lewis, "Axioms for Reading the Landscape," in Meinig, *The Interpretation of Ordinary Landscapes*, 11–32; and Jackson, *Discovering the Vernacular Landscape*. My notion of linking environmental and political change has also been informed by the field of political ecology. For instructive overviews of this field, see Paul Robbins, *Political Ecology: A Critical Introduction* (New York: Blackwell, 2004), especially "Part I: What Is Political Ecology"; and Robbins, "Cultural Ecology," in *A Companion to Cultural*

Geography, ed. James Duncan, Nuala Johnson, and Richard Schein (New York: Blackwell, 2004).

18. See "Cultural History: Caring for the Land and Serving People: George Washington National Forest History," http://www.fs.fed.us/r8/gwj/cultural.

19. On the U.S. Forest Service as embodying both Progressive conservation and Progressive politics, see Hays, *Conservation and the Gospel of Efficiency*, especially chap. 3, "Woodman, Spare That Tree," 27–48. On Pinchot's wise use philosophy guiding early Forest Service management, see Miller, *Gifford Pinchot*, especially chap. 7.

20. On the early forestry work of Camp Roosevelt, see Erle Kauffman, " 'Roosevelt': Forest Camp No. 1," *American Forests* 39, no. 6 (June 1933): 270; Lucy Chumbley, "Recalling the Days: During the Great Depression, CCC Helped Area Man Make a Living," *Northern Virginia Daily*, 26 September 2001, 1; and Carrie Leonard, "Roosevelt's Tree Army," *Curio* (Summer 1984): 42.

21. For a wonderful analysis of Olmsted's philosophy, see W. H. Wilson, *The City Beautiful Movement* (Baltimore, Md.: Johns Hopkins University Press, 1989), especially chap. 1. On similar efforts during the Progressive Era, see Paul Boyer, *Urban Masses and Moral Order in America, 1820–1920* (Cambridge, Mass.: Harvard University Press, 1978), chaps. 15–16, especially 220–221.

22. On recreation development projects undertaken by Camp Roosevelt, see Leonard, "Roosevelt's Tree Army," 42; Chumbley, "Recalling the Days," 1; and Gerald W. Williams, "Camp Roosevelt, NF-1: First CCC Camp in the Nation," at the Camp Roosevelt Legacy Foundation Web site, http://www.cclegacy.org/ccc_history.htm#Camp%20 Roosevelt,%20NF-1.

23. For an example of Marshall's opposition to the CCC, see Bob Marshall to Willard Van Name, 31 July 1933, Bob Marshall Papers, Bancroft Library, University of California at Berkeley, Box 1, Folder 16, as quoted in Sutter, *Driven Wild*, 231.

24. George Washington National Forest contains six designated wilderness areas covering more than 32,000 acres. On these wilderness areas, see Wilderness Society, "About Virginia Wilderness," at http://www.wilderness.org/WhereWeWork/Virginia/ AboutVirginiaWilderness.cfm?TopLevel=VirginiaWilderness.

25. Former Camp Roosevelt CCC enrollee Charles "Moon" Mullins remembers stocking George Washington National Forest with deer and fish. For Mullins's description of such work, see Leonard, "Roosevelt's Tree Army," 42. For descriptions of similar deer-stocking work by CCC camps, see RG 35: CCC, Entry 115: Camp Inspection Reports, North Carolina, Folder: NC, Co. #F1: Pisgah Forest, National Archives and Records Administration (hereafter NARA); and RG 35: CCC, Entry 115: Camp Inspection Reports, North Carolina, Folder: NC, Co. #F28: Brevard, NARA. For additional examples of Corps fish-stocking projects, see RG 35: CCC, Entry 115: Camp Inspection Reports, North Carolina, Folder: NC, Co. #F14: Pisgah Forest, NARA.

26. For a discussion of this term, see Leo Marx, *The Machine in the Garden: Technology and the Pastoral Ideal in America* (New York: Oxford University Press, 1964).

27. On the differing compositions and concerns of the Progressive conservation and postwar environmental movements, see Hays, *Conservation and the Gospel of Efficiency*; and Hays, *Beauty, Health, and Permanence*, 22. For helpful discussions regarding professional conservationists versus lay or amateur conservationists, see Fox, *The American Conservation Movement*; Warren, *Hunter's Game*; Jacoby, *Crimes against Nature*; and Worster, *Dust Bowl*, 200–203.

28. As we will see in chapter 2, Franklin Roosevelt personally checked on the placement of CCC camps, and used Corps work projects as rewards and punishments for political allies and opponents.

29. The responsibilities and authority of many New Deal programs were similarly divided between public works aimed at undertaking physical projects and work relief focused on helping people. For an informative discussion of these dual roles, see Jason Scott Smith, "Building New Deal Liberalism: The Political Economy of Public Works, 1933–1956" (Ph.D. diss., University of California, Berkeley, 2001), 83.

30. There is a well-developed literature on the rise of the welfare state. See especially Lizabeth Cohen, *Making a New Deal: Industrial Workers in Chicago, 1919–1939* (New York: Cambridge University Press, 1990); Alan Dawley, *Struggles for Justice: Moral Responsibility and the Liberal State* (Cambridge, Mass.: Harvard University Press, 1991); Linda Gordon, *Pitied but Not Entitled: Single Mothers and the History of Welfare, 1890–1935* (Cambridge, Mass.: Harvard University Press, 1995); Theda Skocpol, "Political Response to Capitalist Crisis; Skocpol, "Bringing the State Back In: Strategies of Analysis in Current Research," in *Bringing the State Back In*, ed. Peter Evans, Dietrich Reuschemeyer, and Theda Skocpol (New York: Cambridge University Press, 1985); Skocpol, *Protecting Soldiers and Mothers: The Political Origins of Social Policy in the United States* (Cambridge, Mass.: Harvard University Press, 1992); Alan Brinkley, *The End of Reform: New Deal Liberalism in Recession and War* (New York: Knopf, 1996); and Brinkley, "The New Deal and the Idea of the State." See also Phillips, *This Land, This Nation*; and Jason Scott Smith, *Building New Deal Liberalism: The Political Economy of Public Works, 1933–1956* (New York: Cambridge University Press, 2005).

CHAPTER 1

1. The fact that Wilson contacted newspapers to claim credit for thinking of the CCC idea is discussed in a letter from Louis M. Howe to Franklin D. Roosevelt, 25 September 1933, Official File 268, Folder "Oct 1933," Franklin D. Roosevelt Library, Hyde Park, New York (hereafter referred to as FDRL).

2. Robert Fechner to James Farley, 19 January 1937, Official File 268, Folder "Jan–Feb 1937," FDRL. For newspaper accounts of Wilson's attempted suicide, see "Man Slashes Wrists at White House Door," *New York Times*, 8 October 1936, p. 48, col. 3; and "Wrists Cut, Electrician Hopes Wife Will Know He's Living," *Washington Post*, 8 October 1936, p. 6, col. 2.

3. Baker makes his claim in his book *Green Glory* (New York: Wyn, 1949), 66–68. Louis M. Howe to Isabel Erlich, 4 October 1933, Official File 268, Folder "Miscellaneous Sept–Oct 1933," FDRL; Robert Fechner to James Farley, 19 January 1937, Official File 268, Folder "Jan–Feb 1937," FDRL.

4. Depression era accounts that link James's essay to the origin of the CCC include Captain X, "A Civilian Army in the Woods," *Harper's*, March 1934, 487; F. A. Silcox, "Our Adventures in Conservation," *Atlantic Monthly*, November 1937, 714; "Conservation: Poor Young Men," *Time*, 6 February 1939, 10; and Kenneth Holland and Frank Hill, *Youth in the CCC* (Washington, D.C.: American Council on Education, 1942), 16. Also see William James, "The Moral Equivalent of War," *McClure's* 35 (1910): 463–468. James wrote this essay as a speech in 1906 and *McClure's* published it four years later.

5. For a good account of European youth work programs prior to the creation of the CCC, see Holland and Hill, *Youth in the CCC*, 19. On Bulgarian and Swiss youth work programs, also see Silcox, "Our Adventures in Conservation," 714. For programs in

Holland, see Arthur Ringland, "Land Utilization and the Unemployed in Holland," *American Forests* 38, no. 8 (August 1932): 448. And for Germany, see Arthur Ringland, "The CCC in Germany," *Journal of Forestry* 34 (1936): 554–561; "CCC," *Life*, June 1938, 58; and especially Thomas Lekan, *Imagining the Nation in Nature: Landscape Preservation and German Identity, 1885–1945* (Cambridge, Mass.: Harvard University Press, 2004).

6. Jonathan Mitchell, "Roosevelt's Tree Army: I," *New Republic*, 29 May 1935, 64. Also see Silcox, "Our Adventures in Conservation," 717; and "200,000 Wandering Boys," *Fortune*, February 1933, 47. Of the 2 million Americans drifting from town to town on freight cars during the early years of the Great Depression, approximately 250,000 were young people. John Salmond, *The Civilian Conservation Corps, 1933–1942: A New Deal Case Study* (Durham, N.C.: Duke University Press, 1967), 3.

7. For an account of Roosevelt's experiences on his Hyde Park estate, see Nelson Brown, "President Has Long Practiced Forestry," *New York Times*, 30 April 1933, sec. viii, p. 1. On his experiences as New York state senator and governor, see "Conservation," *Time*, 6 February 1939, 10.

8. Franklin Roosevelt to Louis Howe, 10 October 1933, as reprinted in Edgar Nixon, comp. and ed., *Franklin D. Roosevelt and Conservation, 1911–1945* (Hyde Park, N.Y.: FDRL, 1957), 1:143. Nixon has collected most of Roosevelt's correspondences and speeches regarding the conservation of natural resources in this two-volume set.

9. Marguerite LeHand to I. Van Meter, 15 July 1939, as reprinted in Nixon, *FDR and Conservation*, 2:354.

10. For a more detailed account of the events of these weeks, see Salmond, *The CCC*, 10–12.

11. The other two legislative initiatives proposed in Roosevelt's 21 March 1933 congressional address granted aid to states for relief work and established a broad public works labor-creating program similar to the Works Progress Administration. The address is reprinted in its entirety in Nixon, *FDR and Conservation*, 1:143.

12. As reprinted in Nixon, *FDR and Conservation*, 1:143–144.

13. See Samuel Hays, *Conservation and the Gospel of Efficiency: The Progressive Conservation Movement, 1890–1920* (Cambridge, Mass.: Harvard University Press, 1959; repr., New York: Atheneum, 1974), 1–4.

14. Because scientific professionals were central to the Progressive Era conservation movement, reformers rarely if ever recommended conservation work as a curative for the unemployment problems of untrained youths. On the elite character of Progressive conservation, see Hays, *Conservation and the Gospel of Efficiency*, 2–3; Stephen Fox, *The American Conservation Movement: John Muir and His Legacy* (Madison: University of Wisconsin Press, 1981), 110; and Robert Gottlieb, *Forcing the Spring: The Transformation of the American Environmental Movement* (Washington, D.C.: Island, 1993), 56.

15. Here and throughout this volume, I am defining the term "ideology" broadly as a "body of ideas reflecting the social needs of an individual," in this case Franklin Roosevelt. See William Morris, ed., *The American Heritage Dictionary* (Boston: Houghton Mifflin, 1982), 655.

16. Thomas Cox, *This Well-Wooded Land: Americans and Their Forests from Colonial Times to the Present* (Lincoln: University of Nebraska Press, 1985), 215.

17. Franklin Roosevelt to Hendrik William Van Loon, 2 February 1937, President's Personal File, FDRL.

18. Franklin Roosevelt, speech given at Clarksburg, West Virginia, 29 October 1944, as reprinted in Nixon, *FDR and Conservation*, 2:603. See also Fox, *The American Conservation Movement*, 185.

19. As quoted in Thomas Patton, "Franklin Roosevelt and ESF: Training a Forester-President," *Alumni Newsletter, SUNY College of Environmental Science and Forestry* 83 (Winter 1980–1981): 6. Also quoted in Cox, *This Well-Wooded Land*, 215.

20. Roosevelt planted trees at Hyde Park every year except five, 1919–1923, during which he was serving as secretary of the navy in Washington or recovering from polio. For good accounts of FDR's tree-planting efforts at Hyde Park, see Nelson Brown, "The President Practices Forestry," *Journal of Forestry* 41, no. 2 (February 1943): 92–93; Nelson Brown, "President Has Long Practiced Forestry," *New York Times*, 30 April 1933, sec. vii, 1; and Patton, "Franklin Roosevelt and ESF," 397–398. For an insightful examination of how the Hyde Park landscape influenced FDR, see Brian Black, "The Complex Environmentalist: Franklin D. Roosevelt and the Ethos of New Deal Conservation," in *FDR and the Environment*, ed. Henry Henderson and David Wolner (New York: Palgrave Macmillan, 2005), 19–47.

21. Roosevelt mentioned the practice of listing his occupation as a tree grower when voting in the (Poughkeepsie, N.Y.) *Eagle News*, 7 November 1944, p. 4. Also see Fox, *The American Conservation Movement*, 185; and F. Kennon Moody, "FDR and His Neighbors: A Study of the Relationship between Franklin D. Roosevelt and Residents of Dutchess County" (Ph.D. diss., State University of New York, Albany, 1981), 99–100.

22. For a description of FDR's Christmas tree–planting efforts, see Nelson Brown, "The President's Christmas Trees," *American Forests* 47, no. 12 (December 1941): 552; and Anna Riesch-Owen, *Conservation under Franklin D. Roosevelt* (New York: Praeger, 1983), 6.

23. Nelson Brown, "The President Practices Forestry," 93; and Thomas Patton, "Forestry and Politics: Franklin D. Roosevelt as Governor of New York," *New York History* 75 (Oct. 1994): 398.

24. Brown, "The President Practices Forestry," 93.

25. "Resolutions Proposed by the Hon. Franklin D. Roosevelt in the State Senate of New York during the Legislative Session of 1912," in FDR: Papers as New York Senator, Pamphlet File, FDRL. See also Fox, *The American Conservation Movement*, 186.

26. For a good history of the Adirondack Forest Preserve, see Philip Terrie, *Forever Wild: A Cultural History of Wilderness in the Adirondacks* (Philadelphia: Temple University Press, 1985; repr., Syracuse, N.Y.: Syracuse University Press, 1994), chap. 5. For an account of the Roosevelt-Jones Bill, see Nixon, *FDR and Conservation*, 1:11–20.

27. Franklin Roosevelt to Dexter Blagden, 21 February 1912, in Papers as State Senator, Legislative Files, File 26: Conservation Bills, Jan–Feb 1912, FDRL.

28. According to historian Stephen Fox, Roosevelt even referred to Pinchot's slides thirty years after this event. Fox, *The American Conservation Movement*, 185.

29. Hays, *Conservation and the Gospel of Efficiency*, 3. Other works on the Progressive conservation movement include Fox, *The American Conservation Movement*, 107–108; James Penick, Jr., "The Progressives and the Environment: Three Themes from the First Conservation Movement," in *The Progressive Era*, ed. Lewis Gould (Syracuse, N.Y.: Syracuse University Press, 1974); Donald Worster, *Nature's Economy: A History of Ecological Ideas* (New York: Cambridge University Press, 1977); Roderick Nash, *Wilderness and the American Mind* (New Haven, Conn.: Yale University Press, 1967); Gottlieb,

Forcing the Spring; Michael Williams, *Americans and Their Forests: A Historical Geography* (New York: Cambridge University Press, 1989); and Samuel Hays, *Beauty, Health, and Permanence: Environmental Politics in the United States, 1955-1985* (New York: Cambridge University Press, 1987), 13.

30. Richard White, "American Environmental History: The Development of a New Historical Field," *Pacific Historical Review* 54, no. 3 (August 1985): 299.

31. Some scholarship has begun to refute the idea that conservation was a predominately elite movement. See especially Louis Warren, *The Hunter's Game: Poachers and Conservationists in Twentieth-Century America* (New Haven, Conn.: Yale University Press, 1997); Karl Jacoby, *Crimes against Nature: Squatters, Poachers, Thieves, and the Hidden History of American Conservation* (Berkeley: University of California Press, 2003); and Richard Judd, *Common Lands, Common People: The Origins of Conservation in Northern New England* (Cambridge, Mass.: Harvard University Press, 2000).

32. As quoted in Worster, *Nature's Economy*, 266.

33. Gifford Pinchot, *Breaking New Ground* (1974; repr., Seattle: University of Washington Press, 1972), 359, as quoted in Harold Steen, *The U.S. Forest Service: A History* (Seattle: University of Washington Press, 1976), 75.

34. Historian Donald Worster has called Pinchot "the major architect of the Progressive conservation ideology." Worster, *Nature's Economy*, 266. For more on Pinchot's conservationist thinking, see Char Miller, *Gifford Pinchot and the Making of Modern Environmentalism* (Washington, D.C.: Shearwater, 2001), 138-144; Paul Hirt, *A Conspiracy of Optimism: Management of the National Forests since World War II* (Lincoln: University of Nebraska Press, 1999); Williams, *Americans and Their Forests*, 416-422; Hays, *Conservation and the Gospel of Efficiency*, 28-30; Fox, *The American Conservation Movement*, 111; and Nash, *Wilderness and the American Mind*, 134-138.

35. John Muir, *Our National Parks* (Boston: Houghton, Mifflin, 1901), 74; John Muir, *My First Summer in the Sierra* (Boston: Houghton, Mifflin, 1911), 211; John Muir, *John of the Mountains: The Unpublished Journals of John Muir*, ed. Linnie Marsh Wolfe (Boston: Houghton, Mifflin, 1938), 138, as quoted in Nash, *Wilderness and the American Mind*, 125.

36. Muir biographer Stephen Fox labels Muir's vision the "amateur" tradition within the American conservation movement. See especially Fox, *The American Conservation Movement*, chap. 10. Environmental historians disagree over Muir's relationship to the conservation movement of Gifford Pinchot. Some scholars, such as Samuel Hays, do not include Muir in their examination of Progressive Era conservation while others, including Stephen Fox, portray Muir as the driving force of the movement. This volume situates Muir's beliefs as a minority voice, albeit one growing in strength during the New Deal era, within the conservation movement.

37. Pinchot, *Breaking New Ground*, 103, as quoted in Fox, *The American Conservation Movement*, 112. As late as 1901, Muir was writing that "state woodlands [should] not be allowed to lie idle," but are made to "produce as much timber as is possible without spoiling them." Muir, *Our National Parks*, 363.

38. John Muir, *The Yosemite* (New York: The Century Company, 1912), 261-262, as quoted in Nash, *Wilderness and the American Mind*, 168.

39. Numerous environmental historians have identified the Hetch Hetchy controversy as a critical event in the splintering of the conservation movement into conservationist and preservationist camps. See especially Fox, *The American Conservation Movement*, 111-113; Nash, *Wilderness and the American Mind*, 135-138; Penick, "The

Progressives and the Environment," 125–126; Williams, *Americans and Their Forests*, 413–414, 456; and Gottlieb, *Forcing the Spring*, 24–28.

40. As quoted in Patton, "Forestry and Politics," 398.

41. The great majority of scholarship on Progressivism defines the Progressive Era as drawing to a close sometime around 1920. For a discussion of this periodization, see Daniel Rodgers, "In Search of Progressivism," *Reviews in American History* 10, no. 4 (December 1982): 113.

42. Franklin Roosevelt, "Message to the Legislature," 26 January 1931, as reprinted in Nixon, *FDR and Conservation*, 1:79.

43. For good accounts of the political battle over the Hewitt amendment, see Patton, "Forestry and Politics," 407–415; Bernard Bellush, *Franklin D. Roosevelt as Governor of New York* (New York: Columbia University Press, 1955), 95–98; Cox, *This Well-Wooded Land*, 217; "Roosevelt Pleads for Reforestation," *New York Times*, 14 February 1931, p. 4; "Smith Pushes Fight on Forest Measure," *New York Times*, 31 October 1931, p. 3.

44. "Forest Measure Approved: Gov. Roosevelt Adds to His Prestige in Clash with Smith," *New York Times*, 4 November 1931, p. 1. Also see "Roosevelt Hailed for Polls Victory: Friends All over Country Congratulate Him on Vote for Forest Amendment," *New York Times*, 5 November 1931, p. 2.

45. Franklin Roosevelt Speech File, #600, FDRL; also printed as "Return of Jobless from City to Farm Is Roosevelt's Aim," *New York Times*, 17 January 1933.

46. The meeting was held on 5 April 1933. Perry Merrill, *Roosevelt's Forest Army: A History of the Civilian Conservation Corps, 1933–1942* (Montpelier, Vt.: Perry Merrill, 1981), 11.

47. As reprinted in Nixon, *FDR and Conservation*, 1:143. Roosevelt's assessment of the unemployment situation is also discussed in Frank Freidel, *Franklin D. Roosevelt: Launching the New Deal* (Boston: Little, Brown, 1973), 80.

48. Franklin Roosevelt, "Speech before the American Country Life Conference, Ithaca, August 19, 1931," Speech File, #437, FDRL. Also see Franklin Roosevelt, "Back to the Land," *Review of Reviews* 84 (October 1931): 63–64.

49. There is quite an extensive literature on back-to-the-land movements during the first half of the twentieth century. See especially David Shi, *The Simple Life: Plain Living and High Thinking in American Culture* (New York: Oxford University Press, 1985). See also Paul Conkin, *Tomorrow, a New World: The New Deal Community Program* (Ithaca, N.Y.: American Historical Association, 1959); David Danbom, "Romantic Agrarianism in Twentieth-Century America," *Agricultural History* 65, no. 4 (Fall 1991): 1–12; Richard White, "Poor Men on Poor Lands: The Back-to-the-Land Movement of the Early Twentieth Century: A Case Study," *Pacific Historical Review* 49 (Feb. 1980): 105–131; and Blaine Brownell, "The Agrarian and Urban Ideals: Environmental Images in Modern America," *Journal of Popular Culture* 5, no. 3 (Winter 1971): 576–587.

50. Shi, *The Simple Life*, 227.

51. Danbom, "Romantic Agrarianism," 6.

52. John Crowe Ransom, "The Aesthetic of Regionalism," *American Review* 2 (January 1934): 306, as quoted in Idus Newby, "The Southern Agrarians: A View after Thirty Years," *Agricultural History* 37 (July 1963): 148. Other sources on the Nashville Agrarians include Paul Conkin, *The Southern Agrarians* (Knoxville: University of Tennessee Press, 1988); and William Havard and Walter Sullivan, eds., *A Gang of Prophets: The Vanderbilt Agrarians after Fifty Years* (Baton Rouge: Louisiana State University Press, 1982).

53. Howard Bishop, *Landward* 1 (Spring 1933): 3, as quoted in Christopher Kauffman, "W. Howard Bishop, President of the National Catholic Rural Life Conference, 1928–1934," *U.S. Catholic Historian* 8, no. 3 (1989): 138. Other sources on the Catholic Rural Life movement include David O'Brien, *American Catholics and Social Reform: The New Deal Years* (New York: Oxford University Press, 1968); Edward Shapiro, "Catholic Agrarian Thought and the New Deal," *Catholic Historical Review* 65 (October 1979): 583–599; and Edward Shapiro, "Catholic Rural Life and the New Deal Farm Program," *American Benedictine Review* 28 (September 1977).

54. Alan Trachtenberg has called this the "incorporation of America." See Trachtenberg, *The Incorporation of America: Culture and Society in the Gilded Age* (New York: Hill and Wang, 1982).

55. John Dewey, "Intelligence and Morals" (1908), in John Dewey, *The Influence of Darwin on Philosophy* (New York: Holt, 1910), 74, as quoted in Boyer, *Urban Masses*, 225.

56. On the shift from "coercive moral reform" to "environmentalist reform," see Boyer, *Urban Masses*, chaps. 15–16, especially 220–221. For more detailed accounts of various environmentalist reform efforts during the Progressive Era, see the following: for advances in behavioral psychology, see John Burnham, "Psychiatry, Psychology, and the Progressive Movement," *American Quarterly* 12, no. 4 (1960): 457–465; on the city beautiful movement, see William Wilson, *The City Beautiful Movement* (Baltimore, Md.: Johns Hopkins University Press, 1989); on settlement house reform, see Gottlieb, *Forcing the Spring*; on the urban sanitation movement, see Martin Melosi, " 'Out of Sight, Out of Mind': The Environment and Disposal of Municipal Refuse, 1860–1920," *Historian* 35, no. 4 (August 1973): 621–640; and on women's environmentalist efforts, see Maureen Flanagan, "The City Profitable, the City Livable: Environmental Policy, Gender, and Power in Chicago in the 1910s," *Journal of Urban History* 22, no. 2 (January 1996): 163–190.

57. Frederick Law Olmsted, "Public Parks and the Enlargement of Towns," *Journal of Social Science: Containing the Transactions of the American Association*, no. 3 (1871): 76, as quoted in Boyer, *Urban Masses*, 238. For a good analysis of Olmsted's environmentalist philosophy and his influence on the city beautiful movement, see Wilson, *The City Beautiful Movement*, chap. 1.

58. George Kessler, *Report of the Board of Park and Boulevard Commissioners of Kansas City, Missouri* (Kansas City, Kans.: Hudson Kimberely, 1893), excerpted in Charles Glabb, ed., *The American City: A Documentary History* (Homewood, Ill.: Dorsey, 1963), as quoted in Boyer, *Urban Masses*, 239. G. Washington Eggleston, "A Plea for More Parks, and the Preservation of the Sublimities of Nature" (n.p., c. early twentieth century), 10, as quoted in Boyer, *Urban Masses*, 239.

59. Henry Curtis, *The Play Movement and Its Significance* (New York: Macmillan, 1917), 6, 8, 36, 119, as quoted in Boyer, *Urban Masses*, 244. For a good overview of the Progressive playground movement, see Dominick Cavallo, *Muscles and Morals: Organized Playgrounds and Urban Reform, 1880–1920* (Philadelphia: University of Pennsylvania Press, 1981).

60. For a general overview of this nature craze and its three main elements, see Shi, *The Simple Life*, 194. On the country life movement, also see William Bowers, *The Country Life Movement in America, 1900–1920* (Port Washington, N.Y.: Kennikat, 1974), 45. For an examination of the wilderness cult during the early years of the twentieth century, see Nash, *Wilderness and the American Mind*, chap. 9. And for analysis of the

outdoor fresh air movement, see David Macleod, *Building Character in the American Boy: The Boy Scouts, YMCA, and Their Forerunners, 1870–1920* (Madison: University of Wisconsin Press, 1983). T. J. Jackson Lears calls this movement "antimodern" in Lears, *No Place of Grace: Antimodernism and the Transformation of American Culture, 1880–1920* (New York: Pantheon, 1981).

61. Theodore Roosevelt, *The Strenuous Life: Essays and Addresses* (New York: The Century Company, 1905), 7–8, as quoted in Shi, *The Simple Life*, 201.

62. "Camping in the Woodland," *New England Magazine* 18 (1898), as quoted in Shi, *The Simple Life*, 205.

63. Ernest Ingersoll, "Practical Camping," *Outlook* 56 (1897): 324, as quoted in Shi, *The Simple Life*, 206.

64. On the founding of the Boy Scouts, see Macleod, *Building Character*, 131–132; Shi, *The Simple Life*, 208; and John Dean, "Scouting in America: 1910–1990" (Ph.D. diss., University of South Carolina, 1992). For additional information on the Boy Scouts of America, see David Macleod, "Act Your Age: Boyhood, Adolescence, and the Rise of the Boy Scouts of America," *Journal of Social History* 16, no. 2 (1982): 3–20; David Shi, "Ernest Thompson Seton and the Boy Scouts: A Moral Equivalent of War?" *South Atlantic Quarterly* 84, no. 4 (1985): 379–391; Carolyn Wagner, "The Boy Scouts of America: A Model and Mirror of American Society" (Ph.D. diss., Johns Hopkins University, 1979); Jeffrey Hanover, "The Boy Scouts and the Validation of Masculinity," *Journal of Social Issues* 34, no. 1 (1978): 184–195; and Nash, *Wilderness and the American Mind*, 147–149. On the Boy Scouts in Great Britain, see Michael Rosenthal, *The Character Factory: Baden-Powell and the Origins of the Boy Scout Movement* (New York: Pantheon, 1984).

65. According to Paul Boyer, the Boy Scout movement was an integral part of the Progressive Era's positive environmentalist effort. See Boyer, *Urban Masses*, 359n61.

66. Ernest Thompson Seton, *Boy Scouts of America: A Handbook of Woodcraft, Scouting, and Lifecraft* (New York: Doubleday, 1910), xi, xii, 1, 2, as quoted in Nash, *Wilderness and the American Mind*, 148.

67. I have found no secondary scholarship pertaining to Franklin Roosevelt's experiences with the Boy Scouts. See Franklin Roosevelt to Conrad Chapman, 15 June 1925, FDR: Family, Business and Personal, Subject File: Boy Scout Foundation of Greater New York, Correspondence: A–C, FDRL. Other facts were pieced together from the following material: Colin Livingston to Franklin Roosevelt, 16 May 1921, FDR: Family, Business and Personal, Subject File: Boy Scout Foundation of Greater New York, Correspondence: D–M, FDRL; Boy Scout Foundation of Greater New York, "Annual Report, January 1923," FDR: Family, Business and Personal, Subject File: Boy Scout Foundation of Greater New York, Correspondence: N–W, FDRL; and "Roosevelt Quits Presidency of Boy Scout Unit," *New York Herald Tribune*, 22 July 1937, clipping from President's Personal File, #4241, Boy Scout Foundation of Greater New York, FDRL.

68. "Roosevelt Sees Problem of Boys Aided by Scouts," *New York City Evening World*, 2 March 1929, in FDR: Papers as Governor of New York State, Series 1: Correspondence, Boy Scout Foundation of New York, FDRL.

69. Franklin Roosevelt, "Magnitude and Accomplishment of the Boy Scout Movement," address given over radio station WJZ at the luncheon of the Boy Scouts Foundation in New York City, 8 April 1932, Speech File #471, FDRL.

70. Franklin Roosevelt, "How Boy Scout Work Aids Youth," *New York Times*, 12 August 1928, in FDR: Family, Business and Personal, Subject File: Boy Scout Foundation of Greater New York, Correspondence: Proctor, Arthur, W., 1925–1928, FDRL.

71. The Boy Scouts established the first of these campgrounds in 1917. The eighteen campsites functioning in 1922 could accommodate anywhere from 75 to 450 boys each. For statistics concerning the Boy Scout Foundation of Greater New York's campgrounds, see Boy Scout Foundation of Greater New York, "Annual Report, January 1923"; A. C. Olson to Franklin Roosevelt, 27 July 1921, FDR: Family, Business and Personal, Subject File: Boy Scout Foundation of Greater New York, Correspondence: N–W, FDRL; Franklin Roosevelt to James Forbes, 1 August 1921, FDR: Family, Business and Personal, Subject File: Boy Scout Foundation of Greater New York, Correspondence: N–W, FDRL; and A. Schaeffer, Jr., "A Hotel That Is as Large as All Outdoors," *National Hotel Review*, n.d., in FDR: Family, Business and Personal, Subject File: Boy Scout Foundation of Greater New York, Correspondence: N–W, FDRL.

72. Roosevelt, "Magnitude and Accomplishment of the Boy Scout Movement." According to historian David Macleod, during the 1910s and 1920s, the Boy Scouts nationwide were plagued by a lack of campground sites. See Macleod, *Building Character in the American Boy*, 242.

73. Franklin Roosevelt to James Forbes, 1 August 1921, FDR: Family, Business and Personal, Subject File: Boy Scout Foundation of Greater New York, Correspondence: N–W, FDRL.

74. For a description of the Sullivan County Boy Scout campground, see "Roosevelt Sees Problem of Boys Aided by Scouts," *New York City Evening World*, 2 March 1929, n.p.; and "Scouting Solves Juvenile Crime, Says Roosevelt," *Brooklyn New York Eagle*, 2 March 1929, n.p., both found in clipping file, FDR: Papers as Governor of New York State, Series 1: Correspondence, Boy Scouts of America, FDRL.

75. Boy Scouts of America, "Fifteen Million American Boys Call to You . . . " (1929), clipping found in FDR: Papers as Governor of New York State, Series 1: Correspondence, Boy Scouts of America, FDRL.

76. Macleod, *Building Character in the American Boy*, 239.

77. Ibid., 245. For a general description of the destructive character of Boy Scout camping, see ibid., 140, 239.

78. Franklin Roosevelt to George Pratt, 6 September 1922, FDR: Family, Business and Personal, Subject File: Boy Scout Foundation of Greater New York, Correspondence: N–W, FDRL.

79. Roosevelt's request was mentioned in the following letter: Louis Howe to H. A. Gordon, 13 July 1922, FDR: Family, Business and Personal, Subject File: Boy Scout Foundation of Greater New York, Folder: FDR Conservation Camps, FDRL.

80. Director of Camp Museums, Palisades Interstate Park, to H. A. Gordon, 24 July 1922, FDR: Family, Business and Personal, Subject File: Boy Scout Foundation of Greater New York, Proctor, Arthur, W., 1922–1924, FDRL.

81. For the broader context of this shift from woodcraft practices to more conservation-oriented camping, see James Morton Turner, "From Woodcraft to 'Leave No Trace': Wilderness, Consumerism, and Environmentalism in Twentieth-Century America," *Environmental History* 7, no. 3 (2002): 462–484.

82. For a good description of the Franklin D. Roosevelt Conservation Camps, see Chairman, Camp Committee, Boy Scout Foundation of Greater New York, to Louis

Howe, n.d., FDR: Family, Business and Personal, Subject File: Boy Scout Foundation of Greater New York, Folder: FDR Conservation Camps, FDRL. For promotional literature on the conservation camps, see *Scout Camps: F. D. Roosevelt Conservation Camps, Harriman Section, Palisades Interstate Park*, pamphlet found in FDR: Family, Business and Personal, Subject File: Boy Scout Foundation of Greater New York, Folder: FDR Conservation Camps, FDRL.

83. Fay Welch, "Rock Oak Forestry Camp," 1924. This description of the Franklin D. Roosevelt Conservation Camps was attached to a letter from Fay Welch to Edgar Nixon, librarian at the FDR Library, 18 April 1955, 2, FDR: Family, Business and Personal, Subject File: Boy Scout Foundation of Greater New York, Folder: FDR Conservation Camps, FDRL. On Roosevelt's desire to include a forestry program at the Boy Scouts' Sullivan County, New York, campground, see Arthur Proctor to Guernsey Cross, 26 August 1930, FDR: Papers as Governor of New York, Series 1: Correspondence, Boy Scout Foundation of Greater New York, FDRL.

84. On the Dutchess County, New York, project, see Walter Forse to Franklin Roosevelt, 16 December 1931, FDR: Papers as Governor of New York State, Series 1: Correspondence, Boy Scouts of America, FDRL. On the Boy Scouts' nationwide Nut Seed and Tree Planting Project, see "Boy Scouts Are Undertaking Wide Tree-Planting Project," *New York Times*, 20 April 1930, sec. ix, p. 8; and "Boy Scouts Are Embarked on Tree-Planting Campaign," *New York Times*, 1 June 1930, sec. viii, p. 12.

85. Franklin Roosevelt to the New York State Legislature, 25 March 1930, as reprinted in Nixon, *FDR and Conservation*, 1:71.

86. Governor Roosevelt established TERA as part of the Wicks Act of September 1931. For background information on TERA, see Bellush, *Franklin D. Roosevelt as Governor of New York*, 141–149; Barrett Potter, "The Civilian Conservation Corps in New York State: Its Social and Political Impact" (Ph.D. diss., State University of New York, Buffalo, 1973), 25; and John Gibbs, "Tree Planting Aids Unemployed," *American Forests* 39, no. 4 (April 1933): 159–161.

87. Franklin Roosevelt to Ovid Butler, 15 August 1932, as reprinted in Nixon, *FDR and Conservation*, 1:122.

88. "New York Employs 10,000 Men for Tree Planting," *American Forests* 38, no. 8 (August 1932): 467; "State Speeds Jobs in Reforestation," *New York Times*, 25 July 1932, p. 17; and Gibbs, "Tree Planting Aids Unemployed," 159.

89. On TERA conservation work and the 25,000 unemployed men aided by the program, see Gibbs, "Tree Planting Aids Unemployed," 161, 159. In 1932, TERA employed approximately 1,000 New York City men in the Palisades Interstate Park. See "Thousand New York City Men Given Work in Interstate Park," press release from the Commissioners of the Palisades Interstate Park, 1932, Bear Mountain State Park Archives, Bear Mountain, N.Y.

90. On TERA work camps and weekly pay, see Potter, "The Civilian Conservation Corps in New York State," 28. For TERA's role as a CCC selection agent, see ibid., 27. According to Potter, TERA maintained ten camps in central New York for its workers.

91. For an overview of these states' forestry work relief programs, see G. H. Collingwood, "Forestry Aids the Unemployed," *American Forests* 38, no. 10 (October 1932): 550. Other states that helped unemployed families by allowing them to collect cordwood and other wood products from state-owned land include New Hampshire, North Carolina, Connecticut, Louisiana, Utah, Idaho, and Colorado.

92. California governor James Rolph established California's forestry relief work program on 27 November 1931. So successful was this program that its chair, Rexford Black, traveled to Washington, D.C., in early April 1933 to help Secretary of Agriculture Henry Wallace to implement the CCC program. Black also spent a full day with Secretary of Labor Frances Perkins, who was in charge of recruiting CCC enrollees, to explain the recruitment strategy of the California forestry camp program. For statistics on the California program for 1932, see Samuel Blythe, "Camps for Jobless Men," *Saturday Evening Post*, 27 May 1933, 9. Other sources on California's forestry work camps include Winfield Scott, "California's Unemployment Forest Camps," *American Forests* 39, no. 2 (February 1933): 51–54; R. L. Deering, "Camps for the Unemployed in the Forests of California," *Journal of Forestry* 30 (1932): 554–557; Raymond Clar, *California Government and Forestry* (Sacramento, Calif.: Division of Forestry, Department of Conservation, 1969), 2:202. The California program began on 1 December 1931; see Loren Chan, "California during the Early 1930s: The Administration of Governor James Rolph, Jr., 1931-1934," *Southern California Quarterly* 63, no. 3 (1981): 272–276; Otis, *The Forest Service and the Civilian Conservation Corps*, 5; Amelia Fry, *National Forests in California* (Berkeley: University of California Press, 1965), 4; Potter, "The Civilian Conservation Corps in New York State," 29.

93. President Hoover allocated a small amount of funds to unemployment relief work in the national forests in January 1931, approximately one year after Governor Roosevelt asked the New York legislature for an appropriation for tree-planting relief work. On President Hoover's forestry relief efforts, see "Forestry to Help Unemployment," *American Forests* 37, no. 1 (January 1931): 48; and "Work on National Forests Contributes to Relief of Unemployment," *American Forests* 37, no. 4 (April 1931): 232.

94. Franklin Roosevelt, "Informal Extemporaneous Remarks of the President, Ten Mile River Camp of the Boy Scouts of America, Ten Mile River, New York," 23 August 1933, FDR: Speech File #647, FDRL. Although President Herbert Hoover had immediately attacked the reforestation plan, the public responded more favorably. On this public response, see *New York Times*, 6 and 7 July 1932.

95. On FDR's coalition of southerners and urbanites in the 1932 election, see Edgar Eugene Robinson, *They Voted for Roosevelt: The Presidential Vote, 1932–1944* (Stanford, Calif.: Stanford University Press, 1947), 19–20; and Sarah Phillips, "Acres Fit and Unfit: Conservation and Rural Rehabilitation in the New Deal Era" (Ph.D. diss., Boston University, 2004), 109.

96. "Excerpt from Roosevelt's Acceptance Speech, Democratic National Convention, Chicago, July 2, 1932," as reprinted in Nixon, *FDR and Conservation*, 1:112.

CHAPTER 2

1. James McEntee, Federal Security Agency, *Final Report of the Director of the Civilian Conservation Corps, April 1933 through June 30, 1942*, RG 35: CCC, Entry 3: Annual, Special, and Final Reports, NARA, 41.

2. For a summary of CCC conservation work from 1933 to 1942, see ibid., 104–109.

3. "An Emergency Conservation Work (CCC) Chart Prepared by Roosevelt, 3 April 1933," as reprinted in Edgar Nixon, comp. and ed., *Franklin D. Roosevelt and Conservation, 1911–1945* (Hyde Park, N.Y.: FDRL, 1957), 1:136.

4. "An Act for the Relief of Unemployment through the Performance of Useful Public Work, and for Other Purposes," approved 31 March 1933, as reprinted in Nixon, *FDR and Conservation*, 1:147. Such authorization was not new. Rather, it merely expanded the

authority granted by the Weeks Act of 1911, which allowed the Forest Service to purchase private lands to protect the watersheds of navigable streams, and the Clarke-McNary Law of 1924, which in effect broadened the scope of the Weeks Act by permitting the federal government to acquire lands for timber production as well. For good explanations of the Weeks and Clarke-McNary laws, see Harold Steen, *The U.S. Forest Service: A History* (Seattle: University of Washington Press, 1976), 122–131, 185–195; Paul Hirt, *A Conspiracy of Optimism: Management of the National Forests since World War II* (Lincoln: University of Nebraska Press, 1999), 203; and Michael Williams, *Americans and Their Forests: A Historical Geography* (New York: Cambridge University Press, 1989), 308, 454.

5. On FDR's executive orders regarding land purchases under the CCC law, see Henry Wallace to FDR, 16 June 1933, as reprinted in Nixon, *FDR and Conservation*, 1:182; FDR to Representative Prentiss M. Brown of Michigan, 26 June 1936, as reprinted in ibid., 1:525; L. F. Kneipp, "Uncle Sam as a Buyer of Forest Lands," *Journal of Forestry* 31, no. 7 (November 1933): 778–782; and Steen, *The U.S. Forest Service*, 217. For a breakdown of federal land acquisition by region from 1933 to 1936, see Henry Wallace to FDR, 30 July 1936, Official File 1c: Department of Agriculture, Folder: Forest Service, June–July 1936, FDRL. For an account of previous allocations, see Anna Riesch-Owen, *Conservation under Franklin D. Roosevelt* (New York: Praeger, 1983), 107. For the total amount of acres purchased under the CCC law, see James McEntee, Federal Security Agency, *Final Report of the Director of the Civilian Conservation Corps: April 1933 through June 30, 1942*, RG 35: CCC, Entry 3: Annual, Special, and Final Reports, NARA, 37.

6. Robert Fechner, *First Report of the Director of Emergency Conservation Work: For Period April 5, 1933 to September 30, 1933*, RG 35: CCC, Entry 3: Annual, Special, and Final Reports, NARA.

7. Dorothy D. Bromley, "The Forestry Army That Lives by Work: In the Camps of the Conservation Corps 150,000 Youths Find a New Outlook," *New York Times*, 23 July 1933, sec. viii, p. 2.

8. Roosevelt reauthorized the CCC by executive order every six months from 1933 to 1935, and thereafter for one- and two-year periods until the program was discontinued in 1942.

9. Determining the number of CCC conservation projects per six-month enrollment period is difficult for a number of reasons. Not only did the number of camps fluctuate during individual enrollment periods, but a camp was sometimes transferred mid-enrollment period to a different location and hence often to a different department and supervising agency. Not surprisingly, the few secondary sources that examine CCC work camps either avoid an accounting of camp strength by enrollment period altogether or refrain from dividing camps according to the type of land on which the work was performed (i.e., national forests versus state forests versus private forests). For an example of the latter, see especially Conrad Wirth, *Parks, Politics, and the People* (Norman: University of Oklahoma Press, 1980), 149.

In piecing together the statistics on camp numbers and agency affiliations, I have relied on two sources: RG 35: CCC, Entry 3: Annual, Special, and Final Reports, NARA; and RG 35: CCC, Entry 108: Station and Strength Reports, NARA. For enrollment periods 1–5 (1 April 1933–30 September 1935), see RG 35: CCC, Entry 3: Annual, Special, and Final Reports, NARA. These director's reports for the first three enrollment periods and thereafter for each year of CCC activity provide statistical data on camp strength. See especially Robert Fechner, *Summary Report of the Director of Emergency Conservation Work on the Operations of Emergency Conservation Work for the Period Extending from April 5, 1933–June 30, 1935* (Washington, D.C.: U.S. Government Printing Office, 1935), 56–57, located at RG 35: CCC, Entry 3: Annual, Special, and Final Reports, NARA. For enrollment periods 6–19 (1 October 1935–30 September 1942), see RG 35: CCC, Entry 108: Station and Strength Reports, NARA. This series contains monthly camp strength reports, many of which are missing, and spans the CCC's entire nine-year existence. When determining the number of camps and their jurisdictional affiliation from these monthly reports, efforts were made to use the data from the final month of each enrollment period, for consistency's sake. When a report from the final month of an enrollment period was missing, calculations were taken from the monthly report closest to the period's end date. Camp numbers for enrollment periods (EP) were taken from the following monthly strength reports: EP 6, from December 1935 report; EP 7, from June 1936 report; EP 8, from December 1936 report; EP 9, from June 1937 report; EP 10, from December 1937 report; EP 11, from June 1938 report; EP 12, from December 1938 report; EP 13, from June 1939 report; EP 14, from March 1940 report; EP 15, from September 1940 report; EP 16, from February 1941 report; EP 17, from September 1941 report; EP 18, from March 1942 report; EP 19, from May 1942 report.

10. The expansion of CCC conservation projects can be seen by comparing the following: Fechner, *First Report*, 7; Robert Fechner, *Two Years of Emergency Conservation Work: April 5, 1933–March 31, 1935*, RG 35: CCC, Entry 3: Annual, Special, and Final Reports, NARA, 5; Robert Fechner, *Annual Report of the Director of Emergency Conservation Work, Fiscal Year Ending June 30, 1937* (Washington, D.C.: U.S. Government Printing Office, 1937), 8, located at RG 35: CCC, Entry 3: Annual, Special, and Final Reports, NARA.

11. Much of the land purchased through the CCC law became part of the national forest system. On the use of the Corps law to increase the number of national forests, see Thomas Cox, *This Well-Wooded Land: Americans and Their Forests from Colonial Times to the Present* (Lincoln: University of Nebraska Press, 1985), 227.

12. For FDR's use of the term "reforestation camps," see Secretary to the President Louis M. Howe to Representative Howard Smith, 6 May 1933, Official File 268 (CCC), Folder: Miscellaneous, March–May 1933, FDRL. For examples of Fechner using forestry language to describe the CCC, see Emergency Conservation Work, Office of the Director, Washington, D.C., "For Release, Morning Paper of Monday, July 3," Official File 268 (CCC), Folder: CCC July 1933, FDRL; "Accomplishments of Summer Camps and Plans for Winter Camps of the CCC," address by Robert Fechner over the Columbia Broadcasting System, 7 October 1933, Official File 268 (CCC), Folder: November–December 1933, FDRL; Robert Fechner to FDR, 22 December 1933, Official File 268 (CCC), Folder: November–December 1933, FDRL; and Robert Fechner to FDR, 11 April 1934, Official File 268 (CCC), Folder: March–July 1934, FDRL.

13. "Roosevelt's Tree Army: I," *New Republic*, 29 May 1935, 64.

14. Gifford Pinchot, *Forest Devastation: A National Danger and a Plan to Meet It* (Washington, D.C.: Committee for the Application of Forestry, 1919), as quoted in Williams, *Americans and Their Forests*, 444; George Ahern, *Deforested America: Statement of the Present Forest Situation in the United States* (printed privately, 1928), v, as quoted in Williams, *Americans and Their Forests*, 460. Ahern followed up this book with another that examined the timber famine threat state by state. See George Ahern, *Forestry Bankruptcy in America: Each State's Own Story* (Washington, D.C.: Green Lamp League, 1932).

15. My understanding of Gifford Pinchot's role in the timber famine scare comes from Williams, *Americans and Their Forests*, 430, 440–460; and Char Miller, *Gifford Pinchot and the Making of Modern Environmentalism* (Washington, D.C.: Shearwater, 2001), 289–290. On the first use of the term "timber famine," see U.S. Department of Agriculture, *Annual Report* (1878), 245, as quoted in Williams, *Americans and Their Forests*, 430.

16. For an analysis of these statistics, see U.S. Forest Service, *A National Plan for Forestry* (Copeland Report) (Washington, D.C.: U.S. Government Printing Office, 1933), 1:208, 221; and Williams, *Americans and Their Forests*, 440. On the Capper Report of 1920, see U.S. Forest Service, *Timber Depletion, Lumber Prices, Lumber Exports, and Concentration of Timber Ownership* (Capper Report), U.S. Congress, Senate, 66th Cong., 2nd sess., report on S. Res. 311 (Washington, D.C.: U.S. Government Printing Office, 1920), 3, 36, and 70, as quoted in Williams, *Americans and Their Forests*, 438.

17. My conception of a degraded landscape has been influenced by the fields of environmental history and political ecology. Both fields view nature as being in constant flux and therefore difficult to define as degraded or not. Political ecologists in particular view landscape degradation as perceptual and socially defined. A landscape is thus degraded if those inhabiting it view it as such. This was most definitely the case with the forested landscape of the United States during the early years of the Great Depression. For discussions of nature as nonstatic, see Peter Schoonmaker and David Foster, "Some Implications of Paleoecology for Contemporary Ecology," *Botanical Review* 57 (1991): 204–245; Margaret Davis, "Quaternary History and the Stability of Forest Communication," in *Forest Succession*, ed. Darrell West, Herman Shugart, and Daniel Botkin (1981); and Norman Christensen, "Landscape History and Ecological Change," *Journal of Forest History* 33, no. 3 (1989): 116–124. For a discussion of landscape degradation as socially defined, see Piers Blaikie and Harold Brookfield, *Land Degradation and Society* (New York: Methuen, 1987), 1, 15, 23.

18. For a description of the first fifty CCC camps in the nation, see "50 Forest Camps Chosen for Corps," *New York Times*, 12 April 1933, p. 2. For the average percentage of CCC camps assigned to the Department of Agriculture during the Corps' existence, see John Salmond, *The Civilian Conservation Corps, 1933–1942: A New Deal Case Study* (Durham, N.C.: Duke University Press, 1967), 121; Michael Sherraden, "The Civilian Conservation Corps: Effectiveness of the Camps" (Ph.D. diss., University of Michigan, 1979), 4; and Stephen Pyne, *Fire in America: A Cultural History of Wildland and Rural Fire* (Princeton, N.J.: Princeton University Press, 1982), 364. For the average percentage of CCC camps assigned to the Forest Service during the Corps' existence, see Steen, *The U.S. Forest Service*, 215; and David Clary, *Timber and the Forest Service* (Lawrence: University of Kansas Press, 1986), 95.

19. My calculations for the number of camps under the jurisdiction of departments and bureaus comes from a combination of sources. See footnote 9 above.

20. E. W. Tinker, "The President's Emergency Conservation Work," *Journal of Forestry* 32, no. 2 (February 1934): 208.

21. FDR to Robert Fechner, 28 July 1937, as reprinted in Nixon, *FDR and Conservation*, 2:90. Although the law creating the Corps permitted CCC work in privately owned forests, Roosevelt succeeded in limiting the number of such projects. On CCC work in private forests, see "An Act for the Relief of Unemployment through the Performance of Useful Public Work, and for Other Purposes," approved 31 March 1933, as reprinted in Nixon, *FDR and Conservation*, 1:147.

22. On the importance of this shift in federal conservation policy to private land, see Sarah Phillips, "Acres Fit and Unfit: Conservation and Rural Rehabilitation in the New Deal Era" (Ph.D. diss., Boston University, 2004), 267.

23. On the CCC's division of forestry work between "protection" and "development," see Fechner, *First Report*, 10. Other historians who have identified these two main categories of CCC forestry work include Alison Otis, *The Forest Service and the Civilian Conservation Corps, 1933–1942* (Washington, D.C.: U.S. Forest Service, U.S. Department of Agriculture, 1986), 2; and Pyne, *Fire in America*, 365. For a list of the types of forestry work performed by Forest Service CCC camps, see appendix H of Robert Fechner, *Second Report of the Director of Emergency Conservation Work: For the Periods April 5, 1933 to September 30, 1933, and October 1, 1933 to March 31, 1934*, RG 35: CCC, Entry 3: Annual, Special, and Final Reports, NARA, 28–29.

24. The CCC's forest improvement work is explained in detail in Civilian Conservation Corps, *Forest Improvements by the CCC* (Washington, D.C.: U.S. Government Printing Office, 1938).

25. CCC, *Reforestation by the CCC* (Washington, D.C.: U.S. Government Printing Office, 1938), 8.

26. James McEntee, Federal Security Agency, *Final Report of the Director of the Civilian Conservation Corps, April 1933 through June 30, 1942*, RG 35, Entry 3, Annual, Special, and Final Reports, NARA, 105.

27. On CCC nursery work, see CCC, *Reforestation by the CCC*, 6–9.

28. For the yearly increases in the CCC reforestation program, see ibid., 4. For total CCC reforestation statistics, see McEntee, *Final Report*, 44 and 105. For CCC reforestation with respect to planting throughout U.S. history, see Salmond, *The CCC*, 121; and for CCC tree planting in relation to U.S. Depression era population, see Phoebe Cutler, *The Public Landscape of the New Deal* (New Haven, Conn.: Yale University Press, 1985), 95.

29. CCC, *Reforestation by the CCC*, 9–10. For a description of CCC timber stand improvement work, see also Emergency Conservation Work, Office of the Director, Washington, D.C., "Memorandum for the Press, Release to Morning Papers, Monday February 10, 1936," Printed Materials Collection, Civilian Conservation Corps, Press Releases, FDRL, 1.

30. For timber acreage improved by CCC Forest Service camps, see McEntee, *Final Report*, 44 and 105; Emergency Conservation Work, Office of the Director, Washington, D.C., "Memorandum for the Press, Release to Morning Papers, Monday February 10, 1936," Printed Materials Collection, Civilian Conservation Corps, Press Releases, FDRL, 1; and CCC, *Reforestation by the CCC*, 10.

31. CCC, *Forests Protected by the CCC* (Washington, D.C.: U.S. Government Printing Office, 1938), 1.

32. For statistics on CCC fire prevention work completed between 1933 and 1942, see McEntee, *Final Report*, 106. On the Ponderosa Way, see J. H. Price, "The Ponderosa Way," *American Forests* 40, no. 9 (September 1934): 387.

33. These two methods, prevention and suppression, are explained in CCC, *Forests Protected by the CCC*, 1.

34. On CCC firefighting work, see James McEntee, *Final Report*, 44. On "fire-proofing the forests," see Guy McKinney, "Forest-Fire Fighters Gird for a Busy Year," *New York Times*, 24 June 1934, sec. viii, p. 10. Unfortunately, forty-two enrollees and five supervisors lost their lives fighting these forest fires.

35. Perry Merrill, *Roosevelt's Forest Army: A History of the Civilian Conservation Corps, 1933–1942* (Montpelier, Vt.: Perry Merrill, 1981), 41. On CCC disease work, see also CCC, *Forests Protected by the CCC*, 8–12. Other diseases singled out by the Corps include canker and heart rot.

36. For the acreage of CCC work against the gypsy moth, see Merrill, *Roosevelt's Forest Army*, 41. Other insects singled out for eradication by the Corps included grasshoppers, the brown tail moth, the elm beetle, the tip moth, Mormon crickets, white pine weevils, and spruce budworms.

37. On CCC insect work, see CCC, *Forests Protected by the CCC*, 8–12. For the total insect and disease work conducted by the CCC, see McEntee, *Final Report*, 106.

38. Jesse Buell, "Results of C.C.C. Timber Stand Improvement on Southern Appalachian National Forests," *Journal of American Forestry* 41 (1943): 105, 111. For a similar assessment of CCC forestry work and its role in raising timber production, see T. B. Plair, "How the CCC Has Paid Off," *American Forests* 60, no. 2 (February 1954): 44–45.

39. The 1939 Black Hills survey by the Forest Service indicated that tree stands gained 77 percent as much growth in the few years after CCC thinning as they had in the previous forty-five years, while the 1956 study in Arkansas' Ozark National Forest found that CCC improvement work on hardwood and pine stands resulted in a 500 and 170 board-feet per acre advantage, respectively, over nearby untreated sites. See Eugene Shoulders, "Timber Stand Improvement in Ozark Forests: An Appraisal after 15 Years," *Journal of Forestry* 54, no. 12 (December 1956): 827. For the study in North Dakota, see National Park Service, "Director's Report 1939," 71, as noted in Cutler, *Public Landscape*, 96.

40. Roy Headley, "Why Big National Forest Fires?" *American Forests* 40, no. 12 (December 1934): 561.

41. On Democratic strengths and weaknesses during the 1932 presidential election, see John Moore, Jon Preimesberger, and David Tarr, eds., *Congressional Quarterly's Guide to U.S. Elections*, 4th ed., vol. 1 (Washington, D.C.: CQ Press, 2001); and Edgar Eugene Robinson, *They Voted for Roosevelt: The Presidential Vote, 1932–1944* (Stanford, Calif.: Stanford University Press, 1947), 14, 19.

42. Roosevelt's margin of victory in New England (Maine, New Hampshire, Vermont, Massachusetts, Connecticut, and Rhode Island) and the Mid-Atlantic states (New York, New Jersey, and Pennsylvania), which was 0.7 percent and 5 percent, respectively, represented the weakest results by region for the Democratic party in the 1932 presidential election. For an analysis of these results by region, see Robinson, *They Voted for Roosevelt*, 41. On the history of state forest creation in this region, see Raymond Torrey, *State Parks and Recreational Uses of State Forests in the United States* (Washington, D.C.: National Conference on State Parks, 1926), 16–17; and Beatrice Ward Nelson, *State Recreation: Parks, Forests and Game Preserves* (Washington, D.C.: National Conference on State Parks, 1928), 302–431.

43. After New England and the Mid-Atlantic states, these three regions had the weakest turnout for Franklin Roosevelt in the 1932 presidential election. Roosevelt won the Great Lakes states (Ohio, Indiana, Illinois, Michigan, Wisconsin) by 11.5 percent, the Rocky Mountain states (Montana, Idaho, Wyoming, Colorado, New Mexico, Arizona, Utah, Nevada) by 20 percent, and the Pacific region (Washington, Oregon, California) by 21.5 percent. On the 1932 election in these regions, see Robinson, *They Voted for Roosevelt*, 41. For an analysis of the West as a region of swing states during the

early New Deal years, see Jason Scott Smith, "Building New Deal Liberalism: The Political Economy of Public Works, 1933–1956" (Ph.D. diss., University of California, Berkeley, 2001), 204.

44. For an examination of Roosevelt's attempt to woo this rural constituency, see Phillips, "Acres Fit and Unfit," 92.

45. Hugh Bennett, *Soil Conservation* (New York: McGraw-Hill, 1939), 55.

46. Franklin Roosevelt mentioned seeing the dust of the Great Plains in Hyde Park in a speech given on 9 July 1938 in Oklahoma City as reprinted in Nixon, *FDR and Conservation*, 2:246. On the dust storms as a threat to the nation, see the speech by Roosevelt given on 28 September 1938 in Fremont, Nebraska, as reprinted in Nixon, *FDR and Conservation*, 1:438.

47. Roosevelt recommended a soil survey of New York state in "The Land Survey of the State of New York, as Outlined by Governor Franklin D. Roosevelt in His Message to the Legislature, Albany, 26 January 1931," as reprinted in Nixon, *FDR and Conservation* 1:77. He mentioned the need for a national soil survey in a letter to Seattle magazine publisher Miller Freeman, 6 September 1932, as reprinted in Nixon, *FDR and Conservation*, 1:123. Prior to the New Deal, many counties throughout the country had also undertaken soil surveys. On such county-level work, see Douglas Helms, Anne B. W. Effland, and Patricia Durana, eds., *Profiles in the History of the U.S. Soil Survey* (Ames: Iowa State University Press, 2002).

48. Congress established the Soil Erosion Service as a temporary agency on 19 September 1933 and placed it under the jurisdiction of the Department of the Interior. In April 1935 Congress renamed the agency the Soil Conservation Service and transferred it to the Department of Agriculture. See *Supplementary Report of the Land Planning Committee to the National Resources Board* (published in eleven separate parts), part 5, *Soil Erosion: A Critical Problem in American Agriculture, Prepared by the Soil Conservation Service and Bureau of Agricultural Engineering of the United States Department of Agriculture for the Land Planning Committee* (Washington, D.C.: U.S. Government Printing Office, 1935), 19.

49. Ibid., 19–22, 24. For his assessment of the Soil Erosion Service's Reconnaissance Erosion Survey, see Bennett, *Soil Conservation*, 58; and R. Burnell Held and Marion Clawson, *Soil Conservation in Perspective* (Baltimore, Md.: Johns Hopkins University Press, 1965), 157.

50. *Supplementary Report of the Land Planning Committee to the National Resources Board*, part 5, *Soil Erosion: A Critical Problem in American Agriculture*, 23, 105.

51. "At Last—a Soil Erosion Program," *New Republic* 83, no. 1069 (29 May 1935): 68–69.

52. As quoted in Stuart Chase, *Rich Land, Poor Land: A Study of Waste in the Natural Resources of America* (New York: AMS, 1936), 99.

53. Ibid., 37, 88. Historians who portray Chase as a populizer include Arthur Schlesinger, *The Age of Roosevelt: The Crisis of the Old Order, 1919–1933* (Boston: Houghton Mifflin, 1957), 20; James Saeger, "Stuart Chase: At Right Angles to Laissez-faire," *Social Studies* 63, no. 6 (November 1972): 251; and Robert Westbrook, "Tribune of the Technostructure: The Popular Economics of Stuart Chase," *American Quarterly* 32, no. 4 (1980): 389. For another example of the use of this metaphor, see Editorial, "The Earth Disease," *American Forests* 42, no. 5 (May 1936): 213.

54. Environmental historians have recently begun exploring this link between health and landscape. For a helpful historiographical overview of this literature, see Gregg

Mitman, "In Search of Health: Landscape and Disease in American Environmental History," *Environmental History* 10, no. 2 (April 2005): 184–210. See also Gregg Mitman, Michelle Murphy, and Christopher Sellers, eds., "Landscapes of Exposure: Knowledge and Illness in Modern Environments," special edition of *Osiris* 19 (2004); Linda Nash, "Finishing Nature: Harmonizing Bodies and Environments in Late-Nineteenth Century California," *Environmental History* 8, no. 1 (2003): 25–52; Nash, "Transforming the Central Valley: Body, Identity, and Environment in California, 1850–1870" (Ph.D. diss., University of Washington, 2000); and Neil M. Maher, "A New Deal Body Politic: Landscape, Labor, and the Civilian Conservation Corps," *Environmental History* 7, no. 3 (Summer 2002): 435–461. For an analysis of such connections within the field of the history of medicine, see Gregg Mitman, "Hay Fever Holiday: Health, Leisure and Place in Gilded Age America," *Bulletin of the History of Medicine* 77, no. 3 (Fall 2003): 600–635; and Conevery Bolton Valencius, "The Geography of Health and the Making of the American West: Arkansas and Missouri, 1800-1860," in *Medical Geography in Historical Perspective*, ed. Nicolaas Rupke (London: Wellcome Trust Centre for the History of Medicine at UCL, 2000), 121–145.

55. For an insightful discussion of this geography of health on the western frontier, as well as its implications for nation building, see Conevery Bolton Valencius, *The Health of the Country: How American Settlers Understood Themselves and Their Land* (New York: Basic, 2003).

56. On the narrow definition of soil conservation during the early 1930s, see Douglas Helms, "The Civilian Conservation Corps: Demonstrating the Value of Soil Conservation," *Journal of Soil and Water Conservation* 40 (March–April 1985): 184–185. Although during the CCC's first year of operation it dedicated on average 118 of its 1,486 camps to soil erosion projects, the great majority of such soil work took place in national and state forests.

57. To determine the number of camps under the jurisdiction of the SES in April 1934 see Fechner, *Summary Report*, 57.

58. McEntee, *Final Report*, 37.

59. On the administrative aspects of this expansion in CCC work, see Robert Fechner, *Third Report of the Director of Emergency Conservation Work: For the Period April 1, 1934 to September 30, 1934*, RG 35: CCC, Entry 3: Annual, Special, and Final Reports, NARA, 3; "35,890,000 Is Allotted for CCC Drought Aid," *New York Times*, 20 September 1934, 6; and Salmond, *The CCC*, 56.

60. To determine the increase in the number of camps under the jurisdiction of the SES from April 1934 to March 1935, see Fechner, *Summary Report*, 57. These camp numbers were computed by adding the number of regular SES camps for the third, fourth, and fifth enrollment periods to the number of camps assigned to the SES through the drought-relief appropriation. On the number of Forest Service camps reassigned to the SES, see Helms, "The Civilian Conservation Corps: Demonstrating the Value of Soil Conservation," 187.

61. Robert Fechner, "The CCC in Soil Conservation," *Soil Conservation* 1, no. 6 (January 1936): 2.

62. Bennett, *Soil Conservation*, 321.

63. Roosevelt to Thomas Campbell, President, Campbell Farming Corporation, Hardin, Montana, 24 August 1936, as reprinted in Nixon, *FDR and Conservation*, 1:556.

64. Robert Fechner, *Annual Report of the Director of the Civilian Conservation Corps: Fiscal Year Ended June 30, 1938* (Washington, D.C.: U.S. Government Printing Office, 1938), 56, located at RG 35: CCC, Entry 3: Annual, Special, and Final Reports, NARA.

65. Bennett, *Soil Conservation*, 321.

66. Douglas Helms, *The Importance of the Civilian Conservation Corps to the Soil Conservation Service* (Washington, D.C.: U.S. Printing Office, 1983), 6–7.

67. Bennett, *Soil Conservation*, 339. Although Bennett does not split SCS conservation projects as succinctly as I do, in part 2 of his book he divides his program's work into these two categories. For other historians who likewise divide SCS and CCC work, see especially Helms, *The Importance of the Civilian Conservation Corps*, 3.

68. Bennett, *Soil Conservation*, 338.

69. Ibid., 507. On the types of plants used in revegetating gullies, see ibid., 516–518.

70. CCC, *The Work of the CCC in Water Conservation* (Washington, D.C.: U.S. Government Printing Office, 1936), 15. On early CCC gully work, see McEntee, *Final Report*, 45. On the CCC vegetative gully work, see Bennett, *Soil Conservation*, 363.

71. The total gully area on which the CCC performed vegetation work, 1,091,524,603 square yards, was computed by adding the gully area on which the CCC performed new vegetation work (464,830,313 square yards of tree planting and 478,499,555 square yards of grasses) with the gully area on which the CCC maintained existing vegetation plots (125,862,616 square yards of tree planting and 22,332,119 square yards of grasses). For these figures, and the total acreage planted against sheet erosion, see McEntee, *Final Report*, 45, 105.

72. On CCC strip-cropping work, see Bennett, *Soil Conservation*, 346–363. For overall statistics for CCC strip-cropping work, see McEntee, *Final Report*, 45, 105.

73. On the difference between temporary and permanent check dams, see Bennett, *Soil Conservation*, 522–524. For CCC statistics on check dams, see McEntee, *Final Report*, 45, 105.

74. On Soil Conservation Service terracing techniques and climatic variations, see Bennett, *Soil Conservation*, 443.

75. For statistics on CCC terrace work, see McEntee, *Final Report*, 45, 105.

76. Bennett, *Soil Conservation*, 434.

77. On how contouring benefited other types of CCC work, see ibid., 435.

78. McEntee, *Final Report*, 105.

79. Paul Tabor and Arthur Susott, "Zero to Thirty Million Mile-a-Minute Seedlings," *Soil Conservation*, 8:61, as cited in Cutler, *Public Landscape*, 114.

80. Speech by Roosevelt given on 28 September 1938 in Fremont, Nebraska, as reprinted in Nixon, *FDR and Conservation*, 1:438.

81. On the location of the new SCS-CCC camps, see Robert Fechner, "Memorandum for the Press, Release to Afternoon Papers, Saturday, July 27, 1935," Printed Materials Collection, Civilian Conservation Corps, Press Releases, FDRL, 1; Fechner, *Third Report*, 3; and Helms, "The Civilian Conservation Corps: Demonstrating the Value of Soil Conservation," 187.

82. For a description of Roosevelt's Dust Bowl trips and his drought-relief governors' conferences in 1936, see Riesch-Owen, *Conservation under Franklin D. Roosevelt*, 24. For an analysis of Roosevelt's weaker support from Republican-leaning farmers from the Midwest and the Great Plains, see Gertrude Slichter, "Franklin D. Roosevelt and the Farm Problem," *Mississippi Valley Historical Review* 43 (September 1956): 238–258.

83. Salmond, *The CCC*, 68.

84. On the importance of this incident in the presidential election of 1936, see Moore, Preimesberger, and Tarr, *Guide to U.S. Elections*, 265. On Roosevelt's efforts to court

Republican farmers from the Great Plains, see also Phillips, "Acres Fit and Unfit," 99, 164–177, 298.

85. On the role of the automobile in fostering this back-to-nature craze, see Paul Sutter, *Driven Wild: How the Fight against Automobiles Launched the Modern Wilderness Movement* (Seattle: University of Washington Press, 2002).

86. For Arno B. Cammerer's comments on outdoor recreation, see Emergency Conservation Work, "Memorandum for the Press, Release to Sunday Papers, June 9, 1935," Printed Materials Collection, Civilian Conservation Corps, Press Releases, FDRL, 2. On national park and national monument attendance, see U.S. Bureau of the Census, *Historical Statistics of the United States: Colonial Times to 1957* (Washington, D.C.: U.S. Government Printing Office, 1960), 222.

87. *Supplementary Report of the Land Planning Committee to the National Resources Board*, part 11, *Recreational Use of Land in the United States, Prepared by the National Park Service for the Land Planning Committee* (Washington, D.C.: U.S. Government Printing Office, 1938), 7, 70, 209. Although research for this document began in 1934, before Congress passed the Park, Parkway, and Recreation Study Act, it incorporated much material gained from work done under the 1936 act and, according to the National Park Service, may thus "properly be considered the first in a series" of studies resulting from the Park, Parkway, and Recreation Study. For this take on part 11 of the report of the Land Planning Committee, see National Park Service, *A Study of the Park and Recreation Problem of the United States* (Washington, D.C.: U.S. Government Printing Office, 1941), vi. On the Park, Parkway, and Recreation Study Act, see National Park Service, *Procedure for Park, Parkway and Recreational-Area Study* (Washington, D.C.: U.S. Government Printing Office, 1937), foreword, 1, 4.

88. The term "recreation problem of the United States" was used repeatedly in the second report filed under the Park, Parkway, and Recreation Study Act. For this and the CCC's role as curative, see National Park Service, *A Study of the Park and Recreation Problem of the United States*, vi. For an overall description of the Park, Parkway, and Recreation Study Act, see Conrad Wirth, *Parks, Politics, and the People* (Norman: University of Oklahoma, 1980), 166–172.

89. This ambivalence with respect to development, which is evident in the charter of the National Park Service, has been examined by numerous historians. See especially Alfred Runte, *National Parks: The American Experience* (Lincoln: University of Nebraska Press, 1979); Joseph Sax, *Mountains without Handrails: Reflections on National Parks* (Ann Arbor: University of Michigan Press, 1980); and Richard Sellars, *Preserving Nature in National Parks* (New Haven, Conn.: Yale University Press, 1977). The quote is from Douglas Strong, *Dreamers and Defenders: American Conservationists* (Lincoln: University of Nebraska Press, 1971), 116.

90. For Roosevelt's desire to defer CCC park work, see Secretary of the Interior Harold Ickes to Roosevelt, 9 February 1935, Official File 268 (CCC), Folder: Jan–Feb 1935, FDRL, 1.

91. On the expansion of CCC camps under the National Park Service, see "President Widens Authority of PWA," *New York Times*, 9 June 1935, p. 6. See also Emergency Conservation Work, "Memorandum for the Press, Release to Sunday Papers, June 9, 1935," Printed Materials Collection, Civilian Conservation Corps, Press Releases, FDRL, 2.

92. Robert Fechner, "My Hopes for the CCC," *American Forests* 45, no. 1 (January 1939): 12.

93. McEntee uses these categories of recreation work in the CCC's final report. See McEntee, *Final Report*, 43, 104–106.

94. For CCC statistics on visitor centers, lodges, museums, cabins, and shelters, see McEntee, *Final Report*, 104. Also see James Jackson, "Living Legacy of the CCC," *American Forests* 94, nos. 9–10 (Sept.–Oct. 1988): 47.

95. For total statistics of these and other "structural improvements," see McEntee, *Final Report*, 104.

96. Statistics for CCC road and bridge work can be found in ibid., 104. For information on CCC work on the Blue Ridge Parkway, see Linda McClelland, *Presenting Nature: The Historic Landscape Design of the National Park Service, 1916–1942* (Washington, D.C.: National Park Service, 1993), 55, 224–226; and Stanley Abbott, "The Blue Ridge Parkway," *American Forests* 46, no. 6 (June 1940): 249.

97. For general statistics on CCC hiking and horse trails and footbridges, see McEntee, *Final Report*, 104–105. The Appalachian Trail was the brainchild of Benton MacKaye, who pitched the idea to Franklin Roosevelt as early as 1921. On CCC work on the Appalachian and Pacific Crest trails, see Cutler, *Public Landscape*, 58; and "Bridge for Appalachian Trail," *American Forests* 44, no. 10 (October 1938).

98. For total statistics on CCC campground and picnic area work, see McEntee, *Final Report*, 106. On CCC campsite work, see McClelland, *Presenting Nature*, 223; Leslie Lacy, *The Soil Soldiers: The Civilian Conservation Corps in the Great Depression* (Radnor, Pa.: Chilton 1976), 156; Charles Carlin, "The Birches," article in CCC camp newspaper Camp S-56 *Chronicle* (25 May 1935): 12, Official File 268 (CCC), Folder: Miscellaneous April–June 1935, FDRL. For an example of CCC work building cookout stoves, see S. J. Clarke, "A New Camp Stove for Forest Use," *American Forests* 44, no. 9 (September 1938): 418.

99. On the swimming pool at the bottom of the Grand Canyon, see McClelland, *Presenting Nature*, 224–225, 67. For CCC work on artificial lakes, see Cutler, *Public Landscape*, 67; and "New Lakes for Palisades," *American Forests* 40, no. 5 (May 1934): 222. For Corps lake work in Palisades Interstate Park, see also "Find Much to Do in Palisades Park," *New York Times*, 6 August 1933, secs. xi and xii, p. 6. General statistics on CCC water recreation work can be found in McEntee, *Final Report*, 104–106.

100. On increased visitation to national parks, see Civilian Conservation Corps, "Memorandum for the Press, Release to Sunday Papers, July 31, 1983," Printed Materials Collection, Civilian Conservation Corps, Press Release, FDRL, 1. On a similar increase in state park tourism, see National Park Service, *A Study of the Park and Recreation Problem*, 50; "Indiana State Parks Set New Record for Visitors," *American Forests* 41, no. 11 (November 1935): 658; and "Winter Sports in Bear Mountain," *American Forests* 44, no. 1 (January 1938): 61. On general park statistics, see also Bureau of the Census, *Historical Statistics of the United States: Colonial Times to 1957* (Washington, D.C.: U.S. Government Printing Office, 1961), 222–225.

101. CCC, "Memorandum for the Press, Release to Sunday Papers, June 9, 1935," Printed Materials Collection, Civilian Conservation Corps, Press Release, FDRL, 2.

102. National Park Service, *Procedure for Park, Parkway and Recreational-Area Study*, foreword, 3. The *Recreational Use of Land in the United States* report of 1938 also stated that "recreation is dependent upon conservation" (17).

103. For statistics on CCC state park work, see Cutler, *Public Landscape*, 65; and CCC, *The CCC and Its Contribution to a Nation-Wide State Park Recreational Program* (Washington, D.C.: U.S. Government Printing Office, 1937), 8.

104. On the number of CCC camps functioning in Great Smoky Mountains National Park, see Charlotte Pyle, "CCC Camps in Great Smoky Mountains National Park," 1979, unpublished manuscript located at Great Smoky Mountains National Park Library (hereafter GSMNPL), 3; and Walter Miller, "The CCC in East Tennessee and the Great Smoky Mountains National Park," 1974, unpublished manuscript, GSMNPL. 6. On CCC work done in the park, see "Superintendent's Monthly Reports" for the years 1935 through 1942, GSMNPL.

105. On southern support for New Deal conservation programs, see Phillips, "Acres Fit and Unfit," 113–144.

106. McEntee, *Final Report*, 41.

107. Russell Lord, *Hands to Save the Soil* (Washington, D.C.: U.S. Government Printing Office, 1938), 84.

108. McEntee, *Final Report*, 14.

CHAPTER 3

1. Pablo Diaz Albertt, "How the CCC Has Helped Me Improve Myself," RG 35: CCC, Entry 99: Benefit Letters, 1934–1942, Folder: Letters from CCC Enrollees re: Benefits Received from the Corps, National Archives and Records Administration (hereafter NARA).

2. Determining the total number of men who joined the Corps between 1933 and 1942 depends on whether one accounts for the reenrollment of individual enrollees as well as the small number of World War I veterans and Native Americans who were permitted to join the Corps. Here I have decided to follow the lead of the CCC's second director, James McEntee, who in his final report noted that 3,240,393 men joined the CCC during its nine years of operation. This number includes camp personnel, World War I veterans, and Native Americans, and does not double- or triple-count men who reenrolled in the Corps two or three times. See James McEntee, Federal Security Agency, *Final Report of the Director of the Civilian Conservation Corps, April 1933 through June 30, 1942*, RG 35: CCC, Entry 3: Annual, Special, and Final Reports, NARA, 109. On 5 percent of the country's total male population joining the Corps, see John Paige, *The Civilian Conservation Corps and the National Park Service: An Administrative History* (Washington, D.C.: National Park Service, 1985), 126. McEntee states that 15 percent of young men aged eighteen to twenty-five joined the Corps in his *Final Report*, 50.

3. Frederick Katz, "How the Civilian Conservation Corps Has Benefited Me," Record Group 35: CCC, Entry 99: Benefit Letters, 1934–1942, Folder: Miscl. Benefit Letters, NARA; Anonymous, "Beneficial Environment in the C.C.C.," Record Group 35: CCC, Entry 99: Benefit Letters, 1934–1942, Folder: Letters from CCC Enrollees re: Benefits Received While in the Corps, NARA.

4. Frank Ernest Hill, "Salvaging Youth in Distress: The CCC, Having Achieved Notable Results in Upbuilding Thousands, Widens Its Field and Recruits New Forces to Carry On the Task of Conservation," *New York Times Magazine*, 21 April 1935, 22.

5. Albertt, "How the CCC Has Helped Me Improve Myself." For additional statements by enrollees regarding the effect of CCC work on both their bodies and minds, see 2nd Corps Area, "Enrollees' Estimates of Benefits Received and Needs Met in CCC Camps Abstracted from 200 Letters on 'What the CCC Has Done for Me,' " RG 35: CCC, Entry 99: Benefit Letters, 1934–1942, Folder: Miscl. Benefit Letters, NARA. Throughout the program's nine-year existence, CCC administrators sporadically asked enrollees to

write "benefit letters" and send them to Washington, D.C., and although it is difficult to determine if, or to what degree, camp officers influenced the contents of these letters, the variety of responses by enrollees suggests that such influence was minimal.

6. On the importance of the working class for New Deal liberalism, see especially Alan Brinkley, *The End of Reform: New Deal Liberalism in Recession and War* (New York: Vintage, 1995), especially chap. 9, "The New Unionism and the New Liberalism"; Steve Fraser and Gary Gerstle, eds., *The Rise and Fall of the New Deal Order, 1930–1980* (Princeton, N.J.: Princeton University Press, 1989), especially chap. 3, Steve Fraser's "The Labor Question"; and David Brody, *Workers in Industrial America: Essays on the Twentieth Century Struggle* (New York: Oxford University Press, 1981), especially chap. 3, "The Emergence of Mass Production Unionism," and chap. 4, "The New Deal and the Labor Movement."

7. Richard White, " 'Are You an Environmentalist or Do You Work for a Living?': Nature and Work," in *Uncommon Ground: Rethinking the Human Place in Nature*, ed. William Cronon (New York: Norton, 1996), 171–185. On the historical importance of workers' bodies, see Christopher Sellers, *Hazards of the Job: From Industrial Disease to Environmental Health Science* (Chapel Hill: University of North Carolina Press, 1997); and Robert Gottlieb, *Forcing the Spring: The Transformation of the American Environmental Movement* (Washington, D.C.: Island, 1993), especially chap. 2, "Urban and Industrial Roots." Interestingly, Gottlieb's discussion skips the Great Depression era.

8. Franklin Roosevelt to Congress, 21 March 1933, as reprinted in Edgar Nixon, comp. and ed., *Franklin D. Roosevelt and Conservation, 1911–1945* (Hyde Park, N.Y.: FDRL, 1957), 1:143.

9. U.S. Congress, "An Act for the Relief of Unemployment through the Performance of Useful Public Work, and for Other Purposes" (approved 31 March 1933), as reprinted in Nixon, *FDR and Conservation*, 1:146.

10. On labor's "grave apprehension" regarding the CCC bill, see *New York Times*, 22 March 1933, and A. F. Whitney, *New York Times*, 24 March 1933, as quoted in John Salmond, *The Civilian Conservation Corps, 1933–1942: A New Deal Case Study* (Durham, N.C.: Duke University Press, 1967), 14.

11. Two amendments were added to the Senate bill before passage: an antidiscriminatory provision and another repealing the restriction (added by the Senate) on the president's authority to acquire property through the CCC. For a brief discussion of the CCC bill's passage, see Nixon, *FDR and Conservation*, 1:149.

12. For criticism of Green's opposition to the CCC, see Chicago *Tribune*, 27 March 1933; New York *Herald Tribune*, 23 March 1933; and the St. Louis *Post-Dispatch*, 25 March 1933, all as cited in Salmond, *The CCC*, 19.

13. For a description of this inspection tour, including the lunch menu, see *New York Times*, 15 August 1933. On Green's reaction to the trip, see Green to Roosevelt, 18 September 1933, Roosevelt Papers, Official File 142, as quoted in Salmond, *The CCC*, 47. See also Nixon, *FDR and Conservation*, 1:197.

14. On Fechner's early life and career, see "Death Claims F. A. Silcox and Robert Fechner," *American Forests* 46, no. 2 (February 1940): 72–73; "Conservation: Poor Young Men," *Time*, 6 February 1939, 12; "Roosevelt's Tree Army: I," *New Republic*, 29 May 1935, 64; and Salmond, *The CCC*, 27, 76.

15. The totals for each enrollment period are taken from the CCC's annual director's reports, which can be found at RG 35: CCC, Entry 3: Annual, Special, and Final Reports,

NARA. Because the total number of enrollees within each enrollment period fluctuated due to continual discharges and replacements, I have used the average enrollment figures for each period.

16. On the Department of Labor's selection bureaucracy and first-year figures, see Robert Fechner, *First Report of the Director of Emergency Conservation Work: For the Period April 5, 1933, to September 30, 1933*, RG 35: CCC, Entry 3: Annual, Special, and Final Reports, NARA. For the Department of Labor's overall selection of enrollees 1933–1942, see McEntee, *Final Report*, 11, 23–24. On comparisons to World War I, see James McEntee, *Now They Are Men: The Story of the CCC* (Washington, D.C.: National Home Library Foundation, 1940), 15; and Salmond, *The CCC*, 45.

17. Alice Kessler-Harris argues persuasively that this "gendered imagination" of the state resulted in women being excluded from what she calls "economic citizenship." See Alice Kessler-Harris, *In Pursuit of Equity: Women, Men, and the Quest for Economic Citizenship in 20th-Century America* (New York: Oxford University Press, 2001).

18. On Eleanor Roosevelt's attempt to establish CCC camps for women, see "Women's Forest Work Camps May Be Set Up if Enough Ask Them, Says Mrs. Roosevelt," *New York Times*, 24 May 1933, p. 1; and Lillian Sire, "Camps for Women," letter to the editor, *New York Times*, 24 May 1933, p. 5. On Camp Jane Addams (also known as Camp Tera) in Bear Mountain State Park, see "Forest Camp for Women Opens in New York," *American Forests* 39, no. 7 (July 1933): 321; Susan Ware, *Beyond Suffrage: Women in the New Deal* (Cambridge, Mass.: Harvard University Press, 1981), 111; and Barrett Potter, "The Civilian Conservation Corps in New York State: Its Social and Political Impact" (Ph.D. diss., State University of New York, Buffalo, 1973), 75. For information on women's clubs, including the Women's Club of Birmingham in Alabama and the Women's National Democratic Club, that supported a female auxiliary CCC, see Potter, "The Civilian Conservation Corps in New York State," 74; and Alison Otis, *The Forest Service and the Civilian Conservation Corps, 1933–1942* (Washington, D.C.: Department of Agriculture, U.S. Forest Service, 1986), 8. On the Works Progress Administration's brief establishment of ninety camps for approximately 5,000 women, none of whom performed conservation work, see John Krygier, "Visualization, Geography, and Landscape: Visual Methods and the Study of Landscape Dereliction as a Process" (Ph.D. diss., Pennsylvania State University, 1995), 221.

19. Acting by executive order, President Roosevelt relaxed the admittance criteria for these groups in the following order: on 22 April 1933 the quota for local experienced men was set at 35,250 men; on 7 June 1933 the quota for World War I veterans was set at 25,000 men; and on 23 June 1933 the quota for Native Americans was set at 11,618 and raised in August 1933 to 12,702. See Fechner, *First Report*, 2. In 1935, the CCC expanded its age restrictions to allow men aged seventeen to twenty-eight to enroll. See Robert Fechner, *Summary Report of Director, Fiscal Year 1936* (Washington: U.S. Government Printing Office, 1936), 22–23, located at RG 35: CCC, Entry 3: Annual, Special, and Final Reports, NARA.

20. From 1933 to 1935, enrollees from families on relief rolls were given priority for enrollment in the Corps. After 1935, only young men from families on public relief were permitted to join the CCC. See Fechner, *Summary Report of Director, Fiscal Year 1936*, 22.

21. My ideas linking boys and labor have been especially influenced by Ava Baron, "An 'Other' Side of Gender Antagonism at Work: Men, Boys, and the Remasculinization

of Printers' Work, 1830–1920," in *Work Engendered: Toward a New History of American Labor*, ed. Ava Baron (Ithaca, N.Y.: Cornell University Press, 1991).

22. The CCC undertook a census of its enrollees during the week of 18–23 January 1937. See Robert Fechner, *Annual Report of the Director of Emergency Conservation Work, Fiscal Year Ending June 30, 1937* (Washington, D.C.: U.S. Government Printing Office, 1937), located at RG 35: CCC, Entry 3: Annual, Special, and Final Reports, NARA, 5. On the "typical enrollee," see Michael Sherraden, "The Civilian Conservation Corps: Effectiveness of the Camps" (Ph.D. diss., University of Michigan, 1979), 191.

23. McEntee, *Final Report*, 50.

24. The CCC presented its enrollee census material in Fechner, *Annual Report 1937*, 45, 5.

25. Robert Fechner, *Annual Report of the Director of the Civilian Conservation Corps, Fiscal Year Ended June 30, 1938* (Washington, D.C.: U.S. Government Printing Office, 1938), located at RG 35: CCC, Entry 3: Annual, Special, and Final Reports, NARA. On the unskilled nature of Corps enrollees, see Sherraden, "The Civilian Conservation Corps," 192.

26. Frank Ernest Hill, *School in the Camps: The Educational Program of the Civilian Conservation Corps* (New York: American Association for Adult Education, 1935), 71. The CCC also undertook projects involving unskilled labor in an effort to slow the pace of Corps work, ensuring a steady supply of work projects well into the future.

27. James Lowe, "What the Civilian Conservation Corps Has Meant to Me," 15 December 1935, RG 35: CCC, Entry 99: Benefit Letters, 1934–42, Folder: Letters of Commendation from CCC Boys, NARA.

28. The CCC was fond of publicizing "the typical CCC day" and did so often. See especially McEntee, *Now They Are Men*, 37; Fechner, *Annual Report 1937*, 3; and Salmond, *The CCC*, 137–141.

29. On enrollee work per day and week, see Robert Fechner, *Second Report of the Director of Emergency Conservation Work: For the Periods April 5, 1933, to September 30, 1933, and October 1, 1933, to March 31, 1933*, RG 33: CCC, Entry 3: Annual, Special, and Final Reports, NARA, 4.

30. I calculated this by multiplying the total number of enrollees in the Corps over its nine-year life span (3 million) by the average number of weeks each enrollee remained in the CCC (thirty-nine weeks) and then again by forty hours of work per week. For the average number of weeks that enrollees remained in the Corps, see Fechner, *Annual Report 1937*, 5; and Salmond, *The CCC*, 135. In his 1937 annual report (p. 3), Fechner also states that enrollees were permitted to perform overtime work in emergency situations only.

31. Robert Fechner to Franklin Roosevelt, 14 April 1939, as reprinted in Nixon, *FDR and Conservation*, 2:321.

32. Harold Fraine, "The Spirit of the CCC," as reprinted in Ovid Butler, *Youth Rebuilds: Stories from the CCC* (Washington, D.C.: American Forestry Association, 1934), 174. On the urban versus agricultural backgrounds of Corps enrollees, see "They Came From," Division of Research and Statistics, Civilian Conservation Corps, 4 November 1941, RG 35: CCC, Entry 12: "Organization Charts, 1941–1942," NARA.

33. Dan Gately, "To Whom It May Concern," 12 December 1935, RG 35: CCC, Entry 99: Benefit Letters, 1934–42, Folder: Letters from CCC Enrollees re: Benefits Received while in the Corps, NARA; Kenneth Stephans, "My Personal Opinion of the CCC," RG 35: CCC, Entry 99: Benefit Letters, 1934–42, Folder: Letters from CCC Enrollees re: Benefits Received from the Corps, NARA.

34. Anonymous, "Nature," as reprinted in the National Association of Civilian Conservation Corps Alumni, *Chapter Chatter and Comment* (newsletter of the NACCCA Mile High Chapter, Denver, Colorado) 10, no. 10 (October 1995): 5. Enrollees from cities stationed in New Hampshire camps were also surprised, and often frightened, by unfamiliar fauna, in this case foxes. See Robert Woodward as interviewed by David Draves, *Builder of Men: Life in the CCC Camps of New Hampshire* (Portsmouth, N.H.: Randall, 1992), 28.

35. Carl McNees, "Material Aids of a CCC Camp," RG 35: CCC, Entry 99: Benefit Letters, 1934–42, Folder: Letters from CCC Enrollees re: Benefits Received from the Corps, NARA.

36. Robert Ross, "The Revelation," as quoted in Butler, *Youth Rebuilds*, 45.

37. Commissioners of the Palisades Interstate Park, "Conservation Teaching for Interstate Park CCC Camps," press release 8 August 1934, in vertical file located at Bear Mountain State Park Archives, Bear Mountain, New York.

38. On the education level of CCC enrollees, see Hill, *School in the Camps*, 71; and Fechner, *Summary Report of Director, Fiscal Year 1936*, 24. On the use of the term "land sciences," see "President Considering Educational Program for the CCC," *American Forests* 39, no. 12 (December 1933): 561.

39. Wesley Kelley to Educational Advisor, 325th Company, CCC, 30 November 1935, RG 35: CCC, Entry 99: Benefit Letters, 1934–42, Folder: Letters of Commendation from CCC Boys, NARA; Joseph Swezey, "Benefits Derived from the Civilian Conservation Corps," RG 35: CCC, Entry 99: Benefit Letters, 1934–42, Folder: Letters from CCC Enrollees re: Benefits Received from the Corps, NARA, 2; James Cordes, "Material Aids of a CCC Camp," RG 35: CCC, Entry 99: Benefit Letters, 1934–42, Folder: Letters from CCC Enrollees re: Benefits Received from the Corps, NARA.

40. CCC, *Woodsmanship for the Civilian Conservation Corps* (Washington, D.C.: U.S. Government Printing Office, 1939), 3.

41. As quoted in Draves, *Builder of Men*, 122.

42. The CCC itself makes this distinction between informal and formal enrollee education in McEntee, Federal Security Agency, *Final Report of the Director of the Civilian Conservation Corps, April 1933 through June 30, 1942*, RG 35: CCC, Entry 99: Annual, Special, and Final Reports, NARA, 52.

43. Robert Fechner, "The Educational Contribution of the Civilian Conservation Corps," *Phi Delta Kappan: A Journal for the Promotion of Research, Service and Leadership in Education*, Special Number: Education in the Civilian Conservation Corps (June 1937): 307.

44. In one publicity pamphlet, subtitled "Learning by Doing," the Corps stated that "since the beginning of the CCC program, the value of training on the job has been recognized as a vital part of the Corps." See CCC, *Forest Improvements by the CCC* (Washington, D.C.: U.S. Government Printing Office, 1938), 11.

45. U.S. Commissioner of Education John Studebaker, "Editorial Comment," *Phi Delta Kappan: A Journal for the Promotion of Research, Service and Leadership in Education*, Special Number: Education in the Civilian Conservation Corps (June 1937): 298.

46. Salmond, *The CCC*, 87.

47. McEntee, *Now They Are Men*, 47.

48. Robert Fechner, address before the Star Radio Forum, 24 October 1934, Printed Material Collection, Civilian Conservation Corps, Press Releases, FDRL.

49. For a description of this manual, see Thomas Clark, *The Greening of the South: The Recovery of Land and Forest* (Louisville: University Press of Kentucky, 1984), 75.

50. On CCC camp libraries, see Robert Fechner, "Study Hour in the CCC," *New York Times*, 1 October 1933, sec. ix, p. 11; and Salmond, *The CCC*, 139-140. See also Leslie Lacy, *The Soil Soldiers: The Civilian Conservation Corps in the Great Depression* (Radnor, Pa.: Chilton 1976), 70. A total of a half million books circulated throughout the CCC library system.

51. Robert Ross, "The Revelation," as reprinted in Butler, *Youth Rebuilds*, 47.

52. Salmond, *The CCC*, 49.

53. Franklin Roosevelt to Major William Welch, 8 November 1933, Official File 973: Palisades Interstate Park, N.J., FDRL.

54. Director of CCC Camp Education Howard Oxley, "Educational Activities in CCC Camps: Fiscal Year 1936-1937," RG 35: CCC, Entry 107: Division of Research and Statistics, Educational Reports, 1935-42, NARA.

55. On early CCC educational classes and their correlation to Corps conservation work, see Robert Fechner, "Study Hour in the CCC," *New York Times*, 1 October 1933, sec. ix, p. 11; Fechner, *Second Report*; Otis, *The Forest Service and the CCC*, 11; and Samuel Harby, *A Study of Education in the Civilian Conservation Corps Camps of the Second Corps Area: April 1933–March 1937* (Ann Arbor, Mich.: Edwards., 1938), 16.

56. On the variety of courses offered by the CCC in 1935, see Emergency Conservation Work (CCC), "Memorandum for the Press," 13, September 1935, Printed Materials Collection, Civilian Conservation Corps, Press Releases, FDRL. On the CCC's educational goals, see "New Educational Program for Civilian Conservation Corps," *American Forests* 41, no. 11 (November 1935): 648.

57. Fechner, *Annual Report 1937*, 7. On percentages of enrollee participation in the CCC educational program, see ibid.; and Calvin Gower, "The Civilian Conservation Corps and American Education: Threat to Local Control?" *History of Education Quarterly* 7, no.1 (Spring 1967): 62.

58. Harby, *Education in CCC Camps*, 143. While this study examined camps in what the CCC called "the Second Corps Area," which covered the states of Washington, Oregon, Idaho, New Mexico, Utah, Nevada, California, and parts of Wyoming, it is a useful benchmark for the country at large since by this time the CCC's educational program was centralized from Washington, D.C.

59. American Tree Association, "Pack Dedicates 100,000 New Primers to Forest Camps," *Forestry News Digest* (August 1933): 8, clipping from Vertical File, Civilian Conservation Corps, Folder 2, FDRL.

60. Dan Gately, "To Whom It May Concern," 12 December 1935, RG 35: CCC, Entry 99: Benefit Letters, 1934–42, Folder: Letters from CCC Enrollees re: Benefits Received while in the Corps, NARA.

61. Frederick Carlsen, "What the Three C's Mean to Me," RG 35: CCC, Entry 99: Benefit Letters, 1934–42, Folder: Letters from CCC Enrollees re: Benefits Received from the Corps, NARA.

62. Harry Gough, as quoted in "How Enrollees Have Benefited by the CCC," RG 35: CCC, Entry 99: Benefit Letters, 1934–42, Folder: Letters from CCC Enrollees re: Benefits Received from the Corps, NARA.

63. Enrollees Thomas Scott and Paul Stone are quoted in Lacy, *Soil Soldiers*, 130, 126; James Weister, "How the CCC Has Benefited Me," RG 35: CCC, Entry 99: Benefit Letters, 1934–42, Folder: Letters of Commendation from CCC Boys, NARA; James Jensen, "What Am I Getting Out of the CCC?" RG 35: CCC, Entry 99: Benefit Letters, 1934–42, Folder: Misc. Benefit Letters. The enrollee stationed in Rushville, Illinois, is

James Kidwell, "A Task, a Plan and Freedom," *American Forests* 40, no. 1 (January 1934): 23. For examples of CCC enrollees using the terms "scrawny," "weak," and "poorly developed," see the following: James Danner, "What the CCC Taught Me," *Rotarian* (September 1941), clipping in Official File 268 (CCC), Folder: Misc 1941, FDRL; Gerald Street, "Wisdom from the Trees," *American Forests* 40, no. 1 (January 1934): 24; and Morelee Frazier, "CCC Camp S-56-Pa.," RG 35: CCC, Entry 99: Benefit Letters, 1934–42, Folder: Benefit Letters from CCC Enrollees re: Benefits Received from the Corps, NARA.

64. James Kidwell, "What the CCC Has Done for Me," *American Forests* 40, no. 1 (January 1934): 23.

65. Fechner, *Annual Report 1937*, 5.

66. Charles Hiller, "It Taught Me One Way to Be Happy," *American Forests* 40, no. 3 (March 1934): 121.

67. Both Billmyer quotes come from Charles Billmyer, "What the CCC Has Done for Me," RG 35: CCC, Entry 99: Benefit Letters, 1934–42, Folder: Letters from CCC Enrollees re: Benefits Received from the Corps, NARA.

68. James Danner to President Roosevelt, 21 September 1936, Official File 268 (CCC), Folder: Misc. July–September 1936, NARA, 2.

69. Illustrations by C. Moran, *Thousand Islander* (Fishers Landing, N.Y.), September 1937, 1 and 11, Official File 268 (CCC), Folder: CCC Periodicals, August–December 1937.

70. Robert Miller, "It's a Great Life," RG 35: CCC, Division of Planning and Public Relations, "Success Stories, 1936–1941," Box 2, NARA.

71. There were a number of sociological studies conducted during the Great Depression on the links among unemployment, physical deterioration, and the loss of male authority. See especially Mirra Komarovsky, *The Unemployed Man and His Family: The Effects of Unemployment upon the Status of the Men in Fifty-Nine New York Families* (New York: Dryden, 1940), 92–101.

72. On the army's health survey, see McEntee, *Final Report*, 55; and McEntee, *Now They Are Men*, 57–58.

73. Fechner, *First Report*, 5. The CCC's second director made a nearly identical statement in 1940; see McEntee, *Now They Are Men*, 58.

74. On enrollee undernourishment, see Robert Fechner, "Statement before the U.S. Senate Special Committee to Investigate Unemployment," 15 March 1938, Official File 268 (CCC), Folder: January–March 1938, 2. For the statement on "bad environments," see McEntee, *Final Report*, 109.

75. *Forestry News Digest* (July 1933), Folder: American Forestry Association Publications, Vertical Files, FDRL.

76. McEntee, *Now They Are Men*, 57–58.

77. Robert Fechner, "Fechner Clarifies Civilian Status of CCC," *American Forests* 45, no. 10 (October 1939): 511.

78. On this masculinity crisis, see Barbara Melosh, *Engendering Culture: Manhood and Womanhood in New Deal Public Art and Theater* (Washington, D.C.: Smithsonian Institution Press, 1991); Anthony Rotundo, *American Manhood: Transformations in Masculinity from the Revolution to the Modern Era* (New York: Basic, 1993); Gail Bederman, *Manliness and Civilization: A Cultural History of Gender and Race in the United States, 1880–1917* (Chicago: University of Chicago Press, 1995); and George Chauncey, *Gay New York: Gender, Urban Culture and the Making of the Gay Male World, 1890–1940* (New York: Basic, 1994). The Theodore Roosevelt quote comes from *The Strenuous Life: Essays and*

Addresses (New York: The Century Company, 1905), 7–8, as quoted in David Shi, *The Simple Life: Plain Living and High Thinking in American Culture* (New York: Oxford University Press, 1985), 201. For Depression era examples of sociological studies linking unemployment, physical deterioration, and the loss of male authority, see Komarovsky, *The Unemployed Man and His Family*, 92–101; Roger Angell, *The Family Encounters the Depression* (New York: Scribner's, 1936); and Ruth Shonle Cavan and Katherine Howland Ranck, *The Family and the Depression* (Freeport, N.Y.: Books for Libraries Press, 1938).

79. On CCC conditioning camps, see Fechner, *First Report*, 3; and Fechner, *Annual Report 1937*, 2. Fechner discussed the physical examination's rejection rate in *First Report*, 5.

80. Civilian Conservation Corps, *Physical Training Manual* (Washington, D.C.: National Publishers, n.d.), 4.

81. Franklin Roosevelt to Congress, 21 March 1933, as quoted in Nixon, *FDR and Conservation*, 1:143. Also see Darel McConkey, "The Health of John Peavey: An Average Boy, Back from the CCC Camp, Provides His Neighbors an Education on the Youth Movement in America's Forests," *American Forests* 40, no. 11 (November 1934): 511.

82. Harby, *Education in CCC Camps*; and McEntee, *Final Report*, 42.

83. While much of the evidence for this corporeal rejuvenation comes from statements written by enrollees at the behest of the CCC, additional material from newspaper reports, personal letters, reminiscences, and medical data on the health of these young men supports the notion that work in nature dramatically transformed enrollees' bodies.

84. James Danner, "What CCC Taught Me," *Rotarian* (ca. September 1941), clipping in Official File 268 (CCC), Folder: Misc. 1941, FDRL.

85. Enrollees used such language in the many letters sent home and to the federal government. For "sore" and "stiff" muscles, see Battell Loomis, "With the Green Guard: Beginning a Tenderfoot Forester's Impressions of Life in the CCC Camps," *Liberty Magazine*, 14 April 1934, 53. On becoming "stronger," see Arthur Dilgado to Whom It May Concern, 17 December 1935, RG 35: CCC, Entry 99: Benefit Letters, 1934–42, Folder: Letters of Commendation from CCC Boys, NARA. And on developing physically, see Jacob Paslawsky, "What the CCC Has Done for Me," RG 35: CCC, Entry 99: Benefit Letters, 1934–42, Folder: Letters from CCC Enrollee[s] re: Benefits Received from the Corps, NARA.

86. Danner, "What CCC Taught Me," n.p.

87. On the average weight and height gain of CCC enrollees, see McEntee, *Final Report*, 55. See also Joseph Weigel, "Material Value of the CCC," RG 35: CCC, Entry 99: Benefit Letters, 1934–42, Folder: Letters from CCC Enrollees re: Benefits Received while in the Corps, NARA; and James Bennett, as quoted in "Looking and Listening with Vann Kincannon," clipping from *Tupelo Journal* (n.d.), RG 35: CCC, Division of Planning and Public Relations, "Success Stories, 1936–1941," Box 1: Alabama–Wyoming, NARA.

88. McEntee, *Now They Are Men*, 31. The few overweight young men who joined the Corps often lost weight during their time in camp. See especially Myer Schaffner, as quoted in Edwin Hill, *In the Shadow of the Mountain: The Spirit of the CCC* (Pullman: Washington State University Press, 1990), 159.

89. On "pasty-faced" new enrollees, see Walter Woehlke, "Mutiny in a 3-C Camp! A Lively Chronicle of Ups and Downs among 300,000 Young Americans Who Are Learning to Be Men," *Liberty Magazine*, 21 April 1934, clipping from Official File 268 (CCC), Folder: March–July 1934, 52. On "pale" enrollees, see Editorial, "Evolution of an Enrollee," *Trumpeter* (enrollee newspaper from Moormans River, Va.), 2. And on

enrollees having no "good color at all," see James Newton as quoted in Merrill, *Roosevelt's Forest Army*, 102.

90. On enrollee sunburn, see William Carson to Franklin Roosevelt, 20 May 1933, Official File 268 (CCC), Folder: Miscellaneous, March–May 1933, FDRL; and Dorothy Bromley, "The Forestry Army That Lives by Work," *New York Times*, 23 July 1933, sec. viii, p. 2. On enrollee blisters, see anonymous enrollee, "How I Have Benefited," RG 35: CCC, Entry 99: Benefit Letters 1934–1942, Folder: Misc. Benefit Letters, NARA; and Paul Briggs, "My Opportunity in the CCC," RG 35: CCC, Entry 99: Benefit Letters 1934–1942, Folder: Letters from CCC Enrollees re: Benefits Received from the Corps, NARA.

91. Robert Buchanan, as quoted in David Draves, *Builder of Men: Life in the CCC Camps of New Hampshire* (Portsmouth, N.H.: Randall, 1992), 125. For descriptions of enrollees' brown skin, see Freeman Bishop, " 'Remembered Men': The Civilian Conservation Corps—Who and What They Are as Told by One of Them," *American Forests* 39, no. 8 (August 1933): 380; and John Guthrie, "With the Texas Forest Army," *American Forests* 39, no. 12 (December 1933): 576.

92. Harold Buckles, "I Have Learned to Know the Human Race," *American Forests* 40, no. 5 (May 1934): 218.

93. Harry Maynor to James Ellis, Director of Emergency Conservation, 7 June 1934, RG 35: CCC, Entry 99: Benefit Letters, 1934–42, Folder: Letters of Commendation from CCC Boys, NARA.

94. Lee Wilson, as quoted in CCC, "Memorandum for the Press: Colorado" (n.d.), RG 35: CCC, Entry 99: Benefit Letters, 1934–42, Folder: Social Benefits of CCC to Enrollees (Alphabetical by State—Not All States), NARA.

95. On the army's health survey, see McEntee, *Final Report*, 55; and McEntee, *Now They Are Men*, 57–58.

96. Lawrence Lescisco, "My Life in the CCC's," RG 35: CCC, Entry 99: Benefit Letters, 1934–42, Folder: Letters from CCC Enrollees re: Benefits Received from the Corps, NARA.

97. A number of environmental historians have raised concerns regarding the usefulness of such terms, claiming that "nature" is socially constructed. See especially Donald Worster, "The Ecology of Order and Chaos," in his *The Wealth of Nature* (New York: Oxford University Press, 1993), 156–170; Donald Worster, *Nature's Economy: A History of Ecological Ideas*, 1st ed. (Cambridge: Cambridge University Press, 1977), 205–212; and Mart Stewart, *"What Nature Suffers to Groe": Life, Labor, and Landscape on the Georgia Coast, 1680–1920* (Athens: University of Georgia Press, 1996), 8–11.

98. John Goodspeed to M. H. Welling, 31 October 1934, Official File 268 (CCC), Folder: Misc. October–December, 1934, FDRL; Herbert Junep, "Farewell to the CCC," as quoted in Butler, *Youth Rebuilds*, 168.

99. Paul Stone, as quoted in Lacy, *Soil Soldiers*, 126. Also see Virgil McClanahan, "The Advantages of the CCC," RG 35: CCC, Entry 99: Benefit Letters, 1934–42, Folder: Letters from CCC Enrollees re: Benefits Received while in the Corps, NARA. Many enrollees used identical language in describing the influence of a more natural environment on their health. See especially Robert Burns to Franklin Roosevelt, 31 August 1935, Official File 268 (CCC), Folder: Misc. July–October 1935, FDRL; and Valentine Bilovsky, "CCC Life," RG 35: CCC, Entry 99: Benefit Letters, 1934–42, Folder: Letters from CCC Enrollees re: Benefits Received from the Corps, NARA.

100. John McAdams, "Experiences in a CCC Camp," RG 35: CCC, Entry 99: Benefit Letters, 1934–42, Folder: Letters from CCC Enrollees re: Benefits Received from the

Corps, NARA. There are dozens of similar letters from enrollees linking their new physiques and working outdoors to manhood. See especially Pablo Albertt, "How the CCC Has Helped Me Improve Myself," RG 35: CCC, Entry 99: Benefit Letters, 1934–42, Folder: Letters from CCC Enrollees re: Benefits Received from the Corps, NARA; Bob Eddy, "What I Have Gained from CCC Life," RG 35: CCC, Entry 99: Benefit Letters, 1934–42, Folder: Letters from CCC Enrollees re: Benefits Received while in the Corps, NARA; and Farran Zerbe II, "What the Greeks Meant," and Robert Ross, "The Revelation," both as quoted in Butler, *Youth Rebuilds*, 122, 48.

101. Anonymous, "But Wilbur Joined the CCC—and After a Year," *Cottonwood* (New Ulm, Minn.), 7 July 1939, Official File 268 (CCC), Folder: CCC Periodicals, 1938–1939, FDRL.

102. James Brandon, "To the Fourth Corps Area," 7 December 1935, RG 35: CCC, Entry 99: Benefit Letters, 1934–42, Folder: Letters from CCC Enrollees re: Benefits Received from the Corps, NARA.

103. For other examples of CCC enrollees linking their work to a newfound appreciation of conservation, see Rossiter Jones, "Benefits Derived from the CCC," RG 35: CCC, Entry 99: Benefit Letters, 1934–42, Folder: Misc. Benefit Letters, NARA; and James Kidwell, "A CCC Fighter," RG 35: CCC, Entry 101: Success Stories, 1936–1941, Folder: Misc. Prize Winning Stories, Box 2, NARA.

104. Fred Harrison, "What the CCC Has Done for Me," RG 35: CCC, Entry 99: Benefit Letters, 1934–42, Folder: Letters from CCC Enrollees re: Benefits Received from the Corps, NARA.

105. On the elite character of Progressive conservationism, see Samuel Hays, *Conservation and the Gospel of Efficiency: The Progressive Conservation Movement, 1890–1920* (Cambridge, Mass.: Harvard University Press, 1959). On the rural, non-elite wing of Progressive conservationism, see Louis Warren, *The Hunter's Game: Poachers and Conservationists in Twentieth-Century America* (New Haven, Conn.: Yale University Press, 1997), especially 49; Karl Jacoby, *Crimes against Nature: Squatters, Poachers, Thieves, and the Hidden History of American Conservation* (Berkeley: University of California Press, 2003); and Richard Judd, *Common Lands, Common People: The Origins of Conservation in Northern New England* (Cambridge, Mass.: Harvard University Press, 2000).

106. The notion of an amateur wing within the conservation movement comes from Stephen Fox, *The American Conservation Movement: John Muir and His Legacy* (Madison: University of Wisconsin Press, 1981).

107. Robert Fechner, "Fechner Clarifies Civilian Status of CCC," *American Forests* 45, no. 10 (October 1939): 511.

108. McEntee, *Now They Are Men*, 6. The CCC used this language frequently. Fechner warned that unemployment leads to "moral erosion" in youth in Fechner, "Fechner Clarifies Civilian Status of CCC," 511. For similar language, see also CCC educational advisor Scott Leavitt, "The Social and Economic Implications of Conservation," *Phi Delta Kappan: A Journal for the Promotion of Research, Service and Leadership in Education*, Special Number: Education in the Civilian Conservation Corps (June 1937): 326.

109. Robert Ross, "The Revelation," as quoted in Butler, *Youth Rebuilds*, 48.

110. Carl Stark, "Conservation of Men in the CCC from My Own Experiences," 3 June 1941, RG 35: CCC, Entry 99: Benefit Letters, 1934–42, Folder: Letters from CCC Enrollees re: Benefits Received from the Corps, NARA.

111. There are numerous examples of the CCC administration using this phrase and similar language. See especially Robert Fechner, *Two Years of Emergency Conservation*

Work, April 5, 1933–March 31, 1935; Robert Fechner, *Annual Report of the Director of the Civilian Conservation Corps, Fiscal Year Ended June 30, 1939* (Washington, D.C.: U.S. Government Printing Office, 1939); James McEntee, Federal Security Agency, *Annual Report of the Director of the Civilian Conservation Corps, Fiscal Year Ended June 30, 1942*; and McEntee, *Final Report*, all located at RG 35: CCC, Entry 99: Annual, Special, and Final Reports, NARA.

112. This point is made most explicitly by Gregg Mitman in his essay "Hay Fever Holiday: Health, Leisure, and Place in Gilded-Age America," *Bulletin of the History of Medicine* 77 (2003): 634–635. According to Mitman, "the historiography of environmentalism in America has been largely silent on the role that health has played in changing environmental attitudes prior to the Second World War." The history of the CCC helps to fill this historiographical gap.

113. For a thorough examination of this amendment, see John Salmond, "The Civilian Conservation Corps and the Negro," *Journal of American History* 52 (1965): 76; Olen Cole, "African-American Youth in the Program of the Civilian Conservation Corps in California, 1933–1942," *Forest and Conservation History* 35 (July 1991): 121; Calvin Gower, "The Struggle of Blacks for Leadership Positions in the Civilian Conservation Corps: 1933–1942," *Journal of Negro History* 61, no. 2 (April 1976): 123.

114. Colonel Duncan Major to Colonel Louis Howe, 14 August 1933, Official File: 268 (CCC), Folder: Misc., June–Aug 1933, FDRL.

115. Kenneth Stephans, "My Personal Opinion of the CCC," RG 35: CCC, Entry 99: Benefit Letters, 1934–1942, Folder: Letters from CCC Enrollees re: Benefits Received from the Corps, NARA.

116. Franklin Roosevelt, "Address at Roosevelt Park," New York City, 18 October 1936, in *Public Papers*, 5:544–555, as quoted in Gary Gerstle, *American Crucible: Race and Nation in the Twentieth Century* (Princeton, N.J.: Princeton University Press, 2001), 138. On 1920s immigration restrictions and the New Deal's subsequent embrace of recent immigrants, see Gerstle, *American Crucible*, 129, 138–139, 150, 154.

117. The quote by Congressman Martin Dies can be found in the *Congressional Record*, 10 May 1935, 7319–7320, as quoted in Gerstle, *American Crucible*, 160.

118. For background information on the House Special Committee on Un-American Activities, see Gerstle, *American Crucible*, 158–160; and William Leuchtenburg, *Franklin D. Roosevelt and the New Deal, 1932–1940* (New York: Harper Torchbooks, 1963), 280–281.

119. Norman Thomas, *Literary Digest* 115 (15 April 1933): 6, as quoted in Salmond, *The CCC*, 14.

120. "Coughlan Say NRA Is Only Beginning," *New York Times*, 5 February 1934, pp. 2 and 4.

121. Massachusetts State Legislature special commission and Mayor Hague as quoted in Salmond, *The CCC*, 192.

122. On conservative newspapers reporting on CCC enrollees' communist activity, see Elmo Richardson, "Was There Politics in the Civilian Conservation Corps?" *Forest History* 16, no. 2 (July 1972): 13. On the CCC not being conducive to a "democratic society," see "Appraising the Civilian Conservation Corps," *School Review* 42 (September 1935): 488, as quoted in Robert Dubay, "The Civilian Conservation Corps: A Study in Opposition, 1933–1935," *Southern Quarterly* 6, no. 3:357.

123. Fechner, *Annual Report 1939*, 8. Although Bryant Simon does an excellent job linking physical changes in Corps enrollees to their Americanization, he refrains from

examining the central role of the natural environment in this Americanization process. See Bryant Simon, " 'New Men in Body and Soul': The Civilian Conservation Corps and the Transformation of Male Bodies and the Body Politic," in *Seeing Nature through Gender*, ed. Virginia Scharff (Lawrence: University Press of Kansas), 137–138.

124. James McEntee, Federal Security Agency, *Final Report of the Director of the Civilian Conservation Corps, April 1930 through June 1942*, RG 35: CCC, Entry 3: Annual, Special, and Final Reports, NARA, 63.

125. James McEntee, Federal Security Agency, *Final Report of the Director of the Civilian Conservation Corps, April 1930 through June 30, 1942*, RG 35: CCC, Entry 3: Annual, Special, and Final Reports, NARA, 63.

126. Kenneth Stephans, "My Personal Opinion of the CCC," RG 35: CCC, Entry 99: Benefit Letters, 1934–1942, Folder: Letters from CCC Enrollees re: Benefits Received from the Corps, NARA.

127. James Danner to President Franklin Roosevelt, 21 September 1936, Official File, 268 (CCC), Folder: Misc., July–Sept 1936, FDRL, 2.

128. Joseph Paul Jurasek, "The Joy of Living," in Butler, *Youth Rebuilds*, 67.

129. For an example of how Italian Americans developed a "white consciousness" during the New Deal era, see Stefano Luconi, "A Troubled Political Partnership: Italian Americans and African Americans in the New Deal Democratic Coalition," *Proceedings of the American Italian Historical Association* 30 (1999): 133–149. For Irish support for Roosevelt during the 1930s, see Patrick Kennedy, "Chicago's Irish Americans and the Candidacies of Franklin Roosevelt, 1932–1944," *Illinois Historical Journal* 88, no. 4 (1995): 263–278.

130. The classic works on this subject are David Roediger's *The Wages of Whiteness: Race and the Making of the American Working Class* (New York: Verso, 1991); and Matthew Frye Jacobson, *Whiteness of a Different Color: European Immigrants and the Alchemy of Race* (Cambridge, Mass.: Harvard University Press, 1998).

131. For an informative historiographical review of the literature in whiteness studies, see Peter Kolchin, "Whiteness Studies: The New History of Race in America," *Journal of American History* 89, no. 1 (June 2002): 154–173. Environmental historians have begun to examine the role played by the environment in creating whiteness. See especially Annie Coleman, "The Unbearable Whiteness of Skiing," *Pacific Historical Review* 65, no. 4 (November 1996): 583–614; and Sylvia Washington, *Packing Them In: An Archeology of Environmental Racism, 1865–1954* (Lanham, Md.: Lexington, 2004).

132. For a wonderful analysis of the connections among gender, race, and nationalism during the early twentieth century, see Gail Bederman, *Manliness & Civilization: A Cultural History of Gender and Race in the United States, 1880–1917* (Chicago: University of Chicago Press, 1996), especially chap. 5, "Theodore Roosevelt: Manhood, Nation, and 'Civilization.' "

133. There is a long history in the United States of white men achieving manhood by becoming more Indian-like. See especially Richard Slotkin, *Regeneration through Violence: The Mythology of the American Frontier, 1600–1860* (Middletown, Conn.: Wesleyan University Press, 1973); and Richard Slotkin, *The Fatal Environment: The Myth of the Frontier in the Age of Industrialization, 1800–1890* (New York: Atheneum, 1985). For an example of this process during the twentieth century, see Marguerite Shaffer, *See America First: Tourism and National Identity, 1880–1940* (Washington, D.C.: Smithsonian Books, 2001), 230.

134. These discriminatory practices in the CCC are examined in detail in Olen Cole, Jr., *The African-American Experience in the Civilian Conservation Corps* (Gainesville: University of Florida Press, 1999).

135. For further evidence that New Deal programs failed to address racial discrimination, see Sarah Phillips, "Acres Fit and Unfit: Conservation and Rural Rehabilitation in the New Deal Era" (Ph.D. diss., Boston University, 2004), 272; and Jason Scott Smith, "Building New Deal Liberalism: The Political Economy of Public Works, 1933–1956" (Ph.D. diss., University of California, Berkeley, 2001), 19. On the failure of the Corps in particular to address racism, see Cole, *The African-American Experience in the Civilian Conservation Corps*; Allen Kifer, "The Negro under the New Deal" (Ph.D. diss., University of Wisconsin, 1961); George Rawick, "The New Deal and Youth: The Civilian Conservation Corps, the National Youth Administration, and the American Youth Congress" (Ph.D. diss., University of Wisconsin, 1957); John Salmond, "The Civilian Conservation Corps and the Negro," *Journal of American History* 52, no. 1 (June 1965): 75–88; Charles Johnson, "The Army, the Negro and the Civilian Conservation Corps: 1933–1942," *Military Affairs* 36 (October 1972): 82–88; and Calvin Gower, "The Struggle for Black Leadership Positions in the Civilian Conservation Corps: 1933–1942," *Journal of Negro History* 61, no. 2 (1976): 123–135.

136. For a discussion of limits on African Americans' ability to "become white," see Peter Kolchin, "Whiteness Studies: The New History of Race in America," *Journal of American History* 89, no. 1 (2002): 37. This notion that discrimination within the CCC placed African Americans outside the body politic is suggested by Simon, "New Men in Body and Soul," 85.

137. Dorothy Bromley, "The Forestry Army That Lives by Work," *New York Times*, 23 July 1933, sec. viii, p. 2.

138. Mrs. Frank Kelsey to Roosevelt, 18 May 1933, Roosevelt Papers, PPF 522, as quoted in Salmond, *The CCC*, 111.

139. Gerstle discusses Roosevelt's success in the election of 1936 in *American Crucible*, 150.

140. The Houston *Post* as reprinted in *Happy Days: The Official Newspaper of the Civilian Conservation Corps*, 26 December 1936, RG 35: Records of the CCC, Entry 2, General Records of the Emergency Conservation Work and Civilian Conservation Corps, 1933–42, NARA.

141. Pablo Diaz Albertt, "How the CCC Has Helped Me Improve Myself," RG 35: CCC, Entry 99: Benefit Letters, 1934–1942, Folder: Letters from CCC Enrollees re: Benefits Received from the Corps, NARA; and Frederick Katz, "How the Civilian Conservation Corps Has Benefited Me," RG 35: CCC, Entry 99: Benefit Letters, 1934–1942, Folder: Miscl. Benefit Letters, NARA.

142. Albertt, "How the CCC Has Helped Me Improve Myself."

CHAPTER 4

1. Much of this material on CCC participation in the Mountain State Forest Festival comes from Jennifer Seltz, "Making the Forest Work: Constructing a National Landscape in West Virginia, 1880–1942," unpublished manuscript. On Camp North Fork's participation in the festival in 1934, see *Petersburg Builder* (camp newspaper of CCC Company 519), 1 October 1934. On visits by Secretary Dern and President Roosevelt,

see Papers of Henry Dern, Library of Congress Manuscript Division; and Calvin Price, "Forest Festival," *Pocahontas Times*, 1 October 1936.

2. The total for camps built up until 1936 comes from Fred J. Murray, "Paul Bunyan Reads the Record of the CCC," *American Forests* 43, no. 4 (April 1937): 157. My estimate of 5,000 camps is conservative.

3. John Mitchell, "FDR's Tree Army," *Audubon* 85, no. 6 (November 1983): 84.

4. Although only 6.8 percent of the 235 "complaint letters" filed with the CCC mentioned opposition to "black camps," "enrollee race" issues garnered the most discussion within the CCC Advisory Council meetings. For analysis of these complaint letters and the Advisory Council's minutes, see Michael Sherraden, "The Civilian Conservation Corps: Effectiveness of the Camps" (Ph.D. diss., University of Michigan, 1979), 221–222. Other examples of community opposition to African-American camps are numerous. See especially John Salmond, *The Civilian Conservation Corps, 1933–1942: A New Deal Case Study* (Durham, N.C.: Duke University Press, 1967), 91; Captain X, "Problems with the Woodland Army," *Military Engineer* (July–August 1934): 299; and Jerrell Shofner, "Roosevelt's 'Tree Army': The Civilian Conservation Corps in Florida," *Florida Historical Quarterly* 65 (April 1987): 449. The best examination of the African-American experience in the CCC is Owen Cole, *The African-American Experience in the Civilian Conservation Corps* (Tallahassee: University Press of Florida, 1999).

5. For additional material on this anti-urban, anti-immigrant bias, see Ben Dixon MacNeill, "The Melting Pot of CCC Takes 'Em, East, West, North, South and Makes a Sturdy Alloy," *News and Observer* (Raleigh, N.C.), 31 March 1935, 3, Official File 268 (CCC), Folder: Misc (April–June 1935), FDRL; Captain X, "A Civilian Army in the Woods," *Harper's* 168 (March 1934): 490; and Barrett Potter, "The Civilian Conservation Corps in New York State: Its Social and Political Impact" (Ph.D. diss., State University of New York, Buffalo, 1973), 61.

6. According to the complaint letters, this was the most common criticism of new CCC camps, accounting for more than 27 percent of the correspondence. On community criticism of CCC enrollees as outsiders, see Alison Otis, *The Forest Service and the Civilian Conservation Corps, 1933–1942* (Washington, D.C.: U.S. Forest Service, 1986), 2. Examples of local laborers opposing the arrival of CCC camps include Bricklayers and Masons Local, Bloomington, Indiana, to CCC director Robert Fechner, 8 February 1935, RG 35: CCC, Entry 2: General Correspondence, #300: Spencer, Indiana, Box: Sidon-Springville (#596), NARA; and Phoenix Building Trades Council to CCC director J. J. McEntee, 19 November 1937, RG 35: CCC, Entry 2: General Correspondence, #500: Phoenix Building Trades Council, Box 733, NARA.

7. The "street-slum foreigners" quote comes from the Kalispell, Montana, *Daily Inter Lake*, 11 April 1933, as quoted in Michael Ober, "The CCC Experience in Glacier National Park," *Montana: The Magazine of Western History* 26, no. 3 (Summer 1976): 37. For descriptions of Corps enrollees as "corner holders" and "bums," see "The CCC Man and the General Public," *Hi-De-Hi-De-Ho* (camp newspaper of "Colored Company" 4487, Anderson, S.C.), vol. 1, Official File 268 (CCC), Folder: CCC Periodicals (Aug–Dec 1937), FDRL.

8. Sherraden, "The Civilian Conservation Corps," 215.

9. For a description of this congressional debate, see Salmond, *The CCC*, 66.

10. Robert Fechner, "The CCC in Soil Conservation," *Soil Conservation* 1, no. 6 (January 1936): 1. On local demand for CCC camps, see also "Fechner and Council

Honored by the American Forestry Association," *American Forests* 41, no. 5 (May 1935): 241.

11. Roosevelt gave this speech in support of the Roosevelt-Jones Bill. The text of the address located at the FDRL is somewhat different than that reported in the *Troy Record*. See Franklin Roosevelt, "Address before the People's Forum, Troy, New York," 3 March 1912, FDR: Papers as New York Senator, General Subject File, Folder: Speeches by FDR, Oct 1910–May 1912, FDRL; and *Troy Record*, 4 March 1912.

12. In general, historians have refrained from examining the impact of New Deal programs on local communities, focusing instead on how such programs influenced those who participated in them. For an exception to this rule, see Maria Montoya, "The Roots of Economic and Ethnic Divisions in Northern New Mexico: The Case of the Civilian Conservation Corps," *Western Historical Quarterly* 26, no. 1 (1995): 14–34.

13. President Franklin D. Roosevelt to Congress, 3 June 1937, as reprinted in Edgar Nixon, comp. and ed., *Franklin D. Roosevelt and Conservation, 1911–1945* (Hyde Park, N.Y.: FDRL, 1957), 2:68.

14. On the interdependence of environmental, economic, and ideological changes, see Arthur McEvoy, "Toward an Interactive Theory of Nature and Culture: Ecology, Production, and Cognition in the California Fishing Industry," *Environmental History Review* 11 (Winter 1987): 300. McEvoy's theory is expanded upon by Barbara Leibhardt, "Interpretation and Causal Analysis: Theories in Environmental History," *Environmental History Review* 12 (Spring 1988): 23–33. The field of political ecology examines this relationship among nature, economics, and political power on the local level. For a good description of the field, see Peter Taylor, "Appearances Notwithstanding, We Are All Doing Something Like Political Ecology," *Social Epistemology* 11, no. 1 (1997): 111–127.

15. While my conception of local communities relies heavily on geographic proximity, it includes as well the notion that "community" is also a process of social, economic, and political interactions among neighbors. While my "locals" are thus those living near CCC camps, I have tried to make distinctions between different sets of locals within these geographic regions. In particular, I have tried to pay special attention to economic differences and to differences based on access to political power in these communities. On the importance of community history in particular, and social history in general, within the field of environmental history, see Samuel Truett, "Neighbors by Nature: Rethinking Region, Nation, and Environmental History in the U.S.-Mexico Borderlands," *Environmental History* 2, no. 2 (April 1997): 160–178; Alan Taylor, "Unnatural Inequalities: Social and Environmental Histories," *Environmental History* 1, no. 4 (October 1996): 6–19; Karl Jacoby, "Class and Environmental History: Lessons from 'The War in the Adirondacks'," *Environmental History* 2, no. 3 (July 1997): 324–342; and Dan Flores, "Place: An Argument for Bioregional History," *Environmental History Review* 18 (Winter 1994): 1–18.

16. On the size and location of Coon Valley, see Soil Conservation Service, U.S. Department of Agriculture, *Farming against Erosion: The Experiences and Recommendations Resulting from Five Years Effort to Check Erosion in the Coon Creek Area at Coon Valley, Wisconsin* (Madison, Wis.: Soil Conservation Service Office, ca. 1938), 2–3. On the geology of Coon Valley, see U.S. Department of Interior, Soil Erosion Service, "Project Working Plan," 1 March 1934, RG 114: Soil Conservation Service, Entry 42: Project Work Programs, 1935–1937, Regions VI–VIII, Box 5, Folder: Project Working Plan, Coon Creek Wisconsin, March 1, 1934, NARA; Kenneth Davis, "Protecting Fin, Fur,

and Feather in Coon Valley," *Soil Conservation* 2, no. 6 (December 1936): 109; R. H. Musser, "Coon Valley—4 Years After," *Soil Conservation* 4, no. 11 (May 1939): 260.

17. For a description of Coon Valley soils and flora during this period, see Soil Conservation Service, *Farming against Erosion*, 6; and John Marks, "Land Use and Plant Succession in Coon Valley, Wisconsin," *Ecological Monographs* 12, no. 2 (April 1942): 117–121.

18. On the shift from timber cutting to wheat cultivation to dairy farming, see Marks, "Land Use and Plant Succession in Coon Valley, Wisconsin," 121–122; U.S. Department of Interior, Soil Erosion Service, "Project Working Plan," 2; and Soil Conservation Service, *Farming against Erosion*, 3, 10–11.

19. On the founding of these communities and their rail links, see Soil Conservation Service, *Farming against Erosion*, 9.

20. My conception of landscape as a weaving of the natural and the cultural comes from Carl Sauer, "The Morphology of Landscape," *University of California Publications in Geography* 2 (12 October 1925): 19–54; J. B. Jackson, "A New Kind of Space," *Landscape* 18 (Winter 1969): 35–50; and D. W. Meinig, ed., *The Interpretation of Ordinary Landscapes: Geographical Essays* (New York: Oxford University Press, 1979).

21. On straight farming as prideful, see Soil Conservation Service, *Farming against Erosion*, 35. On straight crop rows as a sign of a farmer's ability, see also Neil Maher, " 'Crazy Quilt Farming on Round Land': The Great Depression, the Soil Conservation Service, and the Politics of Landscape Change on the Great Plains during the New Deal Era," *Western Historical Quarterly* 31 (Autumn 2000): 319–339.

22. Soil Conservation Service, *Farming against Erosion*, 52. A small minority of Coon Valley farmers close cropped approximately 10 percent of their land each year. On close cropping in Coon Valley, see Phoebe Cutler, *The Public Landscape of the New Deal* (New Haven, Conn.: Yale University Press, 1985), 113.

23. Stanley W. Trimble and Steven W. Lund, *Soil Conservation and the Reduction of Erosion and Sedimentation in the Coon Creek Basin, Wisconsin*, Geological Survey Professional Paper 1234 (Washington, D.C.: U.S. Government Printing Office, 1982), 2.

24. Soil Conservation Service, *Farming against Erosion*, 52, 10.

25. For a discussion of localism, the national survey, and the American West, see Vernon Carstensen, "Patterns on the American Land," *Publius: The Journal of Federalism* 18, no. 4 (1988): 31–39; J. B. Jackson, "Life and Death of American Landscapes: Jefferson, Thoreau and After," *Landscape* 15 (Winter 1965–1966): 26. Jackson writes, "The National Survey of 1785 was not merely inspired by Jefferson, it was a clear expression of the Jeffersonian dislike of powerful government, centralized in cities."

26. For an insightful examination of this process in the West, see John Mack Faragher, *Sugar Creek: Life on the Illinois Prairie* (New Haven, Conn.: Yale University Press, 1986). Faragher discusses the role of Jefferson's Land Ordinances on the idea of localism on 53–60. have also examined this localism just prior to the New Deal in more detail in my essay "Crazy Quilt Farming on Round Land," 319–339.

27. "Collier's for September 29, 1934," *Collier's*, 29 September 1934, n.p.

28. The Republican presidential vote in these counties is as follows: La Crosse County: 1920 election, 81 percent; 1924 election, 82 percent; 1928 election, 56 percent. Monroe County: 1920 election, 87 percent; 1924 election, 86 percent; 1928 election, 62 percent. Vernon County: 1920 election, 90 percent; 1924 election, 87 percent; 1928 election, 72 percent. For additional statistics on the presidential elections in these counties, see Richard

M. Scammon, ed., *America at the Polls: A Handbook of American Presidential Election Statistics, 1920–1964* (Pittsburgh, Pa.: University Press of Pittsburgh, 1965), 501–503.

29. On erosion's effect on Coon Creek, see Davis, "Protecting Fin, Fur, and Feather in Coon Valley," 110.

30. Trimble and Lund, *Soil Conservation*, 4.

31. See Leopold, "Coon Valley: An Adventure in Cooperative Conservation," *American Forests* 41, no. 5 (May 1935): 206–207. On sheet erosion in Coon Valley, see Soil Conservation Service, *Farming against Erosion*, 21; Musser, "Coon Valley—4 Years After," 260; U.S. Department of Interior, "Project Working Plan," 2; Marks, "Land Use and Plant Succession in Coon Valley, Wisconsin," 127. On the gullies of Coon Creek, see Davis, "Protecting Fin, Fur, and Feather in Coon Valley," 110; and Trimble and Lund, *Soil Conservation*, 23.

32. On Coon Valley's declining crop yields, see Soil Conservation Service, *Farming against Erosion*, 19, 39; Davis, "Protecting Fin, Fur, and Feather in Coon Valley," 110; and Marks, "Land Use and Plant Succession in Coon Valley, Wisconsin," 127.

33. All of this material on the economic consequences of soil erosion in Coon Valley comes from Soil Conservation Service, *Farming against Erosion*, 40–43. The Soil Conservation Service uses the term "standard of living" in this document.

34. See Leopold, "Coon Valley," 206–207.

35. On Leopold's work with the CCC in the Southwest, see Marybeth Lorbiecki, *A Fierce Green Fire* (Helena, Montana: Falcon, 2004), 120.

36. On Leopold's role in helping to establish and in overseeing the Coon Creek Demonstration Area, see Susan Flader and J. Baird Callicott, eds., *The River of the Mother God and Other Essays by Aldo Leopold* (Madison: University of Wisconsin Press, 1991), 218; and Curt Meine, *Aldo Leopold: His Life and Work* (Madison: University of Wisconsin Press, 1991), 313.

37. The arrival of the CCC camp in Coon Valley is described briefly in Soil Conservation Service, *Farming against Erosion*, 71.

38. On Soil Conservation Service demonstration projects nationwide, see Hugh H. Bennett, "A New Farm Movement Takes Rapid Root," *Soil Conservation* 6 (February–March 1941): 193–194; and Cutler, *Public Landscape*, 113.

39. Hugh H. Bennett, *Soil Conservation* (New York: McGraw-Hill, 1939), 317.

40. On demonstration tree plantings at Hyde Park, see *Forestry Practice on the Roosevelt Farm at Hyde Park, Dutchess County, New York* (Syracuse: New York State College of Forestry, Syracuse University, 1931), FDR: Family, Business, and Personal, Subject File: Hyde Park Matters, Roosevelt Estate, Tree Plantings, 1931–1933, FDRL; and Thomas Patton, "Franklin Roosevelt and ESF: Training a Forester-President," *Alumni Newsletter: SUNY College of Environmental Science and Forestry* 83 (Winter 1980–1981): 6.

41. On forestry demonstration areas, see "Demonstration Plots: Forest Service to Improve Small Areas So All May See Value of the Work," *Forestry News Digest* (June 1937): 19. On soil demonstration areas, see Cutler, *Public Landscape*, 109 and 113. On recreational demonstration areas, see Linda McClelland, *Presenting Nature: The Historic Landscape Design of the National Park Service, 1916–1942* (Washington, D.C.: National Park Service, 1993), 195; and Amelia Fry, "The National Park Service and the Civilian Conservation Corps," oral interview series with Newton Drury and Herbert Evison located at the Bancroft Library, University of California at Berkley, 67; and Cutler, *Public Landscape*, 64.

42. Roosevelt to Henry P. Kendall, President, Kendall Company, Boston, 30 June 1939, as reprinted in Nixon, *FDR and Conservation*, 2:352.

43. These statistics come from Hugh Bennett, *Report of the Chief of the Soil Conservation Service, 1938* (Washington, D.C.: U.S. Government Printing Office, 1938), 9.

44. Bennett, *Soil Conservation*, 321.

45. Roosevelt to Robert Fechner, Director, Civilian Conservation Corps, 28 July 1937, as reprinted in Nixon, *FDR and Conservation*, 2:90.

46. Corps director Robert Fechner was equally concerned about CCC work on private land. See especially Robert Fechner, *First Report of the Director of Emergency Conservation Work: For the Period April 5, 1933, to September 30, 1933*, RG 35: CCC, Entry 3: Annual, Special, and Final Reports, NARA, 9.

47. Ibid.

48. For the square mileage of the Coon Creek Demonstration Area, see Soil Conservation Service, *Farming against Erosion*, 2. On the area's acreage, see Soil Conservation Service, "Something about the Coon Creek Soil and Water Conservation Demonstration Project, La Cross[e], Monroe, and Vernon Counties, Wisconsin," Soil Conservation Service Office, Madison, Wis., unpublished report, 2.

49. Soil Conservation Service, *Farming against Erosion*, 46. The map comes from Musser, "Coon Valley—4 Years After," 260.

50. Leopold, "Coon Valley," 207.

51. I calculated the man-hours spent laboring in the Coon Creek Demonstration Area by multiplying the number of enrollees (200) by the number of work hours per day (8) by the number of days per week (5) by the number of weeks per month (4) by the number of months the camp was in operation (37). This is a conservative estimate since it does not account for the workdays of the 413 farming families that labored alongside CCC enrollees.

52. On CCC terracing, see Soil Conservation Service, "Something about the Coon Creek Soil and Water Conservation Demonstration Project," 3. On strip cropping, see Soil Conservation Service, *Report of the Chief of the Soil Conservation Service, 1935* (Washington, D.C.: U.S. Government Printing Office, 1935), 7.

53. Soil Conservation Service, *Farming against Erosion*, 74.

54. Leopold, "Coon Valley," 207.

55. On Leopold's role in the Coon Creek Demonstration Area, see Cutler, *Public Landscape*, 113; and Meine, *Aldo Leopold*, 313.

56. On replanting above a 40 percent grade, see Cutler, *Public Landscape*, 113. On the increased length of crop rotations, see Soil Conservation Service, *Farming against Erosion*, 53. And on the conversion of steep crop land, see ibid., 73.

57. Glennon Loyd, "Iowa's Wirkler and His Victory Farm," *Soil Conservation* 8, no. 1 (July 1942): 10. Although this farmer was from Iowa, his experiences were similar to those in Coon Valley.

58. On CCC work done in Coon Valley's gullies, see Emergency Conservation Work (CCC), "Camp Report: Coon Valley, SCS-1," 2 July 1936, Record Group 35: CCC, Entry 115: Divisions of Investigations, Camp Inspection Reports, 1933–1942, Box 241: Wisconsin, SES-1–SCS-17, Folder: Wisconsin SES 1, Coon Valley, NARA.

59. Leopold, "Coon Valley," 207.

60. Emergency Conservation Work (CCC), "Camp Report: Coon Valley, SCS-1," 27 May 1937, Record Group 35: CCC, Entry 115: Divisions of Investigations, Camp Inspection

Reports, 1933–1942, Box 241: Wisconsin, SES-1-SCS-17, Folder: Wisconsin SES 1, Coon Valley, NARA.

61. Trimble and Lund, *Soil Conservation*, 5.

62. Soil Conservation Service, *Farming against Erosion*, 73.

63. Trimble and Lund, *Soil Conservation*, 4.

64. Ibid., 25.

65. The Soil Conservation Service studied soil erosion by comparing data from 1934 and 1975 for ten sub-basins in Coon Valley, and sedimentation by examining accumulation rates in small reservoirs and deposition rates in the main valley. The study also accounted for climatic fluctuations over the decades. On reductions in upland erosion and sedimentation rates, see ibid., 10, 1. The Soil Conservation Service's conclusion regarding the cause of these improvements can be found in ibid., 1.

66. On increased hay sales, see Soil Conservation Service, *Farming against Erosion*, 85. On increased alfalfa and feed crop production, see Musser, "Coon Valley—4 Years After," 260–261.

67. On increases in butterfat production per cow from 1934 to 1936, see Musser, "Coon Valley—4 Years After," 261. On butterfat sales from 1940 to 1941, see Soil Conservation Service, *Report of the Chief of the Soil Conservation Service, 1942* (Washington, D.C.: U.S. Government Printing Office, 1942), 12.

68. Soil Conservation Service, *Farming against Erosion*, 77, 98. On similar actions by banks in other soil demonstration areas, see A. G. Black, "Soil Conservation Strengthens Credit Ratings," *Soil Conservation* 5, no. 12 (June 1940): 298, 308; and Walter Cothran, "The Banker's Part in Soil Conservation Districts," *Soil Conservation* 6, nos. 8–9 (February–March 1941): 207–208.

69. Cutler, *Public Landscape*, 113. On farm income increases for cooperating farmers in the upper Mississippi region, see Soil Conservation Service, *Report of the Chief of the Soil Conservation Service, 1942*, 21.

70. Soil Conservation Service, *Report of the Chief of the Soil Conservation Service, 1935*, 4.

71. Soil Conservation Service, *Report of the Chief of the Soil Conservation Service, 1940*, 21.

72. Soil Conservation Service, *Farming against Erosion*, 76.

73. Ibid., 86, 97.

74. The CCC used this term to describe the impact of soil demonstration areas in Texas. See CCC, "Material from Soil Conservation Service," President's Personal File, #1820: Speech Material, Civilian Conservation Corps, FDRL, 2.

75. Trimble and Lund, *Soil Conservation*, 29–30.

76. For evidence of similar changes in other soil demonstration areas, see J. G. Lindley, "Soil Conservation and the CCC," *Soil Conservation* 2, no. 12 (June 1937): 285–286. For soil demonstrations in Iowa, see Arthur Bunce, "Some Economic and Social Problems of Soil Conservation," *Soil Conservation* 5, no. 4 (October 1939): 73–76, 82; J. S. Russell, "232 Farmers Are in the Program: Laying Out Contour Lines Simple Matter," (Des Moines, Iowa) *Register*, 18 May 1941, RG: CCC, Entry 68: Division of Planning and Public Relations, Newspaper Clippings, 1937–1942, Box 3: Enrollment-General, NARA; and Loyd, "Iowa's Wirkler and His Victory Farm," 10–11, 17. For demonstrations in the southern plains, see H. H. Finnell and Theodore A. Neubauer, "Farmer Evaluation of Conservation Practices in Southern Plains," *Soil Conservation* 6, no. 7 (January 1941): 172–173. For Ohio, see C. D. Black, "Cooperators Appraise Conservation Program," *Soil Conservation* 6, no. 12 (June 1941): 316. For Oklahoma,

see "Oklahoma Farmers Change Their Minds: They Are Now Willing to Cooperate in Federal Erosion Work," *New York Times*, 25 February 1935, n.p., clipping file located at FDRL. For Missouri, see "Soil Conservation Practices Spread in Maryville Area: Farmers Plant 20,000 Acres of Crops on Contour, A. J. Dinsdale Says," (St. Joseph, Missouri) *News Press*, 4 May 1941, RG: CCC, Entry 68: Division of Planning and Public Relations, Newspaper Clippings, 1937–1942, Box 3: Enrollment-General, NARA.

77. As quoted in Douglas Helms, "The Civilian Conservation Corps: Demonstrating the Value of Soil Conservation," *Journal of Soil and Water Conservation* 40 (March–April 1985): 186.

78. Soil Conservation Service, *Farming against Erosion*, 46. The map comes from Musser, "Coon Valley—4 Years After," 260.

79. During the 1936 presidential election 66 percent, 58 percent, and 56 percent of residents in La Crosse, Monroe, and Vernon counties, respectively, voted for the Democratic party. For additional statistics on the presidential election in these counties, see Scammon, *America at the Polls*, 501–503.

80. Soil Conservation Service, *Farming against Erosion*, 76. On the role and formation of Soil Conservation Districts, see Bennett, *Soil Conservation*, 322.

81. This shift from the local to the federal in western agricultural communities is examined in Donald Worster, *Dust Bowl: The Southern Plains in the 1930s* (New York: Oxford University Press, 1979). See also Maher, "Crazy Quilt Farming on Round Land."

82. Leopold, "Coon Valley," 208.

83. On the geology of the Smokies, see Harry Moore, *A Roadside Guide to the Geology of the Great Smoky Mountains National Park* (Knoxville: University of Tennessee Press, 1988), 23–26; and Rose Houk, *A Natural History Guide: Great Smoky Mountains National Park* (New York: Houghton Mifflin, 1993), 15. On soil fertility in the region, see Margaret Lynn Brown, *The Wild East: A Biography of the Great Smoky Mountains* (Gainesville: University of Florida Press, 2000), 32–33; and Henry Lix, "Short History of the Great Smoky Mountains National Park" (1958), unpublished paper, GSMNPL.

84. On early Euro-American settlement in the Smokies, see Daniel Pierce, *The Great Smokies: From Natural Habitat to National Park* (Knoxville: University of Tennessee Press, 2000), 9–10. On early white settlers in Cataloochee Valley, see Great Smoky Mountains Natural History Association, "Cataloochee: Auto Tour," an interpretive booklet, 1; and Peter Shelburne Givens, "Cataloochee and the Establishment of the Great Smoky Mountains National Park," (master's thesis, Western Carolina University, Cullowhee, N.C., 1978), 44; Elisabeth Powers and Mark Hannah, *Cataloochee, Lost Settlement of the Smokies: The History, Social Customs, and Natural History* (Charleston, S.C.: Powers-Hannah, 1982), 43. On Cades Cove, see Great Smoky Mountains Natural History Association, "Cades Cove: Auto Tour," an interpretive booklet (n.d.), 1; and A. Randolph Shields, *The Cades Cove Story* (Gatlinburg, Tenn.: Great Smoky Mountains Natural History Association, 1977), 12.

85. On the shift in timber production from the North to the South between 1880 and 1920, see especially Michael Williams, *Americans and Their Forests: A Historical Geography* (New York: Cambridge University Press, 1989), chap. 8, "The Lumberman's Assault on the Southern Forest, 1880–1920," 238–288.

86. On logging in the Smokies, see Robert Lambert, "Logging in the Great Smoky Mountains National Park," unpublished report to the superintendent (1958), GSMNPL, 10–14, 16, 26, 29, 40–43; Vic Weals, *Last Train to Elkmont: A Look Back at Life on Little River*

in the Great Smoky Mountains (Knoxville, Tenn.: Olden, 1991), 115; Great Smoky Mountains Natural History Association, "Tremont Logging History: Auto Tour" (Gatlinburg, Tenn.: Great Smoky Mountains Natural History Association); Daniel Pierce, "Boosters, Bureaucrats, Politicians and Philanthropists: Coalition Building in the Establishment of Great Smoky Mountains National Park" (Ph.D. diss., University of Tennessee, Knoxville, 1995), 28.

87. On the Little River Lumber Company, see Weals, *Last Train to Elkmont*, 115. For material on the Parsons Pulp and Lumber Company, see Lambert, "Logging in the Great Smoky Mountains National Park," 31–32.

88. On the lack of reforestation across the South during this period, see Williams, *Americans and Their Forests*, 286.

89. On clear cutting in the Smokies, see Brown, *The Wild East*, 67; and Pierce, *The Great Smokies*, 31.

90. Elizabeth Engleman Black, "A Study of the Diffusion of Culture in a Relatively Isolated Mountain Community" (Ph.D. diss., University of Chicago, 1928), 91, *North Carolina v. Suncrest Lumber Operations*, Logging Records, GSMNPL, as quoted in Brown, *The Wild East*, 69, see also 42.

91. Winfred Cagle, interview by William Weaver, 1973, Oral History Collection, GSMNPL, as quoted in Brown, *The Wild East*, 13.

92. This proposal to limit logging in the Smokies was part of a plan by the Department of the Interior to create Great Smoky Mountains National Park. For examples of local timber company owners expressing opposition to federal intervention in the Smoky Mountains logging industry, see *Knoxville News-Sentinel* and *Knoxville Journal*, 7 December 1925. On lumber company owners' involvement with the Republican party during the 1920s, see Brown, *The Wild East*, 67.

93. In the 1928 election, of the 25,535 residents who voted from the five counties on either side of the Smokies, 17,874 did so for Herbert Hoover (69.9 percent). In the 1932 election, 68 percent, 60 percent, and 77 percent of the residents of Tennessee's Blount, Cocke, and Sevier counties, respectively, voted for the Republican party. For additional statistics on the presidential elections in these counties, see Scammon, *America at the Polls*, 326–327 and 415–416.

94. Paul Fink, *Backpacking Was the Only Way: A Chronicle of Camping Experiences in the Southern Appalachian Mountains* (Johnson City: Research Advisory Council, East Tennessee State University, 1975), 65, as quoted in Brown, *The Wild East*, 61.

95. Earl Franklin, as quoted in Brown, *The Wild East*, 64.

96. On the environmental side effects of clear cutting in the Smokies, see Pierce, *The Great Smokies*, 28; and Brown, *The Wild East*, 61–65.

97. Robert S. Lambert, "Logging in the Great Smoky Mountains: A Report to the Superintendent: October 1, 1958," copy in GSMNPL, as quoted in Pierce, *The Great Smokies*, 24.

98. On the disintegration of the Smokies' subsistence lifestyle during this period, see Brown, *The Wild East*, 72.

99. On the short-term nature of logging in the Smokies, see Pierce, *The Great Smokies*, 33.

100. Lucile Deaderick, ed., *Heart of the Valley: A History of Knoxville, Tennessee* (Knoxville: East Tennessee Historical Society, 1976), 377; Ina Van Noppen and John Van Noppen, *Western North Carolina since the Civil War* (Boone, N.C.: Appalachian Consortium Press, 1973), 387.

101. "Recruiting of Young Men for Reforestation Service Will Begin in Asheville on Monday," *Asheville Advocate*, 28 April 1933, 1.

102. Bob Marshall, "A Proposed Remedy for Our Forestry Illness," *Journal of Forestry* 28, no. 3 (March 1930): 273–280, as quoted in Sutter, *Driven Wild*, 215. On Marshall's time spent in logging communities and his belief in their protection, see Sutter, *Driven Wild*, 204–205, 215.

103. There is some debate as to the actual number of CCC camps functioning in Great Smoky Mountains National Park. Some of this confusion is due to the fact that camps were constantly being moved to other areas of the park or being reassigned to different regions of the country. Adding to this confusion is that many side, or branch, camps seem to have functioned in the more inaccessible areas of the Smokies. For a list of CCC camps in Great Smoky Mountains National Park, see Tennessee and North Carolina Camp Directories, RG 35: CCC, Entry 13: Camp Directories, 1933–1942, NARA. See also Charlotte Pyle, "CCC Camps in Great Smoky Mountains National Park" (1979), unpublished manuscript, GSMNPL, 3; and Walter Miller, "The CCC in East Tennessee and the Great Smoky Mountains National Park" (1974), unpublished manuscript, GSMNPL, 6.

104. On monthly expenditures by CCC camps in nearby economies, see Robert Fechner, *Third Report of the Director of Emergency Conservation Work: For the Period April 1, 1934 to September 30, 1934*, RG 35: CCC, Entry 3: Annual, Special, and Final Reports, NARA, 7.

105. "One Month More," RG 35: CCC, Division of Planning and Public Relations, Success Stories, 1936–1941, Box 2, NARA.

106. On money spent by CCC enrollees locally, see Sherraden, "The Civilian Conservation Corps," 235.

107. Robert Fechner, *Summary Report of Director, Fiscal Year 1936* (Washington, D.C.: U.S. Government Printing Office, 1936), 8, located at RG 35: CCC, Entry 3: Annual, Special, and Final Reports, NARA.

108. "CCC Also Spends," *Business Week*, 4 May 1935, 12.

109. This amount was computed by multiplying the number of CCC camps then in operation (seventeen) by the cost of constructing each camp ($22,000).

110. These estimates were computed by multiplying the annual cost of maintaining each camp ($60,000) by the number of camps in existence each year.

111. This amount was calculated by multiplying the annual cost to maintain a camp ($60,000) by the number of camp-years (eighty-eight) in the Smokies. "Camp-years" are calculated by adding up the number of camps functioning in the Smokies for each year between 1933 and 1942. For the number of camps in existence each year during this period, see the North Carolina and Tennessee camp directories located at RG 35: CCC, Entry 13: Camp Directories, 1933–1942, NARA.

112. This number was calculated by multiplying the annual amount spent by enrollees in each camp ($24,000) by the number of camp-years (eighty-eight) in the Smokies.

113. As quoted in Harley Jolley, *The CCC in the Smokies* (Gatlinburg, Tenn.: Great Smoky Mountains Natural History Association, 2001), 9.

114. Frank Jackson, interview by Glenn Cardwell and Kathleen Manscill, 1981, Oral History Collection, GSMNPL, as quoted in Brown, *The Wild East*, 125.

115. On early CCC work in the Smokies, see Brown, *The Wild East*, 125–127; and Pierce, *The Great Smokies*, 177.

116. Brown, *The Wild East*, 136.

117. On Asheville's role in early outdoor tourism, see ibid., 81.

118. Harvey Broome, *Out under the Sky of the Great Smokies: A Personal Journey* (Knoxville, Tenn.: Greenbrier, 1975), 5, 17, as quoted in Brown, *The Wild East*, 78.

119. W. B. Townsend, for instance, transported tourists into the Smokies on his Little River Lumber Company rail line and turned his employee boardinghouse into a backwoods hotel. On Townsend and similar sorts of local efforts, see Brown, *The Wild East*, 84–85.

120. For the composition and efforts of the Smoky Mountains Conservation Association, see Pierce, *The Great Smokies*, 61–62; Brown, *The Wild East*, 87–88; *Knoxville Sentinel*, 10 October 1923, as quoted in Pierce, *The Great Smokies*, 62.

121. *Knoxville Sentinel*, 10 October 1923, as quoted in Pierce, *The Great Smokies*, 62.

122. Pierce, *The Great Smokies*, 63.

123. On the links between the efforts of the Smoky Mountains Conservation Association and the good roads movement in the South, see Pierce, *The Great Smokies*, 63. Although the Knoxville Automobile Club later changed its name to the East Tennessee Automobile Club, I have maintained the original name here to avoid confusion.

124. As quoted in Carlos Campbell, *Birth of a National Park in the Great Smoky Mountains* (Knoxville: University of Tennessee Press, 1960), 17.

125. On conservation work projects undertaken by CCC enrollees in the Smokies, see the Superintendent's Monthly Reports, located at GSMNPL. This figure for annual man-hours performed by CCC enrollees in the Smokies is a conservative estimate made by taking the 3,500 CCC enrollees stationed in the park in 1934–1935 and multiplying them by a forty-hour work week and then again by a fifty-week year (two weeks allowed for holidays). Total annual man-hours per year come to 7 million.

126. "Superintendent's Monthly Report, September 1935," GSMNPL.

127. On Corps work on the Elkmont bridge, see "Superintendent's Monthly Report, November 1936," GSMNPL; and "Superintendent's Monthly Report, July 1937," GSMNPL.

128. On CCC road work in Cades Cove, see "Superintendent's Monthly Report, January 1934," GSMNPL. For a description of Corps work along Parsons Branch Road, see U.S. Bureau of Public Roads, "Inventory and Inspection Report, Parsons Branch Road," 11 September 1950, GSMNPL.

129. U.S. Bureau of Public Roads, "Inventory and Inspection Reports, Rich Mountain Road," 11 September 1950, GSMNPL.

130. On CCC landscape work along Newfound Gap Road, see King to Eakin, 9 July 1936, File 8: Correspondence, Box: Willis King 1, GSMNPL; and "Superintendent's Monthly Report, January 1934," GSMNPL.

131. "Superintendent's Monthly Report, July 1936," GSMNPL.

132. On CCC work on Clingmans Dome Road, see "Superintendent's Monthly Report, May 1936," GSMNPL. On the expansion of the Clingmans Dome parking area, see "Superintendent's Monthly Report, September 1937," GSMNPL. On Corps labor on the wooden observation tower, see "Superintendent's Monthly Report, May 1950," GSMNPL.

133. Brown, *The Wild East*, 140.

134. On the actions of the Asheville Chamber of Commerce, see Great Smoky Mountains National Park superintendent J. R. Eakin to National Park Service director Horace Albright, 16 February 1932, File 2, Box 310, Entry 7, Record Group 79, NARA. On the

early proposed route see "Planning for Park Highway," *Asheville* (N.C.) *Times*, 3 August 1932, 4.

135. On J. R. Eakin's announcement, see "Plans 40-Mile 'Skyline Road' in Smoky Park," *Knoxville News-Sentinel*, 29 July 1932, n.p.; and Charles Peterson, Assistant Chief Landscape Architect, National Park Service, to Director of National Park Service, 2 December 1932, File 2: Newfound Gap–Clingmans Dome, Correspondence 1932, Box 1: Design and Construction, 1, GSMNPL. On Bob Marshall's role in determining the Skyway's route, see Sutter, *Driven Wild*, 232.

136. On plans for CCC work on the Skyway, see Pierce, *The Great Smokies*, 188.

137. This notion that the Great Smoky Mountains are a constructed wilderness is not new. See Brown, *The Wild East*, 10.

138. There is an extensive literature within environmental history on the relationship between the artificial and the natural. Some of the best contemporary scholarship on this topic includes Jennifer Price, *Flight Maps: Adventures with Nature in Modern America* (New York: Basic, 2000); Susan Davis, *Spectacular Nature: Corporate Culture and the Sea World Experience* (Berkeley: University of California Press, 1997); William Cronon, "The Trouble with Wilderness; or, Getting Back to the Wrong Nature," in *Uncommon Ground: Rethinking the Human Place in Nature*, ed. William Cronon (New York: Norton, 1996); and especially Mark Fiege, *Irrigated Eden: The Making of an Agricultural Landscape in the American West* (Seattle: University of Washington Press, 2000).

139. J. R. Eakin to Victor Cahalane, 24 July 1935, Box 1138, File 175–02, RG 79, NARA, as quoted in Pierce, *The Great Smokies*, 180. On the return of wildlife in Great Smoky Mountains National Park, see Pierce, *The Great Smokies*, 179; and Brown, *The Wild East*, 136. Part of the increase in trout populations was also due to the stocking of streams with fish by the CCC.

140. On the link between segmenting forests and decreasing wildlife habitat, see Nancy Langston, *Forest Dreams, Forest Nightmare: The Paradox of Old Growth in the Inland West* (Seattle: University of Washington Press, 1995), especially chapter 6, "Animals: Domestic and Wild Nature."

141. "Forest Workers Busy in Smokies," *Asheville Advocate*, 29 September 1933, 5.

142. "Superintendent's Report, June 1934"; "Superintendent's Report, June 1940"; and "Superintendent's Report, December 1940," GSMNPL.

143. "Expects Crowds to Visit Park: This Season to Surpass Last in Smoky Mountains Is Belief," *Asheville Advocate*, 23 February 1934, 3.

144. North Carolina State Highway and Public Works Commission, Tennessee State Department of Highways and Public Works, and U.S. Bureau of Public Roads, *Great Smoky Mountains National Park Travel Study* (Washington, D.C.: U.S. Government Printing Office, 1956), 23–26. For other examples of increased tourism expanding the local economy, especially in the area of pioneer crafts and culture, see Brown, *The Wild East*, 191–197.

145. North Carolina Emergency Relief administrator Thomas O'Berry to Frank Persons, U.S. Department of Labor, 5 March 1935, RG 35: CCC, Entry 32: Division of Selection, State Procedural Records, 1933–1942, New York–Carolina, NARA.

146. "Farmers Plant New Pine Trees: Reforestation of Eroded Acres Being Pushed in This Section," *Asheville Advocate*, 4 May 1934, 8.

147. "491 Miles of Foot and Horse Trails Have Been Completed in the Great Smoky Mountains National Park by the CCC Boys," *Appalachian Journal* (Knoxville, Tenn.) 29, no. 3 (March 1936): 1.

148. Mrs. Thomas O'Berry, North Carolina Emergency Relief Administration to W. Frank Persons, U.S. Department of Labor, 5 March 1935, RG 35: CCC, Entry 32: Division of Selection, State Procedural Records, 1933–1942, New York, North Carolina, North Dakota, NARA.

149. In July 1933, 425 boys from Asheville alone tried to enroll in the Corps. See "Recruiting of Young Men for Reforestation Service Will Be Begun in Asheville on Monday," *Asheville Advocate*, 28 April 1933, 1. On the majority of enrollees in the Smoky camps coming from North Carolina and Tennessee, see Brown, *The Wild East*, 123.

150. For the background of the LEM policy and the number of LEMs nationwide, see Salmond, *The CCC*, 34. The Corps also hired LEMs for soil conservation and park construction work. My estimate for the number of LEMs assigned to the Great Smoky Mountains comes from multiplying the number of LEMs assigned to each CCC camp (eight) by the number of camps in the Smokies during between 1933 and 1942 (22). While this would result in 180 LEMs assigned to the Smokies during this period, turnover of these positions would provide work for additional local men, hence my 200-man estimate. On local men gaining work in Corps camps around Asheville, see "Camp Heads Are Assigned," *Asheville Advocate*, 2 June 1933, 1.

151. The margin of victory in presidential elections for the Republican party in Blount County decreased from 36.8 percent in 1932 to 14.8 percent in 1936 to 12.4 percent in 1940. For additional statistics on the presidential elections in these counties, see Scammon, *America at the Polls*, 415, 417.

152. In 1936, residents in Haywood and Swain counties voted by 71 percent and 55 percent, respectively, for Franklin Roosevelt. In 1940, the Democrats in Haywood and Swain increased their numbers to 78 percent and 63 percent, respectively. For additional statistics on the presidential elections in these counties, see Scammon, *America at the Polls*, 328–329.

153. "Radio Address Made by Robert Fechner, Director of the Emergency Conservation Work, over the National Broadcasting Company Red Network at 7:30 P.M., Friday, April 17, 1936," Official File 268 (CCC), Folder: March–June 1937, FDRL, 3.

154. Loyd, "Iowa's Wirkler and His Victory Farm," 10. Here again, Wirkler's experiences in Iowa reflect those of farmers in Coon Valley.

CHAPTER 5

1. "... and it didn't hurt a bit!" advertisement for American Fork and Hoe Company, in *American Forests* 41, no. 1 (January 1935): 35. The CCC camp was under the jurisdiction of the Tennessee Valley Authority.

2. D. B. Smith and Company, advertisement for Indian water pumps, *American Forests* 42, no. 5 (May 1936): 227; Warren Tool Corporation, advertisement for Quik-Werk tools, *American Forests* 39, no. 9 (September 1933): 419; Bartlett Manufacturing Company, advertisement for tree pruners and pole saws, *American Forests* 39, no. 10 (October 1933): 466; and J. I. Case Company, advertisement for the Case plow, *American Forests* 41, no. 9 (September 1935): 553.

3. Mapleine Company, advertisement for maple syrup, *American Forests* 42, no. 7 (July 1936): 332.

4. Morris Cooke to Soil Conservation Service chief Hugh Bennett, n.d., Official File 1r: Soil Conservation Service, FDRL.

5. James McEntee, Federal Security Agency, *Final Report of the Director of the Civilian Conservation Corps*, April 1933 through June 30, 1942, RG 35: CCC, Entry 3: Annual, Special, and Final Reports, NARA, 70.

6. "A Splendid Record," *Pittsburgh Press*, 8 August 1939; and "The CCC's Report Card," *Medford* (Oregon) *Mail Tribune*, 6 August 1939, both as reprinted in Civilian Conservation Corps, *The Nation Appraises the CCC, April, 1933–September, 1939* (Washington, D.C.: U.S. Government Printing Office, 1939), n.p. For additional examples of newspapers praising the Corps, see "CCC Camps Exempt from New Deal Criticism," *Flint* (Michigan) *Journal*, 27 July 1939; *San Francisco Chronicle* as reprinted in the *New York Times*, 18 February 1934; and the *Detroit News* as reprinted in the *New York Times*, 18 February 1934. See also *Literary Digest* 117 (18 August 1934): 8.

7. Rexford Tugwell, *The Democratic Roosevelt* (New York: Doubleday, 1957), 331, as quoted in John Salmond, *The Civilian Conservation Corps, 1933–1942: A New Deal Case Study* (Durham, N.C.: Duke University Press, 1967), 102. On the overwhelming popularity of the Corps, see Salmond, *The CCC*, 106; and Michael Sherraden, "The Civilian Conservation Corps: Effectiveness of the Camps" (Ph.D. diss., University of Michigan, 1979), 8.

8. Salmond, *The CCC*, 23.

9. Robert Dubay, "The Civilian Conservation Corps: A Study in Opposition, 1933–1935," *The Southern Quarterly* 6, no. 3 (XXXX): 350.

10. On the CCC's publicity efforts, see Barrett Potter, "The Civilian Conservation Corps in New York State: Its Social and Political Impact" (Ph.D. diss., State University of New York, Buffalo, 1973), 3, 79, 94.

11. For the CCC's numerous press releases, see Printed Materials Collection, Civilian Conservation Corps, Press Releases, FDRL. On feature articles written by CCC director Robert Fechner and his publicity assistants Guy McKinney and Edgar Brown, see Potter, "The Civilian Conservation Corps in New York State," 79. For a list of pamphlets published by the CCC on its various types of conservation work, see Larry Sypolt, *Civilian Conservation Corps: A Selected Annotated Bibliography* (New York: Praeger, 2005), compiled by the Institute for the History of Technology and Industrial Archaeology, West Virginia University, 124–131. And finally, books that the Corps published or promoted include CCC, *Hands to Save the Soil* (Washington, D.C.: U.S. Government Printing Office, 1938); Ray Hoyt, *We Can Take It: A Short Story of the CCC* (Cincinnati, Ohio: American Book, 1935); Ovid Butler, *Youth Rebuilds: Stories from the CCC* (Washington, D.C.: American Forestry Association, 1934); Kenneth Holland and Frank Hill, *Youth in the CCC* (Washington, D.C.: American Council on Education, 1942); and H. R. Kylie, *CCC Forestry* (Washington, D.C.: U.S. Government Printing Office, 1937).

12. On the CCC's radio committee, see Guy McKinney to William Hassett, 6 March 1935, Official File 268 (CCC), Folder: March–June 1936, FDRL.

13. On the CCC film production organization, see Guy McKinney to Stephen Early, Assistant Secretary to the President, 22 December 1936, Official File 268 (CCC), Folder: September–December 1936, FDRL. For a list of CCC films, see John Paige, *The Civilian Conservation Corps and the National Park Service: An Administrative History* (Washington, D.C.: National Park Service, 1985), 127, 240–241.

14. Works Progress Administration, Federal Theatre CCC Project, "Special to Happy Days" (official newspaper of the CCC), Record Group 35: CCC, Entry: 101, Success Stories: 1936–1941, Miscellaneous: Prize Winning Stories, Box 2, NARA.

15. On conservation work at Camp Roosevelt, see Emergency Conservation Work, Office of the Director, Washington, D.C., "Memorandum for the Press, Release to Morning Papers, Friday, April 17, 1936," Printed Materials Collection, Civilian Conservation Corps, Press Releases, FDRL, 2–3. The numerous press releases that describe Corps work as natural resource conservation can be found at Printed Materials Collection, Civilian Conservation Corps, Press Releases, FDRL. For a listing of many of the feature articles written on the Corps by CCC director Robert Fechner and his staff, see "Civilian Conservation Corps Bibliography: A List of References on the United States Civilian Conservation Corps," compiled by the Office of the Director, CCC, 1939, Bancroft Library, University of California, Berkeley.

16. CCC pamphlets on the Corps' forestry conservation work include CCC, *Reforestation by the CCC* (Washington, D.C.: U.S. Government Printing Office, 1938); CCC, *Forests Protected by the CCC* (Washington, D.C.: U.S. Government Printing Office, 1938); and CCC, *Forest Improvements by the CCC* (Washington, D.C.: U.S. Government Printing Office, 1938).

17. "Radio Address Made by Robert Fechner, Director of Emergency Conservation Work, over the National Broadcasting Company Red Network at 7:30 P.M., Friday, April 17, 1936," Printed Materials Collection, Civilian Conservation Corps, Press Releases, FDRL, 3–4.

18. Paige, *The CCC and the National Park Service*, 240–241. The movies were titled *Pilgrim Forests* and *Land of the Giants*.

19. For CCC press releases describing the Corps' efforts to halt soil erosion in the Dust Bowl, see Emergency Conservation Work, Office of the Director, Washington, D.C., "Memorandum for the Press, Release to Morning Papers, Wednesday, September 19, 1934," Printed Materials Collection, Civilian Conservation Corps, Press Releases, FDRL; and Emergency Conservation Work, Office of the Director, Washington, D.C., "Memorandum for the Press, Release to Morning Papers, Saturday, July 27, 1936," Printed Materials Collection, Civilian Conservation Corps, Press Releases, FDRL. On FDR's tour of the Dust Bowl area, see Edgar Nixon, comp. and ed., *Franklin D. Roosevelt and Conservation, 1911–1945* (Hyde Park, N.Y.: FDRL, 1957), 1: 568.

20. G. H. Gilbertson with H. H. Bennett, "The CCC's Eighth Birthday," *Soil Conservation* 7, no. 4 (April 1941): 263.

21. William Van Dersal, "The Making of 'A Heritage We Guard'," *Soil Conservation* 4, no. 3 (September 1940): 78–81. On other soil conservation films produced by the CCC, including *Running Water* and *Ground Water*, see Paige, *The CCC and the National Park Service*, 240–242.

22. Robert Fechner, "CCC Takes Its Place in the American Scene," *Forestry News Digest* (October 1938): 24.

23. Franklin Roosevelt refers to the CCC in fireside chats delivered on the following dates: 7 May 1933; 24 July 1933; 22 October 1933; 12 October 1937; 14 April 1938; 24 June 1938; and 26 May 1940. For the full texts of these chats, see President's Personal File, Speeches, Boxes 14–99, Folder: Fireside Chat, FDRL. On the Corps' filmmaking, see Guy McKinney to Stephen Early, Assistant to the President, 22 December 1936, Official File 268 (CCC), Folder: September–December 1936, FDRL.

24. For an example of Roosevelt's use of the term "simple conservation," see "Suggestions for the President's Message to Arbor Day Celebration, Nebraska City, Nebraska, 23 April 1934," Official File 183a: Arbor Day, Folder: Arbor Day, 1933–1940, FDRL.

25. Gifford Pinchot, as quoted in Donald Worster, *Nature's Economy: A History of Ecological Ideas* (New York: Cambridge University Press, 1977), 266. And Gifford Pinchot as quoted in Fox, *The American Conservation Movement*, 111. For more on Pinchot's conservationist thinking, see Paul Hirt, *A Conspiracy of Optimism: Management of the National Forests since World War II* (Lincoln: University of Nebraska Press, 1999); Michael Williams, *Americans and Their Forests: A Historical Geography* (New York: Cambridge University Press, 1989), 416–422; Hays, *Conservation and the Gospel of Efficiency*, 28–30; Fox, *The American Conservation Movement*, 111; and Roderick Nash, *Wilderness and the American Mind* (New Haven, Conn.: Yale University Press, 1967), 134–138.

26. On the elite character of the Progressive Era conservation movement, see especially Hays, *Conservation and the Gospel of Efficiency*; and Fox, *The American Conservation Movement*. For examples of local non-elites embracing conservation during the Progressive Era, see Louis Warren, *The Hunter's Game: Poachers and Conservationists in Twentieth-Century America* (New Haven, Conn.: Yale University Press, 1997); Karl Jacoby, *Crimes against Nature: Squatters, Poachers, Thieves, and the Hidden History of American Conservation* (Berkeley: University of California Press, 2003); and Richard Judd, *Common Lands, Common People: The Origins of Conservation in Northern New England* (Cambridge, Mass.: Harvard University Press, 2000).

27. "Rebuilding Paul Bunyan's Empire," *Popular Mechanics Magazine* 73, no. 5 (May 1940): 674. Other magazines that used the Paul Bunyan fable in articles about the CCC include Fred Murray, "Paul Bunyan Reads the Record of the CCC," *American Forests* 43, no. 4 (April 1937): 154–158; and "Paul Bunyan's Rival," *Review of Reviews* (June 1937): 44.

28. Jonathan Mitchell, "Roosevelt's Tree Army: I & II," *New Republic* 83, nos. 1071–1072 (29 May and 12 June 1935): 64–66, 127–129; "New Army Marches 'over Here'," *Christian Science Monitor*, as reprinted in *Forestry News Digest* (April 1933): 9; and Robert Martin, "Army Recruited from Idle Men Wars against Fire and Flood," *Popular Science Monthly* (July 1934): 49–52, 109. See also Johnson Hagood, "Soldiers of the Shield: The Civilian Conservation Corps Stands Square with the National Defense," *American Forests* 40, no. 3 (March 1934): 103–105; and Cecil B. Brown, "Roosevelt's Tree Army," a series of six articles in the *Pittsburgh Press*, 26–31 August 1935, Official File 268 (CCC), Folder: Miscellaneous, July–October 1935, FDRL.

29. Richard Hofstadter, *The Age of Reform* (New York: Vintage, 1955), 23–50.

30. Ivy Howard, "Pioneers of Today," *Soil Conservation* 3, no. 9 (March 1938): 244, 246.

31. Nelson Brown, "When East Goes West: How Thousands of CCC Boys from the Sidewalks of Great Eastern Cities Have Reacted to the Forest Environment of the West," *American Forests* 39, no. 11 (November 1933): 526. For other examples of newspapers and magazines using the agrarian myth to promote the CCC's soil conservation work, see Harold Fraine, "The Spirit of the CCC," *American Forests* 40, no. 6 (June 1934): 256–257, 284; and Dr. Frank Thone, "Are We Creating an American Sahara?" *Washington (D.C.) Evening Star* (12 August 1934): 6; and an untitled article in the *McKeesport (Pa.) News*, 8 November 1937, as quoted in Salmond, *The CCC*, 107.

32. "Roosevelt's Tree Army: Camp Environment Builds Sturdy Characters from City's Loiterers," the second in a series of six articles in the *Pittsburgh Press*, 27 August 1935, Official File 268: (CCC), Folder: Miscellaneous, July–October 1935, FDRL.

33. "The Record of the CCC," (Davenport, Iowa) *Times*, 25 July 1939. For this and numerous other examples of newspapers describing Corps conservation work as the wise

use of natural resources, see Civilian Conservation Corps, *The Nation Appraises the CCC, April, 1933–September, 1939* (Washington, D.C.: U.S. Government Printing Office, 1939).

34. Cecillia Miles Reber, "Our New Kind of Army: Letter to the Editor of the *New York Times*," *New York Times*, 4 June 1933, sec. iv, p. 5.

35. Margaret March-Mount, "Women Push Forestry: In Wisconsin, Michigan and Minnesota They Are Planting and Educating for the Future," *Forestry News Digest* (August 1933): n.p.

36. Margaret March-Mount, "Women as Forest Builders," *American Forests* 48, no. 2 (February 1942): 64. See also "Calumet State Bank Gives Trees: School Pupils to Be Given a Tree to Plant," newspaper clipping from Official File 149: Forestry, Folder: 1933–1934, FDRL; and statement by Postmaster George C. Clemens of Hammond, Indiana, 8 May 1933, clipping from Official File 149: Forestry, Folder: 1933–1934, FDRL.

37. George Barnes, "Conservation and the Classroom: An Introduction to This Issue," *Soil Conservation* 6, no. 4 (October 1940): 87. This entire edition of *Soil Conservation* was dedicated to examining various programs on soil conservation developed by educators throughout the country. During the 1930s, there was also a movement to incorporate forestry conservation, and conservation of natural resources in general, into public school curriculums. On forestry being introduced to public school curriculums, see "Pack Dedicates 100,000 New Primers to Forest Camps," *Forestry News Digest* (August 1933): 9. On natural resource conservation being introduced to school curriculums, see Effie Bathurst, *Curriculum Content in Conservation for Elementary Schools* (Washington, D.C.: U.S. Government Printing Office, 1939); and President of the Educational Conservation Society Harry Vavra, "Outlines of School Courses in Conservation," Official File 177: Conservation Matters, 1935, FDRL.

38. On the soil conservation education programs at the University of Seattle and Reed College, see Frank Harper and C. C. Johnson, "Summer Planning for Winter Studies," *Soil Conservation* 6, no. 4 (October 1940): 105. On the program at Tar Hollow, see F. E. Charles, "Tar Hollow Conservation-Teaching Laboratory," *Soil Conservation* 6, no. 4 (October 1940): 104. On other soil conservation education programs, including those at Kansas State Teachers College, the State Teachers College of Colorado, the University of North Carolina, the University of Kentucky, and the University of Tennessee, see Tom Dale, "Soil Conservation in Elementary and Secondary Schools," *Soil Conservation* 6, no. 4 (October 1940): 101; and Helen Strong, "National Resources and the Work-Shop Idea," *Soil Conservation* 6, no. 4 (October 1940): 104.

39. Many of the schools undertaking soil conservation education began with the premise that "the land was the textbook." See Julia Tappan, "Land Use and the Modern School," *Soil Conservation* 6, no. 4 (October 1940): 89.

40. On soil conservation curriculum development in North Carolina, see Bert Robinson, "Conservation Education in the Southeast," *Soil Conservation* 6, no. 4 (October 1940): 91. For a description of similar programs in other states, see Walter John, "Schools Teach Lessons from the Land," *Soil Conservation* 6, no. 4 (October 1940): 102. On programs in Tennessee, see John Caldwell, "Taking Conservation to the Children," *American Forests* 46, no. 10 (October 1940): 454–456.

41. Harry Vavra, *Outlines of School Courses in Conservation* (Woodside, N.Y.: Educational Conservation Society, 1935), 1.

42. "Indiana Conservation Program Advances," *American Forests* 46, no .7 (July 1940): 330.

43. Franklin Roosevelt to Carl Shoemaker, n.d., Official File 3589: National Wildlife Federation, 1939-1940, FDRL.

44. Robert Fechner, "CCC Takes Its Place in the American Scene," *Forestry News Digest* (October 1938): 24.

45. Civilian Conservation Corps, *The Civilian Conservation Corps and Public Recreation* (Washington, D.C.: U.S. Government Printing Office, 1941), 3. For additional examples of the promotion of recreational areas as natural resources in need of conservation, see Robert Fechner, *Summary Report of Director, Fiscal Year 1936* (Washington, D.C.: U.S. Government Printing Office, 1936), 29, located at RG 35: CCC, Entry 3: Annual, Special, and Final Reports, NARA; and Robert Fechner, *Annual Report of the Director of the Civilian Conservation Corps, Fiscal Year Ended June 30, 1938* (Washington, D.C.: U.S. Government Printing Office, 1938), 52, located at RG 35: CCC, Entry 3: Annual, Special, and Final Reports, NARA; and National Park Service, *Procedure for Park, Parkway and Recreational-Area Study* (Washington, D.C.: U.S. Government Printing Office, 1937), foreword, 3, 17.

46. Civilian Conservation Corps, *The CCC and Its Contribution to a Nation-Wide State Park Recreational Program* (Washington, D.C.: U.S. Government Printing Office, 1937), 3. For other examples of promotional materials by the CCC that describe modern society as enervating, see Civilian Conservation Corps, *Recreational Developments by the CCC in National and State Forests* (Washington, D.C.: U.S. Government Printing Office, 1936), 3; and Civilian Conservation Corps, *Recreational Demonstration Projects: As Illustrated by Chopawamsic, Virginia* (Washington, D.C.: U.S. Government Printing Office, 1937), 6.

47. Civilian Conservation Corps, *The Civilian Conservation Corps and Public Recreation*, 3. On the CCC promoting its recreational work projects as helping to conserve human resources, see also Conrad Wirth, director of CCC state park work, "The Nation-Wide Program for More Recreational Areas Grows under the CCC," *American Forests* 42, no. 11 (November 1936): 505-506; Fanning Hearon, CCC state park work administrator, "The Recreation Renaissance," *Recreation* (September 1935): 289; and Robert Fechner, "CCC Work Valued at $579,000,000," *American Forests* 42, no. 2 (February 1936): 90.

48. W. Frank Persons, "A Selecting Agency Views CCC Work Opportunities," *Soil Conservation* 3, no. 9 (March 1938): 240. For other examples of the Corps promoting the conservation of its enrollees, see Robert Fechner, "The CCC in Soil Conservation," *Soil Conservation* 1, no. 6 (January 1936): 4; R. Y. Stuart, Chief Forester, U.S. Forest Service, "That 250,000-Man Job," *American Forests* 39, no. 5 (May 1933): 195; F. A. Silcox, Chief Forester, U.S. Forest Service, "Our Adventures in Conservation: The CCC," *Atlantic Monthly* 160 (November 1937): 720; and Franklin Roosevelt, fireside chat given on 7 May 1933, President's Personal File, Speeches, Boxes 14-99, Folder: Fireside Chat, FDRL.

49. James Frankland, "New Worlds to Conquer: CCC Roads in Oregon Open Up Entrancing Recreational Areas," *Oregon Motorist* (June 1935): 5-6. See also Charles Mann, "Roads Open New Region," *New York Times*, 4 October 1936, sec. x, p. 4.

50. Hearon, "The Recreation Renaissance," 289-290. See also Cecil Brown, "Country Saved Thousands of Dollars by Conservation Job of Youths," *Pittsburgh Press*, 1 September 1935, clipping from Official File 268 (CCC), Folder: Miscellaneous, July-October 1935, FDRL.

51. Mary Pasco, "Connecticut Improves Her Trout Streams: Civilian Conservation Corps Inaugurates Pioneer Work in Developing an Important Recreation Asset," *American Forests* 40, no. 2 (February 1934): 73.

52. Fred Fletcher of the New York Rod and Gun Editors Association to Franklin Roosevelt, 18 December 1936, President's Personal File, #4301: New York Rod and Gun Editors Association, FDRL; Bet Bull of the Izaak Walton League to Franklin Roosevelt, 11 June 1934, Official File 344: Izaak Walton League, 1933–1944, FDRL; Ned Anderson of the Housatonic Trail Club to Franklin Roosevelt, 6 December 1934, Official File 268 (CCC), Folder: Miscellaneous, October–December 1934, FDRL.

53. John Hatton, "New Things in Conservation," *The Producer: The National Live Stock Monthly* 105, no. 5 (October 1933): 3, 5. For a critique of this broadening of conservation, see "CCC Needs Clearer Policy on Conservation," *American Forests* 44, no. 5 (May 1938): 224.

54. Charles Lathrop Pack, "Blister Busters," *Scientific American* (February 1934): 61.

55. American Institute of Public Opinion, *The Gallup Poll: Public Opinion, 1935–1971* (New York: Random House, 1972), 1:27. Between 11 and 16 May 1936, the Gallup organization asked 1,500 individuals, "are you in favor of continuing the CCC camps?"

56. This second survey, conducted in September 1939, asked 5,146 individuals the following question: "Considering Mr. Roosevelt's six and a half years in office, on the whole do you approve or disapprove of the CCC?" See American Institute of Public Opinion, *The Gallup Poll*, vol. 1.

57. American Institute of Public Opinion, *The Gallup Poll*, vol. 1. In this survey, 28 percent of respondents cited "relief and the W.P.A.," 21 percent listed "banking reforms," and 11 percent viewed the CCC as the Roosevelt administration's greatest accomplishment.

58. *Congressional Record*, 75th Cong., 1st sess., vol. 81, pt. 4, p. 4365; as quoted in Salmond, *The CCC*, 104.

59. Franklin D. Roosevelt, radio broadcast, "Fireside Chat," 7 May 1933, FDRL.

60. On Roosevelt's use of the CCC in his 1936 campaign speeches, see Salmond, *The CCC*, 69.

61. Speech by Roosevelt at the Dedication of Shenandoah National Park, 3 July 1936, as quoted in Nixon, *FDR and Conservation*, 1:537–538. Roosevelt made similar speeches at North Carolina and Tennessee's Great Smoky Mountains National Park before the election of 1940; and he visited New York's Bear Mountain State Park numerous times during campaigns throughout the 1930s and early 1940s. On campaign trips to work project sites in Vermont, New Hampshire, and New York, see Jason Scott Smith, "Building New Deal Liberalism: The Political Economy of Public Works, 1933–1956" (Ph.D. diss., University of California, Berkeley, 2001), 217.

62. During his nine-state Dust Bowl tour, for instance, Roosevelt visited several CCC work projects and publicly received the report from his Great Plains Drought Area Committee as he passed through Bismarck, North Dakota, on a campaign stop. On this stop, see Jean Christie, "New Deal Resources Planning: The Proposals of Morris L. Cooke," *Agricultural History* 53, no. 3 (July 1979): 601. For a similar argument about WPA work projects serving as advertisements for the New Deal, see Smith, "Building New Deal Liberalism," 217.

63. The fact that Leopold opposed the CCC on both wilderness and ecological grounds greatly complicates the conservationist-preservationist split so prevalent in environmental history narratives. For a more in-depth analysis of Leopold's role in defying this dichotomy, see Paul Sutter, *Driven Wild: How the Fight against Automobiles Launched the*

Modern Wilderness Movement (Seattle: University of Washington Press, 2002), especially chap. 3, "A Blank Spot on the Map: Aldo Leopold," 54–99.

64. Aldo Leopold, "Threatened Species: A Proposal for the Wildlife Conference for an Inventory of the Needs of Near-Extinct Birds and Animals," *American Forests* 42, no. 3 (March 1936): 116–119.

65. Leopold, "Engineering and Conservation," lecture delivered on 11 April 1938, as printed in Susan Flader and J. Baird Callicott, eds., *The River of the Mother of God and Other Essays* (Madison: University of Wisconsin Press, 1991), 231.

66. Aldo Leopold gave this talk to the University of Wisconsin's Taylor-Hibbard Economics Club on 1 March 1934. For a transcript of the talk, see Aldo Leopold, "Conservation Economics," *Journal of Forestry* 32, no. 5 (May 1934): 537–544; and Aldo Leopold, "Conservation Economics," *American Game* 23, nos. 4–5 (July–August 1934 and September–October 1934): 56, 63, and 71, 77–78. On the importance of this talk in Leopold's career, see Curt Meine, *Aldo Leopold: His Life and Work* (Madison: University of Wisconsin Press, 1991), 320.

67. Worster, *Nature's Economy*, 232. For background on the history of ecology, see especially Robert P. McIntosh, *The Background of Ecology: Concept and Theory* (Cambridge: Cambridge University Press, 1985); F. N. Egerton, "History of Ecology: Achievements and Opportunities, Part I," *Journal of History of Biology* 16, no. 2 (Summer 1983): 259–310; Egerton, "History of Ecology: Achievements and Opportunities, Part II," *Journal of History of Biology* 18, no. 1 (Spring 1985): 103–143; and Meine, *Aldo Leopold*, 184.

68. Aldo Leopold, "Coon Valley: An Adventure in Cooperative Conservation," *American Forests* 41, no. 5 (May 1935): 205.

69. Aldo Leopold, "The Farmer as Conservationist," *American Forests* 45, no. 6 (June 1939): 298.

70. Leonard Wing, "Naturalize the Forest for Wildlife," *American Forests* 42, no. 6 (June 1936): 260, 261.

71. Professor Merritt L. Fernald, talk given before the Franklin Institute, 20 May 1938, Philadelphia, Pennsylvania, as quoted in "Upsetting Nature's Equilibrium," *Horticulture* 16, no. 12 (15 June 1938): 1. For coverage of Fernald's speech, see "Says CCC Upsets Nature's Balance: Professor M. L. Fernald Holds It Alters Life of Ages and Menaces Rare Plants," *New York Times*, 21 May 1938, p. 1.

72. On the use of CCC funds to hire wildlife biologists to monitor Corps work in national parks, see Richard Sellars, "The Rise and Decline of Ecological Attitudes in National Park Management, 1929–1940, Part I," *George Wright Forum* 10, no. 1 (1993): 68. Sellars calls these wildlife biologists a "kind of minority 'opposition party' " within the Park Service (58).

73. George Wright to National Park Service director Arno Cammerer, 28 February 1934, Central Classified File, RG 79, as quoted in Richard Sellars, "The Rise and Decline of Ecological Attitudes in National Park Management, 1929–1940, Part II: Natural Resource Management under Directors Albright and Cammerer," *George Wright Forum* 10, no. 2 (1993): 103. Here Sellars provides numerous other examples of wildlife biologists opposing CCC fire protection work in national parks.

74. Victor Cahalane to A. E. Demaray, 23 September 1935, Entry 34, RG 79; and Adolph Murie to George Wright, 26 March 1935, Entry 34, RG 79; both as quoted in Sellars, "The Rise and Decline of Ecological Attitudes in National Park Management, 1929–1940, Part II," 106.

75. Aldo Leopold's essays criticizing the CCC were reprinted widely during the mid-1930s. See especially Leopold, "Conservation Economics: Misuse of Land Is Liability against Public Purse," *American Game* 23, nos. 4–5 (July–August and September–October 1934), 56, 63, and 71, 77–78; Leopold, "Coon Valley," 205–208; Leopold, "The Farmer as Conservationist," 295–299, 316, 323.

76. Newspapers covering Fernald's talk include "Says CCC Upsets Nature's Balance," *New York Times*, 21 May 1938, p. 1; and an unnamed Philadelphia newspaper, a clipping from which can be found attached to a letter from Mrs. Edith Pierce to Secretary to the President Stephen Early, 21 May 1938, Official File 268 (CCC), Folder: Miscellaneous, April–June 1938, FDRL.

77. Edward Farrington, "Upsetting Nature's Equilibrium," *Horticulture* 16, no. 12 (15 June 1938): 1.

78. William Vogt, "Mosquito Control and Wild Life: Unwise Drainage, Especially, Has an Important Adverse Effect," *American Game* 24, no. 3 (May–June 1935): 35.

79. C. E. Rachford, "Conservation Army Aids Wild Life," *American Game* 22, no. 1 (January–February 1933): 21.

80. Jean Sherwood Harper to Franklin Roosevelt, 26 May 1937, as reprinted in Nixon, *FDR and Conservation*, 2:66–67. For examples of other letters written by concerned citizens about the CCC's threat to ecological balance, see H. L. Baker to Administrator of the Civilian Conservation Corps, 14 December 1938, RG 35: CCC, Entry 2, File: 100: Baker, H. L., NARA; and Corresponding Secretary of the Death's Door Council of Ellison, Wisconsin, to President Franklin Roosevelt, 11 March 1938, Official File 177: Conservation Matters, 1936, FDRL. The council also sent copies of the letter to Secretary of the Interior Harold Ickes, Wisconsin governor Robert La Follette, and the Wisconsin State Conservation Commission.

81. W. B. Sheppard, "Work of the CCC Is Found Unwise," letter to the editor, *New York Times*, 18 November 1934, sec. iv, p. 5. For other examples, see C. A. B., "Wilderness," letter to the editor, *New York Times*, 1 September 1935, sec. iv, p. 9; and Rosalie Edge, "Forestry Camps Harm Game," letter to the editor, *New York Times*, 11 June 1933, sec. iv, p. 5.

82. Emergency Conservation Committee, *Fighting the Good Fight: An Account of Militant Conservation in Defense of Wild Life including the Report of the Emergency Conservation Committee for the Calendar Year, 1934* (New York: Emergency Conservation Committee, 1934), 14, located at Collection: Rockefeller Family Archives, Record Group 2, Series: Cultural Interests, Box 76, Folder 723, Item: "Fighting the Good Fight," Rockefeller Archive Center (hereafter RAC); Rosalie Edge, *Conservation: How It Works: Notes, News and Comments, Annual Report of the Emergency Conservation Committee for the Year 1939* (New York: Emergency Conservation Committee, 1940), 3, located at Collection: Rockefeller Family Archives, Record Group 2, Series: Cultural Interests, Box 76, Folder 725, Item: "Conservation: How It Works," RAC.

83. Rosalie Edge often wrote letters criticizing the CCC to the editor of the New York Times. See especially Edge, "Forestry Camps Harm Game," *New York Times*, 11 June 1933, sec. iv, p. 5.

84. For examples of the Emergency Conservation Committee criticizing the Audubon Society for its failure to oppose CCC predator control work projects, see the annual reports of the Emergency Conservation Committee located at Collection: Rockefeller Family Archives, Record Group 2, Series: Cultural Interests, RAC.

85. John Baker to Robert Fechner, 23 November 1935, RG 35: CCC, Entry 2: General Correspondence, #500: National Association of Audubon Societies, Box 722, NARA. See also John Baker to Robert Fechner, 5 December 1935, RG 35: CCC, Entry 2: General Correspondence, #500: National Association of Audubon Societies, Box 722, NARA.

86. The Audubon Society asked its members to write letters protesting CCC predator control work in its bimonthly magazine; see "President's Page," *Bird-Lore* 39, no. 4 (July–August 1937): 1. For examples of Audubon Society members writing letters protesting such CCC work, see Nettie Sellinger Pierce, 29 April 1937, RG 35: CCC, Entry 2: General Correspondence, #500: The Burroughs-Audubon Nature Club, Box 709, NARA. This resolution was attached to a letter from the National Association of Audubon Societies' executive director, John Baker, to Robert Fechner, 26 May 1937, RG 35: CCC, Entry 2: General Correspondence, #500: National Association of Audubon Societies, Box 722, NARA.

87. Warren Eaton, "The Depression Army Takes to the Woods," *Bird-Lore* 37, no. 4 (July–August 1935): 255. For other examples of members of the Audubon Society criticizing CCC work on ecological grounds, see "Contributions of Non-Sportsmen to Wild-Life Conservation," *Bird-Lore* 38, no. 2 (March–April 1936): 138–140; "Drainage and Wild Life," *Bird-Lore* 38, no. 2 (March–April 1936): 140; and William Vogt, *Thirst on the Land: A Plea for Water Conservation for the Benefit of Man and Wild Life* (New York: National Association of Audubon Societies, 1937). An Audubon Society letter-writing campaign against CCC mosquito control work is mentioned in a letter from Audubon Society member Charles Butler to Franklin Roosevelt, 22 March 1938, Official File 268 (CCC), Folder: January–March 1938, FDRL.

88. Untitled newspaper as quoted in Eaton, "The Depression Army Takes to the Woods," 261. For a detailed description of the Izaak Walton League's complaints against the CCC and the subsequent investigation by the federal government, see "Memorandum for Regional Forester: Investigation of Izaak Walton League and W. S. Moscrip Complaints," 18 June 1935, RG 35: CCC, General Correspondence, #300: Minnesota (Destroying Wildlife), Box 613: Minnesota–Mississippi, NARA.

89. "Drainage and Wild Life," *Bird-Lore* (March–April 1936): 140.

90. On the creation of the National Wildlife Federation and its efforts against CCC mosquito control work, see Theodore Cart, " 'New Deal' for Wildlife: A Perspective on Federal Conservation Policy, 1933–1940," *Pacific Northwest Quarterly* 63, no. 3 (July 1972): 117.

91. On Marshall's trip to the Great Smokies, see Sutter, *Driven Wild*, 231–232. On plans for CCC work on the Skyway, see Daniel Pierce, *The Great Smokies: From Natural Habitat to National Park* (Knoxville: University of Tennessee Press, 2000), 188.

92. On these other proposals, see Benton MacKaye, "Flankline vs. Skyline," *Appalachia* 20 (1934): 104. On the proposed parkway across the Green Mountains of Vermont, see John Douglas, "The Forest Service, the Depression, and Vermont Political Culture: Implementing New Deal Conservation and Relief Policy," *Forest and Conservation History* 34, no. 4 (October 1990): 171.

93. Marshall to Willard Van Name, 31 July 1933, Bob Marshall Papers, Box 1, Folder 16, as quoted in Sutter, *Driven Wild*, 231. "Emergency funds" was often used as a term for the Corps, since early on the program was called Emergency Conservation Work.

94. Bob Marshall, "The Problem of the Wilderness," *Scientific Monthly* 30, no. 2 (February 1930): 145.

95. With his training in forestry and his dedication to wilderness preservation, Bob Marshall, like Aldo Leopold, also defies the conservationist-preservationist divide so common in environmental history narratives. For a more in-depth analysis of Marshall's role in complicating this dichotomy, see Sutter, *Driven Wild*, especially chap. 6, "The Freedom of the Wilderness: Bob Marshall," 194–238.

96. Marshall, "The Problem of the Wilderness," 143.

97. Bob Marshall to Ferdinand Silcox, 24 June 1935, as quoted in Fox, *The American Conservation Movement*, 210.

98. For the best study of the Wilderness Society and its founding, see Sutter, *Driven Wild*; and Fox, *The American Conservation Movement*, 210. The quote is from Nash, *Wilderness and the American Mind*, 207.

99. MacKaye, "Flankline vs. Skyline," 104–105, as quoted in Sutter, *Driven Wild*, 187.

100. Raymond Torrey, "Truck Trails in the Adirondacks," *Living Wilderness* (September 1935): 3.

101. Bob Marshall, "The Universe of the Wilderness Is Vanishing," *Nature Magazine* 29, no. 4 (April 1937): 239. On Wilderness Society opposition to roads, see also MacKaye, "Flankline vs. Skyline," 104–108.

102. Arthur Morgan, "For a Wilderness Program," *Living Wilderness* (November 1936): 14.

103. Georgia Engelhard to Bob Marshall, 31 January 1937, as reprinted in "Women Members Protest against Elaborate National Park Trails," *Living Wilderness* (December 1937): 10. For similar critiques of CCC trail-building work, see Helen Howell Moorhead to Bob Marshall, 25 January 1937; and Mabel Abercrombie to Wilderness Society president Sterling Yard, 24 January 1937; both as reprinted in "Women Members Protest against Elaborate National Park Trails," 8–10.

104. Robert Sterling Yard, (no title), *Living Wilderness* (September 1935), as quoted in Fox, *The American Conservation Movement*, 211.

105. As quoted in Nash, *Wilderness and the American Mind*, 207.

106. "Manicuring the Wilderness," *Saturday Evening Post*, 8 December 1934, 22.

107. C. S. Cowan, "The CCC Movement and Its Relation to the Clarke-McNary Act," *Journal of Forestry* 34, no. 4 (April 1936): 384.

108. "Truck Trails in the Woods," *New York Times*, 8 October 1935, p. 22.

109. "A New Defender of the Wilderness," *Nature Magazine* 26, no. 3 (September 1935): 178.

110. Fred Morrell, "Straw Men in the Wilderness," *Nature Magazine* 29, no. 3 (March 1937): 174.

111. E. R. Lehnert, "Parking the Wilderness: Besides Being Unfair, CCC Is Held to Be Destroying Nature's Gifts," letter to the editor, *New York Times*, 15 October 1934, p. 16.

112. Stanton Coblentz, "Conservation in Reverse," letter to the editor, *New York Times*, 20 November 1934, p. 20.

113. The actions of the Association for the Protection of the Adirondacks are described in detail in the organization's annual reports for 1933–1935. See "Report of the President of the Association for the Protection of the Adirondacks," Collection: Rockefeller Family Archives, Record Group 2, Series: Cultural Interests, Box 49, Folder 487: Association for the Protection of the Adirondacks, 1902–1936, Item: "Roads in Forest Preserve," RAC. On the association's role in organizing a statewide campaign against CCC work in the forest preserve and Governor Lehman's appointment of an advisory

committee to study such work, see Raymond Torrey, "Adirondack Conservation: Dissatisfaction with the Methods of the CCC," letter to the editor, *New York Times*, 8 October 1935, p. 22; "Truck Trails in the Woods, *New York Times*, 8 October 1935, p. 22; "Gov. Lehman Names Fire Trail Board: Committee Will Advise Osborne on CCC Work in the Adirondacks," *New York Times*, 8 October 1935, p. 43; and "For Forest Trail Inquiry: Osborne Asks Lehman to Act in Conservation Controversy," *New York Times*, 6 October 1935, p. 22. For a good description of this controversy and its role in New York state's conservation history, see Potter, "The Civilian Conservation Corps in New York State," 96–104.

114. Raymond Torrey, "Adirondack Truck Trails Stopped," *Living Wilderness* (November 1936): 15.

115. Walter Eaton, "A Little Wilderness in Vermont," *Living Wilderness* (November 1936): 8–9.

116. Elers Koch, "Three Great Western Wildernesses: What Can Be Done to Save Them?" *Living Wilderness* (September 1935): 9.

117. On the Save the Redwoods League campaign against the CCC, see Schrepfer, *Save the Redwoods: A History of Environmental Reform, 1917–1978* (Madison: University of Wisconsin Press, 1983), 68.

118. The efforts of California's Commonwealth Club are described in the editorial "Roads and the Wilderness," *American Forests* 44, no. 4 (April 1938): 165.

119. On the High Sierra Packers' Association campaign against CCC road building, see Norman Livermore, Jr., "Roads Running Wild," *American Forests* 44, no. 4 (April 1938): 153–155.

120. On the role of roads in the Kings Canyon wilderness controversy, see Fox, *The American Conservation Movement*, 212–217.

121. John Guthrie, "The CCC and American Conservation," *Scientific Monthly* 57 (November 1943): 401, 412.

122. Ibid.

123. For a wonderful examination of this New Deal public landscape, see Phoebe Cutler, *The Public Landscape of the New Deal* (New Haven, Conn.: Yale University Press, 1985).

CHAPTER 6

1. "The Kidnapping—or More and More Democracy," *Des Moines Register*, 21 November 1937 (emphasis original). On the importance of cartoons, including those drawn by Ding Darling, to the field of environmental history, see "Dale Goble, Paul Hirt, and Susan J. Kilgore on Environmental Cartoons," in the Gallery section of *Environmental History* 10, no. 4 (October 2005): 776–793.

2. Much of my thinking concerning Roosevelt's 1937 reorganization plan comes from Richard Polenberg, *Reorganizing Roosevelt's Government: The Controversy over Executive Reorganization, 1936–1939* (Cambridge, Mass.: Harvard University Press, 1966).

3. See ibid., 191.

4. There is an extensive historical literature on the "third New Deal." For informative overviews of this scholarship, see especially John Jeffries, "A 'Third New Deal'?: Liberal Policy and the American State, 1937–1945," *Journal of Policy History* 8, no. 4 (1996): 387–409; John Jeffries, "The 'New' New Deal: FDR and American Liberalism, 1937–1945," *Political Science Quarterly* 105, no. 3 (1990): 397–418. See also Barry Karl,

The Uneasy State: The United States from 1915 to 1945 (Chicago: University of Chicago Press, 1983); Barry Karl, "Constitution and Central Planning: The Third New Deal Revisited," *Supreme Court Review, 1988* 6 (1989): 163–201; and Otis L. Graham, Jr., *Toward A Planned Society: From Roosevelt to Nixon* (New York: Oxford University Press, 1976).

5. John Jeffries argues that this period reflected the changing course of American liberalism in his essay "The 'New' New Deal," 399. For a contemporary account of the defeat as a turning point for Franklin Roosevelt, see New York *World-Telegram,* 9 April 1938, p. 20.

6. Ovid Butler, "Conservation at the Forks: Proposed Reorganization of the Federal Government Raises Questions Vital to Agriculture, Forestry and Other Fields of Conservation," *American Forests* 43, no. 3 (March 1937): 109. For a similar critique of Roosevelt's reorganization plan, see Ovid Butler, "Whither Conservation?" *American Forests* 43, no. 11 (November 1937): 1.

7. For a review of scholarship on the first, second, and third New Deals, see Jeffries, "A 'Third New Deal'?" 387–391.

8. The role of this conservative coalition in Congress is well documented. For its role in the debate of federal reorganization, see Jeffries, "The 'New' New Deal," 405.

9. On Roosevelt's affinity for competition between government bureaus and administrators, see Richard Polenberg, "The Great Conservation Contest," *Forest History* 10, no. 4 (January 1967): 15.

10. Memorandum circulated by Department of the Interior secretary Harold Ickes, "A United States Department of Conservation," as attached to a letter from Department of Agriculture secretary Henry Wallace to President Franklin Roosevelt, Official File 1c: Department of Agriculture, Folder: Forest Service, January 1940, FDRL.

11. Several historians identify these two issues—a lack of centralized authority in the executive branch and a lack of coordination within the Roosevelt administration—as central to the problems associated with the third New Deal. See especially Jeffries, "A 'Third New Deal'?" 388; Otis Graham, "Franklin Roosevelt and the Intended New Deal," in *Essays in Honor of James MacGregor Burns,* ed. Michael R. Beschloss and Thomas E. Cronin (Englewood Cliffs, N.J.: Prentice-Hall, 1989), 85–86; and Barry Karl, *The Uneasy State: The United States from 1915–1945* (Chicago: University of Chicago Press, 1983), esp. 155–181.

12. Emphasis in original. See Ovid Butler, "CCC Needs Clearer Policy on Conservation," *American Forests* 44, no. 5 (May 1938): 224. Foresters were especially alarmed by this trend. See, for instance, the complaints of regional forester C. J. Buck in Polenberg, "The Great Conservation Contest," 20. Other New Deal agencies often blamed for "stealing" power from the Forest Service regarding the conservation of natural resources include the Soil Conservation Service and the Tennessee Valley Authority.

13. Secretary of the Department of the Interior Harold Ickes to Ovid Butler, editor, *American Forests,* in response to editorial titled "Let Mr. Ickes' Answer," *American Forests* 44, no. 3 (March 1938): 114. Here Ickes is quoting, in part, American Forestry Association president George Pratt.

14. For a good synopsis of the relationship between the conservation crisis and the political crisis of the late 1930s, see Polenberg, *Reorganizing Roosevelt's Government,* 25.

15. Ding Darling as quoted in "President Leads Great Conservation Rally," *American Forests* 41, no. 10 (October 1935): 590. For a similar take on the fracturing of conservation, see E. Laurence Palmer, "What Is Conservation," *Guardian: A Bulletin of News and Suggestions*

for *Leaders of Camp Fire Girls* 17, no. 5 (January 1938): part 1, especially the section titled "Conservation Means Different Things to Different People," beginning on p. 2.

16. Aldo Leopold, "Conservation Economics: Misuse of Land Is Liability against Public Purse," *American Game* 23, no. 5 (September–October 1934): 71. On Leopold's similar critique of the CCC, see chap. 5.

17. Butler, "Whither Conservation?" n.p. For additional concerns about a conservation crisis during the late 1930s, see General Federation of Women's Clubs Conservation chairman Mrs. G. H. Boert to President Franklin Roosevelt, 14 November 1937, 1, Official File 177, Conservation Matters, 1937, FDRL.

18. Walter P. Taylor, "What Is Ecology and What Good Is It," *Ecology* 17, no. 3 (July 1936): 339.

19. On the centrality of planning to the New Deal, see Phoebe Cutler, *The Public Landscape of the New Deal* (New Haven, Conn.: Yale University Press, 1985); Clayton Koppes, "Efficiency, Equity, Esthetic: Shifting Themes in American Conservation," in *The Ends of the Earth: Perspectives on Modern Environmental History*, ed. Donald Worster (New York: Cambridge University Press, 1988), 239; Albert Lepawsky, "The Progressives and the Planners," *Public Administration Review* 31, no. 3 (May–June 1971): 299, 301; Graham, *Toward a Planned Society*; Otis Graham, "The Planning Ideal and American Reality: The 1930s," in *The Hofstadter Aegis: A Memorial*, ed. Stanley Elkins and Eric McKitrick (New York: Knopf, 1974); and especially Patrick Reagan, *Designing a New America: The Origins of New Deal Planning, 1890–1943* (Amherst: University of Massachusetts Press, 1999), esp. 7–8.

20. Rexford Tugwell, "Design for Government," Address, Federation of Bar Associations of Western New York, 24 June 1935, in Tugwell, *The Battle for Democracy* (New York: Columbia University Press, 1935), 14, as quoted in Graham, "The Planning Ideal and American Reality," 260.

21. Franklin Roosevelt made this comment in a Jefferson Day speech on April 18, 1932. For a copy of this speech see Samuel I. Rosenman, ed., *The Public Papers and Addresses of Franklin D. Roosevelt*, vol. 1, p. 632, as quoted in Otis Graham, Jr., *Toward a Planned Society: From Roosevelt to Nixon* (New York: Oxford University Press, 1976), 19.

22. Franklin Roosevelt, "President Roosevelt's Own Story of the New Deal: Article No. 11, President Roosevelt on TVA and Regional Planning," FDR: Family, Business, and Personal Papers, Writing and Statement File, Folder: United Feature Syndicate Press Release, FDR Series, 1938, FDRL, 5.

23. Lepawsky, "The Progressives and the Planners," 300.

24. There is a large literature on the Progressive Era conservation movement. On the relationship between the conservation movement and planning, see ibid., 297, 300.

25. There is an enormous literature on Progressive reformers. On the relationship between these urban Progressive reformers and the urban planning movement, see Graham, *Toward a Planned Society*, 7-9; Robert Gottlieb, *Forcing the Spring: The Transformation of the American Environmental Movement* (Washington, D.C.: Island, 1993), 71; Paul Boyer, *Urban Masses and Moral Order in America, 1820–1920* (Cambridge, Mass.: Harvard University Press, 1978), 268; and Lepawsky, "The Progressives and the Planners," 300–301.

26. On Roosevelt's planning at his Hyde Park estate and in the Adirondacks, see chap. 1. On his statewide land use plans, see Roosevelt, "President Roosevelt's Own Story of the New Deal: Article No. 11, President Roosevelt on TVA and Regional Planning," 1.

27. For additional examples of Roosevelt's desire to use planning to conserve natural resources before becoming president, see Sarah Phillips, *This Land, This Nation: Conservation, Rural America, and the New Deal* (New York: Cambridge University Press, 2007), chapter 1, "The New Conservation."

28. On the pre–New Deal planning experiences of Frederic Delano, see Reagan, *Designing a New America*, 36–47.

29. On Roosevelt's use of planning to enact milk reform in New York City, see Franklin Roosevelt, "Growing Up by Plan," *Survey* (1 February 1932): 484; and Daniel Fusfeld, "The Source of New Deal Reformism: A Note," *Ethics* 65, no. 3 (April 1995): 218. On Roosevelt's plans to expand Boy Scout camps, see chap. 1.

30. Roosevelt, "Growing Up by Plan," 483.

31. For an examination of the origins of this third tradition within the American planning movement, see James L. Wescoat, Jr., " 'Watersheds' in Regional Planning," in *The American Planning Tradition: Culture and Policy*, ed. Robert Fishman (Washington, D.C.: Woodrow Wilson Center Press, 2000), 151–152. Wescoat sees Marsh and Powell as seminal figures in the birth of regional planning. On Powell's suggestion that the federal government plan the settlement of the American West, see Donald Worster, *Rivers of Empire: Water, Aridity, and the Growth of the American West* (New York: Oxford University Press, 1985), 132–143.

32. For a history of these men and the creation of the RPAA, see Edward Spann, *Designing Modern America: The Regional Planning Association of America and Its Members* (Columbus: Ohio State University Press, 1996).

33. On the notion of the region as a space for planning, see Mark Luccarelli, *Lewis Mumford and the Ecological Region: The Politics of Planning* (New York: Guilford, 1995). On the deeper history of regionalism, see Robert Dorman, *Revolt of the Provinces: The Regionalist Movement in America, 1920–1945* (Chapel Hill: University of North Carolina Press, 2003). For a good examination of the RPAA's belief in the interconnection of urban and rural planning, see Paul Sutter, *Driven Wild: How the Fight against Automobiles Launched the Modern Wilderness Movement* (Seattle: University of Washington Press, 2002), 160–167.

34. Benton MacKaye, "An Appalachian Trail: A Project in Regional Planning," *Journal of the American Institute of Architects* 9 (October 1921): 327, as quoted in Sutter, *Driven Wild*, 156. On MacKaye's use of the term "new deal," see also Spann, *Designing Modern America*, 153.

35. Spann, *Designing Modern America*, 89.

36. This lunch between Roosevelt and Clarence Stein, as well as the RPAA memo to FDR, is discussed in greater detail in ibid., 127–130, 152.

37. Franklin Roosevelt, *Public Papers and Addresses* (New York: Russell and Russell Publishing, 1969), 28–29, as quoted in Spann, *Designing Modern America*, 151.

38. Roosevelt mentions creating the New York State Power Authority in "President Roosevelt's Own Story of the New Deal: Article No. 11, President Roosevelt on TVA and Regional Planning," 1. On Roosevelt's regional plans for New York state, see Daniel Fusfeld, "The Source of New Deal Reformism: A Note," *Ethics* 65, no. 3 (April 1955): 218–219.

39. Roosevelt, "Growing Up by Plan," 483.

40. Franklin Roosevelt to Congress in Samuel I. Rosenman, ed., *The Public Papers and Addresses of Franklin D. Roosevelt*, 2:122–123, as quoted in Graham, *Toward a Planned Society*, 20–21.

41. On the AAA and the NRA as planning agencies, see Graham, *Toward a Planned Society*, 28–35.

42. Franklin Roosevelt to Congress in Rosenman, *Public Papers and Addresses of Franklin D. Roosevelt*, 2:122–123, as quoted in Graham, *Toward a Planned Society*, 20–21.

43. On the Tennessee Valley before the arrival of the TVA and the CCC, see Leslie Mowitt Headrick and Daniel Schaffer, *A Peace Time Army: The Tennessee Valley Authority–Civilian Conservation Corps, 1933–1942* (Washington, D.C.: Division of Land and Forest Resources, Office of Natural Resources, Tennessee Valley Authority, 1983), 1.

44. Franklin Roosevelt, "Speech by Roosevelt at the Chickamauga Dam Celebration, near Chattanooga, Tennessee, September 2, 1940," as reprinted in Edgar Nixon, comp. and ed., *Franklin D. Roosevelt and Conservation, 1911–1945* (Hyde Park, N.Y.: FDRL, 1957), 2:468.

45. Roosevelt to Congress, 10 April 1933, as quoted in Nixon, *FDR and Conservation*, 1:151.

46. On the exceptional power of the TVA, see Cutler, *Public Landscape*, 138–139.

47. Senator George W. Norris of Nebraska to Roosevelt, 9 September 1939, as reprinted in Nixon, *FDR and Conservation*, 2:944.

48. Roosevelt, "President Roosevelt's Own Story of the New Deal, Article No. 11: President Roosevelt on TVA and Regional Planning," 4.

49. For a wonderful history of this board and its members, see Reagan, *Designing a New America*. See also Jeffries, "The 'New' New Deal," 397–418.

50. On the power of the NRPB, see Roosevelt, "President Roosevelt's Own Story of the New Deal: Article No. 11, President Roosevelt on TVA and Regional Planning," 4.

51. Ibid.

52. Harcourt A. Morgan, Vice Chairman, Board of Directors, Tennessee Valley Authority, to Franklin Roosevelt, 18 February 1938, as reprinted in Nixon, *FDR and Conservation*, 2:179.

53. This map is a snapshot of CCC camps in the Tennessee Valley in June 1941 and therefore does not show all of the nearly thirty Corps camps in existence throughout the Valley during the CCC's nine-year existence. The number of CCC camps assigned to the TVA is discussed in the following correspondence: Harcourt A. Morgan, Vice Chairman, Board of Directors, Tennessee Valley Authority, to Franklin Roosevelt, 18 February 1938; and Franklin Roosevelt to Harcourt A. Morgan, Vice Chairman, Board of Directors, Tennessee Valley Authority, both as reprinted in Nixon, *FDR and Conservation*, 2:179, 188. See also Headrick and Schaffer, *A Peace Time Army*, 2. Because data are reliable for 1933, 1935, and 1938, and because they represent the rise and fall of CCC strength under the TVA, these three years were also used to compute averages for the decade as a whole. In his reply to Morgan's letter, Franklin Roosevelt mentions Forest Service, Soil Conservation Service, and National Park Service CCC camps that, while not counted officially as TVA camps, were nevertheless performing conservation for the TVA.

54. These man-hours were computed by taking the average number of CCC enrollees in TVA camps during the Great Depression (5,000), multiplying that by the number of hours of labor per week (forty), multiplying that by the number of weeks per year (fifty-two), and finally multiplying that by the number of years the CCC labored in the Tennessee Valley (ten).

55. For an overview of CCC work in the Tennessee Valley, see Cutler, *Public Landscape*, 140–142, and for data on TVA camps during these years, see Leslie Headrick and Daniel Schaffer, "A Peace Time Army: The Tennessee Valley Authority—Civilian

Conservation Corps, 1933–1942" (Division of Land and Forest Resources Office of Natural Resources, Tennessee Valley Authority, 1983), 1–23. These numbers were computed by taking the average for the number of camps for the three years 1933, 1935, and 1938, and multiplying it by the 200-man capacity of each CCC camp. These three years have reliable data on camp strength and also represent the rise and fall of CCC enrollment.

56. On CCC soil conservation work in the Tennessee Valley, see Cutler, *Public Landscape*, 142–143; and Civilian Conservation Corps, "Tennessee Valley Authority C.C.C. Camps," Record Group 35: CCC, Entry 12: "Organization Charts, 1941–1942," NARA. For a list of Corps camps working at the Muscle Shoals nitrate plant, see the Alabama list of CCC camps available on the National Association of CCC Alumni Web site at http://www.cccalumni.org/states/alabama1.html.

57. Harcourt A. Morgan, Vice Chairman, Board of Directors, Tennessee Valley Authority, to Franklin Roosevelt, 18 February 1938, as reprinted in Nixon, *FDR and Conservation*, 2:179.

58. On the CCC's recreational development work under the TVA, see Cutler, *Public Landscape*, 138–140; and Brian Black, "Organic Planning: Ecology and Design in the Landscape of the Tennessee Valley Authority, 1933–1945," in *Environmentalism in Landscape Architecture*, ed. Michel Conan (Washington, D.C.: Dumbarton Oaks Research Library and Collection, 2001), 87–88.

59. Interestingly, the Corps was also involved in the construction of Norris, a planned greenbelt town that even included a collective farm. On the town of Norris, see Cutler, *Public Landscape*, 138.

60. Roosevelt, "President Roosevelt's Own Story of the New Deal: Article No. 11, President Roosevelt on TVA and Regional Planning," 1.

61. On Roosevelt asking the National Planning Board to formulate these regional river plans, see Graham, *Toward a Planned Society*, 52–53; and Reagan, *Designing a New America*, 1. On the number of regional and state planning boards created with the help of the NRPB, see Cutler, *Public Landscape*, 135; and Frederic Delano, Chairman, Advisory Committee to the National Resources Committee, to Harold Ickes, 23 November 1935, as quoted in Nixon, *FDR and Conservation*, 1:450.

62. As quoted in Graham, *Toward a Planned Society*, 52.

63. Scholars have noted that at this early date Roosevelt had not yet formulated the more comprehensive kind of planning that would emerge during his later presidency. See especially Lepawsky, "The Progressives and the Planners," 301.

64. On the importance of this Supreme Court decision, see Cutler, *Public Landscape*, 139. On congressional opposition to the "seven little TVAs," see Graham, "The Planning Ideal and American Reality," 269.

65. On this shift from early support for the NRPB during the early 1930s to increasingly vocal opposition during the late 1930s, see Graham, *Toward a Planned Society*, 55–56; Hugh Johnson, editorial, *Washington Daily News*, August 1937, as quoted in Richard Kalish, "National Resource Planning, 1933–1939" (Ph.D. diss., University of Colorado, 1963), 243.

66. Benton MacKaye to Stuart Chase, 20 July 1935, as quoted in Spann, *Designing Modern America*, 158.

67. Roosevelt as quoted in Polenberg, "The Great Conservation Contest," 16.

68. On the composition of the President's Committee on Administrative Management, see "Many Changes in Conservation Set-Up Indicated," *Forestry News Digest* (February 1937): 1; and Polenberg, "The Great Conservation Contest," 16.

69. Report of the President's Committee on Administrative Management, as quoted in Polenberg, "The Great Conservation Contest," 16, 21.

70. Polenberg, *Reorganizing Roosevelt's Government*, 21.

71. *New York Times*, 17 January 1937, p. 7, as quoted in Polenberg, *Reorganizing Roosevelt's Government*, 28. Several historians have examined this political battle between the Departments of Agriculture and Interior. See especially Hal Rothman, " 'A Regular Ding-Dong Fight': Agency Culture and Evolution in the NPS-USFS Dispute, 1916–1937," *Western Historical Quarterly* 20, no. 2 (May 1989): 142.

72. Harold Ickes to Franklin Roosevelt, as reprinted in Nixon, *FDR and Conservation*, 2:421.

73. Bob Armstrong, Jr., to Mrs. Eleanor Roosevelt, 27 November 1937, Official File 177: Conservation Matters, 1937, FDRL, 1. For a description of the meeting at the Palmer House, see Irving Brant, Horace Albright, Richard Lieber, and Tom Wallace to President Franklin Roosevelt, 17 November 1937, Official File 177a: Conservation Matters, Department of Conservation, FDRL. On this group's subsequent meeting with President Roosevelt, see Polenberg, "Conservation and Reorganization," *Agricultural History* 39, no. 4 (1965): 238.

74. Franklin Roosevelt, *Public Papers and Addresses*, 5:668–674; as quoted in Polenberg, *Reorganizing Roosevelt's Government*, 43.

75. Ibid.

76. *Report of the President's Committee on Administrative Management* (Washington, D.C.: U.S. Government Printing Office, 1937), 53, as quoted in Polenberg, *Reorganizing Roosevelt's Government*, 21.

77. Harold Ickes, Secret Diary, 1:584, as quoted in Polenberg, *Reorganizing Roosevelt's Government*, 105.

78. "Remarks of the President, Bismarck, North Dakota, 27 August 1936," 1, Speech File, #896, FDRL.

79. For a more thorough discussion of this ecological critique of the CCC, see chap. 5.

80. On the difference between the science and philosophy of ecology, see Randall Beeman and James Pritchard, *A Green and Permanent Land: Ecology and Agriculture in the Twentieth Century* (Lawrence: University Press of Kansas, 2001), 35, 40.

81. Rexford Tugwell, "The Outlines of Permanent Agriculture" (ca. 1935), Tugwell Papers, Box 69, as quoted in Beeman and Prichard, *A Green and Permanent Land*, 23.

82. "Remarks of the President, Bismarck, North Dakota, 27 August 1936," 1, Speech File, #896, FDRL.

83. Paul Sears, "Science and the New Landscape," *Harper's*, July 1939, 207, as quoted in Black, "Organic Planning," 91.

84. Tennessee Valley Authority, *Forests and Human Welfare*, 1940, as quoted in Black, "Organic Planning," 91.

85. Brian Black sees such efforts by the TVA as an example of what he calls "organic planning." In his insightful essay, however, Black refrains from examining the periodization of this new type of planning. My research suggests that this shift toward what I am calling "ecological planning" occurred toward the end of the decade. See Black, "Organic Planning."

86. "President Roosevelt's Own Story of the New Deal: Article No. 11, President Roosevelt on TVA and Regional Planning," 4.

87. Roosevelt as quoted in Graham, *Toward a Planned Society*, 61.

88. Others have identified this rise of ecological thinking during the 1930s, but not linked it directly to New Deal planning. See, for instance, Koppes, "Efficiency, Equity, Esthetics," 240; Graham, "The Planning Ideal and American Reality," 267; and Donald Worster, *Nature's Economy: A History of Ecological Ideas* (New York: Cambridge University Press, 1985), 320.

89. On the local impact of the regional planning movement, see Spann, *Designing Modern America*, especially chap. 18.

90. Rosenman, *Public Papers and Addresses of Franklin D. Roosevelt*, 1:697, as quoted in Graham, "The Planning Ideal and American Reality," 261.

91. Others have claimed that New Deal planning was unique, but not because of its inclusion of ecological ideologies. See especially Reagan, *Designing a New America*, 5.

92. President's Committee on Administrative Management, *Report* (Washington, D.C.: U.S. Government Printing Office, 1937), as quoted in Polenberg, "The Great Conservation Contest," 16.

93. "Ickes Sees More Efficiency in Works Bill Plan," *Forestry News Digest* (August 1935): 2.

94. Franklin Roosevelt to Harold Ickes, 8 July 1941, Roosevelt Papers, Official File 149, as quoted in Polenberg, *Reorganizing Roosevelt's Government*, 107.

95. Aldo Leopold, "Conservation Economics: Misuse of Land Is Liability against Public Purse," *American Game* 23, no. 5 (September–October 1934): 71.

96. Robert Fechner, *Summary Report of Director, Fiscal Year 1936* (Washington, D.C.: U.S. Government Printing Office, 1936), located at RG 35: CCC, Entry 3: Annual, Final, and Special Reports, NARA.

97. Morris Llewellyn Cooke, "On Total Conservation," introductory remarks made at a symposium on "The Administrative Task of Conservation: Public and Private," at Irving Auditorium, 18 September 1940, University of Pennsylvania, transcript located at Special Collections, Dartmouth College Library, Hanover, N.H., 2. On Cooke as an ardent New Deal conservationist, see Jean Christie, "New Deal Resources Planning: The Proposals of Morris L. Cooke," *Agricultural History* 53, no. 3 (July 1979): 598.

98. Cooke, "On Total Conservation," 5.

99. Ibid., 3.

100. Cooke uses this language, and these ecological metaphors, throughout his "On Total Conservation" talk. See especially the first paragraph of Cooke, "On Total Conservation," 1. The ecologist Paul Sears also called for more ecological science in CCC conservation work. See Paul Sears, "What Is Ecology and What Good Is It?" *Ecology* 17, no. 3 (July 1936): 337.

101. Cooke, "On Total Conservation," 2.

102. Cooke discusses these four groups, which I argue represent four different conservationist ideologies, in his symposium speech. See ibid., 5.

103. Ibid., 1.

104. Ibid., 6.

105. Ibid., 5.

106. For evidence of the idea of total conservation among New Dealers, see Hugh Bennett, "Total Conservation: An Introduction to This Issue by H. H. Bennett, Chief, Soil Conservation Service," *Soil Conservation* 7, no. 10 (April 1942): 233; David Lilienthal to Franklin Roosevelt, as cited in Black, "Organic Planning," 72–73; and Benton Mac-Kaye to Clarence Stein, 13 August 1940, Dartmouth College Special Collections Library,

Collection ML5, Box 185, Folder 48, Hanover, N.H. For a more extensive examination of this idea among soil conservationists, including Rexford Tugwell, see Beeman and Prichard, *A Green and Permanent Land*, 11.

107. Harold Ickes quoted in "Ickes Sees More Efficiency in Works Bill Plan while Silcox Calls Conservation Unity a Fallacy," *Forestry News Digest* (August 1935): 5.

108. For a brief description of the history of the Society of American Foresters, see Richard Davis, *Encyclopedia of American Forest and Conservation History* (New York: Macmillan, 1983), 1:612. On the Society of American Foresters' letter-writing campaign and Gifford Pinchot's involvement in it, see Polenberg, "The Great Conservation Contest," 21; and Richard Polenberg, "Conservation and Reorganization: The Forest Service Lobby, 1937–1938," *Agricultural History* 39, no. 4 (1965): 235.

109. For a more detailed examination of the Society of American Foresters' lobbying campaign, see Polenberg, "Conservation and Reorganization," 235–237.

110. Harold Ickes as quoted in Polenberg, "The Great Conservation Contest," 21. For examples of anti–Conservation Department letters from farmers, ranchers, timber interests, and especially foresters, see RG: Society of American Foresters, Box 53, Folder 13–14: "1937: Reorganization Letters," Forest History Society; Official File 1c: Department of Agriculture, Folder: Replies to Governor Pinchot, FDRL; and Official File 1c: Department of Agriculture, Folder: Forest Service, 1939, FDRL.

111. *Report of the President's Committee on Administrative Management* (Washington, D.C.: U.S. Government Printing Office, 1937), 53, as quoted in Polenberg, *Reorganizing Roosevelt's Government*, 105.

112. *Congressional Record*, 75th Congress, 1st sess., 7695, 7692–7693, 8857, as quoted in Polenberg, *Reorganizing Roosevelt's Government*, 50.

113. Gifford Pinchot to William F. Finley, 29 March 1940, Pinchot MSS, Box 1901, as quoted in Polenberg, *Reorganizing Roosevelt's Government*, 104.

114. Select Committee, Hearings, 147, as quoted in Polenberg, *Reorganizing Roosevelt's Government*, 85.

115. Gifford Pinchot to Franklin Roosevelt, 18 April 1933, Roosevelt Papers, President's Personal File, 289, as quoted in Polenberg, *Reorganizing Roosevelt's Government*, 107.

116. Society of American Foresters president H. H. Chapman, "Reorganization and the Forest Service," *Journal of Forestry* 35, no. 5 (May 1937): 429.

117. Secretary of War George Dern, as quoted in Graham, "The Planning Ideal and American Reality," 269.

118. New York *World-Telegram*, 9 April 1938, p. 20, as quoted in Polenberg, *Reorganizing Roosevelt's Government*, 175.

119. Friends of the Land brochure, Official File 177: Conservation Matters, 1940–1945, FDRL, 1–2. For a brief history of Friends of the Land, see Beeman and Prichard, *A Green and Permanent Land*, 67.

120. William Vogt, "The Survival of Man," *Conservation in the Americas* 5 (October 1947), 1–8, as quoted in Beeman and Prichard, *Green and Permanent Land*, 57 (emphasis mine).

121. Friends of the Land brochure, 1–2. The "moral equivalent of war" reference speaks directly to the essay of the same title by William James that many contemporaries believed, incorrectly, inspired the idea for the CCC. Franklin Roosevelt claimed to have never read the James essay. See chap. 1 for a more detailed discussion of this essay.

122. On the rise of special interest politics during the later New Deal years, see Jeffries, "A Third 'New Deal'?" 398; Graham, "The Planning Ideal and American Reality," 283; and Graham, *Toward a Planned Society*, 63–68.

EPILOGUE

1. Camp Roosevelt was closed on May 25, 1942. This description of the dismantling of Camp Roosevelt, especially the flag lowering ceremony, is partly conjecture on my part from a reading of several sources, including Carrie Leonard, "Roosevelt's Tree Army: Fifty-One Years Ago, the Nation's First Civilian Conservation Corps Camp Opened Near Edinburg," *Curio* (Summer 1984): 44; "Camp Roosevelt, NF-1: First CCC Camp in the Nation," http://ccclegacy.org/ccc_brief_history.htm, 5; and "C.C.C. Nine Years Old Mobilizes for Forest Protection," *Shenandoah Herald*, 17 April 1942.

2. On the lingering visual remnants of Camp Roosevelt, see Leonard, "Roosevelt's Tree Army," 44.

3. "Conservation in Congress," *American Forests* 48, no. 8 (August 1942): 330. On the House vote also see "Congress End of CCC, *Time*, 15 June 1942, 10; and John Salmond, *The Civilian Conservation Corps, 1933–1942: A New Deal Case Study* (Durham, N.C.: Duke University Press, 1967), 216.

4. President Franklin Roosevelt to Senator Elbert D. Thomas, 16 March 1942, Official File, #268 (CCC), Folder CCC, 1942–45, FDRL, 2. For other examples of the president promoting the CCC as helping to prepare the nation for World War II, see the following letters and speeches by Roosevelt in Edgar Nixon, comp. and ed., *Franklin D. Roosevelt and Conservation, 1911–1945* (Hyde Park, N.Y.: FDRL, 1957), 2:548, 557, 604.

5. James McEntee, *Annual Report of the Director of the Civilian Conservation Corps: Fiscal Year Ended June 30, 1940* (Washington, D.C.: U.S. Government Printing Office, 1940), 3, located at RG 35: CCC, Entry 3: Annual, Special, and Final Reports, NARA. For other examples of the CCC promoting its role in helping the country prepare for World War II, see McEntee, *Annual Report 1940*, 14; McEntee, *Final Report of the Director of the Civilian Conservation Corps, April 1933 through June 30, 1942*, RG 35: CCC, Entry 3: Annual, Special, and Final Reports, NARA, 41; McEntee, "The CCC and National Defense," *American Forests* 46, no. 7 (July 1940): 309–310, 320, 324, 335; and Federal Security Agency, Civilian Conservation Corps, "Memorandum for the Press, Release to P.M. Papers, Saturday, October 26, 1940," Printed Materials Collection, Civilian Conservation Corps, Press Releases, FDRL.

6. Edwin Hill, *In the Shadow of the Mountain: The Spirit of the CCC* (Pullman: Washington State University Press, 1990), 136.

7. On this expansion in CCC work into the military arena, see John Paige, *The Civilian Conservation Corps and the National Park Service* (Washington, D.C.: National Park Service, U.S. Department of the Interior, 1985), 29–31.

8. On the CCC's Victory War Program, see McEntee, *Annual Report 1940*, 4.

9. On the number of camps assigned to the military in 1942, see Conrad Wirth, *Parks, Politics, and the People* (Norman: University of Oklahoma Press, 1980), 144. On the Corps' national defense efforts see also Civilian Conservation Corps, *Civilian Conservation Corps: Contributing to the Defense of the Nation* (Washington, D.C.: Federal Security Agency, 1941), pamphlet located in vertical file, folder: U.S. Civilian Conservation Corps, FDRL.

10. "The New Frontier," editorial in *American Forests*, 46, no. 7 (July 1940): 295.

11. "Senate Ends CCC on House Demand," *New York Times*, 1 July 1942, p. 16. See also McEntee, *Annual Report 1942*, 1.

12. For a brief description of these corps, see table titled "1995–96 Youth Corps–NPS Partnerships, October 1996," National Association of Service and Conservation Corps, Washington D.C.

13. On the increase in forestry classes at the University of Idaho and the University of Mississippi, see CCC administrator Guy McKinney to U.S. Forest Service employee Mr. Charles Randall, 1 February 1935, RG 35: CCC, Entry 2: General Correspondence, File 400: University of Mississippi, NARA. On other enrollees who went on to pursue conservation-related degrees see Phoebe Cutler, *The Public Landscape of the New Deal* (New Haven, Conn.: Yale University Press, 1985), 94. Cutler writes, "The CCC left a patrimony of men dedicated to the outdoors and skilled in appropriate trades. Many CCC youths continued on in the park and forest line of work."

14. On Wisconsin's prison conservation camp program, see Seegar Swanson, "Trees Build Men: Wisconsin's Experiment in Growing Trees in Prison Camps Is Proving Two-Way Benefit," *American Forests*, 48, no. 4 (April 1942): 158–60, 180. On California's program, see Raymond Clar, *California Government and Forestry* (Sacramento, Calif.: Division of Forestry, Department of Conservation, 1969), 2:265. And on New York's inmate conservation program, see Barrett Potter, "The Civilian Conservation Corps in New York State: Its Social and Political Impact" (Ph.D. diss., State University of New York, Buffalo), 242–44.

15. On California's CCC, see Thomas Bass, "A Reborn CCC Shapes Young Lives with an Old Idea," *Smithsonian* 14, no. 1 (1983): 56–64. On New Hampshire's CCC, see David Draves, *Builder of Men: Life in the CCC Camps of New Hampshire* (Portsmouth, N.H.: Randall, 1992), 363. On Michigan's CCC program, see "Michigan CCC Dedicates Second Residential Camp," *NACCCA Journal* 22, no. 9 (September 1999): 1. And on Arizona's, Montana's, and Washington's CCC programs, see table titled "1995–96 Youth Corps–NPS Partnerships, October 1996," National Association of Service and Conservation Corps, Washington D.C.

16. On enrollees pursing careers in conservation after 1942, see Camp P-15, Jefferson, Maine, 24 February 1939, RG 35: CCC, Entry 101: Success Stories, 1936–1941, Miscellaneous Prize Winning Stories, Box 2, NARA; "A CCC Recruit Finds a Career in the Forest Service," RG 35: CCC, Entry 56: Success Stories, 1939, Folder: Success Stories Letter of Instruction # 66, Quarterly Report, 1/12/39, Box 1, NARA; and "Extra Duty Marks Beginning of Long Climb From Enrollee to Park Service Official, Oklahoma Section, *Happy Days* (CCC camp newspaper), 9 July 1938, RG 35: CCC, Entry 101: Success Stories, 1936–1941, Happy Days, Box 2, NARA.

17. Chuck Krall as quoted in Perry Merrill, *Roosevelt's Forest Army: A History of the Civilian Conservation Corps, 1933–1942* (Montpelier, Vt.: Perry Merrill, 1981), 93.

18. On enrollees from Camp City Creek in Highland, California, taking jobs with the Forest Service, see Commander W. E. Druebert to Mrs. Ida K. Brooks, 21 December 1938, RG 35: CCC, Entry 101: Success Stories, 1936–1941, Folder: California, NARA. There are numerous reports of former CCC enrollees taking government jobs in conservation-related fields. See especially Cutler, *Public Landscape*, 94–95; Amelia Fry, "The National Park Service and the Civilian Conservation Corps," oral interview located at the Bancroft Library, University of California at Berkeley, 1963; Merrill, *Roosevelt's Forest Army*, 67; "Extra Duty Marks Beginning of Long Climb From Enrollee to Park Service Official,"

anonymous, *Happy Days* [Oklahoma Section], 9 July 1938, 16; "A CCC Recruit Finds a Career in the Forestry Service," anonymous, RG 35: CCC, Entry 56: Success Stories, 1939, Folder: Success Stories Letter of Instruction #66, Quarterly Report, 1/12/39, Box 1, NARA; "Quarterly Report of Former CCC Enrollees Who Have Attained Outstanding Success in Private Life," C. H. McCay, 5 June 1939, RG 35: CCC, Entry 56: Success Stories, 1939, Folder: Success Stories, Letter of Instruction #66, Quarterly Report, 1/12/39, Box 1, NARA.

19. Congress, House of Representatives, Committee on Education and Labor, *Act to Reestablish a Civilian Conservation Corps*, 1950, 81st Cong., 2nd sess., H.R. 7462, Congressional Record (28 February 1950). On Senator Moynihan's attempt to create the American Conservation Corps, see "At Issue: A Conservation Corps for Today," *American Forests* 104, nos. 9–10 (September–October 1998): 14–15.

20. For information on the Job Corps, see NACCCA President, "Job Corps Has More Direct Relationship to Original CCC," *NACCCA Journal* 23, no. 4 (April 2000): 3. As of April 2000, there were 118 such centers and approximately 70,000 American youths participating in the Job Corps program each year. See also Cutler, *Public Landscape*, 154; Sherraden, "The Civilian Conservation Corps: Effectiveness of the Camps" (Ph.D. diss., University of Michigan, 1979), iv, 10; and Salmond, *The CCC*, 222. For a discussion of the Youth Conservation Corps and the Young Adult Conservation Corps and their similarity to the New Deal's CCC, see Sherraden, "The Civilian Conservation Corps," 9–13, 252–253; and James Jackson, "Focus: Living Legacy of the CCC, *American Forests* 94, nos. 9–10 (September/October 1988): 37–47. On the history of the Youth Conservation Corps, see David Nye, *The History of the Youth Conservation Corps* (Durham: The Forest History Society, 1980). The Reagan Administration abolished both the Youth Conservation Corps and the Young Adult Conservation Corps programs in 1981 and vetoed a similar program called the American Conservation Corps in 1983. On the American Conservation Corps see Letters to the Editor, "The American Conservation Corps," *Washington Post*, 12 March 1983; and "Jobless Youth and Useful Work," *New York Times*, 12 March 1983.

21. "AmeriCorps Volunteers Assist CCC 'Grandparents,' " *NACCCA Journal* 22, no. 8 (August 1999): 1. On the similarities between AmeriCorps and the New Deal's CCC see Alan Greenblatt, "The Call to Service," *Washington Monthly* (April 1994): 19–22.

22. On the preponderance of government conservation at the federal level prior to the New Deal era see Samuel Hays, *Conservation and the Gospel of Efficiency: The Progressive Conservation Movement, 1890–1920* (Cambridge: Harvard University Press, 1960).

23. There is an extensive literature on the rise of interest group politics. For the emergence of special interests during the New Deal era see John Jeffries, "A 'Third New Deal'?: Liberal Policy and the American State, 1937–1945," *Journal of Policy History* 8, no. 4 (1996): 398; Otis Graham, "The Planning Ideal and American Reality: The 1930s," in *The Hofstadter Aegis: A Memorial*, ed. Stanley Elkins and Eric McKitrick (New York: Knopf, 1974), 283; and Otis Graham, *Toward a Planned Society: From Roosevelt to Nixon* (New York: Oxford University Press, 1976), 63–68. For a good overview on the deep history of interest group politics in America see Elizabeth Clemens, *The People's Lobby: Organizational Innovation and the Rise of Interest Group Politics in the United States, 1890–1925* (Chicago: University of Chicago Press, 1997).

24. On the shift in postwar politics to an emphasis on "quality of life" issues see Adam Rome, " 'Give Earth a Chance': The Environmental Movement and the Sixties," *Journal of American History* 90, no. 2 (September 2003): 525–54.

25. On the Ex. Civilian Conservation Corps Workers see George DeLorenzo to Franklin Roosevelt, 29 January, 1935, Official File, #266 (CCC), Folder: Misc. Jan.–March 1935, FDRL. On the American Conservation Enrollees, see Director of American Conservation Enrollees Neil Metcalfe to President Franklin Roosevelt, 5 April 1938, Official File, #268 (CCC), Folder: Miscellaneous, April–June 1938, FDRL.

26. On the Citizens for Conservation and Trustees of the Earth, see Potter, "The Civilian Conservation Corps in New York State," 240.

27. The National Association of Civilian Conservation Corps Alumni (NACCCA) still exists, is located in St. Louis, and publishes a newspaper titled the *NACCCA Journal*. On NACCCA membership in 1981 see Cutler, *Public Landscape*, 94.

28. Norma Ryland Graves, "The Little Green Guards," *American Forests* 48, no. 11 (November 1942): 506.

29. For a brief history of the Student Conservation Association, see *History of the Youth Corps Movement*, pamphlet published by the National Association of Service and Conservation Corps, Washington D.C. For a description of the Durham Service Corps, see Joseph N. Boyce, "Rescue Mission: Principles of Depression-Era Corps Are Tested on Troubled Youths in Durham, N.C.," *Wall Street Journal*, 25 November 1992, 1, A8.

30. National Parks Association, *A Worthwhile Summer in Your National Parks*, Collection: Rockefeller Family Archives, Record Group: 2, Series: Cultural, Box: 87, Folder: 808, RAC.

31. Graves, "The Little Green Guards," 506.

32. Joseph N. Boyce, "Rescue Mission," 1.

33. National Parks Association, *A Worthwhile Summer*.

34. On the work of the American Conservation Enrollees see Neil Metcalfe to Franklin Roosevelt, 5 April 1938, Official File, #268 (CCC), Folder: Misc., April–June, 1938, FDRL.

35. On the work of Citizens for Conservation and Trustees of the Earth see Barettt Potter, "The Civilian Conservation Corps in New York State" (Ph.D. diss., State University of Buffalo, 1973), 240–41.

36. On the Student Conservation Association and its work preserving wilderness areas see *SCA: Changing Lives through Service to Nature*, publicity brochure, in possession of author.

37. Environmental historians have written extensively about the Echo Park dam controversy. See especially Mark Harvey, *A Symbol of Wilderness: Echo Park and the American Conservation Movement*, 2nd ed. (Seattle: University of Washington Press, 2000). See also Roderick Nash, *Wilderness and the American Mind* (New Haven, Conn.: Yale University Press, 1967), 209–19; and Stephen Fox, *The American Conservation Movement* (Madison: University of Wisconsin Press, 1981), 281–86.

38. Roosevelt's role in enlarging Dinosaur National Monument is discussed by Harvey, *A Symbol of Wilderness*, 14.

39. *Vernal Express/Roosevelt Standard*, "Scenic Edition," 18 August 1938; and *Vernal Express*, 28 July 1938, as quoted in Harvey, *A Symbol of Wilderness*, 14–15.

40. On Dinosaur National Monument's isolation, see Fox, *The American Conservation Movement*, 281; Rothman, *The Greening of a Nation?* 40, and Harvey, *A Symbol of Wilderness*, 15, 24. Here Harvey also includes an informative discussion of how national monument status limited federal funding and recreational development projects at Dinosaur.

41. The four camps in the Dinosaur National Monument region can be found on the map titled "Fiscal Year 1940, Civilian Conservation Corps Camps," RG 35: CCC, Entry 3: Annual Reports, Year Ending 1940, NARA.

42. On the CCC's road-building projects in Utah's canyon country, see Jared Farmer, *Glen Canyon Dammed: Inventing Lake Powell and the Canyon Country* (Tucson: University of Arizona Press, 1999), 46. On CCC recreational development work in eastern Utah see the numerous inspection reports for each camp in the area at RG 35: CCC, Entry 115: Camp Inspection Reports, Folder: Utah, NARA. On the same work in western Colorado, see RG 35: CCC, Entry 115: Camp Inspection Reports, Folder: Colorado, NARA.

43. The quote is by Sierra Club member Richard Leonard in his memoir, as quoted in Fox, *The American Conservation Movement*, 281. For rising visitation rates at Dinosaur National Monument see Fox, *The American Conservation Movement*, 284.

44. On the Bureau of Reclamation's early surveys of Dinosaur National Monument, see Harvey, *A Symbol of Wilderness*, 29–30.

45. Harvey, *A Symbol of Wilderness*, 75.

46. On National Park Service and the Sierra Club's opposition to the Echo Park Dam, see Harvey, *A Symbol of Wilderness*, 67–68, 164–65.

47. On the Wilderness Society's opposition to the dam at Echo Park, see Harvey, *A Symbol of Wilderness*, 52–53, 106. See also Benton MacKaye, "Dam Site vs. Norm Site," *Scientific Monthly* 71 (1950): 244, as quoted in Nash, *Wilderness and the American Mind*, 214.

48. On the role of roads in the Kings Canyon wilderness controversy see Fox, *The American Conservation Movement*, 212–17.

49. "Summary of Situation Regarding Dinosaur National Monument, May 1954," a six-page letter most probably written by the Emergency Committee on Natural Resources to the Rockefeller Family. For a copy of this letter, see Collection: Rockefeller Family Archives, Record Group: 2, Series: Cultural Interests, Box: 80, Folder: 755, RAC.

50. On the Izaak Walton League's opposition to the Echo Park dam on recreational grounds, especially with respect to hunting, see Harvey, *A Symbol of Wilderness*, 53–54. For other examples of recreationists opposing the Echo Park dam see Nash, *Wilderness and the American Mind*, 213.

51. Bernard DeVoto, "Shall We Let Them Ruin Our National Parks?" *Saturday Evening Post*, 223 (1950), 44, as quoted in Nash, *Wilderness and the American Mind*, 214.

52. On opposition to the Echo Park dam by the National Wildlife Federation and Rosalie Edge, see Harvey, *A Symbol of Wilderness*, 213, 271, 290.

53. On the Audubon Society's opposition to the dam in Dinosaur National Park, see Harvey, *A Symbol of Wilderness*, 54, 171.

54. This quote appears on the banner of the Denver, Colorado, chapter of the National Association of Civilian Conservation Corps Alumni. See *Chapter Chatter and Comment* 12, no. 4 (April 1997), Vertical File, Folder #2: Civilian Conservation Corps, FDRL.

INDEX

Italicized page numbers refer to illustrations.

and planning, *193*, 198–200, 202–5, 208–9, 293n85, 294n100
and post-World War II era, 218–19, 224
economic efficiency. *See* efficient natural resource use
Edge, Rosalie, 170, 199, 224, 284n83
education (CCC), 13, 84, 86–91, *87*, *89*, 213, 257n58
educational advisors, 89–91, 96
Educational Conservation Society, 160
educational system, American, 86–87, 159–60, 280nn37, 39
effeminacy, 95–96
efficient natural resource use, 4–5, 7, 11–12
and Dinosaur National Monument, 222
and evolution of CCC, 54–56, 66–67, 70, 75
and human conservation in CCC work, 103–6, *104*, *105*
at Hyde Park (N.Y.) estate, 22–24, *23*
and local communities, 117
and national debate about CCC, 157–61
and Pinchot, 4–5, 7, 25–27, 157, 161
and post-World War II era, 217
and reorganization proposal, 208
and Roosevelt as N.Y. governor, 28
Eggleston, George Washington, 32
Eliot, Charles II, 188
Elizabeth Furnace recreation area, 8
Elkmont Vehicle Bridge (Great Smoky Mountains), *142–43*
Emergency Conservation Committee, 170–72, 199, 224
Emerson, Ralph Waldo, 26
Engelhard, Georgia, 174
environmentalism, 5–6, 8, 10–11, 15, 229n12
and Dinosaur National Monument, 220
and local communities, *144–45*, 149, 216–19
and planning, 184, 197
and Progressive Era influences, 32–36, 41
erosion, soil. *See* soil conservation
Escape from Babylon (Owen), 30
ethnicity, 106, 110–13, 154, 263nn130,132
European youth work programs, 18
evening classes (CCC), 88–91. *See also* education (CCC)
Ex Civilian Conservation Corps Workers, 216
executive authority. *See* presidential power
exotic species, 9, 22, 168–69, 219

families of CCC enrollees, 19, 82–83, 95, *95*, 100, *101*, 254n20
"Farmer as Conservationist, The" (Leopold), 167
farms, 11–13. *See also* subsistence agriculture
abandonment of, 28, 39, 136
and Catholic Rural Life movement, 31
and media coverage, 156
and national debate about CCC
ecological balance vs. conservation, 167
media coverage, 156–58
and planning, 191, 202
and Roosevelt as N.Y. governor, 28

and soil conservation by CCC, 61–67, *68–69*, 75, 117
in Coon Valley (Wis.), 118–31, *120–21*, *128–29*, *132*, 148–49
Farrington, Edward, 169
fascism, 107–8, 206
feature films. *See* motion pictures
Fechner, Robert, 4, 18
and CCC work, 83–84, 255n30
bodily transformations, 93, 95, 96, 103
education, 86, 88, 90
human conservation, 110
and evolution of CCC, 45
forestry, 48–49, 52–54
soil conservation, 61–62, 64
and local communities, 117, 125, 148, 269n46
and national debate about CCC
ecological balance vs. conservation, 170
human resources conservation, 161–62
media coverage, 154–57, 160
and organized labor, 79–80, *81*, 154
and planning, 185–86, 202–3, 205
federal government, 4–6, 8, 11, 14–15. *See also names of government entities*
and land purchases, 44–45, *46–47*, 48, 241–42n4
and local communities, 119, 122, 149–50
Coon Valley (Wis.), *128–29*, 130–31, 267n26
Great Smoky Mountains, 134, 136, 147
National Plan for American Forestry (1932), 50
and reorganization proposal, 181–84, *182*, 196–207
Federal Security Agency, 212
Federal Theatre Project, 107, 155
"Federation Forests," 159
fence building, 43
Fernald, Merritt L., 168–69, 171, 179, 198
film. *See* motion pictures
Fink, Paul, 135
firebreaks, 52, 55, 137, 146, 217
fire fighting, 8, 38, 55–56, 84, 155, 245n34
fire lookout towers, 55, 137, 156, 217
fire prevention, 55–56, 137, 149, 168, 174
fire roads, 8, 55, 137, 174, 176
fires. *See* forest fires
fireside chats, 157, 164
Fish, Hamilton, 206
fish stocking, 9, 43, 137, 231n25, 275n139
Five Acres and Independence (Kains), 30
"Flankline vs. Skyline" (MacKaye), 174
Flight from the City (Borsodi), 30
flood control, 7
in Great Smoky Mountains, 146
and origination of idea for CCC, 20, 40
and overtime labor, 84
and planning, 191, 194, 207
food at CCC camps, 98
forest fires, 7–8, 55, 135, 141, 147, 151, 212–13, 245n34

presidential power, 184–86, 195, 197–98, 206, 208
programmatic coordination, 185–87, 195–96, 198, 201
regional, 189–95, *193*, 199–200
reorganization proposal, 181–84, *182*, 196–209
and Progressive Era influences, 17–41, 187–88
  Boy Scouts of America, 34–41, *35*, 88, 188
  at Hyde Park (N.Y.) estate, 21–22, *23*, 27, 234n20. *See also* Springwood
  origination of idea for CCC, 17–25, 28–31, 40–41, 295n121
  TERA (N.Y.), 39–40, 240n86, 241n93
and war effort, 212–14
Roosevelt, Frederic Delano, 188, 192
Roosevelt, Sara, 21
Roosevelt, Theodore, 32–34, 38, 95–96, 187–88
Roosevelt-Jones Bill (N.Y.), 23–25, 41, 52, 63, 266n11
"Roosevelt's Tree Army," 49, 157
Ross, Robert, 85, 88, 103
rural communities, 14. *See also* farms; local communities and CCC camps
  and evolution of CCC, 44, 57, *58–59*, 74
  and Progressive Era influences, 29–36, 41
  Boy Scouts of America, 34–36, 40
"rural-life bureaus," 31
Russell Sage Foundation, 188

San Francisco (Calif.) water supply, 4, 26–27
sanitary facilities, 71
Saturday Evening Post, 175, 224
Save the Redwoods League, 177
schools. *See* educational system, American
"Science and the New Landscape" (Sears), 199
Scientific American, 163
scientific forestry, 4–5, 8, 11, 24–28, 233n14. *See also* efficient natural resource use
  and Boy Scouts, 37–38
  and national debate about CCC, 166
  and TERA (N.Y.), 39–41
Scientific Monthly magazine, 172, 178–79
Scott, Thomas, 92
Sears, Paul, 166, 199, 294n100
sedimentation, 127, 270n65
seed collection/distribution, 38, 53–54
Selway-Salmon River valley (Idaho), 177
Sequoia National Park (Calif.), 73, 100
Seton, Ernest Thompson, 33–34, *35*, 36
"Shall We Let Them Ruin Our National Parks" (DeVoto), 224
sheet erosion, 64, 122, 125–26
Shelford, Victor, 166
Shenandoah National Park (Va.), 74, 79, *81*, 141, 164, 172, 179
Shenandoah Valley, 7–8
Sheppard, W. B., 170
Shi, David, 32
Sierra Club, 4–5, 26–27, 173, 177–78, 223

Sierra Nevada Mountains, 55, 73, 177, 223
Silcox, Ferdinand, 173, 181
Simmons, Virgil, 160
"simple conservation," 157, 161, 179, 202, 218, 222
Skyway (Great Smoky Mountains), 141, 150, 172–73
Smith, Adam, 187
Smith, Al, 28
Smith, Roger, 166
Smoky Mountains. *See* Great Smoky Mountains
snakes, 85, 88
social control, 31–32, 37
social injustices, 216
Socialist party, 107, 154
Society of American Foresters, 56, 205, 207
soil conservation, 3, 7, 12–13
  and CCC work, 85, *89*, 90–91, 102
  and evolution of CCC, 43, *53*, 57, 60–67, *62*, *63*, *68–69*, 75–76, 248n60, 249nn67, 71
  and local communities, 117
    Coon Valley (Wis.), 118–31, *120–21*, *128–29*, *132*, 148–49, 267n22, 270n65
    Great Smoky Mountains, 146–47
  and national debate about CCC
    ecological balance vs. conservation, 167
    efficient natural resource use, 160–61
    media coverage, 156–59
    public interest in, 159–61
  and planning
    programmatic coordination, 185–86
    reorganization proposal, 207
    Tennessee Valley Authority (TVA), *193*, 194
  and Progressive Era influences, 20–21, 24
Soil Conservation magazine, 156, 158, 204, 280n37
Soil Conservation Service (SCS), 6, 215
  and CCC alumni, 215
  and evolution of CCC, *50*, *51*, *53*, 62–66, *62*, *63*, 247n48, 249n67
  and local communities, 117–18
    Coon Valley (Wis.), 123–24, 127, 130–31, *132*, 270n65
  and national debate about CCC
    media coverage, 156
    public interest in conservation, 164
    schools, 159–60
  and Tennessee Valley Authority (TVA), 192, 195
Soil Erosion Service (SES), *50*, *51*, 60–62, *62*, *63*, 247n48
soil surveys, 60, 190, 247n47
Sons of Daniel Boone, 33, 36
spawning, 163
special interests. *See* interest group politics
Springwood estate. *See* Hyde Park (N.Y.) estate
square agriculture, 119, 122, 126–27, *128–29*, 149
standard of living, 122–23